M000159460

PERSIAN AND ARABIC LITERARY COMMUNITIES IN THE SEVENTEENTH CENTURY

I.B. Tauris Studies in Medieval and Early Modern Persian Literature

Dominic Parviz Brookshaw (Series Editor)

This series provides a forum for cutting-edge scholarship from established and emerging scholars in the field of Persian literary studies. It publishes monographs which challenge received understandings of the primary source material and offer new ways of approaching both familiar and obscure texts. The series editor and advisory board encourage submissions from authors who adopt a comparative approach to the study of Persian literature that spans genres, periods, regions and/or languages; however, studies of distinct periods and individual poets (or clusters of poets) will also be considered. The temporal scope of the series is the first millennium of literary production in New Persian, circa 850–1850, encompassing the medieval (or pre-modern) and the early modern periods. The geographical range is the full expanse of the Persianate world, from Anatolia and the Caucasus in the west, through Iran and Afghanistan, to Central and South Asia in the east.

Series Editor

Dominic Parviz Brookshaw, Professor of Persian Literature and Iranian Culture, University of Oxford, UK

Advisory Board

Leili Anvar, Associate Professor of Persian, INALCO, Paris, France

Shahzad Bashir, Aga Khan Professor of Islamic Humanities, Brown University, USA

Alyssa Gabbay, Associate Professor of Religious Studies, University of North Carolina, Greensboro, USA

Sunil Sharma, Professor of Persianate and Comparative Literature, Boston University, USA

Christine van Ruymbeke, Ali Reza and Mohamed Soudavar Professor of Persian Studies, University of Cambridge, UK

Published and Forthcoming Titles

Persian and Arabic Literary Communities in the Seventeenth Century, James Whi

PERSIAN AND ARABIC LITERARY COMMUNITIES IN THE SEVENTEENTH CENTURY

Migrant Poets between Arabia, Iran and India

James White

I.B. TAURIS

LONDON • NEW YORK • OXFORD • NEW DELHI • SYDNEY

I.B. TAURIS
Bloomsbury Publishing Plc
50 Bedford Square, London, WC1B 3DP, UK
1385 Broadway, New York, NY 10018, USA
29 Earlsfort Terrace, Dublin 2, Ireland

BLOOMSBURY, I.B. TAURIS and the I.B. Tauris logo are trademarks of
Bloomsbury Publishing Plc

First published in Great Britain 2023

Copyright © James White, 2023

James White has asserted his right under the Copyright, Designs and Patents Act,
1988, to be identified as Author of this work.

For legal purposes the Acknowledgements on p. x constitute an extension of this
copyright page.

Series design by Adriana Brioso
Cover image © The Witsen Album, with 49 miniatures of rulers, 1686.
Rijksmuseum, Amsterdam.

All rights reserved. No part of this publication may be reproduced or transmitted in any
form or by any means, electronic or mechanical, including photocopying, recording, or any
information storage or retrieval system, without prior permission in writing from
the publishers.

Bloomsbury Publishing Plc does not have any control over, or responsibility for, any third-
party websites referred to or in this book. All internet addresses given in this book were
correct at the time of going to press. The author and publisher regret any inconvenience
caused if addresses have changed or sites have ceased to exist, but can accept no
responsibility for any such changes.

A catalogue record for this book is available from the British Library.

ISBN: HB: 978-0-7556-4456-8
ePDF: 978-0-7556-4457-5
eBook: 978-0-7556-4458-2

Series: I.B. Tauris Studies in Medieval and Early Modern Literature

Typeset by Deanta Global Publishing Services, Chennai, India

To find out more about our authors and books visit www.bloomsbury.com and
sign up for our newsletters.

In memory of my mother,
and to my father,
with love.

CONTENTS

FIGURES

ACKNOWLEDGEMENTS

Work on this book has bridged my stint as an Alexander von Humboldt Foundation fellow at the Department for Arabic and Semitic Studies, Freie Universität Berlin, and my time as Departmental Lecturer of Persian Literature at the Faculty of Asian and Middle Eastern Studies, Oxford University. I am enormously grateful to my colleagues in Berlin, and to my colleagues and students in Oxford, for many conversations which have made me pause and reflect on my research. I would particularly like to thank Dominic Brookshaw for his encouragement over the past years; Julia Bray for her long-standing guidance through the corpus of premodern Arabic poetry; and Beatrice Gruendler for agreeing to bring my von Humboldt project to the Freie Universität. In addition, I would like to express my gratitude to Edmund Herzig, Sahba Shayani, Mahsa Aghdas Zadeh, Farniyaz Zaker, Isabel Toral, Jan van Ginkel, Mahmoud Kozae, Khouloud Khalfallah, Theodore S. Beers, Rima Redwan, Johannes Stephan and Christopher Bahl; and I must thank Paul Losensky for his very helpful and detailed comments on Chapter 6. I would also like to acknowledge the Alexander von Humboldt Foundation for its material support during my time in Berlin.

At Bloomsbury, I must thank my editors, Rory Gormley and Yasmin Garcha, for shepherding this book through to publication; and the anonymous reviewers who read and commented on my manuscript. Finally, I would like to express my gratitude to the archivists, curators and reading room staff of the manuscript libraries that I visited while conducting this research.

A NOTE ON TRANSLITERATION AND DATES

The system of transliteration to which I adhere throughout this book is a modified form of *IJMES*. As per the style guidelines of the series, overdots and underdots are not used. Macrons are employed to indicate long vowels in the transliteration of quotations from poetry, artistic prose and the Qur'an. In all other instances, including in the transliteration of personal names, ranks (e.g. *sultan*, *amir*), book titles, place names and geographical terms, technical terms, poetic forms, poetic metres, numbers and months of the year, no diacritical marks are used at all.

Dates are provided in the *hijri* calendar and Common Era notation in the format AH/CE. The seventeenth century of the Common Era largely coincides with the eleventh century of the Hijra.

A NOTE ON GEOGRAPHICAL TERMINOLOGY

The names 'Arabia', 'Iran' and 'India' are applied in the title of this book as shorthand terms to describe the regions of the western, northern and eastern littoral of the Arabian Sea. It is important to emphasize that these three broad zones should not be considered monolithic or discrete political dispensations, that borders shifted considerably during the seventeenth century, and that changing political control affected the circulation of poets. In the Arabian Peninsula, the north remained under Ottoman suzerainty;[1] the cities of Mecca and Medina and the surrounding region of the Hijaz were controlled by the *sharifs* of Mecca;[2] after the expulsion of the Ottomans in 1044–5/1635, upland Yemen was united under the Qasimi Imamate;[3] Hadramawt recognized Qasimi suzerainty, but was ruled by the Kathiri sultans;[4] the Portuguese had control of Muscat until 1060/1650, when the Imam Sultan b. Sayf of the Ya'ariba re-established Omani authority.[5]

Iran was ruled by the Safavid dynasty, who, during the reign of Shah 'Abbas I (r. 995/1587–1038/1629), exerted political authority over an area extending from Diyarbakır and Baghdad in the west to Qandahar in the east, and from Yerevan in the north to Bahrain in the south.[6] However, conflict with the Ottomans, the Toqay-Timurid Khanate of Central Asia, the Mughals and the Portuguese meant that the boundaries of the Safavid state changed. Qandahar passed from Mughal to Safavid hands, with the Safavids taking the city in 1058/1649.[7] Baghdad was lost to the Ottomans in 1047/1638.[8] Bahrain was captured from the Portuguese in 1011/1602.[9] Although the suzerainty of the Safavids extended far beyond the borders of the modern nation of Iran, many areas of their state were semi-independent. The region of 'Arabistan, for example, which covered a similar territory to the modern-day province of Khuzistan, was ruled by a local dynasty, the Musha'sha', who acknowledged the nominal authority of the Safavids.[10]

In South Asia, during most of the seventeenth century, the domains of the expansionist Mughal Empire stretched from Kabul in the northwest to Bengal in the east, and to Ahmadnagar in the south.[11] On the Deccan plateau, the 'Adilshahi sultanate of Bijapur and the Qutbshahi sultanate of Golkonda remained nominally independent of the Mughals until 1097/1686 and 1098/1687 respectively.[12] One should also remember that centres of political authority changed during the seventeenth century. For example, the Mughal emperor Awrangzib (r. 1068/1658–1118/1707) was absent from his capital at Delhi during the second half of his reign, as he campaigned against the Deccan sultanates and the Marathas.[13]

Partly due to changing political geography, but also due to their own itineraries and perspectives, the seventeenth-century authors who are discussed in this book did not all use the same nomenclature or subscribe to the same conceptualization of geographical space. The use of different terms was not simply tied to language.

For Ibn Ma'sum, active in Arabic in Golkonda before its annexation by the Mughals, the Deccan was part of *al-Diyar al-Hindiyya* ('the land of India').[14] Nizam al-Din Ahmad Sa'idi Shirazi, also writing in Golkonda but in Persian, speaks of individuals travelling from the Qutbshahi domains to *Hindustan*, equating the latter word with the Mughal north.[15] Nasrabadi, writing in Persian in Iran, often introduces a distinction between physical and political geography when discussing South Asia, sometimes using the word *Hindustan* to designate South Asia as a region, and the words *Hind* and *Dakan* to mean the polities that covered it (the Mughal Empire and the Deccan sultanates).[16] However, at other moments, he also equates *Hindustan* with the Mughal domains, contrasting them with *Vilayat-i Dakan* (the dominion of the Deccan).[17] Safi ibn Vali, who performed pilgrimage to Mecca in the year 1087/1676 under Mughal patronage, writes of *Bilad va Amsar-i Hind* ('the countries and lands of India').[18]

Seventeenth-century authors also applied the term *Iran* in different ways, sometimes using it to refer to the Safavid body politic, and at other times employing it to describe the land which the Safavids controlled. Despite being the descendant of a Safavid princess, Ibn Ma'sum uses the term *Faris* ('Persia') and *al-'Ajam* ('non-Arabs', or 'Persians') when writing of Iranian authors and the Safavid state too (he calls Shah 'Abbas I *Sultan al-'Ajam*, or 'the sultan of the Persians').[19] Nasrabadi refers to the courtiers and commanders of the Safavid state as *Muqarraban va Umara'-yi Iran* ('the courtiers and commanders of Iran'), but speaks of *'Iraq* and *Khurasan* when referring to the western and eastern lands of the Safavid domains.[20]

At the same time, we can find overlapping representations of space shared between the works of different authors: Ibn Ma'sum invokes a geographical rather than political mode of thinking when describing the region of the Hijaz (*al-Hijaz*).[21] Safi ibn Vali also uses a geographical frame when referring to *Hijaz* ('the Hijaz') and *Tihama* ('the Tihama').[22] Both authors think in partly political terms when they speak of *Bilad al-Yaman* ('the country of Yemen') and *Vilayat-i Yaman* ('the dominion of Yemen').[23]

Thus, representations of space reflect both the physical location of the authors, and their own prejudices, networks and concerns. Readers are therefore asked to remember that for the historical figures discussed in this book, terms cognate with 'Arabia', 'Iran' and 'India' would have elicited a variety of interpretations.

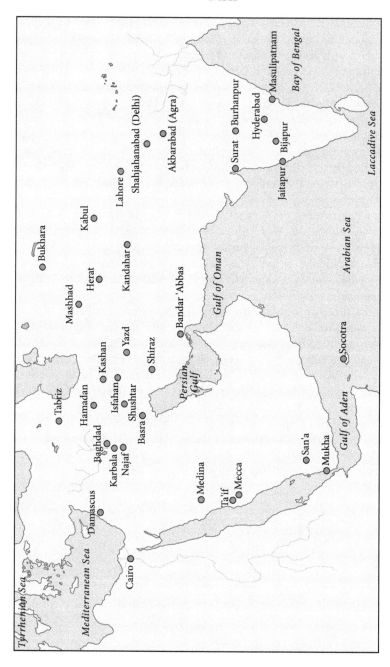

Figure 1 Map of the Arabian Sea.

A SUMMARY LIST OF KEY HISTORICAL FIGURES

Ibn Ma'sum al-Madani (1052/1642–1119/1707). A poet, philologist and Shi'i thinker who wrote in Arabic, and the author of the biographical anthology of seventeenth-century Arabic poetry entitled *Sulafat al-'Asr fi Mahasin A'yan al-'Asr* (*The First Wine of the Press, on the Merits of the Leading Men of the Age*). Raised in Mecca, Ibn Ma'sum emigrated to Hyderabad in the Deccan as a teenager. This was because his father, Nizam al-Din Ahmad al-Husayni (1027/1618–1085/1674), had become the confidant and son-in-law of Sultan 'Abd Allah (r. 1035/1626–1083/1672), ruler of the Qutbshahi sultanate of Hyderabad and Golkonda. Ibn Ma'sum spent forty-five years in India, initially as a prince of the Qutbshahi court, and then as a provincial bureaucrat under Mughal rule. In the last years of his life, he left India for good, and travelled back to Mecca, then performed pilgrimage to the Shi'i shrine cities of Iraq and finally moved to Safavid Iran, the homeland of his paternal ancestors. He bought a house in Shiraz, in the affluent district of Bazar-i Murgh, where he died in 1119/1707.

Ibrahim b. Salih al-Hindi (d. 1101/1689–90), known by his pen name as al-Sarim al-Hindi. A poet and scribe in the employ of the Qasimi Imams of Yemen, and the author of a collected volume of Arabic verse which survives in manuscript. Al-Sarim al-Hindi's father, Salih al-Muhtadi, was a member of the Banya, the class of Hindu and Jain brokers who acted as middlemen in the trading system of the Arabian Sea, and latterly a convert to Islam. Al-Sarim himself grew up in Yemen, and was trained in Arabic literary culture from a young age. In his poetry, he helped to explore and to fix an identity for the Qasimi Imams, particularly Isma'il al-Mutawakkil (r. 1044/1644–1087/1676) and al-Mahdi Ahmad (r. 1087/1676–1092/1681). Al-Sarim was a good friend of the father of al-Haymi al-Kawkabani (d. 1151/1738–9), eighteenth-century Yemen's most prominent literary biographer. Al-Sarim is the subject of an entry in Ibn Ma'sum's *Sulafat al-'Asr*.

Al-Hurr al-'Amili (1033/1624–1104/1693). A prominent jurist, theologian and biographer, al-Hurr was born in Jabal 'Amil, a district in the mountains of southern Lebanon known for its historical Shi'i community. He emigrated to Safavid Iran in his forties and became *Shaykh al-Islam* at the shrine of the Imam Riza in Mashhad. In addition to his theological scholarship, al-Hurr was also an accomplished Arabic poet, and took a great deal of interest in the Arabic poetry of his contemporaries, as is shown in his biographical work, *Amal al-Amil fi Dhikr 'Ulama Jabal 'Amil* (*The Hope of the Hopeful, Recalling the Religious Scholars of Jabal 'Amil*). Al-Hurr is the subject of an entry in Ibn Ma'sum's *Sulafat al-'Asr*.

Muhammad Tahir Nasrabadi (1027/1617-18 – after 1099/1687–8). Born into a once-influential family of landowners whose estate was at Nasrabad, just south of the Safavid capital at Isfahan, Nasrabadi was one of seventeenth-century Iran's most prominent editors, essayists and publishers. His biographical anthology (*tazkira*) of contemporary Persian verse was the result of many years of corresponding with, and meeting, poets, particularly in Isfahan's coffee houses and mosques. Towards the end of his life, Nasrabadi founded his own coffee house in the suburb of Lunban, where poets came and sought him out. He was a great friend of Sa'ib (*c*. 1000/1592–1086–7/1676), the most illustrious Persian poet of the later seventeenth century.

Salik Yazdi (d. 1081/1671). A professional poet active in Persian, Salik was born in Yazd, in Iran, and began his career in Shiraz and Isfahan, before setting out for the Deccan, where he found employment at the court of Sultan 'Abd Allah the Qutbshah. There he encountered a number of other migrant poets from Iran, including Faraj Allah al-Shushtari. Salik's main patrons in Golkonda were the *Mir Jumla* (prime minister) Muhammad Sa'id Ardistani, and Ardistani's son, Muhammad Amin. When these two men defected to the side of the Mughals in 1066/1655, Salik followed them north to Delhi, where he died. Salik is the subject of an entry in Nasrabadi's *tazkira*.

Ilahi Hamadani (d. *c*. 1063/1653). Another professional poet active in Persian, Ilahi was born in Asadabad in Iran, probably in the last decade of the sixteenth century. As a young man, he emigrated to India, where he initially found employment at the Mughal court. He then moved to Kabul, where he developed an association with Zafar Khan Ahsan (d. 1073/1662–3), the Mughal governor of the city. Along with Ahsan, his companions in Kabul included a young Sa'ib. When Ahsan was reassigned to govern Kashmir, Ilahi went into retirement there, constructing a garden which became a famous location for poetic gatherings. Ilahi is the subject of an entry in Nasrabadi's *tazkira*.

Nur al-Din Muhammad Sharif Kashani (d. 1123/1711–12), known by his pen name Najib. The son of a draper, Najib grew up in Kashan, and then came to Isfahan as a young, aspiring poet. Biographies indicate that he spent some time in Yerevan, working for the Safavid governor of the city, before emigrating to Kashmir, where he became associated with the Mughal prince Akbar (d. 1119/1707). Najib returned to Isfahan, and was soon followed by Akbar, who had revolted against his father, the emperor Awrangzib (d. 1118/1707), and so sought sanctuary with the Safavids, to whom he was related on his mother's side. The Safavid statesman Muhammad Tahir Vahid (d. 1112/1701) assigned Najib to accompany (and to inform on) Akbar during the latter's stay in Isfahan. Najib published his memoirs of his time with Akbar under the title *Tarikh-i Kishikkhana-yi Humayun* (*The History of the Royal Guardhouse*). Najib is the subject of an entry in Nasrabadi's *tazkira*.

Part I

DISTANT READINGS IN SEVENTEENTH-CENTURY
MIGRATION

INTRODUCTION

CONNECTED LITERARY HISTORY

Migration, mobility and the world of the seventeenth century

In the collections of Amsterdam's Rijksmuseum is an album of paintings that was compiled in India in 1686.[1] Many of the images inside are individual portraits of ministers of the court of the Qutbshahs, a dynasty of Shi'i Muslim sultans who ruled over Golkonda and Hyderabad in India's southern Deccan region between the early sixteenth century and 1098/1687, when the Mughal ruler Awrangzib (r. 1068/1658–1118/1707) absorbed their kingdom into his expanding empire. The album was probably assembled for European audiences in Hyderabad as a pictorial history of the elites of India's ruling houses: the portraits are annotated in Portuguese and Dutch with information on the men who are represented, reflecting the fact that European powers had carved out a significant role for themselves in shipping and trade across the Indian Ocean by the middle of the seventeenth century, and were interested in absorbing as much knowledge as possible about the political history of South Asia.[2] One of the portraits depicts a grey-bearded man in his sixties, clad in a striped robe and a cap, with a shawl over his shoulders (Figure 2). He gazes towards stage left, his look weary but self-assured. The inscription in Dutch beneath the painting reads: 'Mirza Ahmad, son in law of Sultan 'Abd Allah, chief vizier of the whole kingdom'.

This annotation, and the inscriptions accompanying copies of this painting in other albums, allow me to identify the portrait as a representation of Nizam al-Din Ahmad b. Ma'sum al-Husayni (d. 1085/1674), the chief minister of Golkonda between 1656 and 1672, who eventually fell from power in the regime change that followed the death of his employer and father-in-law, the Qutbshah 'Abd Allah (r. 1035/1626–1083/1672). Nizam al-Din Ahmad is a fascinating figure, and his life encapsulates the processes of migration, community formation and transcultural literary production which this book investigates. He was not from a local family of Hyderabad, but had journeyed at the relatively young age of twenty-seven from his home, 2,500 miles away in the Arabian Peninsula, to become a leading minister of state in the Deccan. When he arrived in India, he quickly established himself as a reference point for other émigrés. A sponsor of Arabic culture, with a marked interest in mathematics and astronomy, he patronized a circle of poets who came to the court of the Qutbshahs from Mecca and Medina, Yemen, Iraq, Bahrain

Figure 2 Nizam al-Din Ahmad. Rijkmuseum RP-T-00-3186-24,26 CC0.

and Iran, creating an Arabic literary network which connected the urban centres around the littoral of the Arabian Sea.

In Hyderabad, Nizam al-Din Ahmad's Arabic circle took shape alongside, even inside, communities that were also composing literary texts in Persian, Dakhni and Telugu.[3] The city was what Francesca Orsini terms a 'multilingual local', and what Karen Thornber calls a 'contact nebula': a space in which writers active in different languages transformed one another's texts.[4] Dakhni and Telugu functioned as 'cosmopolitan vernacular' languages under the Qutbshahs, meaning that they were both languages of daily communication for Hyderabad's population, and that they were also used to compose literary texts.[5] At the court of Sultan ʿAbd Allah, Dakhni romances, which often responded to Persian models, were consumed alongside a rich corpus of Telugu song cycles, and Telugu poems, some of which expanded beyond the traditional themes of Telugu literature and addressed quintessentially Shiʿi topics, such as the martyrdom of the Imam Husayn.[6]

Like Dakhni and Telugu, Persian and Arabic also functioned as local literary languages in Sultan ʿAbd Allah's Hyderabad: they were used as a means of exchange among communities of writers at the court of the Qutbshahs who were addressing one another and domestic audiences. Many of these writers were migrants from Arabia and Iran, for whom Arabic, Persian or both languages were at once vernacular idioms of daily communication and languages of high culture. At the same time, the literary works which these small communities in Hyderabad produced fed into a much larger, transregional system of literary production in Persian and Arabic, creating globalizing idioms that actively linked writers in India with readers in Arabia and Iran. In this book, I examine the interplay between these localizing and globalizing tendencies that made Persian and Arabic cosmopolitan languages of high culture during the seventeenth century, not just in south India but all around the littoral of the Arabian Sea. One of my central points of enquiry is the question of why authors sought to write in a way that enabled their Persian and Arabic texts to circulate transregionally, even as they composed for specific groups of interlocutors in their immediate environs, creating what Ronit Ricci calls a 'web of prior texts and new interpretations that were crucial to the establishment of both local and global . . . identities'.[7]

It does not automatically stand to reason that seventeenth-century writers *should* have adopted consciously globalizing idioms which engaged – formally and intellectually – with the literary past when they composed Persian and Arabic texts. Many other authors active in the two languages *did* experiment with linguistic register and with form, producing literary works that reflected the version of the language which they heard around them and which spoke to the needs of their immediate communities, a process of 'double distancing' in which 'the pleasures of the local tongue' were celebrated.[8] The choice to use globalizing idioms meant not only embracing standardized linguistic registers but also working with established corpora of literary forms and themes which had been developed for over 1,100 years in the case of Arabic and for over 750 years in the case of Persian. In both literary cultures, the most common globalizing genres of the seventeenth century all used verse forms. They include the panegyric (generally written in the *qasida* form in both Arabic and Persian, but sometimes also composed using strophic or short forms in Persian), the lyric (often composed using the *qit'a* in Arabic, and almost always using the *ghazal* in Persian) and the narrative poem (often composed in *rajaz* verse in Arabic, and using the *masnavi* in Persian). Authors also composed elegies, poems about friendship, satires and lyric epigrams in both languages.

As Sheldon Pollock writes, 'creating or experiencing literature that is meant for a large world or a small place is a tacit declaration of one's affiliation with that world or place.'[9] The authors of Arabic and Persian literary texts who concern me here were declaring their affiliation with Pollock's 'large world'. Thibaut d'Hubert argues that it was 'the will to carve out a new, deprofessionalized space for literacy' that fostered the use of regionally inflected literary idioms' in the early modern Indian Ocean arena.[10] By the same token, authors who composed globalizing Arabic and Persian texts were seeking to preserve this world of professionalism by creating a 'communal and confederational site of discussion'.[11] In this respect, their activities parallel those of authors who composed in other cosmopolitan idioms because of their durability and the freight of associations with which they were charged. Certain patrons at the Mughal court, for example, opted to sponsor the production of works in Sanskrit, because it presented an established series of 'options for imagining and enacting imperial power'.[12] Other cosmopolitan literary tongues opened up different avenues: for example, Brajbhasa – a form of Hindi that had been shaped into a predominantly literary idiom – gave writers in north India ways of interacting 'with the Persianate world of Mughal India in ways that were foreclosed by classical tradition'.[13]

Nizam al-Din Ahmad's multi-layered use of Arabic may seem to us today to represent a 'hybrid' identity, but the use of such a term risks delimiting our view of the Arabic language, its historical reach and Nizam al-Din Ahmad's own orientation. In many ways, he stands outside the 'paradigmatic categories' that nineteenth- and twentieth-century historiography and modern nationalisms have imposed on our understanding of the early modern period,[14] and his experiences invite us to think about what Gayatri Spivak calls the 'unacknowledged prehistory' of comparative literature and comparative frames of thinking.[15] He was related to a long line of *sayyids* (descendants of the Prophet Muhammad) who had spent many generations in Iran. His five times great-grandfather, the *amir* Sadr al-Din Muhammad Dashtaki (d. 903/1498), was a religious scholar and landowner who had endowed the Mansuriyya Madrasa (Islamic college) in Shiraz, Iran.[16] His great-grandfather, Ibrahim b. Salam Allah (d. 990/1582-3), had married into the royal family of Safavid Iran (907/1501–1135/1722) by wedding Gawhar Shad Baygum, the daughter of Prince Ibrahim Mirza (d. 984/1577).[17] The children born from this union had set about creating an international network. While a branch of the family remained in Fars, one son, Nasir al-Din (d. 1023/1614–15) emigrated to the cities of Ta'if and Mecca in the Arabian Peninsula, along with his nephew (Nizam al-Din Ahmad's father), Muhammad Maʿsum (d. 1032/1622-3).[18] The family prospered as scholars and merchants. Their ability to assume authority wherever they set up camp is a quality that they shared with other *sayyids*, who migrated extensively in the early modern period, establishing themselves as mercantile and political actors in an area extending from North Africa to the Malay Archipelago, and in some instances also founding states.[19]

Nizam al-Din Ahmad himself was born in the town of Ta'if, in the province of Mecca, on 4th Shaʿban 1027/27 July 1618.[20] The eighteenth-century man of letters ʿAbbas al-Makki (d. *c.* 1180/1766-7) reports that Nizam al-Din Ahmad studied a range of subjects with renowned teachers, including *fiqh* (Islamic jurisprudence), *hadith* (statements attributed to the Prophet Muhammad), the Arabic language and logic, and that he possessed a prodigious memory, which made him a skilled transmitter of knowledge.[21] Nizam al-Din Ahmad's background and abilities allowed him to make a successful match with the daughter of a leading Meccan jurist and merchant, Muhammad b. Ahmad al-Manufi (d. 1044/1634-5), who had lectured on religious law in Damascus and had been patronized by Murad IV (r. 1032/1623–1049/1640), sultan of the Ottoman Empire (1299–1922 CE).[22] Al-Manufi was a Sunni, and so the marriage was not only international but also ecumenical.[23] Nizam al-Din Ahmad was building a multifaceted identity which supported his mobility.

It may strike readers as curious that a man who began life with no connection to India, and who did not speak Dakhni or Telugu, was chosen to assume power in Golkonda, but during the seventeenth century, the polities of the western Indian Ocean formed a zone of circulation, in which religion, trade and state building stimulated mass migration. It was routine to journey between the Arabian Peninsula, Iran and India. Nizam al-Din Ahmad's first wife – al-Manufi's daughter, whose name is not given in the sources – was independently well travelled before she even met her husband. She was the widow of *mulla* ʿAli b. *mulla* Qasim b. Niʿmat Allah al-Shirazi al-Makki, a Meccan philologist and rhetorician of Iranian descent who had spent time in India.[24] After *mulla* ʿAli's death, she had journeyed to both Iran and India, but had eventually returned to Mecca, where her marriage to Nizam al-Din Ahmad took place.[25] Émigré scholars of Arabic from both Iran and the Arabian Peninsula had also been present in Golkonda at the beginning of the seventeenth century.[26]

After his arrival in the Deccan in 1055/1645–6, Nizam al-Din Ahmad made a second, polygynous marriage to one of Sultan ʿAbd Allah's daughters, who is named in some sources as Fatima.[27] The wedding precipitated his rise to power and allowed him to become a munificent patron of Arabic letters. Nizam al-Din Ahmad was able to tighten his grip on power further when the *Mir Jumla* (prime minister) Muhammad Saʿid Ardistani, another *sayyid*, defected to the side of India's preeminent political dynasty, the Mughals, in 1066/1656.[28] Nizam al-Din Ahmad then emerged as one of the most influential figures at the Qutbshahi court, along with Sultan ʿAbd Allah's mother and regent, Hayat Bakhshi Baygum, who died in 1077/1667.[29] He was appointed to the post of ʿAyn al-Mulk ('Eye of the Kingdom'), a position which purportedly made him outrank all other ministers.[30] The daily news reports of Hyderabad indicate that he had a particular role as a gatekeeper who facilitated introductions between foreign merchants and the sultan.[31] He lived for some time in the fortress of Golkonda, the seat of government, where the Qutbshahs had their apartments, and, in testament to his wealth, he had a mansion constructed for himself in the city of Hyderabad in 1069/1658–9.[32] His influence came to an end with the death of Sultan ʿAbd Allah in 1083/1672 and the subsequent struggle for succession, which saw him incarcerated by the military commander Sayyid Muzaffar, another émigré from Iran.[33] Nizam al-Din Ahmad was murdered – poisoned, it seems – in prison in 1085/1674.[34]

For as long as he was able to exercise authority in Golkonda, Nizam al-Din Ahmad tried to use his position to expand his family's political and economic interests in the states around the littoral of the Arabian Sea. This was a high-risk scheme, as is evidenced by Nizam al-Din Ahmad's ultimate imprisonment and death, but he was able to justify his interests for a long time thanks to the transregional migrations of his forebears. Previously unstudied letters demonstrate that while he was at the height of his powers, Nizam al-Din Ahmad was in correspondence with the most important state religious officials of the Safavid dynasty, Khalifa Sultan (d. 1064/1654), and Mirza Mahdi (d. 1081/1670–1), to whom he addressed several petitions, in which he staked his claims to the ownership of landed property in Iran.[35] One entrepreneurial petition, which seems to have gone unanswered, outlined Nizam al-Din Ahmad's rights to all the property that had been owned by his paternal grandmother, the Safavid princess Gawhar Shad Baygum, despite the fact that this property had come under Safavid state control. In his letter, Nizam al-Din Ahmad requests that the management of the property be transferred to his agent in Iran, Muhammad Muqima, and that the income deriving from the holdings be handed to Nizam al-Din Ahmad's family in Mecca.[36] Hypothetically, if this request were to have been granted, it is likely that it would have made Nizam al-Din Ahmad and his sons some of the wealthiest landowners in Iran.

A separate request, which was actually approved in 1066/1655–6, demanded that another one of Nizam al-Din Ahmad's agents in Iran, Sayyid Muhammad al-Bahrani, be handed control of the property, endowments and land in Shiraz and Khurasan that had been owned by Nizam al-Din Ahmad's recently deceased paternal uncle.[37] These holdings included the Mansuriyya Madrasa, the religious school which had been founded by Nizam al-Din Ahmad's ancestor, Sadr al-Din Muhammad Dashtaki.[38] While Nizam al-Din Ahmad's petitions give some indication that his immediate family's absence from Iran had hindered them from claiming their inheritance, they also vividly show how he tried to build a globalized portfolio of holdings for himself and his sons, and thereby to increase his economic and political influence transregionally.

Nizam al-Din Ahmad may have supported his literary circle financially, but it was his son, ʿAli Sadr al-Din Ibn Maʿsum al-Husayni al-Hasani (1052/1642 – before Ramadan 1119/November 1707) (henceforth Ibn Maʿsum), who turned it into a bounded community by imagining it in textual form.[39] Nizam al-Din Ahmad had left his young son behind when he was establishing himself in India, and so Ibn Maʿsum grew up in Mecca, attending study circles at which scholars from all over the Islamic world met and debated topics in religion, the law, and Arabic philology.[40] When Nizam al-Din Ahmad had secured his position as chief minister at the court of the Qutbshahs, he summoned Ibn Maʿsum. After his arrival in the Deccan in 1068/1657, at the age of fifteen, Ibn Maʿsum did not abandon his studies but expanded them, training with two specialists in the fields of *fiqh*, *hadith*, Qurʾanic exegesis, biography, Arabic grammar and prosody, who had travelled from the Shiʿi scholarly centres of Jabal ʿAmil (in modern-day Lebanon) and Bahrain to join the entourage of Nizam al-Din Ahmad.[41] Ibn Maʿsum's education should therefore partly be seen as a diasporic and Indian phenomenon.

Today, Ibn Maʿsum is better known than his father, thanks to the large body of extant Arabic works which he wrote.[42] His identity was closely connected to his status as a *sayyid* and as a scholar of Twelver Shiʿism, and many of his works, not just those that are about explicitly religious topics, such as his short treatise on *hadith* transmitted by his ancestors, but also those which are about Arabic language and literature, project and reflect the presence of a connected, professional Shiʿi community around the Arabian Sea.[43] Just like his father, Ibn Maʿsum sought to use his philological and religious authority to link the littoral of the western Indian Ocean economically. In around 1114/1702–3, having spent over forty-five years in India, initially as a prince of the realm and then as a provincial bureaucrat, Ibn Maʿsum returned to the Arabian Peninsula and then made his way for the first time to the country of his ancestors, Iran. The impetus for this journey seems to have been primarily financial. On arriving in Mecca, Ibn Maʿsum inventoried his family's property there and ensured that the inalienable charitable endowment on it was registered in the names of his sons.[44] Having journeyed on to Iraq and inspired a biographer there, Muhammad ʿAli al-Khayqani, to write a continuation of his work, he finally arrived in Iran.[45] There, he made a pilgrimage to the shrine of the Imam Riza at Mashhad, in the vicinity of which he purchased agricultural property, again endowing it to his offspring.[46] He then headed to Shiraz, where he entered into a new legal dispute over the ownership of the Mansuriyya Madrasa and its holdings.[47] He won this case and ensured that his three adult sons, who had travelled with him, would inherit the property.[48] The *madrasa* itself is an excellent example of how the circulation of knowledge and the movement of capital were imbricated in one another.

Ibn Maʿsum's migrations open up a way into exploring the intersection between textual production, circulation and the literary canon. Most particularly in the Deccan, but also in Iran, Ibn Maʿsum's spatial distance from the traditional centres of Arabic learning further to the west encouraged him to take a panoramic view of the Arabic literary corpus, much like the scholars al-Thaʿalibi (d. 429/1037–8) before him, and Azad Bilgrami (d. 1200/1786) after him, both of whom also spent most of their lives in lands where Arabic was not a vernacular for the majority.[49] This panoramic perspective is best embodied by Ibn Maʿsum's global biographical anthology of the Arabic poetry of his contemporaries, entitled, in the previously unknown autograph manuscript, *Sulafat al-ʿAsr fi Mahasin Aʿyan al-ʿAsr* (*The First Wine of the Press, on the Merits of the Leading Men of the Age*).[50] *Sulafat al-ʿAsr* is made up of 129 individual biographical entries, each one of which offers a summary of the given subject's life and career, and selections of his poetry. The individual entries are in turn subsumed into five chapters, which each represent a region: (1) Mecca and Medina; (2) Syria and Egypt; (3) Yemen; (4) Iran, Iraq and Bahrain; (5) North Africa. The biographical subjects are mostly sorted into these geographically oriented sections on the basis of the location from which they migrated rather than their destination, creating 'paternal and learned lineages'.[51] For example, there are poets placed into the chapter on Syria and Egypt who travelled to the Deccan in the course of their careers. This means that the five regions are not discrete: networks overlap between them, creating an ecumene of circulation that extended from North Africa to India.

Ibn Maʿsum's decision to compose *Sulafat al-ʿAsr* certainly owes something to the conventions of scholarship in his own time. When he was a child, the Egyptian scholar al-Khafaji (d. 1069/1659) had composed a biographical anthology of contemporary poetry entitled *Rayhanat al-Alibbaʾ wa-Zahrat al-Hayat al-Dunya* (*The Sweet Basil of the Learned and the Blossom of Earthly Life*), and Ibn Maʿsum reveals in his introduction to *Sulafat al-ʿAsr* that he was inspired – and irritated – when he received a copy of this book, as he himself had been planning to write a similar volume since his early teens.[52] He presents *Sulafat al-ʿAsr* as a corrective to the *Rayhana*, designed to publicize information about men of learning and erudition who formed part of his own network.[53] In a sense, therefore, the work is about promoting an intellectual movement, and about framing biographical information that was in circulation for its own ends.[54]

Yet, seen from the perspective of world literary studies, *Sulafat al-ʿAsr* offers an insight into the processes by which literatures select, present and circulate texts, building cultural capital and levels of recognition which allow them to assert their independence as transnational idioms.[55] While it is certainly important that Arabic literary culture (*adab*) had an illustrious history stretching back more than 1,100 years in the Middle East by the time that Ibn Maʿsum was writing, the question of its authority in South Asia is another matter. Although Arabic is often imagined to have acted as a lingua franca wherever there were Muslim populations, the reality for anyone navigating the early modern world would have been more akin to Foucault's 'heterotopia': as Nile Green argues, the western Indian Ocean's 'social and linguistic realities' meant that cosmopolitanism was always contested, and the ability of migrant scholars to find interlocutors in the diaspora who shared exactly the same worldview as them was not a given.[56]

Ibn Maʿsum's selections of the poetry of his contemporaries in *Sulafat al-ʿAsr* show how he and the writers with whom he was in dialogue related to the conventions of globalizing Arabic literary production from its traditional centres further to the west, but at the same time, their work was not a pale imitation of something as monolithic as 'metropolitan style'. The anthology therefore encourages us to look beyond a model of centres and margins, in which writers in the diaspora merely reproduce the work of the centre, and instead uncover a version of Arabic literature which is worldly because it manages to effect a balance between addressing the diverse social contexts in which it is composed and maintaining a dialogue with the transnational. Although it relates to a different, postcolonial environment, Elleke Boehmer's concept of imitation with the intention 'to explore new worlds', provides a useful frame for understanding how migrant poets of the seventeenth century related to canonical works of Arabic and Persian verse.[57] Rather than seeing early modern Arabic and Persian classicizing poems as derivative reiterations of medieval convention, we should be open to considering their possible facility for expressing dissonance, dislocation and a new artistic identity. Here, Wai-Chee Dimock's idea of 'deep time', through which literary texts bind 'continents and millennia into many loops of relations', becomes a productive framework for considering how seventeenth-century writers did not simply imitate the texts of the classical corpora but, rather, sought to embody them.[58]

As Ibn Maʿsum was mapping the corpus of contemporary Arabic poetry from Hyderabad, another man living just under 2,000 miles to the north west, in Isfahan, the capital of Safavid Iran, had committed to doing a methodologically identical task, charting the corpus of contemporary Persian poetry by using a form of biographical anthology that was broadly cognate with *Sulafat al-ʿAsr*.[59] Muhammad Tahir Nasrabadi (1027/1617–18 – after 1099/1687–8), read the first draft of *Tazkira-yi Nasrabadi* (*Nasrabadi's Biographical Anthology*) with his amanuensis, Sabz ʿAli Baba Ahmadi, in 1086/1676, only four and a half years after Ibn Maʿsum had completed the same process with his own copyist, Saʿid b. Darwish b. ʿAli al-Kujarati.[60] The main difference between his anthology and *Sulafat al-ʿAsr* is that Nasrabadi treats many more poets in less detail than Ibn Maʿsum, with just over 900 biographical entries in the main body of the *tazkira*. This is manifestly not a comment on the numbers of seventeenth-century poets writing in Arabic or in Persian, simply a choice on the part of the anthologists. A further difference between the two anthologies is that Nasrabadi uses sociological categories to divide his subjects, beginning with the kings of the age, then proceeding through the leading courtiers of Iran and India, before coming to calligraphers, dervishes and, finally, the professional poets of Iran, Iraq, Central Asia and India. We have no indication that Nasrabadi and Ibn Maʿsum knew of each other's enterprises, although, as we shall see in Chapter 1, there were very few degrees of separation between them. The reason why they both decided to compose such works depends in part on the fact that the biographical anthology was simply a common vehicle for presenting and classifying knowledge in both premodern Arabic and premodern Persian literary culture, and in part on the fact that both men were witnesses to the same social phenomenon of mass migration and diasporic literary production in the Indian Ocean. A partly geographical, partly sociological frame for classifying and describing literary production helped the anthologists to make sense of this globalizing system.

A member of a family of once-influential landowners and court administrators who had fallen on hard times, Nasrabadi was a consummate insider in Safavid high society who nevertheless managed to observe his contemporaries as though he were an outsider. In his autobiography, which he appends to his anthology, Nasrabadi bitterly complains of his family's fall from power and their perceived marginalization as a result of the Safavid state's decision to take control of the *vaqf* (charitable endowment) on their ancestral landed property during the reign of Shah Tahmasp (930/1524–984/1576).[61] The family lived on the income that they derived from their holdings, and so this move effectively stripped them of a large portion of their wealth.[62] Nasrabadi's account of his own life is marked by a strong sense of exclusion. He writes that his father was a good man but had been distressed by financial concerns and died when Nasrabadi himself was seventeen.[63] In his grief, Nasrabadi turned in on himself and developed addictions to gambling and narcotics.[64] However, he began to frequent coffee houses, which acted as a nexus of sociability where courtiers, the nobility, professional poets and the ordinary inhabitants of Isfahan came together, and he met a group of poets among whom he felt a sense of belonging.[65] Notably, he writes that he received no formal training in the art of poetry but, rather, became poeticized through association with others.[66] He was primarily a critic, an editor and an essayist, but he did compose a limited amount of his own verse.[67] In later life, when his renown as a literary figure had grown, he founded his own coffee house behind the mosque at Lunban, in a suburb of Isfahan, where poets would seek him out.[68] He also spent a considerable amount of time on his family estate at Nasrabad, a small village to the southeast of Isfahan.

The fact that Nasrabadi experienced isolation and dislocation while living at the geographical heart of the Safavid Empire invites us to consider the boundaries of the community that he established with contemporary poets. It is true that Nasrabadi was writing at a time when the Safavid state was pursuing policies of centralization, and simultaneously fostering an Iranian national identity through the promulgation of Twelver Shiʿism and the Persian language, which was far from the only language spoken in premodern Iran. It is also true that Nasrabadi anchors his anthology in the Safavid capital of Isfahan, on some level equating the practice of Persian poetry with the exercise of Safavid political power. However, the demographics of the *tazkira* depend on flows of people from the Iranian provinces to Isfahan, from Isfahan to Iran's port cities, and between Iran, the Arabian Peninsula, Central Asia and India. The anthology is not founded on a sense of national literary community but, rather, on an idea of connections between individuals who were in constant motion – 'indefinitely stretchable nets of kinship and clientship', to borrow an expression from Benedict Anderson.[69] Like *Sulafat al-ʿAsr*, Nasrabadi's *tazkira* is designed to help literature circulate on a global scale. The poems that it contains can be related to one another through their use of common formal and thematic conventions, but the anthology is not a project designed to argue that Safavid Iran 'influenced' literary style in other political dispensations. Rather, it shows the plurality of voices transforming classical literary convention. It is this balancing act between creating a corpus of poetry that depends on shared features and accommodating differences that makes Nasrabadi a worldly author.[70] Although there are many features of Nasrabadi's life which might lead us to distinguish him from Ibn Maʿsum, both anthologists shared a panoramic view of literary activity in their chosen language of high culture.

Globalizing literatures: Transnational community in the anthologies

Every act of composing a text is dependent on reading the work of others, no matter whether an author is emulative or iconoclastic (since one can only deliberately reject the past if one knows it).[71] Yet writers do not have access to the same, universal body of works. The materials that they read are shaped by the basic practicalities of what is available to them. Seventeenth-century Arabic and Persian book culture was dependent on manuscripts, which often presented varying recensions of texts, even when it came to the classics.[72] Contemporary, freshly composed works of literature generally circulated semi-privately, in authors' notebooks (also called commonplaces) or in manuscript *divans/diwans* (collected works) which were not subject to mass reproduction. This tied the process of reading to the practice of sociability, because it was only by meeting people or corresponding with them and reading the texts that they permitted one to see that one could maximize one's own knowledge of the contemporary corpus.[73] A vivid illustration of the importance of channels of diffusion is made by Nasrabadi, who writes of a close acquaintance, named Mulla ʿAli Bayg, who had spent a considerable amount of time in Nasrabad, had taught the young Nasrabadi calligraphy, and had retired to the village.[74] Despite the long-lasting connection between the two men, Nasrabadi struggled to gain access to Mulla ʿAli Bayg's collected works, as the only manuscript copy of them was owned by one of Nasrabadi's relatives, who refused to let the anthologist consult it until the *tazkira* was nearing completion.[75] Conversely, Nasrabadi corresponded with the poet ʿInayat Khan Ashna, a nobleman of the Mughal court, who sent him his collected works in manuscript.[76] These two anecdotes show that a sense of community is not inherently tied to the local.

The ease which Nasrabadi experienced in obtaining texts from India, where he never travelled, and the difficulties which he faced in extracting manuscripts from members of his own family, point to some of the fault lines that can create or divide communities. As Jean-Luc Nancy intimates, the very idea of community can be constructed in different ways – socially, politically or anthropologically.[77] All communities are in some sense affective, as their limits are demarcated ideologically: decisions always have to be made about who does not belong. Competing models of community interact with one another, as we shall see in cases where patrons who were politically powerful bowed to the literary authority of professional authors. A literary community, meaning a group of writers who are connected through sociability and intertextuality, can be local, transregional, global or a mixture of all three. If it is transregional or global, enabled through networks of migration and correspondence, then one may be tempted to infer that it is a supra-political entity, a 'Republic of Letters'. There are compelling reasons why this term has become popular in recent scholarship: Evrim Binbaş emphasizes a sociological aspect of the model, pointing to the autonomy of writers embedded in 'networks of peers who shared similar aesthetic, religious, political, and ideological persuasions'.[78] For his part, Muhsin al-Musawi underscores the importance of anthological book culture, describing postclassical Arabic letters as a 'massive cultural archive of 'institutionalized' and 'reading' communities'.[79] While these arguments are well taken, and give a sense of the enormous space for communication opened up by the mobility of people and texts, we may also wish to explore points of asymmetry and imbalance in the Republic of Letters, focusing not just on 'community cohesion' but also, to use Peter Burke's phrasing, 'on the means by which communities are constructed or reconstructed'.[80] Since the language that one chooses to write in is not the only marker of one's identity and outlook,[81] we also need to think about how communities can be particularized. As cultures of knowledge broadened during the late medieval period to encompass urban society as a whole, settlements around the Arabian Sea became host to multiple communities with their own archives and interlocutors.[82]

Sulafat al-'Asr and *Tazkira-yi Nasrabadi* draw attention to how the interplay between political borders and the flow of people, texts and capital formed and delimited literary communities in the western Indian Ocean region during the seventeenth century. Both Ibn Ma'sum and Nasrabadi use terminology which shows the very particular connections that characterized their relationships with their peers, evoking mental images that range from the lines on a family tree or a graph of relations, to the inclination of bodies to one another at a social gathering. Ibn Ma'sum writes that a league ('isaba, from the root '-s-b, 'to tie or bind') of poets has been deemed to excel in every age;[83] that he has recorded in his book the names of a community (jama'a, from the root j-m-', 'to collect or bring together') of poets from the people (ahl, from the root a-h-l, 'to marry or be familiar with') of the current century;[84] and that the anthology is restricted to the best poetry produced by this cohort (fi'a, from the root f-a-', 'to incline favourably towards').[85] When describing the five main geographically oriented sections of *Sulafat al-'Asr*, he continues with his usage of the word *ahl*, with its connotations of kinship and familiarity. Nasrabadi describes the cohort of writers who helped him to develop his sense of self as a 'ring' or 'circle' (*halqa*), as a 'community' or a 'collective' (*majma ', jam '*), a 'group' (*guruh*), his 'friends' (*dustan*) and his 'companions' (*ashab*), while characterizing literary critics as a 'class' (*tabaqa*) and talking about the 'web' (*silk*) of poets.[86] Together, these terms suggest that literary production depends on connections between individuals, in which inter-marriage, physical proximity, sociability through mingling at gatherings and a common purpose bind writers together into a network. They connote a supranational collective but imply that participation in it was not open to everyone. Adherence to valorized aesthetic standards was a prerequisite for joining.

Given that their concept of community is predicated not only on inclusion but also on exclusion, it is unsurprising that both anthologists share an idea of living in an age of decline: if they did not recognize others, then, logically, certain others would not recognize them. Playing with highly economic language that reflects the devaluation of silver coinage in Iran in the 1670s, Nasrabadi says that, on the scales by which the poets of the age are judged, poetic speech had become akin to petty cash in his day, and the worth of the critic, like devalued silver, had depreciated to that of stone. He speaks of a ready market in poor judgement, and of the unsaleability of the goods of speech and the wares of craftsmanship.[87] Similarly, Ibn Ma'sum describes South Asia as a region whose 'Arabs, Persians and Indians have not instituted a market for culture', a quotation to which we will return.[88] There is a tension here between shared ideals and unsociability, and between assimilation and segregation. The principle of degradation brings us to the now rightly much maligned concept that the states of the Middle East and South Asia were affected by forms of social and cultural decline during the early modern period. The utility of this argument to colonial narratives is obvious, and the past fifty years have seen it roundly interrogated and rebuffed in scholarship on early modern politics and cultural history.[89] Nevertheless, it is interesting to see the anthologists make the claim to living in an era of cultural depression. If the value of literature is not understood by society at large, then the basis for literary community becomes more restricted, and the grounds for mutual recognition more refined. In decrying a supposed lack of appreciation for contemporary literature, the anthologists cast themselves as the architects of their communities, who have constructed them textually. At the same time, they are making the more fundamental point that aesthetic values are not shared by everyone.

Where do the fault lines in taste therefore lie? In the eyes of the anthologists, any individual in any territory can contribute to the corpus in a way which allows them to communicate with their peers. Literary community is therefore global. Yet it is not universal. This effectively makes the production of early modern Arabic and Persian literature into an issue of textual circulation through networks that spanned a decentred territory. And it is indeed true that we find no single city around the littoral of the Arabian Sea that acted as the centre of literary production to the exclusion of others. This is one reason why texts that responded to one another enjoyed currency in the period: formally appreciable dialogues could be understood within a system of transregional exchange and codified the social relationships to which they testified.

Although the composition of response poems that shared imagery, rhyme and metre with their models may have aided in their circulation and brought writers closer together, the highly formal quality of the intertextual relationships that we see in globalizing seventeenth-century verse in both Arabic and Persian is among the reasons why some critics active in the nineteenth and twentieth centuries dismissed this material as artificial, overly complicated and derivative, and consequently avoided studying and editing it. The most polemical works of scholarship have characterized postclassical Arabic poetry as suffering from 'alienation', stylistic rigidity and a preoccupation with pushing rhetorical devices to create new effects;[90] and a number of mid-twentieth-century critics condemned Persian poetry composed in the period *c.* 1550–1750 on the same counts.[91] The term 'the Indian style' (*sabk-i hindi*) was popularized by the Iranian literary critic Malik al-Shuʿaraʾ Bahar (d. 1951) as a shorthand way of describing all Persian poetry composed in the early modern period, which he dismissed as obsessed with rhetorical artifice and lacking in a natural sense of fluency.[92] Subsequent scholarship has attempted a more balanced reassessment of the aesthetics of early modern Persian poetry, but the term *sabk-i hindi* is still often used, either as a general term for verse composed in the period *c.* 1550–1750, or to describe a particular philosophy within early modern poetry – most famously typified by the work of Bidil (d. 1133/1721) – that stands out for its 'markedly meditative manner', which blends reflections on formal commonplaces and pre-existing conceits with stimuli traditionally regarded as original and diverse';[93] a labyrinthine and 'baroque' mode of expression resulting in 'alienation';[94] 'subtleties of thoughts and themes'[95] and 'a philosophical subtlety'.[96]

A number of seventeenth-century poets of Persian deliberately represented themselves as proponents of a poetic avant-garde, which they themselves described as a 'fresh' (*taza*) way of writing.[97] Yet many of them did not come to a consensus about aesthetics: Saʾib (d. 1086–7/1676), for example, praises Naziri (d. 1021/1612–13) and Jalal Asir (d. 1049/1639), but declares his own superiority over ʿUrfi (d. 999/1591), who is conventionally regarded in modern scholarship as a harbinger of the fresh mode.[98] As we would expect with any accretive change in artistic style that is subsequently re-analysed as a coherent movement, the fresh mode was formed through the disagreements of its own practitioners rather than by their unanimity.[99] What is more, the fresh mode was – unsurprisingly – far from the only expressive idiom in seventeenth-century Persian poetry. Other poets of the period were just as invested in thinking through the future of literature, but did not identify themselves as members of an avant-garde.[100] Similarly, while some seventeenth-century poets active in Arabic consciously developed 'new poetic currents', not all authors were so invested in creating a form of 'modernism'.[101] This does not necessarily mean that they were conservative or archaizing in their style, simply that they were part of other formations. Literary culture was pluralistic, and aesthetics were negotiated via communities, even as writers continued to use classical convention for their inspiration.[102] Even if the aesthetics of the canon represent 'the values of the hegemonic culture' – in this case, the values of pedagogical cultures – that did not prevent authors from building on the canon in distinctive and individualistic ways in their own work.[103]

The study of intertextuality therefore emerges as a way in which we can not only overcome prejudicial readings of seventeenth-century poetry but also gain a greater sense of its diversity. Both those modern scholars who dismissed early modern Arabic and Persian poetry and those contemporary ones who have sought to rehabilitate it have somewhat tended to particularize the problem of imitation, as though other literatures have always regarded originality as the hallmark of genius.[104] Yet imitation was a central aspect of the theory and practice of poetry in many cultures during the late medieval and early modern periods, including in Italy, where Bembo (d. 1547) advised the budding writer to imitate 'the single best [classical] author in each genre of writing';[105] and in China, where the *fugu* (return to antiquity) movement became prominent from the sixteenth century.[106] Crucially, in both cases, as in the coeval Indian Ocean arena, authors connected themselves to or distinguished themselves from classical convention through a process of negotiation over ideas about fluency, naturalism and creativity: it was impossible to ignore the weight of the past.[107] Even in the twentieth century, the themes of 'diminished achievement, of weakness in the shadow of departed giants, of the past as a burden', characterized understandings of modern, Western art, which has generally been regarded as sophisticated, dynamic and playful.[108]

Social networks and intertextuality

Although the term 'intertextuality' is now often used to designate an allusive relationship between two or more texts, Julia Kristeva's original coinage of the word emphasized the idea that each work of literature is a mosaic of fragments formed from all discourse, an argument which explicitly denies authors agency in shaping their work, and which rejects the concept of filiation, according to which an author borrows discrete elements from one or more identifiable predecessors.[109] This model has been interrogated, most famously in Harold Bloom's *The Anxiety of Influence*, which contended the opposite: that great works of literature are formed when an author challenges and overcomes an identifiable forebear through the act of misinterpretation.[110] Ultimately, these two seemingly antithetical positions can be usefully integrated: an author can consciously intend to respond to an identifiable forebear while inevitably and unconsciously reproducing phrasing and imagery drawn from across the corpus.

As we shall see throughout this book, biographical anthologies were often the vehicle through which poems came to reach new cities, and they were actively used as sources of inspiration by seventeenth-century poets. They therefore not only documented but also informed literary production. The grouping of the biographical entries in these works into chapters that are bounded by geography (e.g. 'poets of Yemen') and space and class (e.g. 'officials of the Safavid court') is founded on the assumption that contact between authors generates connections between texts. If social interaction played no role in shaping intertextuality, or if connections between texts were impossible to trace, it would have sufficed to arrange the entries alphabetically – as some compilers of biographical dictionaries did – or to have dispensed with the biographical and spatial elements altogether. Instead, biographical anthologies emphasize the importance of interactions (in space or in time) to literary creativity, advancing a form of 'epistemological anthropocentrism'.[111] Individuality arises as the manner in which an author maintains a dialogue with his peers in a network while asserting his own voice.[112] A poet who cannot be related to others falls outside the practice of sociability and hence outside the world of the biographical anthology too.

Biographical anthologies would therefore seem to argue that – to invert Barthes – filiation is not a myth, and that texts make traceable allusions to one another.[113] There are two main reasons why the anthologists who adopted this method of life writing, including Ibn Ma'sum and Nasrabadi, are able to pursue this thesis. The first reason is that the kinds of intertextuality which interest them are often explicit and identifiable: the use of the same metre and rhyme by two poets, direct quotation of a verse, or the transformation of a line of prose into poetry. The second is that the poetry which they quote often had a socially embedded life: it was composed within and shared at gatherings, whether at royal courts, coffee houses, the homes of the nobility, or pleasure-grounds. At such meetings, poets would frequently work with a theme and a common metre and rhyme, producing texts which shared formal features.[114] This context of production brought intertextuality and intersubjectivity together in parallel: a *majlis* (pl. *majalis*, gathering or symposium) was a meeting of minds as well as a forum for making connected texts, and in choosing to reference another author's work, poets were often implicitly endorsing or appropriating the characters and ideas of their interlocutors.[115] A definition of mimesis as the imitation not just of other people's texts but other people's personas too is key to this understanding of intertextuality.

The now common idea that intertextuality is within the eye of the beholder depends on the recognition that readers have differing fields of reference. We can only distinguish allusions to other works of literature if we have read and internalized those works. This inherent subjectivity goes hand in hand with the notion that discourse consists of fragments which writers reconstitute from what they have read and heard. While it could, therefore, be contended that the study of allusive relationships between texts is a lost cause, which can only reveal the habits of the scholar undertaking the research, I argue that an examination of intertextual practice which both reconstructs the social connections between authors and uncovers their reading patterns can help to uncover forms of allusive relationship that are deliberate, traceable, responsive and designed to establish dialogues. This is why I follow Ibn Ma'sum and Nasrabadi in studying intertextuality in parallel with social interaction in this book. Poems that borrow the rhyme, metre, imagery and rhetorical devices of their models allow us to track the spread of dialogues across regions, developing a view of the geographical extent of a world of circulation, while looser and more subtle forms of allusion, which are harder to identify when the works of linked contemporaries are not cross-read, can potentially tell us a great deal about how concepts of originality and invention operated in the early modern period.

Throughout this book, I employ the term 'emulative' intertextuality to describe the use of shared formal markers and discursive features, including rhyme, metre, imagery, rhetorical devices, and often but not always in the case of Persian lyric and panegyric verse, a refrain (*radif*), all features which create an explicit link between a poem and its model(s).[116] I use the term 'emulative' because it carries an implication of community, suggesting that authors are imitating the sight and sound of one another.[117] Although literary emulation has often been seen as a site of generational conflict, in which the imitator is attempting to surpass or outdo the model competitively, a more appropriate comparison may be the cognitive development of children as they emulate their parents.[118] Infants not only mimic the physical movements of adults but also match 'adult emotional states via "affect attunement"', the mimicry of physical postures and emotional behaviours until they become internalized.[119] In the same way, poets who emulated their peers or their predecessors were attempting to hone and to fix an emotive and an intellectual argument through imitation. The act of literary emulation becomes one of mimesis, a process of 'learning', but also one of 'discovery'.[120] Lara Harb demonstrates that within the system of Aristotelian poetics championed by thinkers such as Ibn Sina (d. 428/1037), our realization of 'similarity between the likeness and the original' is the source of the wonder that we as readers find in mimesis.[121] Hence, the practice of emulative intertextuality can be a fundamentally creative endeavour, exciting the reader's astonishment and perplexity. As an act, it is produced through the conscious design of the author but anticipates 'the comprehending response of the reader'.[122]

Emulative intertextuality was commonly practised by poets who were active in the same performance contexts, but there are also many examples of poets constructing emulative intertextual connections with pieces that were in circulation in manuscript. Emulation of a poem in manuscript can suggest either a form of diachronic intertextuality or a dialogue with a poet living in a geographically distant land. In such cases, the mimetic function remains, signifying the imitation of the persona that the model author projects in his writing.

Emulative intertextuality can be contrasted with what I term here 'masked' intertextuality, which implies a de-emphasized connection that can operate on the level of imagery or rhetoric. Masked intertextuality occurs most frequently with references to a fairly defined corpus of texts which we might call 'canonical', in the sense that any poet who had a middling education would have had some exposure to them, regardless of the territory in which they lived. Such canonical texts, forming a 'reference culture', include the *Mu'allaqat*, the collected poetry in Abu Tammam's (d. 231/845 or 232/846) *Hamasa*, the *diwan* of Abu Nuwas (d. c. 198–200/813–815), and the verse of al-Mutanabbi (d. 354/965) in the case of Arabic; and the poetry of Anvari (d. 585/1189 or 587/1191), Sa'di (d. 691/1292), Hafiz (d. 790/1391) and Jami (d. 898/1492) in the case of Persian.[123] Familiarity with texts like these meant that poets who received training in classicizing culture shared certain frames of reference with their peers who were active in the same language in other regions.

This is not to suggest that poets across the entire Arabian Sea arena were regularly schooled in both the corpus of Arabic letters and the corpus of Persian letters, although, as we shall see, there certainly were individuals who grew up with an equal command of Arabic and Persian literary history.[124] Nor is it to imply that curricula were identical across the western Indian Ocean region, even if *madrasa* students in the Ottoman, Safavid and Mughal empires were often taught using the same textbooks.[125] Nevertheless, poets of Arabic who studied in the Levant, North Arabia, Yemen, Iraq, Iran and India would have all had some exposure to an overlapping set of canonical literary texts, as would poets of Persian growing up in Iran, Central Asia and South Asia.

A poetics of dislocation

Ultimately, the grounds for a reading of seventeenth-century Arabic and Persian poetry in tandem with one another are not simply comparative, which might be justified because of the two literatures' engagement with shared techniques of what Earl Miner called 'lyric intensification' over the course of their long history of interaction, since the emergence of New Persian literature in the multilingual environment of late-ninth-century Khurasan.[126] Nor, in a more particularized sense, is it just that seventeenth-century poets used the panegyric *qasida* to explore notions of kingship in the two languages, and reworked the topoi of monothematic lyric verse to create comparable representations of wine consumption and eroticized beloveds, although that is also the case. Rather, my interest is in the fact that Arabic and Persian literary texts were produced within a transnational phenomenon of dislocation during the seventeenth century. At 'the very tangible level of mobile persons and mobile texts',[127] movement, circulation and the decentring of the locus of literary authority encouraged poets in both languages to use familiar forms to create 'a new structure of feeling' within overlapping physical spaces across the Arabian Sea.[128]

In this book, I have deliberately chosen to study migrant poets, actors who negotiated foreign political dispensations and created their own, new worlds, since migration is 'a focal point for theoretical reflections about individual and cultural identity'.[129] For the poets under discussion, migration involved navigating not only the sense of estrangement which confronts anyone who settles in a new country, but also a literary alienation, a need to create an expressive idiom which allowed them to communicate with those around them. These figures are better placed to reveal the points of fracture and asymmetry in the process of literary creativity than poets who remained put, because they brought with them multiple frames of reference. The way in which they attuned themselves ideologically and emotionally to their interlocutors allows us to pinpoint aesthetics in the making and thereby to gain a more nuanced understanding of the very concept of literary community. I argue that this approach can help us to write a 'genealogy of here and now' – our globalized present.[130]

The body of this book consists of six case studies of literary communities that were formed in the decades surrounding the compilation of *Sulafat al-ʿAsr* and *Tazkira-yi Nasrabadi*, and whose members are featured in the anthologies. Chapters 2–4 are devoted to Arabic literary communities in south India (Chapter 2), Yemen (Chapter 3) and Iran (Chapter 4). Chapters 5–7 are concerned with Persian literary communities in south India (Chapter 5), north India (Chapter 6) and Iran (Chapter 7). The case studies are designed with a sense of geographical balance in mind, in order to develop a holistic picture of literary production as a transregional phenomenon, and in order to test where the limits of the arena of circulation that I am describing lay. Each of the literary communities featured in the case studies can be related to the others through international networks. Not only do the subjects of the chapters feature in the anthologies, but in many instances, they were also aware of their contemporaries discussed in the other chapters. In order to reconstruct linkages of this kind, I have had to expand my focus beyond the collected works of seventeenth-century poets that have been printed, as the published corpus is not sufficiently comprehensive for this sort of study.

Consequently, two-thirds of the poets whose work is examined here are almost entirely unknown to scholarship, featuring briefly in bio-bibliographical surveys or in manuscript catalogues. In many cases, it has been necessary to spend time reconstructing the biographies of these figures in order to even be able to classify them as migrant poets. However, my twin focus on biography and texts in this book is not designed to argue for a biographical reading of literature, which would see poems as expressions of moments in the lives of their authors. Rather, it is intended to reconstruct the web of social interactions between the subjects, their fellow poets and their patrons, in order to understand how they use intertextuality. Chapter 1 delves into the demographic and economic factors which stimulated migration in the seventeenth-century western Indian Ocean, in order to reconstruct the extratextual world in which these literary communities took shape.

Chapter 1

SOCIETY IN MOTION

THE PROSOPOGRAPHY AND ECONOMICS OF SEVENTEENTH-CENTURY MIGRATORY NETWORKS ACROSS THE ARABIAN SEA

A foundational study of early modern migration across the Arabian Sea is Ahmad Gulchin Ma'ani's (d. 2000) *Karvan-i Hind* (*The Caravan Bound for India*).[1] This biographical dictionary of poets who left Iran for South Asia between the late medieval period and the eighteenth century combs through many *tazkiras* and *divans* in order to create as expansive a source-book as possible, identifying 353 poets who migrated eastwards in the long seventeenth century, from the accession of the Mughal emperor Jahangir in 1014/1605 to the death of Awrangzib in 1118/1707. A meticulous work of scholarship, *Karvan-i Hind* simultaneously manages to complicate and to reinforce commonplaces about diasporic literary communities. While its singular focus on movement away from Iran towards South Asia gives us a great deal of information about how the demographics of migration and the profiles of Iranian migrant poets changed over time, it implies – perhaps unintentionally – that the 'flow' of writers was 'unidirectional',[2] that India's courts were the period's only significant centres of literary production, and that Persian literary talent was exclusively Iranian. Additionally, although Gulchin Ma'ani's monolingual approach cannot be criticized, I argue that we should extend his findings by examining how writers active in differing languages circulated around the Arabian Sea, since maritime contacts bring cultures together and are inherently multilingual: language is 'the luggage of the individual travelling around the world'.[3] In this chapter, I collect data derived from *Sulafat al-'Asr* and *Tazkira-yi Nasrabadi* to create a picture of migratory patterns around the western Indian Ocean, demonstrating the extent to which the movement of people and capital turned the region into an arena of circulation. While the use of two directly contemporary biographical anthologies could be said to narrow the focus of our enquiry, hindering us from developing a totalizing view of migration over the longue durée, it allows us to reconstruct exactly how authors were connected to one another in the focused period of time from *c.* 1620 to 1675 CE. The fact that Nasrabadi and Ibn Ma'sum were writing within a few years of one another, and that both include a class of Shi'i scholars among their biographical subjects, some of whom feature in both anthologies, means that their texts can be said to dovetail, sharing points of continuity while fanning out in different directions. In a certain sense, they therefore document one bifurcating, transnational system of authors.

The seventeenth century in historical context

In his introduction to *Sulafat al-ʿAsr*, Ibn Maʿsum writes that the idea for his anthology has turned out to be a 'damp squib in a country whose Arabs, Persians and Indians have not instituted a market for culture'.[4] He also divorces himself from his surroundings at the end of his chapter on the poets of Syria and Egypt, quoting Ibn al-Qirriyya (d. 84/703) as saying that 'India is distant and far-off, a land of tyrannical unbelievers'.[5] It is difficult to get around the fact that these remarks are exclusive: they draw distinctions based on lineage, religion and political systems, emphasize disjunction rather than connectivity, could be taken to imply that Ibn Maʿsum thought of himself intellectually in an Arabian setting rather than in an Indian context, and seemingly place value in the sentiments of a late antique figure who died before the widespread arrival of Islam in South Asia.[6] This is a curious idea when one considers that the Qutbshahi sultanate was both politically and confessionally amenable to Ibn Maʿsum. Nevertheless, the comments do invite two questions which are fundamental to the study of migration and literary production in the seventeenth century. The first concerns the extent to which diasporic communities – whether mercantile, professional, political, religious or a mixture of all four – were able to create a 'market for culture' independently, without some form of accommodation with the systems of patronage that already existed in their adopted countries. The second revolves around the issue of whether the early modern Arabian Sea can really be considered a discrete zone, constituted through flows of people, capital and trade. In order to consider this question in more depth, we have to examine the migratory patterns of the seventeenth century in historical context.

India had already acted as a magnet for émigré scholars of Arabic for centuries prior to the arrival of Nizam al-Din Ahmad and Ibn Maʿsum in the Deccan. From the medieval period, the Muslim dynasties which ruled from Delhi, Gujarat, Bengal and the Deccan had established mosques and Islamic colleges, propagated the teaching of the Islamic sciences, hired scribes to copy the Qurʾan and others to recite it, and engaged in diplomatic correspondence in Arabic with the rulers of Mecca.[7] These actions all necessitated an inbound flow of Arabic speakers, and so scholars came from locations such as Egypt, North Arabia and Yemen, in order to teach and to seek patronage.[8] A significant number of dynasties also sought to bolster their authority by patronizing charismatic Muslim religious leaders, who established themselves as spiritual preceptors in regions such as Gujarat.[9] More broadly, medieval transoceanic trade also brought Arabic speakers to regions such as Malabar that were not controlled by Muslim dynasties.[10] Migrants settled and married locals, turning Arabic into a local language with transregional roots.[11] The pursuit of commerce, scholarship and political power created a knowledge economy that linked India with centres of Arabic-Islamic scholarship further to the west.[12] The movement was bidirectional. Numerous thinkers emigrated from India to Arabia, including ʿAli al-Muttaqi (d. 975/1567), who grew up as a Chishti Sufi in Burhanpur in Khandesh, and spent the final decades of his life as a multilingual scholar in Mecca.[13] Additionally, some of the Indian sultanates sponsored the establishment of colleges in Mecca, such as the *Kulbarkiyya* (named after Gulbarga in the Deccan), which was founded by the Bahmanids (748/1347–933/1527).[14] A scholarly and mercantile elite formed just one social component of a much larger flow of people: slavery too brought many individuals who learned Arabic from East Africa to India.[15] Crucially, waves of migration were continuous, and each new generation reconfigured relationships between South Asia and the Middle East.[16]

A high proportion of the scholars who travelled from the Arab lands to the Deccan – and to India more broadly – authored books after their arrival. The pedagogical texts that they produced, including commentaries on Arabic grammar, contributed to the spread of Arabic literacy among the Muslim populace of the region and functioned as sites in which the entire history of Arabic philological knowledge could be debated.[17] Such works represented a way of forming a broad community through education and the practice of religion. However, some of the émigrés also set about creating literary networks in India, in which they and their interlocutors composed new works of Arabic poetry and prose.[18] They were supported in this endeavour by the enormous number of Arabic texts which circulated to India in manuscript and were then recopied. These texts encompassed many different genres, including medicine, historiography, biography, poetry and *adab*, *hadith* and Qurʾanic exegesis. Although a statistical study is beyond the scope of this book, one may point to manuscript catalogues to give some sense of the scale and diversity of the Arabic texts that were read in early modern South Asia. The Arabic catalogue of the Khuda Bakhsh Library in Patna, for example, stretches to twenty-eight volumes in the old series alone, incorporating literary manuscripts varying from canonical texts like commentaries on the *Muʿallaqat* and the *diwan* of al-Mutanabbi, through collections of Mamluk erotic epigrams, to perhaps unexpected works, such as the *diwan* of Niqulaʾus al-Saʾigh (d. 1756), a Greek Catholic monk and 'the most gifted Christian poet in Arabic of the early 18th century'.[19] These manuscripts represent what we might follow Shahab Ahmed in calling an 'aestheticized' corpus.[20] They are a vast and little studied resource which forces us to entirely rethink the conventional assumption that because it was a language of religion and not a vernacular for the vast majority of Muslims in early modern South Asia, Arabic must have had a limited set of social and intellectual uses.

The migratory routes from the lands that are recognized today as the 'Arab world' should be considered an important part of a circulatory system which also connected South Asia with Iran and Central Asia, fostering the mobility of people and objects, including manuscripts.[21] This system encouraged the migration of all social classes, not only those that might be thought of as 'elites', such as political leaders, merchants and scholars, but also more subaltern groups, including figures who subsisted on charity.[22] Islamic polities in medieval and early modern South Asia have often been characterized as 'Persianate', to use Marshall Hodgson's now popular term, which reflects the facts that dynasties such as the Delhi Sultanate (*c.* 607/1211–932/1526) and the Mughal Empire (932/1526–1857) adopted Persian as a courtly language; and that they adapted the bureaucratic systems of the Central Asian dynasties that used Persian as their language of administration.[23] From the early eleventh century, when Lahore became a major political centre of the Ghaznavid Empire, Persian literary production began to flourish throughout South Asia, in contexts ranging from courts to Sufi *khanagah*s (lodges) and *qasba*s (fortified villages).[24] Movement from Iran and Central Asia to India followed many routes, including not just to the north, but also to the Deccan.[25]

The migration of speakers of Arabic and Persian to India led to the creation of transnational political and religious structures, and to the investment of economies in one another. A good example of this phenomenon is the Qutbshahi sultanate, whose royal family traced their origins to the early-fifteenth-century Turkic Qaraqoyunlu rulers of Tabriz and Baghdad.[26] The dynasty's links with Iran were continuous and ongoing, and the name of the shah of Iran was traditionally pronounced before the name of the Qutbshah in the sermon (*khutba*) at Friday prayers in Golkonda.[27] Even in the seventeenth century, many of the state's principal officers were migrants from Iran, including the prime minister (*Mir Jumla*) Mir Muhammad Saʿid Ardistani (d. 1073/1663), who had spent his early life in Isfahan, and Niknam Khan (d. 1083/1672), commander in chief of Golkonda's military.[28] Safavid Iran invested heavily in Golkonda's economy, and constituted one of its major trading partners.[29]

Arabic and Persian can therefore be characterized as supranational idioms of culture in early modern South Asia, in the sense that their use transcended any one particular social or confessional group and linked India with the lands across the Arabian Sea. Neither was used as a vernacular by the vast majority of India's populace, and this aided in their adoption as languages of high culture. At the same time, both did function as a language of daily communication for certain families.

Although we might be tempted to assume that the situation in Iran and Arabia was radically different – with Persian being both the vernacular and the language of high culture in Iran, and Arabic the language of daily communication and culture in Arabia – a different set of circumstances pertained in many communities. The populace of Safavid Iran spoke a variety of languages, including, in addition to Persian, Turkic, Armenian, Georgian, Kurdish and Arabic, and a raft of languages that were more localized, such as Gilaki and Tati.[30] According to the reports of Carmelite missionaries in the early seventeenth century, in Qazvin – the one-time Safavid capital – the only language that the city's entire populace was united in understanding was Turkic.[31] The main language of the Safavid court was also Turkic, which was spoken by the Qizilbash military and political elite.[32] Turkic was used as a literary language too, to the extent that Nasrabadi, who admits to not knowing it, discusses Turkic verse on a couple of occasions.[33] From a certain perspective, therefore, Persian can be seen as a unifying language of high culture in early modern Iran, rather than as the only idiom of cultural production.

Arabic was also important in Safavid Iran beyond purely religious settings. I calculate that 8 per cent (*c.* 950 out of 11,752), of the titles listed under the heading *diwan/divan* in the union catalogue of manuscripts in Iranian collections are written in Arabic.[34] This figure concerns literary production only, not texts on Qur'anic exegesis, Islamic law or other disciplines with which Arabic is associated in religious contexts.[35] It implies a substantial body of writers and readers of Arabic literature in Iran, not just during the 'Abbasid era (132/750–656/1258), when Arabic had been a language of political power, but also in the late medieval and early modern periods. Of the seventy manuscript copies of the *diwan* of al-Mutanabbi (d. 354/965) that are held in Iranian libraries, sixteen were made during the Safavid era, and twenty-one during the later eighteenth and nineteenth centuries.[36] Such manuscripts suggest the persistence of Arabic as a language of high culture in defined scholarly, literary and bureaucratic contexts in Iran, throughout the early modern period. In instances, its usage may have been strictly learned and artificial, but this was not always the case. As in South Asia, the reading and writing of Arabic cut across social and confessional groups. Future reconstructions of the role of Arabic in early modern Iran and South Asia will need to elaborate on how its function as a language of prestige was shaped by interaction between migrant groups and local populations.

We also have to expand and complicate our understanding of language use in the Arabian Peninsula. During the late sixteenth and seventeenth centuries, a significant number of Iranian families settled in Mecca and Medina. Ibn Ma'sum's own grandfather, who emigrated from Shiraz, is a good example of this phenomenon, but there are more cases, to the extent that at least fourteen biographical subjects in the sections of *Sulafat al-'Asr* devoted to the two holy cities were wholly or partly of Iranian descent, including scholars who traced their lineage to Tabaristan;[37] Shiraz;[38] Isfara'in[39] and Bust.[40] Additionally, in his chapter on Iran, Ibn Ma'sum mentions a further two figures who left the country to settle in Mecca.[41] While these writers composed their scholarly works in Arabic, it does not seem likely that they would have entirely abandoned using Persian as their vernacular after their arrival in Arabia. Even though Nizam al-Din Ahmad and Ibn Ma'sum both seem to have composed poetry exclusively in Arabic, extant archival documents, such as letters and legal papers, show that they both retained and used their family's knowledge of Persian. Further evidence for a community of Persian speakers in Arabia is provided by Nasrabadi, who gives information on poets who emigrated to Mecca and settled there, either permanently or for an extended number of years.[42] He tells us that the poet Hajji Muhammad lived in Mecca for twenty-two years, running a jeweller's shop at Bab al-Salam, and that he adopted the pen name 'Makki' ('Meccan') in his Persian verse.[43] Hajji Muhammad returned to Isfahan only after the death of the *sharif* (most probably Zayd, r. 1040/1631–1076/1666) when Mecca was affected by political and social instability.[44]

Even more intriguing evidence comes in the form of an anthology of Persian poetry by one of Nasrabadi's biographical subjects, Nazim Tabrizi (d. 1083/1672–3).[45] This work, which remains in manuscript, was completed by Nazim in Mecca in 1036/1626-7.[46] It consists of poems drawn from the historical Persian corpus, including verse by poets such as Mas'ud Sa'd Salman (d. *c.* 515/1121–2), 'Iraqi (d. 668/1289) and 'Ubayd-i Zakani (d. 772/1370–1). Its composition was fed by networks of circulation that crossed the Arabian Sea: the literary biographer Muhammad Darabi, a contemporary of Nasrabadi, relates that when Nazim had been in Yemen, he had obtained an accurate manuscript of poems by 'Urfi (d. 999/1591) which had come from the library of 'Urfi's patron, the Mughal statesman 'Abd al-Rahim Khan-i Khanan (d. 1036/1627).[47] Although it is certain that Iranian émigré groups in the two holy cities and Yemen adopted Arabic as a second language, the fact that Nazim read and edited Persian materials there encourages us to reimagine the Arabian Peninsula as a multilingual space.

The biographical anthologies: Subjective networks

In order to move beyond a general picture of historical trends in migration and appreciate how seventeenth-century poets were connected to one another, we have to analyse the structure of *Tazkira-yi Nasrabadi* and *Sulafat al-'Asr*, and consider the anthologists' concerns, interests and prejudices. We should always bear in mind the subjectivity inherent in biographical anthologies: as Mana Kia writes, compilers such as Nasrabadi 'selected and emphasized details about their collectives in the service of particular representational preoccupations'.[48] These works effectively map out communities based on networks of authors, and, just as importantly, intertextual relationships between the poems that these networks composed.

Excluding its conclusion, which is devoted to verse chronograms and follows a different format from the rest of the anthology, *Tazkira-yi Nasrabadi* contains entries on just over 900 poets active between the very end of the sixteenth century and 1091/1680. The biographical entries are extremely short – even the longest ones are a maximum of four pages – and they consist of contextual information on the origins and careers of each poet, followed by a limited selection of their verse. Nasrabadi's critical approach is rooted in individual images and rhetorical devices, and for this reason he does not give poems in their entirety, only isolated lines extracted from different pieces.[49] Some entries include just a single line of poetry, others up to sixty, with each line generally being drawn from a different poem. Unlike some other early modern Persian biographical anthologies, such as Taqi Kashi's (fl. late sixteenth to early seventeenth centuries) *Khulasat al-Ash'ar*, which contains very extensive selections from the work of each biographical subject and is an enormously useful source-book of poems, *Tazkira-yi Nasrabadi* invites readers – whether premodern or modern – to use it as a kind of catalogue, which must be read in conjunction with *divan*s through a process of referencing and cross-referencing.[50] *Sulafat al-'Asr* is devoted to far fewer writers, treating 129 poets active between the late sixteenth century and 1082/1671, the year of composition, but it treats their output in detail, often giving *qasa'id* and *qita'* in full, and tracing emulative intertextual connections between authors.

One of the most obvious ways in which *Tazkira-yi Nasrabadi* and *Sulafat al-'Asr* demonstrate their subjectivity is in the demography of the poets whom they survey. Both anthologies have a total disregard for female poets. Although a few women are featured in passing, they are mentioned only in relation to the biographical subjects, who are, without exception, men, and those women who are discussed are either the mothers of poets, royals who acted as patrons, or courtesans who had relationships with poets.[51] The two texts are also exclusive in their focus on Muslims, particularly Twelver Shi'is, and non-Muslims, including Jews, Zoroastrians, Christians and Hindus – all religious communities which produced authors writing in Persian or Arabic – are passed over, apart from in a couple of cases where the biographical subjects were converts or became involved in elite Muslim networks.[52] It is also important to stress that the anthologists only disclose the information that they deem to be germane or interesting, or which was available to them through their sources, and so they do not always provide the reader with the same level of detail for each poet. In *Tazkira-yi Nasrabadi*, for example, the anthologist sometimes states that a poet had been to Mecca, but in certain cases the reader infers this because the figure in question is referred to using the title *hajj* or *hajji*.[53] These inconsistencies are natural for texts rooted in social networks, and oblige us to interpret demography through the eyes of the anthologists.

The subjectivities of the two anthologists also extend to their approaches to space and place. Nasrabadi was highly mobile. As he states in his autobiography (the last entry in the main body of the anthology), he had done *hajj* to Mecca, and pilgrimage to the shrine of the Imam Riza (the eighth Twelver Imam) at Mashhad.[54] Furthermore, he had family in India. His paternal grandfather had settled at the court of the Mughal emperor Jahangir, and one of his uncles and one of his nephews were in India at the time of the anthology's composition.[55] Nevertheless, his *tazkira* takes the Safavid capital of Isfahan, in whose environs he grew up and spent most of his life, as its unstated centre of exchange. This is quite different from making it the centre of literary production. Cities that were in close proximity to the capital, such as Shiraz, Yazd, Qum and Kashan, feature prominently, as does Mashhad, in the *beglerbeg* of Khurasan, and Tabriz, in the *beglerbeg* of Azarbayjan. Relatively little space is given to non-Iranian poets who migrated inwards to Iran, or who remained outside Iran, and those who are included came to the anthologist's attention directly, or through his sources. A conservative estimate, based on Nasrabadi's explicit statements, would suggest that he had met 7.9 per cent (72) of the poets whom he mentions;[56] and had corresponded directly with a few more,[57] but it seems probable that the actual figures are somewhat higher. Many of these personal contacts were well travelled, both within and outside Iran, and they brought with them their own networks, meaning that there are minimal degrees of separation between the anthologist and the vast majority of his subjects. A good example of this phenomenon is Nasrabadi's friend *mulla* 'Ali Riza Tajalli, who was both a student of the religious scholar Aqa Husayn Khvansari – who taught in Isfahan – and a former tutor to the Mughal nobleman Ibrahim Khan, the son of 'Ali Mardan Khan (d. 1067/1657), an Iranian nobleman who had left for India after surrendering the fortress of Qandahar to the Mughals.[58] It is possible that Tajalli acted as Nasrabadi's source for information on a further twelve students of Aqa Husayn Khvansari and a further three poets who were in the service of Ibrahim Khan.[59]

One of the most striking aspects of Nasrabadi's *tazkira* is its demonstration of the fact that literary production cut across classes in Safavid Iran. The following table surveys the professions of all of the biographical subjects in the *tazkira*:

Professions of Seventeenth-Century Poets, per Nasrabadi

Rank	Profession	No. of Poets
1	Professional poet (living derived primarily or exclusively from verse, or evidence of other professional activity wanting).[1]	213
2	Member of the religious establishment (incl. professions as diverse as jurist, Qur'an reciter, preacher, *Shaykh al-Islam*, etc.).[2]	156
3	Functionary (e.g. chancellery official), provincial politician (e.g. *vizir*, *kalantar*), agent or representative of a politician.[3]	119
4	Governor, senior minister of state.[4]	53
5	*Sayyid* (living derived from social status, e.g. through relating family *hadith* or through a state-issued stipend).[5]	52
6	Nobleman or gentleman poet (living derived from inherited wealth or income from holdings).[6]	45
7	Craftsman (e.g. leather worker, ceramist, goldsmith; incl. guild head).[7]	42
8	Dervish.[8]	33
9	Merchant.[9]	29
10	Tradesman (e.g. farrier), labourer (e.g. bricklayer), wholesaler, shopkeeper.[10]	17
= 11	Scribe, secretary.[11]	15
= 11	Painter or calligrapher.[12]	15
= 11	Host of a salon, courtly hanger-on, companion to another poet.[13]	15
= 14	Doctor of medicine.[14]	11
= 14	Copyist, bookbinder.[15]	11
16	Musician.[16]	10
= 17	Superintendent of a shrine, keeper of a mosque, administrator in charge of *vaqf* disbursements.[17]	8
= 17	Prince of the realm.[18]	8
= 17	Man of letters (incl. lexicographer, etc.).[19]	8
20	Military- or guards-man.[20]	7
= 21	Librarian.[21]	5
= 21	*Shahnama* reciter or storyteller.[22]	5
23	Tutor to royal children.[23]	4
= 24	King.[24]	3
= 24	Ambassador.[25]	3
= 24	Historian (incl. author of historical *masnavis*).[26]	3
= 24	Astronomer or astrologer.[27]	3
28	School teacher.[28]	3
29	Geomancer.[29]	2
= 30	Industrialist.[30]	1
= 30	Spiritual preceptor.[31]	1
= 30	Architect.[32]	1
= 30	Dogsbody.[33]	1
= 30	Publican.[34]	1
= 30	Banker.[35]	1

[1] *TN*, 309; 312; 316; 319; 322; 325; 327; 331; 337; 339; 341; 343; 344; 345; 347; 348; 349; 350; 351; 353; 354; 356; 359; 360; 363; 365 (two entries); 366; 370 (two entries); 371; 372; 374; 375; 376; 377; 378; 381 (two entries); 383; 386; 388; 389; 390; 391 (two entries); 394; 395; 396 (two entries); 399 (two entries); 400 (two entries); 401 (two entries); 404 (two entries); 406; 408; 409 (three entries); 414; 415; 417; 418 (two entries); 420; 422; 423 (two entries); 424 (two entries); 428; 429; 430; 431; 432; 438; 439 (two entries); 442 (two entries); 443 (two entries); 444 (two entries); 445; 446; 447 (two entries); 448; 449 (two entries); 450; 451; 454; 458; 459; 460; 461; 463 (two entries); 464 (two entries); 465 (two entries); 467; 469; 470; 471; 472; 476; 478; 479 (two entries); 481; 488; 490; 492; 503; 504; 509; 510; 511; 512;

513 (two entries); 514; 515; 518; 519; 520; 525; 527; 530; 531; 532; 534 (two entries); 539; 546; 547; 549; 551; 552; 553; 556; 560; 562; 563 (two entries); 566; 569 (two entries); 570 (three entries); 571; 573; 580; 581; 582; 583; 584; 586; 587; 593; 604; 615 (two entries); 617; 625; 626; 627 (two entries); 628; 630 (three entries); 631 (three entries); 632 (two entries); 634; 635; 637; 638 (three entries); 639; 640 (two entries); 641; 642 (three entries); 643 (two entries); 645; 648; 649; 650 (two entries); 651 (three entries); 654 (two entries); 655 (two entries).

[2] *TN*, 149; 168; 209; 217; 218; 220 (two entries); 221; 223; 224; 225 (two entries); 227; 228 (two entries); 229; 231 (two entries); 232 (two entries); 233; 234; 235; 236; 237; 238; 239; 240; 244; 245; 247; 248 (two entries); 249; 250; 251; 252; 254; 255 (two entries); 256; 261 (two entries); 262; 263; 264 (two entries); 267; 268; 271; 272; 273; 274; 275; 276; 277 (two entries); 278 (two entries); 279 (two entries); 280 (two entries); 281; 282; 283 (two entries); 284; 285; 286 (two entries); 287; 288; 289 (three entries); 290 (two entries); 291; 292; 293; 294 (three entries); 372; 385; 397; 398; 406; 421; 422; 437; 440 (two entries); 452; 461; 473; 475; 491; 494; 497; 499; 501; 503; 505 (two entries); 515; 516; 518; 525; 529 (two entries); 531; 537; 538; 540; 541; 542; 545; 550; 552; 554; 563; 568 (two entries); 571; 579; 583; 585; 589; 590; 592 (two entries); 602; 614; 615; 620; 621; 622; 623; 625; 629 (two entries); 635; 636 (three entries); 640; 641 (three entries); 644; 646; 648; 649; 652.

[3] *TN*, 88; 98; 99; 100; 101 (two entries); 102; 103; 104; 106; 107 (two entries); 108; 109 (two entries); 110 (two entries); 111; 112; 113; 114; 115 (two entries); 116; 117 (two entries); 118 (two entries); 119; 120 (two entries); 121; 122 (two entries); 123; 124 (two entries); 126 (two entries); 127; 128; 129 (two entries); 130 (two entries); 131; 132; 133; 139 (two entries); 141; 142; 143; 144; 149; 150; 154; 155 (two entries); 157; 158; 159; 160; 161; 162; 163; 164; 166; 167 (two entries); 169; 170; 173; 174; 175 (two entries); 176; 177 (two entries); 178 (two entries); 184; 186 (two entries); 187; 188; 189 (two entries); 190 (two entries); 191; 193 (two entries); 201 (two entries); 202; 209; 210; 212; 233; 244; 270 (two entries); 480; 497; 498; 548; 566; 581; 588; 591; 594; 626; 633; 659; 660 (two entries); 661; 662.

[4] *TN*, 23; 24; 25; 26; 29; 31; 32; 33; 34 (two entries); 36 (two entries); 37; 38; 40 (two entries); 41; 42 (two entries); 43; 44 (three entries); 45; 46; 47 (two entries); 48 (two entries); 49 (three entries); 50; 51 (two entries); 52; 53; 54 (two entries); 55; 58; 59; 75; 77; 78; 79; 80; 83; 84 (two entries); 94; 96; 622.

[5] *TN*, 137; 138; 140; 142; 145; 146 (two entries); 147 (two entries); 148; 150; 154; 162; 163; 165 (three entries); 166; 176; 179; 184; 188; 210; 253; 269; 272; 286; 359; 362; 367; 373; 383; 411; 414; 423; 426; 427 (two entries); 466 (two entries); 486; 487; 496; 508; 545; 548; 564; 574; 578; 588; 601; 613.

[6] *TN*, 60 (two entries); 61 (three entries); 62; 64; 65 (two entries); 66 (two entries); 67 (two entries); 71; 72; 74; 78; 79; 81; 84; 85 (two entries); 87; 89; 90; 91; 93 (two entries); 160; 179 (two entries); 180; 194; 197; 205; 274; 277; 392; 454; 594; 598; 599; 663; 664 (two entries).

[7] *TN*, 69; 178; 206 (two entries); 212 (two entries); 398; 406; 410; 416; 432 (two entries); 434; 445; 451; 465; 472; 477; 493; 520; 521; 523; 528; 535; 536; 540 (two entries); 541; 544 (two entries); 547; 553; 557; 558; 559; 560 (two entries); 606; 608; 610; 612; 629.

[8] *TN*, 300; 301; 302 (two entries); 303 (three entries); 304 (two entries); 397; 402; 405; 413; 417; 438 (two entries); 441; 453; 541; 543; 551; 571; 577 (two entries); 578; 590; 600; 602; 605; 618; 620; 632; 637.

[9] *TN*, 169; 170; 171 (two entries); 172; 173; 180; 181; 192; 193; 194; 195; 197; 198; 199; 204; 340; 357; 358; 407; 510; 519; 527; 535; 536; 558; 565; 569; 600.

[10] *TN*, 204; 207; 433; 526; 538; 549; 585; 599; 600; 602; 607; 608; 609; 611; 615; 618; 620.

[11] *TN*, 266 (two entries); 364; 375; 463; 483; 501; 539; 542; 544; 573; 624; 628; 630; 631.

[12] *TN*, 200; 202; 296; 297 (two entries); 298 (two entries); 416; 420; 474; 517; 524; 580; 591; 593.

[13] *TN*, 203; 211; 292; 408; 419; 457; 506; 561; 582; 590; 616; 619; 621; 633; 634.

[14] *TN*, 70; 71; 86 (two entries); 95; 241; 288; 462; 532; 545; 604.

[15] *TN*, 211; 287; 489; 522; 543; 552; 555 (two entries); 559; 567; 606.

[16] *TN*, 293; 369; 434; 453; 458; 460; 581; 607; 610; 611.

[17] *TN*, 213; 285; 290; 301; 433; 436 (two entries); 485.

[18] *TN*, 13; 14; 15; 16; 17; 18 (two entries); 19.

[19] *TN*, 265; 393; 412; 428; 429; 482; 535; 654.

[20] *TN*, 63; 68; 69; 73 (two entries); 208; 537.

[21] *TN*, 56; 105; 298; 346; 379.

[22] *TN*, 207; 435 (two entries); 462; 572.

[23] *TN*, 242; 258; 281; 455.

[24] *TN*, 11; 12; 14.

[25] *TN*, 92; 624; 639.

[26] *TN*, 147; 260 (two entries).

[27] *TN*, 403; 436; 637.

[28] *TN*, 420; 576; 597.

[29] *TN*, 415; 476.

[30] *TN*, 198.

[31] *TN*, 88.

[32] *TN*, 198.

[33] *TN*, 456.

[34] *TN*, 213.

[35] *TN*, 416.

As *Sulafat al-ʿAsr* treats a smaller number of poets than Nasrabadi's anthology, we might also expect it to be more limited to the compiler's direct acquaintances, and this may be the case: a conservative estimate, based on the information that the anthologist reveals, indicates that Ibn Maʿsum had met 25 (19.3 per cent) of his entrants.[60] It cannot be said that the biographical subjects in *Sulafat al-ʿAsr* belonged to a single class, but Ibn Maʿsum does display a marked interest in men who, like him, were Shiʿis and *sayyids*, and who possessed a particular intellectual profile, belonging to a group of scholars who were trained in the religious sciences, philology and Arabic grammar. The anthology contains many more such figures than professional poets. Like Nasrabadi, Ibn Maʿsum harnessed the networks that his contacts brought with them. One way in which he did this was through consulting their notebooks (*tadhakir*), in which they asked their acquaintances to jot down poems. Ibn Maʿsum tells us that he consulted the notebook of Taj al-Din al-Maliki (d. 1066/1655), the Imam of the Maliki *madhhab* (doctrinal school) at the Sanctuary in Mecca, from which he derived information about poets of Mecca and Medina.[61] He also consulted the notebook of the judge Muhammad Daraz al-Makki, who had been posted to Yemen by the Ottomans.[62] This *tadhkira* appears to have been Ibn Maʿsum's only source of information regarding the Yemeni poet ʿAbd al-Rahman b. al-Mahdi al-ʿAqabi.[63] It is possible that Ibn Maʿsum consulted these sources and transcribed passages from them while he was in Arabia during his early teens.

Given that Ibn Maʿsum grew up in Mecca and emigrated to India as a young man, making influential literary connections in Yemen on the way, we might assume that *Sulafat al-ʿAsr* would have a more bifocal quality than *Tazkira-yi Nasrabadi*. The division of *Sulafat al-ʿAsr* into five geographically arranged chapters creates a superficial impression of equanimity, but there is, of course, a subjective geographical pull to the text. Ideological, personal and practical factors make Mecca into one the anthology's major hubs. Ibn Maʿsum regarded Mecca as the pivot of his world because it was the home of his religious faith, because the poets of pre- and early Islamic Arabia were major stylistic models for him and his contemporaries, and because he had grown up there. Seven of the biographical subjects in *Sulafat al-ʿAsr* are men of an older generation whom Ibn Maʿsum encountered in Mecca during his youth, some of them in scholarly reading circles.[64] Mecca was also pivotal to him because it was a hub of circulation and information exchange thanks to the annual *hajj*, which attracted Muslims from all over the old world. His chapter on North Africa is mostly derived from the scholar al-Maqqari's (d. 1041/1632) works, including not just the famous *Nafh al-Tib min Ghusn al-Andalus al-Ratib* (*The Scent of Perfume from the Succulent Branch of al-Andalus*), but also *Fath al-Mutaʿal fi Madh al-Niʿal* (*The Victory of the Lofty, in Praise of the Sandals*), an anthology of Maghribi texts on the Prophet and his sandals, and *Rawdat al-As* (*The Garden of Myrtle*), a biographical work on al-Maqqari's contemporaries in Marrakesh and Fez.[65] Al-Maqqari had done *hajj* and visited Mecca, and so Ibn Maʿsum's use of his work most probably reflects the circulation of books to India by way of the Arabian Peninsula, rather than directly from North Africa.[66] Similarly, Mecca seems to be one of the conduits through which information reached Ibn Maʿsum about the poets of Syria and Egypt: of the thirty-eight poets featured in that chapter, at least twelve had been in Mecca and can be located in a web of the anthologist's mutual contacts.[67]

Although Ibn Maʿsum does not devote a chapter to India, *Sulafat al-ʿAsr* is also slanted towards the poets who surrounded him at the court of the Qutbshahs. It is simply that the entries on them are slotted into the chapters on the regions from which they had emigrated.[68] Out of the 129 poets featured in *Sulafat al-ʿAsr*, 17 (13.1 per cent) are explicitly mentioned as having been in Golkonda and as having dedicated Arabic verse to Ibn Maʿsum's father, Nizam al-Din Ahmad. Six came from the Arabian Peninsula;[69] two from the Jabal ʿAmil region in greater Syria;[70] one from Yemen;[71] two from Iran;[72] three from Bahrain;[73] and three from Iraq.[74] Although some of these figures stayed in Golkonda for an extended period of time, others travelled on elsewhere, establishing connections with Ibn Maʿsum and Nizam al-Din Ahmad which continued by letter after their departure from Golkonda.[75] A further seven figures do not seem to have migrated to India, but they contributed to the broader, international network of the Golkonda circle by sending missives to its members from Iran and Arabia.[76]

Patterns in migration

The supranational perspective of both Ibn Maʿsum and Nasrabadi suggests that migration and mobility played a significant role in seventeenth-century letters, and this is indeed the case. The internal migration of poets within the Safavid domains was key to the dynamics of literary production in Iran, and most of Nasrabadi's biographical subjects who remained in the country were highly mobile. Although a lack of paved roads made Iran into 'a number of regional economies represented by major towns with their hinterland', the flow of poets between the borderlands and the central domains was relatively free.[77] Under Shah ʿAbbas I (r. 995/1587–1038/1629), state policies of forced migration from the country's periphery had created new districts in Isfahan, such as ʿAbbasabad, which rehoused families of merchants and craftsmen from Tabriz. Nasrabadi devotes entries to twenty-three Tabrizis of ʿAbbasabad.[78] Conflict with the Ottomans over Iraq in the west, and with the Mughals over Qandahar in the east, also encouraged the circulation of poets, some of whom were military men and so travelled out, and others of whom were displaced and so travelled in.[79] Another major stimulus for internal migration was pilgrimage. In Iraq, Najaf and Karbalaʾ, two of the most important pilgrimage destinations for Twelver Shiʿis, were mostly under Ottoman control throughout the seventeenth century, and there are relatively few references to poets travelling there.[80] However, the shrine of the Imam Riza at Mashhad was a major destination for poets from all over the Safavid domains.

Nasrabadi leaves us in no doubt that the principal destination for internal migrants in seventeenth-century Iran was Isfahan, the Safavid capital. The following table shows the professions of arrivals in Isfahan, as indicated in the anthology. It suggests that only a small proportion of writers came to Isfahan seeking careers as professional poets. Most were drawn there in order to study the religious sciences at one of the state *madrasa*s, or were involved in the life of the royal court, as high-ranking bureaucrats, ministers of state or secretaries. Trade and the crafts also represented significant reasons why poets travelled to Isfahan.

In general, these statistics give some indication of the degree of centralization that Safavid Iran experienced in the seventeenth century. The biographies of the individual poets indicate that many of them tried to find success in Isfahan before considering emigration to India or Arabia.

Professions of Iranian Poet Migrants to Isfahan, per Nasrabadi

Rank	Profession	No. of migrants
1	Religious scholar (incl. judge, preacher, etc.)[1]	65
2	High-ranking bureaucrat (*vizir, kalantar*).[2]	23
= 3	Professional Poet (living derived primarily or exclusively from verse, or evidence of other professional activity wanting).[3]	8
= 3	Calligrapher, bookbinder, copyist.[4]	8
5	Craftsman (incl. guild head).[5]	7
= 6	Tradesman (incl. weaver, farrier).[6]	6
= 6	Dervish.[7]	6
8	Governor, senior minister of state.[8]	5
9	Secretary.[9]	4
= 10	Court employee (incl. *Shahnama* reciter).[10]	2
= 10	Gentleman poet.[11]	2
= 10	Doctor of medicine.[12]	2
= 10	Merchant.[13]	2
= 14	Man of letters.[14]	1
= 14	Bookseller.[15]	1
= 14	*Maddah* (panegyrist of the Prophet and his family).[16]	1
= 14	Practitioner of the occult sciences.[17]	1
= 14	Painter.[18]	1
= 14	Dogsbody.[19]	1
= 14	Publican.[20]	1
= 14	Pensioner.[21]	1
= 14	Tutor to royal children.[22]	1

[1] *TN*, 165; 167 (two entries); 168; 220 (two entries); 221; 223; 227; 231; 233; 234; 235; 237; 238; 242; 248; 249; 252; 253; 261; 264 (two entries); 267; 268; 269; 270 (two entries); 272; 279; 280; 283; 284; 285; 292; 293; 294; 372; 397; 402; 406; 444; 457; 459; 465; 473; 487; 491; 497; 499; 501; 503; 505 (two entries); 512; 518; 522; 525; 532; 538; 548; 552; 554; 579; 588.

[2] *TN*, 109; 116; 119; 120; 121; 139; 144; 146; 150; 154; 159; 161; 162; 176; 184; 186; 197; 255; 497; 549; 556; 566; 591.

[3] *TN*, 341; 378; 391; 479; 504; 551; 553; 583.

[4] *TN*, 296; 297 (two entries); 410; 489; 522; 559; 570.

[5] *TN*, 434; 464; 465; 528; 559; 610; 616.

[6] *TN*, 458; 477; 519; 521; 523; 526.

[7] *TN*, 303; 304; 520; 551; 578; 602.

[8] *TN*, 34; 47; 49; 51; 72.

[9] *TN*, 266; 463; 501; 581.

[10] *TN*, 506; 587.

[11] *TN*, 205; 578.

[12] *TN*, 288; 515.

[13] *TN*, 169; 172.

[14] *TN*, 265.

[15] *TN*, 585.

[16] *TN*, 613.

[17] *TN*, 574.

[18] *TN*, 591.

[19] *TN*, 456.

[20] *TN*, 213.

[21] *TN*, 466.

[22] *TN*, 454.

Despite Nasrabadi's proximity to the Safavid capital, transnational migration features prominently in the anthology. Broadly speaking, the geographical area which he charts extends from the Levant in the west to India in the east, although we gain occasional glimpses of a more truly global world: mention is made of a poet who was shipwrecked and spent time in Europe, and another who was sent on a diplomatic mission to Ethiopia.[81] Of the poets featured, a remarkably high number, 176 (19.6 per cent), travelled from Iran to India, of whom 157 went to Mughal north India;[82] and 21 travelled to the Deccan sultanates, mostly to Shi'i Golkonda.[83] This figure exceeds the number of poets who migrated from other locations in Iran to Isfahan, indicating that India was an attractive destination for provincial Iranians. We may speculate that

Most Common Professions of Migrant Iranian Poets in India, per Nasrabadi

Rank	Profession	No. of Migrants
1	Professional poet (living derived primarily or exclusively from verse, or evidence of other professional activity wanting).[1]	60
2	Political figure (officer of state, governor, high-ranking bureaucrat or courtier, gentry with court employment, etc.)[2]	25
3	Merchant or trader on business.[3]	24
4	Religious scholar.[4]	20
5	Nobleman, *sayyid*, or professional driven to leave Iran due to straightened financial circumstances.[5]	12
6	Man of letters (e.g. court secretary, lexicographer, prose author but not professional poet).[6]	11
7	Craftsman (incl. guild head).[7]	7
= 8	Tutor to elite children.[8]	4
= 8	Court librarian, painter or calligrapher.[9]	4
= 10	Varying professions, but driven to leave Iran because of religious or social persecution.[10]	2
= 10	Representative in business or diplomatic affairs (*hajib*).[11]	2
= 10	Professional musician.[12]	2
= 13	Servant.[13]	1
= 13	No profession or employment.[14]	1
= 13	Dervish.[15]	1

[1] *TN*, 260 (two entries); 312; 316; 319; 322; 325; 327; 344; 348; 356; 359; 360; 363; 365; 366; 367; 370; 383; 397; 399; 401; 404 (two entries); 408 (two entries); 411; 429; 430; 438 (two entries); 439; 443; 444; 445; 448; 449; 467; 469; 471; 478; 479; 481; 492; 520; 543; 551; 552; 553; 563; 566; 570 (two entries); 571 (two entries); 572; 574; 577; 600; 617.
[2] *TN*, 52; 69; 75; 79; 84; 85 (two entries); 86; 88; 90; 91; 94; 123; 139; 160; 173; 174; 175; 190 (two entries), 202, 231; 537; 660; 662.
[3] *TN*, 119; 170; 171; 188; 192; 194; 195; 197; 199; 204; 211; 212; 229; 340; 357; 407; 510; 527; 558; 559; 569; 588; 603; 615.
[4] *TN*, 167; 221; 228; 261; 267; 272; 290; 291; 440; 442; 475; 485; 540; 568; 569 (two entries); 571; 583; 585; 620.
[5] *TN*, 139; 142; 147; 180; 186; 252; 392; 461; 464; 472; 486; 593.
[6] *TN*, 147; 191; 265; 379; 412; 429; 463; 464; 476; 482; 573.
[7] *TN*, 403; 406; 553; 558; 560; 607; 608.
[8] *TN*, 242; 258; 278; 281.
[9] *TN*, 298 (two entries), 346, 416.
[10] *TN*, 413; 473.
[11] *TN*, 104; 105.
[12] *TN*, 434; 610.
[13] *TN*, 137.
[14] *TN*, 441.
[15] *TN*, 600.

those who lived in eastern Iranian cities such as Mashhad may have found it just as easy to migrate to north India as to western Iran. As the table above shows, there are many more professional poets among the migrants to India than in the cohort who moved to Isfahan. Politics and trade come in second and third place respectively, indicating the importance of the Mughal Empire to Iranian mercantile activity, and the durative elite networks which connected the Safavid, Mughal and Deccani courts. Merchants represent a small proportion of subjects in the anthology as a whole, but a significant minority of the migrant poets, showing the importance of trade to transnational movement. Many of the émigrés in the remaining categories can be classed as skilled specialists, such as royal tutors, painters and musicians, who possessed talents which were in demand with Indian patrons.

The duration of these migratory journeys differed. Some poets left Iran with the intention of settling in India, but a substantial minority made return trips for financial or professional gain, with no aim of residing permanently in South Asia. Of the 176 poets who are recorded as having gone from Iran to India in Nasrabadi's *tazkira*, 52 (29.5 per cent of the sub-group) returned to Iran after a while or made multiple trips between Iran and India.[84] Most of these return trips should be considered ventures rooted in commercial speculation. It is difficult to quantify exactly how many migrant poets travelled to earn through composing verse alone, and how many journeyed for trade, because the two undertakings were not mutually exclusive. In fact, if an individual was voyaging by sea, it was relatively common for them to seek some profit in the journey by transporting goods for sale, even if they were not a wholesale merchant by profession. Shapur Tihrani, a prominent poet who was by no means a dilettante, travelled to India for mercantile activity (*tijarat*), but also made inroads at the Mughal court through composing lyric and panegyric poetry.[85] Munsif, another leading poet who also went to India, actually derived his principal income through trade.[86] This is not to suggest that poetry was simply a tool for cultivating relationships that could seal business deals, but rather that its production overlapped with commercial flows. For some, it was another tool in their armoury, a way to diversify their income.

The next most popular destination from Iran in Nasrabadi's anthology is Mecca, to which forty-two (4.6 per cent) of the biographical subjects travelled.[87] Of these, half (21) visited both Mecca and India, some on the same trip, and others on separate journeys.[88] Given the importance of Mecca as Islam's single most significant centre of pilgrimage, and its role as a hub of religious scholarship in the early modern period, the high proportion of migrants who were involved in the religious economy as scholars and *madrasa* professors is unsurprising. However, it is particularly noteworthy that merchants and traders on business represent the single most populous category, and that a relatively large number of professional poets also travelled to the Arabian Peninsula. In many cases, members of these two professions visited Mecca on their way between Iran and India, or vice versa.

Most Common Professions of Migrant Iranian Poets in Mecca, per Nasrabadi

Rank	Profession	No. of Migrants
1	Merchant or trader on business.[1]	10
2	Religious scholar, *madrasa* professor.[2]	9
3	Professional Poet (living derived primarily or exclusively from verse, or evidence of other professional activity wanting).[3]	8
4	Court official.[4]	5
5	Student of religion, dervish.[5]	4
= 6	Scribe.[6]	3
= 6	Craftsman.[7]	3

[1] *TN*, 172; 175; 197; 198; 199; 207; 510; 558; 594; 615.
[2] *TN*, 442; 450; 459; 491; 583; 585; 589; 620; 648.
[3] *TN*, 325; 366; 367; 381; 429; 490; 492; 617.
[4] *TN*, 96; 113; 160; 175; 549.
[5] *TN*, 228; 261; 290; 304.
[6] *TN*, 375; 463; 501.
[7] *TN*, 189; 406; 544.

The high degree of mobility between Iran, Arabia and India stands in contrast to a much more limited flow of people between the Safavid realm and the hostile states of the Ottoman Empire and the Toqay-Timurid Khanate of Central Asia. Only five poets travelled from Iran to Ottoman Anatolia, Syria or Egypt;[89] and just one went from Iran to the Toqay-Timurid Khanate, and thence to India.[90] Going the other way, one travelled from Ottoman Syria to Iran;[91] four went from the Toqay-Timurid Khanate to Iran[92] and one from the Toqay-Timurid Khanate to both Iran and India.[93] Although war is likely to have seriously reduced mobility between Anatolia, Iran and Transoxiana, it is important to emphasize that these figures do not necessarily represent the actual demographics of migration in the seventeenth century, or the most popular migratory routes, but rather Nasrabadi's perspective. This is reflected in the fact that only six poets who feature in the anthology were citizens of Indian polities who travelled to Iran;[94] only one poet grew up in India and travelled to the Arabian Peninsula, bypassing Iran altogether;[95] and only one migrated from the Toqay-Timurid Khanate to India.[96] As the following table shows, those migrants from Central Asia and India to Iran who were on Nasrabadi's radar were mostly high-ranking bureaucrats or diplomats, such as his friend Maliha (d. after 1104/1692–3), the author of the anthology *Muzakkir al-Ashab* (*The Recaller of [His] Companions*), who accompanied the Toqay-Timurid embassy from Bukhara to Isfahan in around 1088/1677–8.[97] There are, however, also several professional poets listed in the table, including Shawkat Bukhari (d. 1107/1695–6).

Most Common Professions of Migrant Central Asian and Indian Poets in Iran, per Nasrabadi

Rank	Profession	No. of Migrants
= 1	Diplomat.[1]	3
= 1	Professional poet (living derived primarily or exclusively from verse, or evidence of other professional activity wanting).[2]	3
3	Governor or *amir*.[3]	2
= 4	Scribe.[4]	1
= 4	Bureaucrat.[5]	1
= 4	Religious scholar.[6]	1

[1] *TN*, 92; 624; 639.
[2] *TN*, 560; 643; 652.
[3] *TN*, 79; 93.
[4] *TN*, 624.
[5] *TN*, 159.
[6] *TN*, 292.

Despite the fact that Ibn Ma'sum's focus is, in sociological terms, narrower than that of Nasrabadi, *Sulafat al-'Asr* displays a number of parallels with the *tazkira* in its representation of the demographics of migration. As the following table shows, the majority of émigrés in Mecca and Medina, who mostly came from Egypt and the Levant, belonged to a class of religious scholars. So much is unsurprising. However, they are almost equalled in number by the aggregate of other professions: men of letters, musicians, doctors and dilettante noblemen. Just as the *tazkira* testifies to the involvement of the holy cities in transregional trade and literary production, the diversity of the professions in this group indicates that Mecca and Medina offered opportunities for employment beyond the production of religious knowledge.

Most Common Professions of Migrant Poets in Mecca and Medina, per Ibn Ma'sum

Rank	Profession	No. of Migrants
1	*Imam, mufti, faqih*, philologist, grammarian.[1]	8
2	*Adib* (professional man of letters).[2]	6
= 3	Musician.[3]	1
= 3	Medical doctor.[4]	1

[1] *SA*, 2:462; 2:478; 2:503; 2:511; 2:596; 2:636 (two entries); 2:740.
[2] *SA*, 1:432; 2:481; 2:614; 2:746; 2:906; 2:930.
[3] *SA*, 2:680.
[4] *SA*, 2:680.

The profiles of the émigrés in the following table suggest that Yemen was drawn into transregional networks by way of Mecca. Although the numbers of poets who left the countries of their birth and settled in Yemen are not high, they are sufficient to indicate that the Qasimi Imams acted as an important source of patronage in the region.

Migrant authors of Arabic poetry in Yemen, per Ibn Ma'sum

Rank	Profession	No. of Migrants
= 1	*Imam, mufti, faqih*, philologist, grammarian.[1]	1
= 1	*Adib* (professional man of letters).[2]	1
= 1	Judge.[3]	1
= 1	Political leader.[4]	1
= 1	Professional poet.[5]	1

[1] *SA*, 1:120.
[2] *SA*, 2:917.
[3] *SA*, 1:199.
[4] *SA*, 1:61.
[5] *SA*, 1:413.

Significantly, just as India is the single most popular destination for émigré professional poets in Nasrabadi's *tazkira*, so too is it the most common destination for émigré professional men of letters (*udaba'*) in *Sulafat al-ʿAsr*. These professional men of letters were almost all in the employ of Nizam al-Din Ahmad. Like the professional poets active in Persian, mercantile interests played a role in guiding some of them to the court of Golkonda. A clear case of overlapping professional personas can be identified in figures such as *sayyid* Abu ʿAbd Allah Muhammad b. ʿAbd Allah al-Husayni b. Ibrahim b. Shababa al-Bahrani (date of death unknown), who sought out Nizam al-Din Ahmad and praised him.[98] When al-Bahrani travelled on to Iran, Nizam al-Din Ahmad appointed him as his agent and legal representative.[99] He subsequently became a *Shaykh al-islam* in the Safavid domains.[100] Further biographical information is given in one of the poet's own *qasaʾid*, where he states explicitly that he travelled to India after his studies in order to trade.[101] Al-Bahrani therefore pursued at least three identities which were not mutually exclusive: those of a merchant, a religious scholar and a poet. Like Shapur Tihrani, al-Bahrani shows how migrant poets in India sustained their professional literary production with mercantile activity. The total of twenty-three émigrés includes an additional six figures who were not part of the Golkonda circle, and who found employment in the Mughal Empire.

Migrant authors of Arabic poetry in India (both the Deccan and the Mughal Empire), per Ibn Ma'sum

Rank	Profession	No. of Migrants
1	*Adib* (professional man of letters).[1]	13
2	*Imam, mufti, faqih*, philologist, grammarian.[2]	4
3	Medical doctor.[3]	3
4	Political leader.[4]	2
5	Professional poet.[5]	1

[1] *SA*, 1:331; 1 :401; 1:421; 1:423; 1:427; 2:514; 2:533; 2:743; 2:805; 2:816; 2:837; 2:877; 2 :895.
[2] *SA*, 1:300; 1:315; 2:784; 2:863.
[3] *SA*, 1 :276 ; 2:570; 2:781.
[4] *SA*, 1:41; 1:78.
[5] *SA*, 2:893.

A further point of continuity between *Sulafat al-ʿAsr* and *Tazkira-yi Nasrabadi* is that Ibn Maʿsum does not discuss many migrants who left other regions for Ottoman Syria, Egypt or Anatolia. Of the three who are featured, one is Ahmad b. Masʿud, a member of the family of the *sharif*s of Dhawi Barakat, who travelled to Anatolia in order to drum up support from the Ottoman sultan Murad IV for his claim to being the rightful ruler of Mecca; and another was Ibn Maʿsum's own grandfather, al-Manufi (d. 1044/1634). In other words, the former was a famous political actor, and the latter was a relative of the anthologist. Otherwise, the Levant, Egypt and Anatolia largely seem to have fallen outside Ibn Maʿsum's own zone of circulation around the littoral of the Arabian Sea. This would tend to suggest that the arena of the western Indian Ocean had defined parameters.[102]

Migrant authors of Arabic poetry in Syria, Egypt and Anatolia, per Ibn Maʿsum

Rank	Profession	No. of Migrants
1	*Adib* (professional man of letters).[1]	2
2	Political leader.[2]	1

[1] *SA*, 1:227 ; 2:668.
[2] *SA*, 1:61.

By way of contrast, Ibn Maʿsum has more details on migrants who left the Arabian Peninsula and the Levant for Iran, Iraq and Bahrain, which he treats as a single region. Although Iraq was mostly under Ottoman rule, Ibn Maʿsum was interested in Shiʿi scholars from the cities of Najaf and Karbalaʾ, many of whom left to teach in Safavid Iran. Bahrain too was a major centre of Shiʿi scholarship, which was in the Safavid sphere of influence even before Shah ʿAbbas I expelled the Portuguese from the islands in 1622. Because Ibn Maʿsum treats Iran, Iraq and Bahrain as a single region, the following table ignores 'internal' migrants, including the Bahraini legal scholars Ibn Majid (d. 1028/1618) and al-Khatti al-Bahrani (d. 1028/1618), who both became renowned in Iran, and instead highlights the prominence of poets from the Arabian Peninsula and the Levant who came to the Safavid domains. It is notable that they were not all religious scholars. As I insinuated earlier in the chapter, the presence of several *udabaʾ* speaks to the consumption of Arabic literature in Safavid Iran outside purely religious environments.

Migrant authors of Arabic poetry in Iran, Iraq and Bahrain, per Ibn Maʿsum

Rank	Profession	No. of Migrants
= 1	*Imam, mufti, faqih*, philologist, grammarian.[1]	3
= 1	*Adib* (professional man of letters).[2]	3
3	*Shaykh al-islam*.[3]	2

[1] *SA*, 1:300; 1:315; 2:523.
[2] *SA*, 2:514; 2:533; 2:590.
[3] *SA*, 2:485; 2:589.

Taken as a whole, the information presented in these tables suggests several important ideas. First, it indicates that the littoral of the Arabian Sea did constitute a zone of circulation, which intersected with flows between other regions (such as the Mediterranean, East Africa and South-East Asia), but which, in poetic terms, could be construed as distinct. Second, the tables demonstrate that emigration from Arabia and Iran to India was noticeably 'professional', meaning that South Asia was the preferred destination of migrant poets who wanted to earn through the composition of verse. This is perhaps the single biggest factor in explaining why the western Indian Ocean constituted a discrete arena in terms of literary production.

This picture would undoubtedly change if one superimposed data drawn from other coeval and near-contemporary anthologies, such as Maliha's (d. after 1104/1692–3) *Muzakkir al-Ashab*, or al-Muhibbi's (d. 1111/1699) *Nafhat al-Rayhana*, onto the map that can be gleaned from Nasrabadi and Ibn Ma'sum. Al-Muhibbi, for example, who despite predeceasing Ibn Ma'sum wrote after him, incorporates authors whom he had encountered in *Sulafat al-'Asr* into his anthology, sometimes referring to Ibn Ma'sum and Nizam al-Din Ahmad and repeating the phraseology of entries in Ibn Ma'sum's text.[103] Nevertheless, *Nafhat al-Rayhana* is anchored in regions which lay on the fringes of Ibn Ma'sum's network, including parts of the Levant and Anatolia. Another example is the Persian *tazkira* of Mutribi (d. *c.* 1040/1630–1), which is focused on Central Asia and even contains information on scholars who emigrated from Yemen to Bukhara, a migratory axis entirely ignored in the texts that are my focus here.[104] Even if biographical anthologies 'operate as interrelated fragments of a genre both in compilative and in (re-)creative continuity', *Sulafat al-'Asr* and *Tazkira-yi Nasrabadi* are rooted in networks of authors who were closely linked to the anthologists.[105] Our next task is to present a more detailed picture of the basis for the bounded nature of these networks.

Poetry as a commodity: The value of verse in a transregional market

While the migration of poets from Arabia to India is so little investigated that it does not seem possible to speak of a dominant hypothesis, past scholarship has tended to emphasize questions of society and ideology when discussing the migration of poets from Iran to India in the early modern period. Modern commentators have variously claimed that the Safavids only patronized religious panegyrics in praise of the Prophet and the Twelver Imams, effectively ending traditional structures of literary production and forcing budding Iranian poets to seek support in South Asia;[106] and that India offered a more tolerant and socially liberal environment than Iran.[107] While the former hypothesis is unsustainable, it is true that in the primary sources we find references to poets who abandoned the Safavid domains for personal reasons: Mir Muhammad Mu'min was charged with apostasy (*ilhad*) and escaped to India, while it seems probable that Mulla Shawkati and Muhammad Qasim left Iran because of persecution directed at them due to their sexuality.[108] It is, however, possible to read too much into these anecdotes. Regarding sexuality, for example, although the Safavid state did in numerous instances execute or mutilate people who had been found to have had same-sex affairs, Nasrabadi indicates that male–male relationships at least were commonly accepted in Isfahan.[109] Furthermore, the Mughal state often displayed a similar degree of intolerance to the Safavid one. It is most likely that those who left Iran due to persecution simply did so because they would have been beyond the reach of the Safavid authorities in India.

There are only a few cases in Nasrabadi's *tazkira* in which individuals emigrated primarily due to threats against their lives. The data that I have presented earlier would tend to indicate that the vast majority of migrant poets travelled for economic gain. Indeed, I argue that economic questions of how and how much seventeenth-century poets earned from the sale of their work are key to understanding the process of migration during the period, and to establishing how the formation of a transregional marketplace and the creation of transnational literatures go hand in hand.[110] To the extent that the sources allow, a reconstruction of the sums paid for poems in the different states around the littoral of the Arabian Sea has the potential to cast light on the relative values that communities of patrons and readers accorded to poetry, and to reveal in which ways India offered a more lucrative market for poets than Iran and Arabia. A fuller understanding of additional factors, such as the cost of living in the different states, and rates of taxation, would ideally inform this view, but as no economic history of early modern Arabic and Persian literary production has been written thus far, we have to proceed from the data available. Nasrabadi's *tazkira* is comparatively rich in information about prices and salaries, while *Sulafat al-ʿAsr* is not, and so the following description presents a more detailed picture of Iran and India than it can of the Arabian Peninsula. It is a matter for speculation whether Ibn Maʿsum's position as a prince of the realm in Golkonda made him less interested in discussing, or more reticent to discuss, costs. When we analyse the prices paid for poems given by Nasrabadi, we have to bear in mind that the majority of the poets who feature in the two anthologies derived their main income from fields such as religious scholarship, the practice of a craft, or work in trade and industry. Furthermore, only a relatively small proportion of the transactions made around the littoral of the Arabian Sea during the seventeenth century would have been paid for with coin. Forms of compensation such as payment in food and objects constituted the majority of transactions across society as a whole, particularly in provincial settings.[111]

Yet even if a system of barter predominated among the general population, there are only a couple of instances in the anthologies where we find evidence of poems being exchanged for goods, and it is not entirely clear whether these were serious or facetious transactions: they are most probably to be seen as part of a habitus of mendicancy that professional poets adopted.[112] Many individuals were rewarded with monetary payment for their poetry. The sums allotted varied according to the relative social standing of the poet and his audience, and the affective impact which a poem had on its auditors. If a poet had social capital and was performing for a wealthy audience, then the rewards could be great. Shah ʿAbbas I was obviously capable of extreme generosity if the mood took him: when the poet Shani Takallu composed a piece in combined praise of the Shah and

'Ali b. Abi Talib, he was rewarded with his bodyweight in coin.[113] This practice, known as 'weighing in gold' (*zarkishi*), was a courtly phenomenon in Central Asia and India too, albeit one which occurred relatively rarely.[114] Mulla Turabi Balkhi, who was a recluse at a shrine in Balkh, was also rewarded with his bodyweight in coin when he praised Imam Quli Khan, the ruler of Bukhara, with a single *qasida*.[115] Despite the Persian name, it is most probable that *zarkishi* refers to receiving one's bodyweight in silver currency. To receive one's bodyweight in solid gold would have been simply a gesture on the part of patrons, as it would have been irredeemable and could only have been hoarded or smelted to make luxury objects.[116] Gold presentation coins were minted in this period, but they enjoyed very little circulation due to their high value.[117]

One-off rewards for poems were handed out frequently in Safavid Iran. Mirza Muqim Bukhari, who was in the service of the Toqay-Timurid Khan of Bukhara, 'Abd al-'Aziz (r. 1055/1645–1091/1680), came as his ambassador to Isfahan, and pronounced a *qasida* in praise of Shah Sulayman (r. 1076/1666–1105/1694), whose entourage rewarded him with a one-off gift of forty *tumans* (equivalent to 2,000 silver 'abbasi coins).[118] In a semi-private setting, the Safavid royal librarian and painter Sadiqi Bayg Afshar once rewarded the poet Mulla Ghururi for a single *qasida* by paying him with five *tumans* and two pen-and-ink compositions drawn in his own hand, which he said were of a type regularly purchased from him by Indian merchants at a rate of three *tumans* each, making his total gift in cash and paintings worth about sixteen *tumans* (equivalent to 800 silver 'abbasi coins).[119] Although Nasrabadi implies that Sadiqi Bayg was capricious in making this offer, the anecdote nevertheless shows that the practice of assaying the financial value of poems and comparing their worth with material objects was ingrained in society. Sadiqi Bayg was not alone. The poet Salim Tihrani (d. 1057/1647–8), who was notoriously difficult company, performed for the governor of Fars in Shiraz but managed to insult him. In order to get rid of the poet, the governor's *vizir* rewarded him with five *tumans* (equivalent to 250 silver 'abbasi coins) and a head-to-toe robe of honour (*khil'at*).[120] Both the sum offered by Sadiqi Bayg and the one given by the governor of Fars would have been a significant reward for a single poem. Nasrabadi says that one of his contemporaries, the poet Mulla Hatim, once remarked that *ghazal* poems were worth one *dinar* (1/10,000th of a *tuman*) each – a facetious comment designed to imply that they had no monetary value, but one which nevertheless throws into relief the generosity of the patrons mentioned above.[121] We do not have enough examples to name a standard price for poems purchased within the patronage system in Safavid Iran, but it is possible that figures such as 12,000 *dinars* (equivalent to sixty silver 'abbasi coins), a figure paid by the *vizir* of Lahijan to the poet Naji Lahiji, may have been considered unremarkable.[122]

The main form of reward which poets hoped their verse could bring them was a fixed income, which was desirable because it was sustainable. It was common for poets to be allotted a salary, a stipend through charitable trust, or feudal tenure of land, all types of payment that had the potential to generate income throughout their lives. Such rewards could either be doled out for continuing service, or act as ongoing recompense for a single piece of work. In Iran, Shah ʿAbbas I gave the poet and performer Mulla Bikhudi Janabadi a salary of forty *tumans* (equivalent to 2,000 silver coins) for reciting Firdawsi's *Shahnama* in courtly gatherings.[123] Musavvir, a poet who happened to be a son-in-law of the renowned painted Riza-yi ʿAbbasi, was in receipt of a stipend from the *vizir* Sarutaqi (d. 1055/1645).[124] Beyond the court, Fazli Jirbadqani, a student of the major poet Shifaʾi (d. 1037/1628), received an ongoing stipend from Imam Quli Khan, the governor of Fars, seemingly to write eulogies for him.[125] Mirza Muqim served Manuchihr Khan, the governor of Lur-i Kuchik, and was rewarded with a district in Luristan as a fiefdom (*tuyul*).[126] Later on in the century, Muqima Maqsud, a poet in the entourage of Shah Sulayman, received a stipend of twelve *tumans* (equivalent to 600 silver coins) from the court.[127]

Together, these examples give some indication of the range of ongoing stipends which were given to poets, but also of the variety of contexts in which they were held. Not just the king, but high-ranking bureaucrats too could act as patrons, and not just in the capital, but also in the provinces, broadening opportunities for employment across Safavid Iran. The values of the stipends that were issued by the court were not necessarily higher than those paid out by bureaucrats or provincial governors. These monetary rewards would have placed their recipients firmly within the ranks of the professional classes: in the 1640s, a one-off gift of five *tumans* (equivalent to 250 silver ʿ*abbasi* coins) would have represented about six months' salary for a master bricklayer in Isfahan.[128] An annual income of 600 silver ʿ*abbasi* coins would have been double the salary of an interpreter in the employ of the Dutch East India Company (VOC) in Isfahan.[129] A one-off gift of 800 silver ʿ*abbasi* coins was almost three times the annual salary of a groom in the employ of the VOC.[130]

The assignment of stipends could be a fickle business, particularly during the reign of Shah ʿAbbas I, when a well-judged poem of an overtly ideological nature was sometimes enough to secure a salary. Sharmi Qazvini, who was a tailor in the ʿAbbasabad district of Isfahan, was given a stipend by the king for having written a single, polemically anti-Sunni *rubaʿi*.[131] Mir ʿAqil ʿKawsari', a *sayyid* of Hamadan known for his extreme Shiʿism, was given cash and a *suyurghal* by Shah ʿAbbas I for demonstrating his devotion to ʿAli b. Abi Talib in verse.[132] Although there does not seem to have been a single stimulus, the *qalandar* Baba Sultan ʿLivaʾi' was also rewarded with a stipend by Shah ʿAbbas I, and was, furthermore, assigned the dervish lodge (*takiyya*) of Haydar in the central Chahar Bagh district of Isfahan.[133] The flip side of this generosity was that stipends could be removed without warning. Masʿuda was given a licence which allowed him to draw an income from auctioning coal and wood (both expensive commodities) in Isfahan.[134] The licence was suddenly suspended, then Masʿuda managed to have it reinstated when he composed a chronogram on the accession of Shah ʿAbbas II (r. 1052/1642–1077/1666), then it was suspended yet again during the vizierate of Mirza Mahdi (d. 1081/1670–1). These continual changes of fortune left the poet 'very poor'. A happier story is told of Hashri Tabrizi, who lived off a stipend in the ʿAbbasabad district of Isfahan. Hashri's stipend was suddenly discontinued, but he managed to complain in a poem to the *sadr*, Habib Allah, who assigned him a new one of thirty *tuman*s (equivalent to 1500 silver *'abbasi* coins).[135]

One final type of continuing support on which some poets in Safavid Iran drew was *vaqf*, in which land or property was endowed to institutions, and the yields therefrom were used to fund the salaries of the people who were on the payrolls of those institutions. Shaykh Shah Nazar, a poet of Qumsha, in the Isfahan area, had spent his substantial inheritance, travelled to India and, on his return to Isfahan, fell in love with a courtesan, on whom he exhausted the remains of his wealth.[136] At the end of his life, he was beset by poverty, and lived off the *vaqf* of the *imamzada*.[137] Hasan 'Zinati' of Natanz, another poet who also happened to be a *sayyid*, received a limited pension from *vaqf*.[138]

It has to be remembered that, like all economies, the economies of the Safavid and Mughal empires, the Ottoman Hijaz, Yemen and the Deccan sultanates were in constant flux over the course of the seventeenth century, and so financial concerns which motivated poets to travel in *c.* 1615 cannot automatically be thought to have pertained in *c.* 1670. The relative performance of national economies may be one factor which encouraged emigration, particularly from Iran, where the value of coin became increasingly adulterated throughout the century. The poet Qudrati even composed a *masnavi* on the devaluation of currency in Isfahan during the reign of Shah 'Abbas II, writing:[139]

چنان گشته خوار از خلایق درم * که شخص غنی گشته صاحب کرم
چو شیر است نقش فلوس این زمان * ز بیمش گریزند پیر و جوان

The *dirham* [silver coinage] is now so abject in men's eyes * That the rich spend lavishly.
The inscription on copper coinage has now become like a lion * Old and young alike flee before it.

Those who emigrated to India found a system of literary production that had many points of continuity with Safavid practices. One way in which poets in the Mughal Empire could achieve a sustainable income was through appointment to a *mansab*, an official rank of state, which entailed either a regular salary drawn in cash from the treasury or, in the higher echelons, the right to the land revenue and tax on a locality which had been assigned to the beneficiary.[140] Even though men of rank were required to perform an office of state, the institution of Mughal *mansabdari* was highly significant to literary production.[141] Nasrabadi reports that Mirza Salih, a *sayyid* from Burujard who had been a local *vizir* in Iran, attained the rank of 500 *zat* (the personal rank of *mansabdari*) under the Mughals, a grade which in a slightly earlier period had attracted a salary of 2,500 rupees per month.[142] Mirza Amin, who was from a family of Tabriz, became a secretary (*bakhshi*) in Mughal service and attained the rank of 1,000 *zat*, a grade associated with a salary of 7,700 rupees per month under the emperor Akbar (d. 1014/1605).[143] Mirroring practices in Iran, men who sought to earn a living in the Mughal domains through poetry alone could sometimes be retained on a stipend by their patrons. Mirza ʿAbd Allah ʿUlfat, from Khurasan, migrated to India as a young man and worked for Jaʿfar Khan Qazvini, who allotted him a stipend of one hundred and fifty rupees per month.[144] During the reign of Jahangir (r. 1014/1605–1037/1627), the monarch whom Jaʿfar Khan served, a *tuman* was worth thirty rupees, which would mean that Ulfat received a stipend equivalent to sixty *tuman*s (or 3,000 silver *ʿabbasi* coins) annually, almost double some of the stipends that we have seen were allotted in Iran.[145]

One of the few cases in Nasrabadi's biographical anthology where a poet's incomes in different states are compared is that of the relatively well-known writer Mir Razi Danish. A *sayyid* from Mashhad, he travelled with his father Abu Turab to North India. The father died, and Mir Razi Danish stayed on to serve Shah Jahan. Nasrabadi reports that Prince Dara Shukuh (d. 1069/1659) rewarded Mirza Razi Danish with 100 *tuman*s (equivalent to 5,000 silver *ʿabbasi* coins) for a single line of poetry.[146] This is presumably the anthologist's own approximate conversion from rupees, or a conversion made by his sources. Mirza Razi Danish then migrated from North India to the Deccan, where he was well received by Sultan ʿAbd Allah, the Qutb Shah. He subsequently returned to Mashhad, and Sultan ʿAbd Allah assigned him an annual stipend of twelve *tuman*s (equivalent to 600 silver *ʿabbasi* coins), to be delivered to him in Iran every year by an agent.[147] The purpose of the stipend was for Mirza Razi Danish to perform pious acts at the shrine of the Imam Riza in Mashhad in lieu of Sultan ʿAbd Allah.[148]

This evidence suggests that a broadly comparable understanding of the financial value of poetry and a similar level of demand for it may have existed in the different states, but that the highest prices paid for verse in India exceeded those generally given in Iran. The ability of Iranian patrons to make good on their valuations would have also been compromised quite substantially in the period *c.* 1660–1710, the decades surrounding the completion of *Sulafat al-ʿAsr* and *Takzira-yi Nasrabadi*, when Safavid Iran suffered from chronic shortages of bullion.[149] During the 1670s, Mughal India was not affected by limited silver supplies to the same extent.[150] This would have meant that, even if courtly patrons paid comparable amounts for verse, poets would have earned differently in the Safavid and Mughal empires in real terms. As currency value and exchange were predicated on the metal content of coinage, a poet who emigrated from Iran, accrued wealth in India and then returned to Iran could have then been able to 'upsell' his earnings in this period by profiting from the exchange of his purer Indian coins.[151] Similarly, until the collapse of the Qutbshahi sultanate in 1098/1687, Golkonda's main unit of currency was a gold coin, the *hun*, which was renowned for the purity of its metal content.[152] That this made Golkonda into an attractive destination for those poets who were entrepreneurial enough to exploit financial inequalities is suggested by a poet called Mir Maʿsum (no relation of Ibn Maʿsum), who states:[153]

عمر اگر امان دهد میروم از ره دکن * روپیه تا بدست من هون نشود نمیشود

If my life is to be secure, I must head to the Deccan * Until the rupees
in my palm become *hun*s, I won't make it.

Mir Maʿsum's line underscores an important point about the nature of the economy of the early modern western Indian Ocean: it was a connected system, and sums accrued in one kingdom could be sent to another. Even as bullion shortages encouraged the Safavids to control the export of specie, Nasrabadi's anecdotes indicate that remittances to Iran from abroad were possible and common.[154] Smuggling appears to have been mundane,[155] but the circulation of capital between states was also supported by an international network of *sarraf*s (bankers) and groups such as the Banya, the expatriate Hindu and Jain moneylenders who set up shop throughout Iran and Arabia.[156] When moving between states, travellers could carry promissory notes and have them redeemed for cash at their destination, on payment of interest.[157]

There are several anecdotes which illustrate how this degree of economic entanglement affected poets. Mulla Muqimi 'Hilmi' of Kashan emigrated to the Mughal domains and served Prince Dara Shukuh.[158] The emperor Awrangzib later gave Hilmi a permit to go to Arabia in order to perform *hajj*, and the poet died on pilgrimage.[159] Before his death, Hilmi had made an Arab merchant named Shaykh Badr al-Din his executor (*vasi*), and Mirza Ibrahim Qaʾini, an Iranian resident in Mecca, the overseer (*nazir*) of his will.[160] Between them, the two administrators fulfilled Hilmi's wishes and had his estate, consisting of several books and 700 rupees, split between the poor and his beneficiary, who lived in India.[161] An equally mobile poet was Muʾmina 'Nisbat', who grew up in Nayruz in Iran.[162] Having spent time in Isfahan, Nisbat went to India, where he was patronized by the émigré noblemen Danishmand Khan and Jaʿfar Khan. With the wealth that he managed to accrue under Mughal patronage, he returned to Isfahan, did *hajj* to Mecca and from there went once more to India. When he died, his property, which was worth nearly a thousand *tuman*s (equivalent to 50,000 silver *ʿabbasi* coins), was brought back to Isfahan and divided among his beneficiaries.[163]

These stories point to the existence of three factors that are vital to transnational networking: a shared legal system – in this case, Islamic law – which allowed the poets' wills to be recognized in the different states; a transportation system which made transregional travel economically feasible; and the freedom to export wealth. Yet, ultimately, this was a question of individual circumstances and ambitions. Some poets were content with their lot and stayed where they were, including Mir Sanad, a *sayyid* from Kashan, who received a stipend from the tax revenue of his local district and lived by the city's idyllic Fin garden.[164] Others decided to travel. Salik Qazvini, for example, earned well in India and returned to Iran, but his relatives then spent the wealth that he had accrued, and he decided to emigrate again. He eventually came back to Iran, ill, and was offered a stipend of twelve *tuman*s (equivalent to 600 silver *ʿabbasi* coins) by the *vaqiʿa-nivis* (the court historiographer, Muhammad Tahir Vahid), but refused it.[165]

The revisionist thesis which the foregoing evidence suggests is not that seventeenth-century poets were forced to migrate because employment was only to be found in India, but, rather, that equivalent institutions of patronage, a common legal infrastructure, financial mobility and relatively affordable transport *encouraged* them to travel and made the littoral of the Arabian Sea one large theatre of opportunity, actively connecting cities in different political dispensations. We have seen that Safavid Iran had a robust market for poetry in Isfahan and provincial centres like Mashhad, and that poets' earnings could be substantial when compared with the salaries of other professions. However, higher stipends and gifts of value, lower living costs and an even greater number of centres of literary production in India encouraged poets to travel there. To migrate was not to abandon one's former life. Indeed, the ability to remit wealth to dependents who had stayed behind would have made it tempting for families to hedge their bets and send their members in different directions. The eighteenth-century scholar Yusuf al-Bahrani (d. 1186/1772) reports that one of Ibn Ma'sum's teachers, Ja'far b. Kamal al-Bahrani (d. 1088/1677–8), struck just such a deal with his brother, who remained in Shiraz while Ja'far himself set out for Hyderabad, on the understanding that whichever of the two men first met with success would care for the other.[166] Therefore, although I do not claim that the causes of migration in this period are reducible to economic factors alone, the evidence indicates that there were clear financial benefits to migration for those willing to look for employment overseas, and that economics contributed to the involvement of Arabic and Persian literature within a transregional marketplace. Even if one regards the second half of the seventeenth century as a time of economic depression in part of the zone studied here, most particularly in Safavid Iran, financial instability contributed to making this period into a time of transnational growth in literary terms by actively encouraging the formation of diasporas.

From one author to another: One network or two?

As Ibn Ma'sum and Nasrabadi compiled their anthologies within five years of one another, charting literary production across a common geographical area, we have to ask whether the biographical subjects of *Sulafat al-'Asr* and *Tazkira-yi Nasrabadi* represent two entirely separate, monolingual networks of authors, a single, bilingual network, or two networks which overlapped in part, like a Venn diagram. I argue that analysing the points of continuity between literary networks in two languages encourages us to destabilize canonical hierarchies, instead focusing on serendipitous connections between poets and revealing how major authors could be linked through minor ones. This in turn affects our understanding of intertextuality, obliging us to consider circulation in terms of the actual social connections that writers made, rather than concentrating exclusively on borrowings made between poets who have subsequently been canonized as 'greats'.

While there certainly are instances in which coteries of prominent poets kept company with one another, migration often created diverse, uneven and socially asymmetrical communities. A rare surviving witness to this kind of entanglement is the *jung* (miscellany) of the Iranian poet and merchant Fayyaz, a brother of the religious scholar Muhammad Baqir Sabzavari (d. 1090/1679).[167]

Like many other poets and men of letters, who carried commonplace-books (*bayaz*, *majmu'a* or *safina* in Persian, *tadhkira* in Arabic) on their travels, Fayyaz took his miscellany with him on his business trips. He assembled the manuscript between 1048/1638–9 and 1076/1665–6, as he journeyed between Safavid Iran, Arabia, the Mughal Empire and the Qutbshahi sultanate, where he was hosted by Nizam al-Din Ahmad Gilani, the royal physician to Sultan 'Abd Allah.[168] Whenever he encountered authors during his travels, Fayyaz asked them to inscribe verse or Shi'i exegetical texts in his miscellany, with the result that the manuscript contains notes in Arabic and in Persian in the hands of upwards of thirty-seven poets and scholars of the period. The document gives us a material sense of migration's role in creating literary communities. It contains entries made in the port cities of Bandar 'Abbas (in Safavid Iran), Surat (on Mughal India's west coast), and Masulipatnam (the Qutbshahi sultanate's main port, on India's southeast coast) showing how encounters happened as travellers embarked, disembarked and waited for passage.[169]

Twelve writers who left their inscriptions in Fayyaz's miscellany were also part of Nasrabadi's network as it is reflected in his *tazkira*. They do not belong to a single social group, nor were they of equal prominence, and yet they were brought together in some form of community by Fayyaz himself.[170] Some of them lived in the different cities to which Fayyaz travelled, such as Muhammad Riza Chalabi 'Unvan[171] and Sa'd al-Din Muhammad Raqim,[172] both of whom were from Mashhad, which Fayyaz must have visited repeatedly, including in 1066/1656.[173] Another group consists of poets connected to Golkonda, including Faraj Allah al-Shushtari, who noted down extracts of *tafsir* and *akhbar* for Fayyaz in Hyderabad in 1054/1644–5;[174] Salik Yazdi, who inscribed his poetry in Hyderabad in 1055/1645–6;[175] and Jawhari, who added extracts of his own poetry in the port of Masulipatnam in 1057/1647.[176] As I explore in Chapter 5, Salik responded emulatively to Faraj Allah's poetry, and Fayyaz's manuscript is good evidence of how their inhabitation of the same space fostered links between their work. Faraj Allah was also bilingual, and features as a biographical subject in *Sulafat al-'Asr*, so we can see how Fayyaz's interactions further enmeshed multilingual networks in one another.

At the same time, Fayyaz also managed to find and convince famous poets to inscribe his miscellany, including Mirza Fasihi of Herat;[177] Sa'ib, who added poems in his own hand in 1059/1649;[178] Ibrahim Adham (the son of the sixteenth-century poet Mir Razi Artimani), who died in prison in India;[179] and 'Abd al-Vasi' Aqdas, the son of Qudsi, who made notes in the volume in 1066/1655–6.[180] Aqdas was chief superintendent of the Mughal emperor Awrangzib's goldsmithy, and so Fayyaz's connection to him may have its roots in commerce. Another two poets who feature in the miscellany, Kalb-i 'Ali Tabrizi,[181] and Rashida-yi Zargar,[182] were goldsmiths, and their inclusion is probably also linked to Fayyaz's mercantile activities.

Navigating Fayyaz's own network forces us to drop our preconceptions of who the most important poets were and instead see the world through his own hierarchy, rooted in the spaces that he navigated and his business trips. It also demonstrates how multifarious the connections between individuals can be. We come to similar conclusions if we attempt a thought experiment: how can we get from Nasrabadi to Ibn Maʿsum in as few social connections as possible? Numerous ways become apparent:

Nasrabadi knew Saʾib, who had been patronized by Zafar Khan Ahsan in North India.[183] Zafar Khan Ahsan's son, ʿInayat Khan Ashna, had patronized Kalim, who had spent time in the Deccan, where he had been patronized by Muhammad Saʿid Ardistani and his son Muhammad Amin, who together acted as patrons to Salik Yazdi, who knew Faraj Allah Shushtari, whom Ibn Maʿsum met in Golkonda.[184] This gets us from Nasrabadi to Ibn Maʿsum in eight moves, using patron–client relationships. We can halve the number of social connections by going through approximately the same chain of people, but replacing patronage with commerce: Nasrabadi knew Saʾib,[185] who met Fayyaz,[186] who met Faraj Allah Shushtari,[187] who met Ibn Maʿsum.[188] This gets us from Nasrabadi to Ibn Maʿsum in four literary relationships. If we shift fields again, we can get from one anthologist to the other in the same number of moves via a courtly route: Ibn Maʿsum knew *sayyid* ʿAbd Allah b. Muhammad al-Bahrani, who was in the retinue of Nizam al-Din Ahmad.[189] *Sayyid* ʿAbd Allah wrote an Arabic panegyric in praise of Muhammad Tahir Qazvini (d. 1112/1701), who was court epistolographer to the Safavid Sultan Sulayman.[190] Nasrabadi knew Muhammad Tahir Qazvini's elder brother, Mirza Fasih.[191]

We can reduce the number of intermediaries even further, pursuing two routes: going via Golkonda, Nasrabadi met the poet Ulfati Savaji when the latter returned to Isfahan from the Deccan.[192] Ulfati had compiled a treatise on poetics and rhetoric for the Qutbshah ʿAbd Allah, who patronized Ibn Maʿsum and his father Nizam al-Din Ahmad.[193] This gets us from Nasrabadi to Ibn Maʿsum in three moves, using a patron–client network. Alternatively, we can go via Mecca and a theological network: Ibn Maʿsum had attended the study circle of the prominent Iranian theologian Muhammad Baqir Khurasani [Sabzavari], when the latter had stayed at the Sanctuary in Mecca in 1063/1052–3.[194] Muhammad Baqir's nephew, Mirza Mirak, came to the mosque at Lunban and visited Nasrabadi.[195] This gets us from Ibn Maʿsum to Nasrabadi in three moves.

Given that we can move from Nasrabadi to Ibn Maʿsum and vice versa along a number of paths which almost all depend on poetic exchange but which exploit differing kinds of professional relationships (patronage, politics, trade and religious learning), and given that the connections which I have plotted here are by no means exhaustive, I argue that there is a fairly extensive bilingual network imbricated within the larger, monolingual networks which *Sulafat al-ʿAsr* and *Tazkira-yi Nasrabadi* document. This bilingual network is cosmopolitan in the sense that Arabic and Persian do not observe hard geographical borders within it: thus, Sayyid ʿAbd Allah's panegyric in praise of Muhammad Tahir Qazvini takes Arabic to the heart of the Safavid court, while, in a different hierarchy, Ibn Maʿsum is the last in a chain of patron–client relationships that were otherwise conducted exclusively in Persian.

The body of this book is devoted to understanding how the patterns in migration and social interaction which I have outlined in this chapter were reflected in the texts that poets composed. In addition to asking which canonical poets of the past were most frequently used as models in classicizing seventeenth-century poetry, we have also to understand that encounters between contemporaries fostered mutual borrowings, and that for many writers, the primary purpose of composing verse was to engage with their fellows. By focusing on the intersection between poets' lives – their itineraries, their interactions with their patrons, their peers and their audiences – and their poetry, we can reconstruct the mechanics of the texts and see how they functioned in the extratextual world. This involves setting aside our own preconceptions of good and bad poetry and major and minor poets, and instead aligning our geopoetical viewpoint with that of the poets themselves. The following chapters show how the borrowings which well-known writers like Ibn Ma'sum and Sa'ib made from lesser-known authors like al-Jawhari and Ilahi are just as significant as the 'influences' which went the other way.

Part II

CLOSE READINGS OF LITERARY NETWORKS

Chapter 2

HYDERABAD

IBN MAʿSUM

The arrival of Ibn Maʿsum in India

Ibn Maʿsum arrived in Golkanda in 1068/1657, when he was fifteen years old.[1] Accompanied by an emissary from the Qutbshahi court, he had journeyed from Mecca to the Yemeni coast, from there by a privately captained ship to the small port of Jaitapur, just north of Goa, and then overland, through territory controlled by the ʿAdilshahi dynasty of Bijapur, to Hyderabad. The voyage as a whole appears to have been carefully coordinated and to have been kept secret, suggesting that he was regarded as a politically sensitive figure. After he had arrived in the Qutbshahi sultanate, he was quickly assimilated into the structures of the court through marriage, as is indicated by a previously unknown sermon which his teacher Jaʿfar b. Kamal al-Din al-Bahrani pronounced at his wedding.[2] Ibn Maʿsum's bride is not named in this text, but it is most likely that she was a member of the Qutbshahi royal family. Through this or further marriages, Ibn Maʿsum had at least four sons, three of whom survived into adulthood. One of them, who identifies himself in an owner's note on one of Ibn Maʿsum's holograph manuscripts, was called Rana (meaning Rajah) Muhammad Jawad, suggesting that he was given a princely title in Golkonda.[3] A second was named Abu Ismaʿil Ibrahim.[4] A third is identified on the fly-leaf of another of Ibn Maʿsum's holograph manuscripts as Muhammad Majd al-Din.[5] The fourth is known from court documents as Sayyid Salam Allah.[6] Both Ibn Maʿsum's marriage and his siring of children would have been central to his creation of a transregional network.

We know a considerable amount about Ibn Maʿsum's voyage from Arabia to India because he used the facts of the journey as the inspiration for a literary travelogue, which he called *Salwat al-Gharib wa-Uswat al-Arib* (*The Outsider's Consolation and the Intelligent Man's Exemplum*). Completed in Golkonda, in 1074/1664, when the author was twenty-two, *Salwat al-Gharib* is the most discussed of Ibn Maʿsum's works among modern scholars.[7] One of the key conceits of the book is the employment of the historical corpus of Arabic literature to render the strange familiar, hence its title. As Ibn Maʿsum progresses on the narrative of his journey, he encounters places, flora, fauna and people that are previously unknown to him, but he is able to interpret this new reality through the Arabic poetry that he has studied. The work as a whole can be seen as an act of internalizing the corpus, mastering it and building on it but also, more importantly, as an act of textualizing the world. A good example of this is Ibn Maʿsum's admiring description of the first time that he ever saw an elephant, at a rest house on the fringes of the Deccan.[8] Wondering 'at its marvellous constitution and strange appearance', he seeks to reach some understanding of it by finding an entire series of quotations about pachyderms that had been composed by earlier authors, such as the man of letters, geographer and historian al-Masʿudi (d. 345/946), who had himself travelled in India, and the scholar al-Turtushi (d. *c.* 520/1126), who only ever made it as far east as Baghdad.[9] He also includes an entire series of descriptive poems about elephants produced at the court of the Buyid vizier al-Sahib ibn ʿAbbad (d. 385/995) in Isfahan,[10] as well as the following short piece by an author of Mamluk Cairo and Damascus, Ibn Fadl Allah al-ʿUmari (d. 749/1349):[11]

هذا هو الفيل الذي * يبدو العجيب لنا به
ليل قد افترس النها * را فبان في أنيابه

Here is the elephant which * Delights us.
A night that pounced on the * Day, then disappeared in his tusks.

Using this poem, he builds one of his own in the same metre, basing it on the same simile:[12]

يا حبذا الفيل الذي شاهدته * وشهدت منه ما نما لي ذكره
فكأنه وكأن أبيض نابه * ليل تبلج للنواظر فجره

What a fine elephant it was that I saw * And which I saw do things that
made me recall it more and more.
It and its white tusks are like * A night whose dawn unfolds for the onlooker.

Poems such as these should be seen as attempts to innovate and to play with the corpus in an Indian context, a reorientation enabled by a mastery of convention. They form part of a broader complex of literary activities which Ibn Maʿsum undertook in India, depending on access to a comprehensive selection of Arabic texts in manuscript, and on discourse with a sizable community of other authors active in Arabic at the court of the Qutbshahs. His best-known works, including *Sulafat al-ʿAsr*, *Anwar al-Rabiʿ* and *Salwat al-Gharib*, are all anthological – they tessellate together fragments compiled from many different Arabic manuscripts, both canonical and contemporary. A good number of the extracts which he cites throughout *Anwar al-Rabiʿ* and *Salwat al-Gharib* are themselves drawn from earlier anthologies, reducing the number of sources on which he was dependent. It is also possible that many of the Arabic manuscripts which he encountered in Golkonda would have belonged to his father, and that he may have brought his own small library with him when he emigrated from Mecca. These caveats aside, the breadth and the variety of Ibn Maʿsum's works testify to the quantity and diversity of Arabic manuscripts which had arrived in Golkonda from across the Arabian Sea and from other cities within South Asia, and which were available to him as he worked.[13]

We gain a fresh insight into the course of Ibn Ma'sum's literary activities during his time at the court of the Qutbshahs thanks to nine manuscripts, some of which are autographs and holographs of his works, and some of which are volumes that he commissioned and read.[14] These volumes are previously unstudied, and they have not been brought together as a corpus before. The autograph manuscript of *Sulafat al-'Asr* survives, as do no less than two holographs and an autograph of *Anwar al-Rabi'*, a partial holograph of *Nafthat al-Masdur* (*The Expectoration of the Consumptive*), and manuscripts of other works (*Salwat al-Gharib* and *Mawdi' al-Rashad*) which are contemporary with the author. Since holographs and autographs are normally rare survivals, it is unusual to have so many extant manuscripts that were either copied or authenticated by a single author. It is possible that later generations attached importance to Ibn Ma'sum's hand because of his significance within Twelver Shi'i scholarly circles, and so looked after these volumes with care, much as the holographs of famous Mamluk scholars like al-Safadi (d. 764/1363) and al-Maqrizi (d. 845/1442) were valued by subsequent generations.[15]

Extant volumes which formed part of Ibn Ma'sum's personal collection of manuscripts in India include two books which tell us something about his intellectual development as a scholar of Shi'i thought and Arabic letters. One is a copy of Volume Two of Mahmud b. Abi l-Hasan al-Naysaburi's (d. *c*. 1130 CE) *Khalq al-Insan* (*The Creation of Man*) – a Qur'anic commentary – containing a list of contents in the hand of Ibn Ma'sum, and a series of poems that he jotted on the blank opening pages.[16] He dates his own additions to Sha'ban 1077/January 1667 and Safar 1081/July 1670, noting his ownership of the volume, and the fact that he consulted it repeatedly for the purpose of study.[17]

The second volume is a multi-text manuscript that was copied for him in Shawwal 1082/December 1671 by Sa'id b. Darwish Kujarati (i.e. Gujarati, who was also known by the *nisba* Ahmadabadi), who transcribed the autograph of *Sulafat al-'Asr* that same year as well.[18] This manuscript consists of several works on Twelver Shi'i tradition and pedagogy, including the so-called *Creed* of Ibn Babawayh (d. 381/991); *Kitab al-Ghayba* (*The Book of the Occultation [of the Twelfth Imam]*) by al-Shaykh al-Tusi (d. 459 or 460/1066–7); *Kashf al-Riba 'an Ahkam al-Ghiba* (*The Removal of Doubt from Judgements Pertaining to Slander*) and *Munyat al-Murid fi Adab al-Mufid wa-l-Mustafid* (*The Disciple's Desire, on The Conduct of Instructor and Instructed*), both by al-Shahid al-Thani (d. 965/1557–8 or 966/1558–9);[19] and *Wusul al-Akhyar ila Usul al-Akhbar* (*The Best [Scholars'] Attainment of the Principles of [Hadith] Traditions*) by Husayn b. 'Abd al-Samad al-'Amili (d. 984/1576–7). In terms of content, the volume connects Ibn Ma'sum with canonical Twelver thought from Iran, and with coeval 'Amili networks, in which both of his two principal teachers in Golkonda participated. We can see this book as part of Ibn Ma'sum's education, but also as part of broader attempts to link the Qutbshahi sultanate into an international Twelver discourse. Ibn Ma'sum's main employment in Golkonda seems to have been in upholding this discourse through his role as a *sadr* (religious leader) and an *amir* (official of state).

The study of the Qur'an and *hadith* went hand-in-hand with philology. The earliest extant manuscript associated with Ibn Ma'sum is a copy of *Mawdi' al-Rashad fi Sharh al-Irshad* (*The Application of Guidance, in Explication of al-Irshad*), his commentary on a work of Arabic grammar by al-Taftazani (d. 793/1390).[20] The manuscript is dated 8th Muharram 1070/5 September 1659, which would mean that Ibn Ma'sum wrote the work in his mid-teens, within a couple of years of his arrival in India. The composition of this commentary seems to have had several functions. The first may have been as a practical exercise, for the author to hone his scholarly technique. The second may have been to cement his authority as a scholar of Arabic in Golkonda.[21] Yet another purpose may have been to further the cause of the Arabic language in the Qutbshahi sultanate, and to instruct an audience which had not grown up speaking or writing it in its grammar.

Although Ibn Ma'sum's annotations in his copy of *Khalq al-Insan* indicate that he continued to study indefinitely, he began to compile his major works from 1074/1664, the year in which he drafted both *Salwat al-Gharib* and *Nafthat al-Masdur*, an anthology on migration and homesickness. Only a portion of the latter work survives, and it is possible that the text never made it beyond the draft stage, because there is a significant amount of crossover between the extracts cited in it and *Salwat al-Gharib*.[22]

From about 1077/1666 to 1082/1672, Ibn Ma'sum worked on two major projects – *Sulafat al-'Asr* and *Anwar al-Rabi'* – the second of which is a monumental, seven-volume auto-commentary on Ibn Ma'sum's own *badi'iyya* (a poem in which each line showcases a different rhetorical device). *Anwar al-Rabi'* is a highly intertextual work which responds to earlier poems of the *badi'iyya* type by authors like Safi al-Din al-Hilli (d. *c.* 750/1349) and Ibn Hijja al-Hamawi (d. 837/1434), and which synthesizes and extends a millennium of rhetorical thought, arguing for 'the rhetorical endeavor . . . as a gateway to literate knowledge'.[23] This dating of *Anwar al-Rabi'* is a reassessment of the evidence. It was always known that Ibn Ma'sum had composed the *badi'iyya* on which *Anwar al-Rabi'* is based in 1077/1666–7, but it was assumed that the auto-commentary was not composed until 1093/1683, after Ibn Ma'sum had left Golkonda.[24] However, the earliest dated copy of *Anwar al-Rabi'* is a holograph, consisting of about a third of the text, made in 1081/1670, indicating that Ibn Ma'sum actually drafted a very large proportion of *Anwar al-Rabi'* straight after composing the *badi'iyya*, while he was still at the court of the Qutbshahs.[25] The next dated manuscript, an autograph of the full text of *Anwar al-Rabi'*, was copied by Ahmad b. Muhammad b. 'Abd al-Sajjad al-Huwayzi (evidently an émigré from the town of Huwayza in Khuzistan, and hence most probably a bilingual speaker of Arabic and Persian) in 1104/1692–3, and was then checked and approved by Ibn Ma'sum over the course of several reading sessions, the last one of which occurred in Muharram 1106/August 1694.[26] The overwhelming impression given by these dates is that while Ibn Ma'sum may technically have completed *Anwar al-Rabi'* in 1093/1683, the work was mostly written earlier, under Qutbshahi patronage, and then finalized after a long gap. This makes sense, considering the support for his literary and linguistic scholarship that Ibn Ma'sum received in Golkonda, and the fact that he seems to have been imprisoned in Hyderabad between the death of Sultan ʿAbd Allah in 1083/1672–3 and Shaʿban 1092/August 1681, the month in which he purportedly travelled north to the Mughal domains.[27] This period of incarceration would have prevented him from publishing the text.

Nizam al-Din Ahmad and Sultan ʿAbd Allah: Arabic panegyrics at a multilingual court

Ibn Maʿsum's work on *Sulafat al-ʿAsr* was conducted during the 1660s, and the text was completed in 1082/1671, at the height of Nizam al-Din Ahmad's power over Golkonda. Ibn Maʿsum devotes the very first biographical entry of the anthology, in the section on poets of Mecca, to his father. This act is certainly designed to mark his esteem for Nizam al-Din Ahmad, and to highlight the importance of the compiler's own network. It also underscores, perhaps deliberately, a dislocation between origin and destination which plays an important role in the anthology. The first poem that Ibn Maʿsum reproduces is a *qasida* which Nizam al-Din Ahmad composed in praise of his father-in-law, Sultan ʿAbd Allah.[28] It is a curious piece which opens up a series of questions about how Arabic verse was performed and received in Golkonda, and which makes one wonder whether Sultan ʿAbd Allah's education meant that he was capable of understanding the tropes of Arabic verse and how they could be manipulated, since, as Muhsin al-Musawi argues, the *qasida* form has 'a strong functional drive that happens to carve and then mold a dominant politics'.[29] The poem is clearly designed as a performative statement of a bond between the two men, evoking their complementary personae, Nizam al-Din Ahmad's fealty, their kinship through marriage, and calling for ʿAbd Allah's loyalty. In its structure and themes, it weaves together elements of self-vaunting (*mufakhara*) and praise of the poet's protector, and figures the poet as an emissary of his people, in a way which recalls the earliest *jahili qasaʾid*.[30] It is also clearly designed to communicate a political statement, which would demand that ʿAbd Allah understood it on some level. The text is too crafted to have operated simply as a phatic piece that derived its significance from the ceremony of its performance.

The poem begins with an evocation of all that Nizam al-Din Ahmad has left behind: the dwelling places of the Hijaz, and the beloveds who haunt it, Salma, Hind, Zaynab and Layla. These women, who appear in the Arabic corpus from its very earliest poems, were almost transformed by later, medieval poets such as Ibn al-Farid (d. 632/1235) into metonyms for the landscape of the Arabian Peninsula, creating a 'topology of nostalgia'.[31] In one *qasida*, for example, Ibn al-Farid writes:[32]

أبرق بدا من جانب الغور لامع * أم ارتفعت عن وجه ليلى البراقع
أنار الغضا ضاءت وسلمى بذي الغضا * أم ابتسمت عما حكته المدامعه

Was it lightning that I saw, flashing from the direction of the Jordan Valley * Or did the veil rise from Layla's face?
Did a blazing fire spark as Salma dwelt in Najd,[33] * Or did she smile through her tears?

In drawing these intertextual references, Nizam al-Din Ahmad ties love and longing inexorably to Mecca, his point of departure.

The next section of Nizam al-Din Ahmad's poem describes one beloved of the Hijaz in particular, a woman 'of curved hip and jet-black hair', wearing a necklace of jewels:[34]

يريك سناء البدر والشمس وجهها * نعم ونجوم الليل في جيدها عقدي

> Whose face shows you the glittering moon and sun * And at whose throat hang
> the night stars on a chain.

This figure is idealized, and familiar from the erotic introductory sections (*nasibs*) of many earlier and contemporary *qasaʾid*, but it is hard, given the context into which Ibn Maʿsum has placed the poem, not to see her on some level as a representation of Nizam al-Din Ahmad's new, royal wife. Such an interpretation depends on an understanding of conventional poetic images as being deployed on multiple levels, both drawing reference to their expression in the corpus and rendering the poet, the patron and the primary audience 'dramatized historical personae'.[35]

The *qasida* moves from erotic introit to praise, bridging themes by claiming that:[36]

بلى ليس بعد الدار يا صاحي ضائرا * إذا كان عبد الله منتجع الوفد

> Distance from one's abode is no loss, my newly sober friend, * If ʿAbd Allah is
> your destination.

The sultan's martial prowess is lauded, as are his aura of majesty, his dominion, and his lineage. The Qutbshahs are such that:[37]

صغيرهم في المهد للملك خاطب * كبيرهم للنيرات على المهد

> The infants among them address themselves to dominion in their cradles *
> and the grown men tread an easy path to the stars.

Nizam al-Din Ahmad then elucidates his relationship with his father-in-law, emphasizing how dependent the sultan has become on him, and how integral he is to the functions of the state. Despite his illustrious lineage:[38]

على أنني قد صرت بعض عبيده * ومن حزبه ومن أسنته الملد
ومن بعض غلمان له أو عشيرة * ومن جنده أو من صوارمه القد

> I have become one of [the sultan's] slaves, * A member of his party, one of
> his fine teeth,
> One of his attendants or a kinsman, * One of his soldiers, or one of his cutting
> swords.

The language that Nizam al-Din Ahmad uses, referring to himself as one of the sultan's slaves and as a member of his 'party' (*hizb*), parallels the political relationships between charismatic émigré Arab *shaykh*s and Indian kings that we find in other early modern states, such as Muzaffarid Gujarat.[39] The affirmation of the bond between the two men leads into a warning that Nizam al-Din Ahmad is beset by enemies:[40]

وتالله لا أخشى لكيدهم أذئ * لعلمي أن الكيد مع كيدهم يكدي

By God, I fear no harm from their trickery * Knowing as I do that cunning will treat their ruse meanly.

The poet appeals to the sultan, who has acted as his refuge, not to listen to the words of those who would slander him, and then ends by invoking a higher authority, the Prophet. A rhetorical and geographical circle is completed in the statement that the Prophet's family trace their beginning to 'the acacias of the river valley, the ben trees, and the sweet myrtle' in Mecca, the words which end the first half-line of the poem.[41] The narrative of the poem has taken us from the Arabian Peninsula to India and back again, proclaiming South Asia as a centre for the patronage of Arabic literature, yet binding us to Arabia through a sense of 'deep time'.

Space and language: Arabic literary production in Golkonda

Sulafat al-ʿAsr includes a great deal of information which can be pieced together to give an overview of Arabic literary activity in Golkonda during the latter half of the seventeenth century, showing how it fitted into the multilingual landscape of the Qutbshahi court, alongside writings in Persian, Dakhni, and Telugu.[42] The Qutbshahis traced their lineage to the Turkic Qaraqoyunlu rulers of fifteenth-century western Iran, and so Arabic was for them a supranational idiom of religion and high culture, rather than a vernacular.[43] Nevertheless, beyond the *qasida* that Nizam al-Din Ahmad wrote in praise of Sultan ʿAbd Allah, there is evidence to suggest that other high-ranking officials of the Qutbshahi court patronized the production of poetry in Arabic. A eulogy by the Iraqi poet al-Haykali is described by Ibn Maʿsum as having been composed for 'one of the viziers of our master the sultan'.[44] The fact that al-Haykali praises the past generosity of the dedicatee (*mamduh*) in this piece is suggestive of a sustained history of patronage, and it is unfortunate that Ibn Maʿsum's edition of the *qasida* cuts out any reference to the vizier's name, beyond the epithet *ibn al-akramayn* ('son of most noble parents').[45] A separate prose piece is equally intriguing. Jamal al-Din Muhammad b. ʿAbd Allah al-Najafi al-Maliki, a poet of the Golkonda circle who had previously spent time at other courts in India, sent an Arabic letter of congratulation to the nobleman Fazil Khan in 1071/1660–1, when the latter was presented with a sword.[46] This figure may be Fazil Khan ʿAla al-Mulk Tuni, lord chamberlain to the Mughal emperor Shah Jahan. Fazil Khan's seal is preserved in an important manuscript of the Arabic grammatical commentary *al-Sharh al-Radi* (by Radi al-Din al-Astarabadhi, d. 684/1285 or 686/1288) which circulated among members of Shah Jahan's court.[47] We know that Fazil Khan was in correspondence with Nizam al-Din Ahmad Gilani, royal physician to Sultan 'Abd Allah the Qutbshah, and so al-Najafi al-Maliki's poem may provide some evidence to demonstrate how Arabic literary networks not only linked Golkonda with the Middle East, but also with Mughal north India.[48]

The remaining material from Golkonda which is preserved in *Sulafat al-'Asr* is concentrated on the circle of Nizam al-Din Ahmad, who, as we have seen, seems to have enjoyed a significant degree of autonomy within the power structures of the court. He was also able to institute an assembly (*majlis*), where poets and critics of Arabic verse encountered one another. Much of the classicizing poetry that was produced in and around this circle was written in praise of Nizam al-Din himself: he was a political leader, to whom it was conventional to address panegyric verse, the host of a salon, who brought authors together, and a religious leader who commanded the respect of the Shi'i scholarly community. The comparison that the contemporary commentator al-Hurr al-'Amili (d. 1104/1693) makes between Nizam al-Din Ahmad and the Buyid vizier and man of letters al-Sahib Ibn 'Abbad (d. 385/995), who by the early modern period had become proverbial, is therefore a reasoned one, intended to emphasize Nizam al-Din Ahmad's control over the field of Arabic letters in Golkonda, his serious, critical interest in poetry, his role as a correspondent with leading intellectual figures of the period, and his Shi'ism.[49]

Majlis is a term with a long history, broad enough in its meaning to designate anything from highly formal, and sober, assemblies, to bacchanalian gatherings, to poetic workshops, or a mixture of all three. Indeed, it is this concatenation of different modes of behaviour and learning within a single space, ensuring that attendees circulated both scholarly knowledge and political and business news, that made *majalis* such an important social institution.[50] The spectrum of attendees at such events could also vary, from an intimate gathering of hand-picked invitees to a more porous formation.[51] While Ibn Ma'sum's comments make it clear that Nizam al-Din Ahmad's *majalis* were important to his literary life, it is difficult to establish whether they followed a standard format, and whether they usually took place in the fortress of Golkonda or at the family mansion. We know that they were quite hierarchical, since Ibn Ma'sum writes that there was a place of honour, which was afforded to Ibn Barakat.[52] We also know that they could be convened at night, since one such nocturnal gathering is mentioned, 'at which the mighty would gather and the circle of our friends would be reunited'.[53] Our most complete picture of one of Nizam al-Din Ahmad's *majalis* comes in an anecdote which Ibn Ma'sum recounts about a gathering that took place one day. He recalls that Nizam al-Din Ahmad rode out to a garden in the company of the poet Hasan b. 'Ali b. Shadqam and an armed guard.[54] When they had arrived and secured the area, Nizam al-Din Ahmad called for Ibn Ma'sum, who came in a cavalcade of troops.[55] Ibn Ma'sum gives this information because the cloud of dust kicked up by the cavalcade is the pretext for a quotation which Ibn Shadqam makes from the great poet al-Mutanabbi

(d. 354/965).[56] The multiple references to guardsmen suggest that Arabic literary life in Golkonda may have taken place in highly regimented and politically controlled spaces, reflecting Nizam al-Din Ahmad's role as the leader of a court faction.[57] The anecdote also highlights the intertextual and learned quality of Nizam al-Din Ahmad's gatherings, and indeed we find further indications that the *majalis* which Ibn Ma'sum attended focused on honing skills such as *iqtirah* (extemporization), and literary commentary.[58] The kinds of emulative and masked intertextuality which are discussed throughout this book would have also constituted a key point in the literary-critical discussions that Ibn Ma'sum and his father held.

Only in rare cases does the extant evidence speak of Arabic poets of Golkonda operating across literary languages. However, one poet attached to Nizam al-Din Ahmad, Faraj Allah al-Shushtari, did just this. Al-Shushtari's extant Persian compositions, which consist entirely of *ghazals* and *ruba'iyyat*, are studied in more detail in Chapter 5. Here it should be noted that there is a clear crossover, in the use of imagery and in the cultivation of an emotional mood, between his lyric Persian texts and the *nasib* sections of his two Arabic *qasida* poems, both in praise of Nizam al-Din Ahmad, which are preserved in *Sulafat al-'Asr*. In the introit to his first Arabic *qasida*, for example, Faraj Allah recalls the flood-plains of the Tigris and the Euphrates around Baghdad – and the beloveds whom he has left there:[59]

ما بين دجلة و الفرات مراتع * هي للنفوس معارج وسماء

**

أكبادنا نار الغضا من بعدهم * تذكي الأسى وجفوننا أنواء

The prairies between the Tigris and the Euphrates * Are places of angelic
ascent and a heaven for our souls.

**

My liver blazes with a euphorbial fire, distance-sparked, * Kindling sorrow
as my tears well.

In one of his Persian *ghazals* we find comparable articulations of love-longing and nostalgia for Iraq, such as:[60]

جگر ز درد و دل از داغ و لب ز افغان پر * نکرد کس چو فرج عاشقی باستعداد
ز یاد دجله دلم بوی مصر میشنود * از آن جهت که مرا یوسفی است در بغداد

My liver aches, my heart is branded, my lips moan * Someone like Faraj
is not ready for love
My heart senses Egypt when I remember the Tigris * For my Yusuf
is in Baghdad.

Although these lines form part of larger pieces, which are in dialogue with the separate conventions and topoi of the Arabic and Persian corpora, and although these particular images have masked intertextual links to the work of earlier poets such as Abu Nuwas (d. between 198/813 and 200/815) and Hafiz (d. 792/1390), I argue that the mutual intelligibility of themes between the kinds of Arabic poems that were being produced in Golkonda and the corpus of Persian poetry that was being digested and expanded in the same spaces would have made Arabic letters more comprehensible within a comparative framework, and therefore more approachable for courtly audiences in early modern India.[61] Continuities in genre and theme with the conventions of other literatures – most particularly Persian – should be considered a decisive factor in encouraging multilingual elites to patronize the production of Arabic literature in states like the Qutbshahi sultanate.

Rather than seeing the court of Golkonda as a tightly controlled field where the course of literary production was dictated by the Qutbshahs alone, this evidence instead invites us to envisage multiple sites of production, each with a differing constitution but overlapping membership. These points of crossover are evidently present in Ibn Maʿsum's mind when he describes his encounter with Faraj Allah:[62]

أحد مفلقي شعراء العجم الذي طلع نبت مقالهم في روض البلاغة ونجم. علا في البراعة شعره فغلا في سوق الأدب سعره. رأيته بمجلس الوالد وقد جاوز السبعين وهو يهدي السرح من بيانه إلى عيون العين وديوانه في هذا الأوان يزاحم بعلو طبقته كيوان وفيه كل معنى مستبدع ولفظ هم للحسن مستقر ومستودع ونظمه بالعربية محرز خصل الإجادة.

He is one of the leading Persian poets, whose collective speech grew in the garden of eloquence and blossomed. His poetry ascended in skill, and his value in the market of *adab* increased. I saw him in my father's assembly when he was over seventy, as he led the herd of his speech towards the wellspring-like eyes of the assembled company.[63] His [Persian] *dīwān* now rivals Saturn in eminence, containing every inventive image, and phrases which are the resting places and storehouses of beauty. His Arabic verse wins the stakes of quality.

Beyond the obvious implication of these comments, that Ibn Maʿsum knew Persian, and that Persian may have been spoken to some extent in his father's gatherings, they also show that he thought analytically about Persian as a literary language and considered it natural to use the terminology of Arabic criticism to evaluate verse in Persian.[64] These findings open up the question of the broader participation of multilingual actors at the Qutbshahi court in composing and critiquing texts. They also encourage us to ask which kinds of Arabic poems would have reached a larger, multilingual audience in Golkonda, through venues such as semi-public *majalis* or scholarly lectures held in the environs of civic spaces like Hyderabad's Mecca Mosque, and which would have had a more limited circulation, for example in the notes which individuals sent to one another.

The constitution of Nizam al-Din Ahmad's circle

As we saw in Chapter 1, out of the 129 poets featured in *Sulafat al-ʿAsr*, 17 are explicitly mentioned as having been in Golkonda and as having dedicated Arabic verse to Nizam al-Din Ahmad, and there are additional figures who contributed to Nizam al-Din Ahmad's broader, international network by corresponding with him from Iran and Arabia.[65] There is, undeniably, a sectarian aspect to this migration, most obviously in the form of the men who travelled from Jabal ʿAmil and Bahrain, both major educational centres producing Shiʿi scholars at this time. However, it was not simply a case of Shiʿi poets seeking patronage at a Shiʿi court. Indeed, religious identity may not have been the primary motivating factor which encouraged these men to migrate to the Deccan.

One reason which helps to explain the higher proportion of poets from the Arabian Peninsula who came seeking Nizam al-Din Ahmad's protection is kinship. Included in the tally are al-Sayyid Muhammad Yahya, who was Ibn Maʿsum's full brother, and Shihab al-Din Ahmad Ibn al-Mulla ʿAli, a son of Ibn Maʿsum's mother from her first marriage.[66] Shihab al-Din Ahmad actively sought Nizam al-Din Ahmad out in India, addressing a *qasida* to him in which he evokes his departure from Mecca and his journey to his patron, much as Nizam al-Din Ahmad does in his eulogy to Sultan ʿAbd Allah.[67]

It seems probable that some of the other figures who came to Golkonda from Mecca and Medina were long-term acquaintances of Nizam al-Din Ahmad. One of them, ʿImad al-Din b. Barakat b. Jaʿfar b. Barakat b. Abi Nammay al-Hasani (d. 1069/1659), was a member of Mecca's aristocracy.[68] Since Nizam al-Din Ahmad was prominent in Mecca during his youth, and since he was given a letter of recommendation written on behalf of the *sharif* Zayd b. Muhsin – indicating that he was close to Mecca's ruling house – it seems probable that Nizam al-Din Ahmad had known Ibn Barakat prior to his emigration.[69] Ibn Barakat exchanged poems with both Nizam al-Din Ahmad and Ibn Maʿsum which can be characterized as *ikhwaniyyat* (poems of brotherly affection).[70] Nizam al-Din Ahmad responded to one of these pieces with a full-length *qasida*, in which he praises Ibn Barakat as an equal and a brother, at one point describing a missive from him in the following terms:[71]

إذ أتت من أخ شقيق المعالي * فائق الأصل غرة في الزمان
ضافي الود صافي القلب قرماً * كعبة قد علا على كيوان
ذاكراً لي فيها تزايد شوق * وولوعاً به مدى الأزمان
ففهمت الذي نحاه ولكن * ليت شعري يدري بما قد دهاني

When a *kaʿba* which excelled Saturn in eminence * Arrived from my eminent brother,
Superior in his lineage, the blaze on the forehead of the era * A noble, abundant in his love and pure of heart,
Who recalled for me how he had missed me more and more * And longed for me over the course of time,
I understood what it was that guided him * Yet would that I knew that he understood what has befallen me.

In contrast to the *qasaʾid* written in praise of Nizam al-Din Ahmad by court functionaries and scholars, such poems may point to a context of production and reception that was relatively informal, though not entirely private. It is likely that these pieces were written in order to be circulated, to advertise the bonds of loyalty and patronage between the two men.

In testament to the mobility of actors in the seventeenth century, there are other poets of Mecca, such as al-Shaykh Ahmad ibn Muhammad ʿAli al-Jawhari (d. 1079/1668), who first met Nizam al-Din Ahmad in India.[72] Al-Jawhari did not leave Mecca in order to seek the patronage of Nizam al-Din Ahmad; indeed, Ibn Maʿsum reports that he had travelled to India as a boy in the company of his father, and that he had spent around twenty years there.[73] However, it seems that he came to Golkonda shortly after Nizam al-Din Ahmad's instalment there, and that he entered his service.[74] In around 1067/1656, al-Jawhari returned to the Arabian Peninsula, still in the company of his father, in order to do *hajj*.[75] Ibn Maʿsum first encountered him that year in the port of Mukha in Yemen, as he was travelling out to join Nizam al-Din Ahmad and al-Jawhari was returning. Al-Jawhari was to make a second trip to India later in life. Finding the political situation in Mecca untenable, he travelled to Shiraz, from where he corresponded with Nizam al-Din Ahmad, and he then returned to the Deccan.[76] The poems which al-Jawhari exchanged with Nizam al-Din Ahmad and Ibn Maʿsum range from formal praise poems to shorter pieces of reciprocal endorsement.

Mutual benefit: Verse endorsements

Cumulatively, the biographies and verse of the men who formed part of the Golkonda circle suggest a durative network based around shifting patterns in mobility and employment. It is unlikely that Nizam al-Din Ahmad, Ibn Maʿsum and the seventeen poets ever gathered all together in one room at once and wrote poetry as a collective. While some of them spent many years in Golkonda, others, like Muhammad b. ʿAbd Allah al-Bahrani, seem to have passed through, using a sojourn there as a stepping-stone to advance their careers in lands further westwards.[77] The fact that they could do this is testament to the extent of the networks which Nizam al-Din Ahmad and the Qutbshahi court cultivated in Iran and Arabia.

At its most practical, the poetry that these men composed was a vehicle to express their allegiance to Nizam al-Din Ahmad, and even simply a way to attract his attention, no small matter within the stratified world of a court.[78] Some of the poems are in fact verse endorsements (*taqariz*, s. *taqriz*), which authors could collect, almost like references from employers today, and keep as proof of the esteem in which the community held them.[79] *Taqariz* are normally understood as prose or prosimetric paratexts – and Ibn Maʿsum does sometimes use the verb *qarraza* and its derivatives in this sense[80] – but he also employs the root several times to describe poems.[81] It was not just that Nizam al-Din Ahmad issued endorsements to the poets who visited him; they lauded his verse too. One function of these endorsements may have been to testify to contemporary scholars elsewhere that Golkonda really did belong on the map of Arabic learning. Another motive may have been for professional men of letters to show that they admired the quality of Nizam al-Din Ahmad's poetry and accepted him as their equal in artistry. For example, the man of letters and poet ʿAli b. Hasan al-Marzuqi al-Yamani wrote a verse endorsement of (*qarraza*) lines which Nizam al-Din Ahmad had sent to him enquiring after his health. Al-Yamani's poem, which is ostensibly addressed to another poet of the court, ʿAfif al-Din ʿAbd Allah b. Husayn b. Jashil al-Thaqafi, praises Nizam al-Din Ahmad's lines, saying that:[82]

حارت الألباب في تأليفه * ومعانيه التي لا تكتسب

Minds are astonished at their composition * And their imagery, which cannot be grasped.

The same poem also asks for financial reward, showing how the issue of an endorsement could be used to mutual benefit.[83]

The relationships of reciprocal esteem which verse endorsements codified and advertised were not always conducted with Nizam al-Din Ahmad. The poet Jamal al-Din Muhammad b. ʿAbd Allah al-Najafi wrote a *qasida* in praise of his peer Hasan b. ʿAli b. Shadqam, a member of a family who had been in transregional motion between Arabia and India for several generations.[84] Similarly, he also exchanged poems with Ibn Maʿsum, in which the two men lauded one another's eloquence, verse and bearing as men of letters.[85] As Ibn Maʿsum was drafting an anthology devoted to contemporary poetry around the time of the poem's composition, his endorsements must have carried considerable weight.

It is worth emphasizing that much of the vocabulary which Ibn Maʿsum uses in his introductory comments on each poet in *Sulafat al-ʿAsr* shares formal features and imagery with prose *taqariz*, such as comparisons between the author under discussion and illustrious writers of the past, descriptions of how beautiful a particular poet's work is to hear and to behold on the page, and discussions of how the subject's renown has travelled far and wide.[86] Hence, one way to approach the anthology as a whole would be to see it as an exercise in publicizing a network of contemporaries linked through reciprocal endorsement. There is one poet of Golkonda, ʿIsa b. Husayn b. Shujaʿ al-Najafi, the very first to seek Nizam al-Din Ahmad out and praise him, about whom Ibn Maʿsum writes rather sarcastically and critically, saying:[87]

أحد من عانى الشعر ونظم. وخضم فيه الكلام وقضم. له أشعار لم يتغن بتنقيحها وتهذيبها.

He was someone who took great pains over poetry and re-arranged [what he had written]. He gnawed and nibbled on speech. There are some poems by him that he could never stop editing and emending.

This negative evaluation, which Ibn Maʿsum supports with a critique of defects in the rhyme of al-Najafi's verse, brings into relief the extent to which the praise which the anthologist heaps on most of the other biographical subjects in his anthology is not an automatic, dictated by the conventions of the genre; it is a deliberate choice.[88] It also hints at the competing concerns which underpin the composition of a biographical anthology. Al-Najafi is probably included not for his own sake, but rather to comment on the extent of Nizam al-Din Ahmad's network.

The contours of the corpus

An examination of the forms and genres of the Golkonda corpus has the potential to reveal much about the contexts which Arabic literary production occupied there. Types of verse and themes which occur repeatedly may reflect exchanges which happened at gatherings such as the *majlis* of Nizam al-Din Ahmad, whereas those which appear once or twice only may be more closely connected to correspondence, and to the networks which linked the writers of Golkonda to the places from which they had emigrated. While some caution is required because Ibn Ma'sum often extracts thematic sections from longer poems, one of the clearest distinguishing features of the corpus is the comparative lack of short lyric pieces, such as *qita'*, *maqati'* and *dubayt* verse, forms of poetry which in other cities, like Cairo and Damascus, appealed to a broad cross section of society and could be adapted to differing performance or reading contexts.[89] The *diwan* of Manjak Basha of Damascus (d. 1080/1669–70), for example, is full of such lyrics.[90] Yet we can only say with certainty that four poets of the Golkonda circle wrote such pieces. One was Nizam al-Din Ahmad himself, who composed a lyric poem of a type which Ibn Ma'sum calls *mushajjar* ('figured in the shape of a tree').[91] This is a kind of acrostic, in which the first letters of each line spell out a name.[92] Such poems seem to have been in fashion among the scholarly classes in Mecca during Nizam al-Din Ahmad's youth, and *Sulafat al-'Asr* contains several examples of this type of verse composed there, as well as one example from Cairo.[93] Although they are not exactly comparable with the riddling exchanges made among contemporary seventeenth-century scholars of Aleppo, the function of sharing poems of the *mushajjar* type was also rooted in 'playful communication' between members of the scholarly class.[94] Nizam al-Din Ahmad's *mushajjara*, which spells out the female name 'Khadija', seems to be more in dialogue with these Meccan pieces than with any of the lyric texts which Ibn Ma'sum reproduces from Golkonda. Nizam al-Din Ahmad also composed a second lyric piece, which may be an independent *qit'a*, about a male beloved suffering from ophthalmia, a theme with a long lineage in 'Abbasid and Mamluk lyrics.[95] This is a thematic field which Ibn Ma'sum developed in his own poetry too.[96]

Another two lyric poems which may reflect the international networks of their author are by the Iranian émigré Abu l-Husayn b. Ibrahim al-Shirazi. A dialogue with his home city is developed in al-Shirazi's pieces, which include a *mu'arada* to one of Sa'di Shirazi's (d. 691/1292) Arabic poems, beginning:[97]

يا نديمي قم بليلٍ * وأسقني وأسق الندامى

خلني أسهر ليلي * ودع الناس نيامى

Come at dark, my boon-companion * Pour me a goblet of wine, and a goblet for
my fellows.
Let me spend all night awake * And leave the world asleep.

Al-Shirazi's other lyric piece possesses a distinctly urban character, describing a
male beloved:[98]

من أودع الشهد والسلاف فمه * والجوهر الفرد فيه من قسمه
**
كتمت حبي عن الوشاة فما * ظن به كاشح ولا علمه

Whose mouth tastes of honey and wine * Revealing a precious pearl to
those who part his lips
**
I concealed my love of him from slanderers. My secret enemy, * Unawares,
does not suspect him.

Such poems depict an urban world of romantic adventures, where love takes shape
publicly, on streets and in squares, under the watchful eyes of onlookers (*ruqaba'*)
and slanderers (*wushah*), and hence they were often popular in major cities.[99]
Ibn Ma'sum reproduces a short piece by the poet and anthologist al-Khafaji (d.
1069/1659), who spent his life between Cairo and Damascus, which is based
around similar tropes of beholding, and describing, a male beloved:[100]

وظبي من السمور ألبس فروة * وماس كما هزت الصبا سحرة سروا
وإلا عيون الناس من دهشة به * نخلف أهداباً فتحسبها فروا

I swear by a gazelle dressed in sable fur, * Who swayed just as the east wind
caresses the cypress at dawn,
Were it not for the people staring in astonishment at him * We would shed our
eyelashes [in crying], so [thickly], you would think them a pelt.

The one set of epigrams (*maqati'*) by a member of the Golkonda circle which we
find in *Sulafat al-'Asr* are by Ahmad b. Muhammad 'Ali al-Jawhari, and come
from his book *La'ali al-Jawhari* (*The Jeweller's Pearls*). Some of these poems are
gnomic; others are lyrical, such as:[101]

ولقد سقتنا البابلية إذ رأت * أنا نحدثنا لنسبر حسنها
خمراً أدارتها العيون فأذهبت * منا العقول ولم تفارق دنها

When she saw that we were conversing with her * To gauge her beauty, the
woman of Babel poured out for us
A wine, which our eyes passed around, and which * Intoxicated us before it had
even left the jar.

We can tell that *La'ali al-Jawhari* was composed after al-Jawhari's arrival in India – or perhaps on his first return from India to the Arabian Peninsula – because the poet includes several topical, descriptive epigrams about his travels, such as:[102]

شبهت أمواج بحر الهند حين رست * به السفائن من هند ومن صين
بأسطر فوق قرطاس قد اتسقت * والسفن فيها علامات السلاطين

When the ships from China and India rested at anchor * I compared the
waves of the Arabian Sea
To lines drafted on paper * And the boats on its waters to the monograms
of kings.

And:[103]

ولو أن أرض الهند في الحسن جنة * وسكانها حور وأملكها وحدي
لما قستها يوماً ببطحاء مكة * ولا اخترت عن سعدى بديّلاً هوى هند

Though India is a paradise of beauty, * And its inhabitants are houris and its
rulers are unequalled,
I would never compare it with the plain of Mecca for an instant * Nor would I
exchange India's heat for my happiness.

The last half-line of this poem is an amphiboly on the names of beloveds who feature in classical poetry, and it can also be read as 'I would never exchange love of Hind for Su'da'. The double meaning of the word *hind* as 'India' and an archetypal beloved of Arabia was exploited by the Golkonda circle frequently, as it evoked their trajectory, simultaneously recalling the land in which they found themselves and their spiritual home.[104]

The aforementioned examples show the close link between the writers' personal networks, their itineraries and the kinds of poetry that they composed. Thinking in connected terms helps to steer a course between the assumption that the style in which an author writes is determined by their origins, and its antithesis, the idea that cosmopolitanism liberates an author to adopt any mode of writing. The poets of Golkonda faced definite choices when they composed, because the selections which they made in their use of forms, themes and rhetorical devices defined them in relation to their contemporaries and the historical corpus of Arabic verse. Perhaps the clearest way in which each poet could articulate his own distinction while connecting himself to others was by authoring an emulative response to a circulating poem. In using the same metre and rhyme scheme as the original, the poets heighten, rather than diminish, the reader's sense of their individuality, which becomes clear through their use of imagery and rhetoric.

Numerous examples of emulative chains of poems are preserved in *Sulafat al-'Asr*, illustrating how the circle of Nizam al-Din Ahmad forged connections with one another, with their contemporaries elsewhere, and with the poets of the past.[105] One particularly productive set of responses is based around the construction of full-length *qasaʾid* which continue a single 'clasp' line by the early Islamic poet Abu Dahbal al-Jumahi (d. after 96/715):[106]

وأبرزتها بطحاء مكة بعدما * أصات المنادي بالصلاة فاعتما

I brought her out onto the plain of Mecca, after * The herald had made the call to prayer and left.

Abu Dahbal's line is from the beginning of one of his *qasida* poems and depicts the narrator's departure on his fleet camel. The line was subsequently used by the eleventh-century *adib* and Shiʿi scholar al-Sharif al-Murtada (d. 436/1044) in what Ibn Maʿsum terms an 'imitation' (*iqtifaʾ*), literally meaning, 'following in somebody's tracks'. In his poem, al-Sharif al-Murtada reinterprets the allusion of Abu Dahbal's line, reading it as a depiction of a beautiful woman. In a markedly different way from the original, al-Sharif al-Murtada develops a cycle of themes concerning the scent of the beloved, her shining face, the desire that men feel for her as she moves and speaks, the narrator's compulsion to depart, abandoning the possibility of love with her, and his nostalgia for her.[107]

Perhaps attracted by the fact that al-Sharif al-Murtada's poem united early Islamic Arabia with a renowned Shiʿi scholar, several poets of the sixteenth and seventeenth centuries responded to it. Although it is possible to find echoes of this poem in pieces composed in the Levant during the late sixteenth century, a set of these responses form what Benedek Péri calls a 'paraphrase network' – a group of texts that respond not only to their ultimate model but also to one another.[108] A paraphrase network is both textual and social, and represents the deliberate construction of a literary genealogy by writers who wished to associate themselves with earlier members of the chain. The first whom Ibn Maʿsum names is al-Sayyid Muhammad b. Hasan b. Shadqam al-Husayni, a man of letters from Medina whose father had travelled extensively in India, and another of whose relatives, Hasan b. ʿAli, was a member of the Golkonda circle. Chronologically, the next to reply was al-Sayyid Hatim b. al-Sayyid Ahmad al-Ahdal al-Husayni (d. 1013/1604), a Sufi and poet of Yemen who corresponded with the ʿAydarus clan in Gujarat.[109] Finally, Ibn Maʿsum himself and Ahmad al-Jawhari also wrote responses.

Each member of this thousand-year chain builds on the work of his forebears by accretion. Abu Dahbal, the author of the model, speaks of his camel galloping to outstrip the dawn, as night folds in its wings, one roseate, the other pitch-black, over al-Bazwaʾ'.[110] This image is not in the 'clasp' line which begins each of the subsequently authored poems, and is found three lines later in the original poem. Yet the later poets did pick up on this motif, suggesting that they sought out the poem in a source such as Abu l-Faraj al-Isfahani's (d. *c.* 363/972) *Kitab al-Aghani* (*The Book of Songs*), in which the text is preserved.[111] The antithesis in colours is transformed in al-Sharif al-Murtada's poem into a contrast between the pale faces of the beautiful women of Medina and the dark henna which they are too modest to wear.[112] Ibn Shadqam builds on both of his predecessors, returning us to Abu Dahbal's image of the lightening day by saying that the beloved is so bright that she illuminates the moon, and by referring to her milk-white visage and dark lips.[113] He also adds in a second antithesis: the beloved is the sun and her black hair the night, her face the full moon which never wanes.[114]

Hatim b. Ahmad al-Ahdal's engagement with the themes in this section of the poem is mediated through Ibn Shadqam. This is important because it suggests that he did not decide to compose an imitation of al-Sharif al-Murtada independently, but was prompted to do so by exposure to his contemporary's poem. Al-Ahdal abandons the colour antithesis of the earlier pieces, instead moving straight into developing the theme of the meadow, which is an invention of Ibn Shadqam's poem. Whereas Ibn Shadqam writes that the beloved causes a garden to blossom everywhere she walks, trailing love-longing in her wake as she passes among the red earth, al-Ahdal formulates the following representation:[115]

وسرحت عيني في رياض خدودها * فشاهدت روضاً كالربيع منمنما
سقته مياه الحسن فازداد بهجة * وغادر قلبي بالحطيم محطما

I let my eye wander over the meadows of her cheeks * Seeing a garden dewy
like spring.
The waters of beauty flowed there, increasing its lustre * And leaving my heart
rent in al-Hatim.

He also retains Ibn Shadqam's second antithesis, between light and dark, or veiling and unveiling, saying:[116]

فتاة تعير الشمس بهجة وجهها * سناها بغير الحسن لن يتلثما

A woman, the lustre of whose face lends the sun * Its brilliance, but not its
beauty, which cannot be veiled.

For his part, Ibn Ma'sum strengthens the connection to Abu Dahbal, bringing back in the element of the camel-driver and the dawn at the end of the journey:[117]

ولما سرت للركب نفحة طيبها * تغنى بها حاديهم وترنما
وشام محياها للحجيج على السرى * فيمم مغناها ولبى وأحرما
أناة هي الشمس المنيرة في الضحى * ولكنها تبدو إذ الليل أظلما

When the caravan caught her scent on the breeze * The camel-driver sang
of her in a gentle murmur.
The pilgrims looked for her face over the course of the night * As they wended
their way to her abode, announcing their presence to God and
purifying themselves
A graceful woman who is the brilliant sun at noon * Yet who appears
when night has fallen.

His lines also retain and strengthen elements of Ibn Shadqam's poem. They do this implicitly, since the image of the beloved appearing at night to be beheld by the pilgrims depends on Ibn Shadqam's idea that her face is the moon. They also do it explicitly, by retaining Ibn Shadqam's second antithesis between dark and light. Al-Ahdal is also brought into the dialogue in the line:[118]

وأسفر عنها الصبح لما تلثمت * ولو أسفرت للصبح يوماً تلثما

The dawn revealed her when she put on her veil, * Yet if she were ever to show
herself to the dawn, it would be veiled.

In the final response, by al-Jawhari, the poet condenses the ideas of his predecessors. Ibn Maʿsum's implicit reference to Ibn Shadqam's metaphorical representation of the beloved as the moon is simplified and made explicit, and his invention of the caravan of pilgrims is retained:[119]

فشاهدت من لو أبصر البدر وجهها * لكان به مضنىً ولوعاً ومغرما
ولو عرضت ركب الحجيج تصده * للبى لما يدعو هواها وأحرما

I saw a woman for whom the full moon would * Pine, ardent and infatuated,
if it glimpsed her face.
If she appeared to a caravan of pilgrims, blocking its path, * The pilgrims
would announce themselves to God and purify themselves when they
proclaimed their love for her.

The pastoral imagery of Ibn Shadqam and al-Ahdal's poems is packed into a single line, turning the beloved into a garden:[120]

وأعذب من صوب الغمامة مرشفاً * وأضواء من لمع البروق تبسما

Sweeter to kiss than rain on fresh herbage * Brighter than the flash
of lightning in her smile.

Having acknowledged his forebears briefly, giving the most weigh to Ibn Maʿsum, al-Jawhari distinguishes himself by transforming the ending of his poem. In the antecedents, the conclusion to the *qasaʾid* as they are transmitted by Ibn Maʿsum is generally lyrical. Al-Sharif al-Murtada and Ibn Shadqam transition through the feelings of the narrator, towards the *rahil*, or departure. Al-Ahdal remains firmly in the bounds of lyric ekphrasis. Ibn Maʿsum hints towards the inner world of the poet with the statement that the beloved cannot remain flesh and blood. However, for al-Jawhari, the beloved is the pretext for a discourse on worldly vanity: conquerors are laid low through their love for the beloved, and:[121]

تظل الملوك الصيد تعثر بالثرى * إذا قاربوا أو شاهدوا ذلك الحمى

Kings become prey, stumbling in the dust, * When they approach or behold
that protected pasture.

What this comparison between the *qasa'id* shows is that the poets are using
emulative intertextuality in order to construct an intellectual, artistic and aesthetic
genealogy, in so doing linking themselves and the locations in which they were
writing. Each choice of image and rhetoric that they make is consciously designed
to acknowledge their forebears and their contemporaries, to emphasize the weight
of historical acts which affect the present, and to mark their own contribution to
the chain. Each poem not only recognizes its immediate forebear, but also the
entire corpus of antecedents.[122] This takes us back to the pieces which I discussed
earlier in the chapter, such as the verse commendations and Nizam al-Din
Ahmad's encomium to Sultan 'Abd Allah, which offer blunter ways of building a
community. These may have been easier to grasp, but they were in many ways not
as inclusive a tool as the response poems. The circle which Ibn Ma'sum and his
father constructed – the former through writing, the latter through patronage –
was designed to connect Golkonda to other centres of learning, and make it a node
in a network around the Arabian Sea. Some of the texts produced by members of
the circle are in dialogue with literary production in their home cities, and may be
designed to codify the long-distance networks of their authors. Others result from
communal meetings in Golkonda, but are also intended to promote and sustain a
transregional conversation.

After the fall: Ibn Ma'sum and Arabic literary communities in provincial Burhanpur

A central problem in examining the work of Ibn Ma'sum is establishing those
points at which Arabic literary production in early modern India became a public
phenomenon that attracted diverse audiences and was drawn into multilingual
literary practice, and those at which it was a largely private affair, driven by
communication between émigrés. Although the Arabic circle of Golkonda was
well supported by an elite and intersected with literary life at the court of the
Qutbshahs more generally, the fact that its backers were also its most prominent
participants may have made it unusual. We need to consider the extent to which
authors such as Ibn Ma'sum would have been in contact with, and aware of, the
output of other figures writing in Arabic in early modern India, including poets like
the Tamil author Shaykh Sadaqat Allah, who dedicated an Arabic picture poem in
the shape of a leaf to the emperor Awrangzib.[123] There is some intersection between
the work of Ibn Ma'sum and Shaykh Sadaqat Allah in certain, limited respects.
For example, both authors composed amplifications of canonical Arabic poems in
praise of the Prophet.[124] For this reason, it is worth closing the present chapter with

an examination of Ibn Maʿsum's literary activities in the twenty-two or so years (*c.* 1092/1681–1114/1702–3) that he spent in India following his departure from Golkonda, when he was obliged to participate in Mughal structures of loyalty and reward as a protégé rather than as a patron.

The dearth of autobiographical information in Ibn Maʿsum's later works means that we are mostly dependent on biographical sources for our understanding of what happened to him during the second stage of his life in India, before he decided to leave for Arabia and Iran in about 1114/1702–3. This in turn affects the extent to which we can reconstruct the communities in which he participated. An important source of information is Azad Bilgrami's (d. 1200/1786) *Subhat al-Marjan fi Athar Hindustan* (*The Coral Rosary, on the Monuments of India*), part of which is a biographical dictionary of learned men who wrote in Arabic in India. Azad states that he visited Hyderabad in 1165/1751–2, and there encountered Ibn Maʿsum's nephew, who showed him a written biography of his uncle.[125] According to this account, Ibn Maʿsum was imprisoned along with his father in Golkonda after the death of Sultan ʿAbd Allah (in 1083/1672–3). While Nizam al-Din Ahmad was murdered in prison (according to a poem in Ibn Maʿsum's *diwan*, this occurred in Safar 1085/May 1674),[126] Azad reports that Ibn Maʿsum managed to escape, but only in Shaʿban 1092/August 1681, after about seven years of incarceration.[127] When he did eventually flee Golkonda, he travelled to Burhanpur, a town to the north of the Deccan which acted as the Mughals' main garrison in their expansion southwards.[128] There he met the Mughal emperor Awrangzib (d. 1118/1707), who gave him the title of Sayyid ʿAli Khan and awarded him the distinguished, but not top-flight, rank (*mansab*) of one thousand five hundred, at the *du asba* (two-horse) grade, a post within the Mughal military bureaucracy which attracted additional pay but enjoined the postholder to have each man whom he enlisted bring two horses to each muster.[129] He was then appointed to military roles, guarding strategic fortresses in Awrangabad and Berar, both on the Deccan frontier, before becoming the head of the chancellery at Burhanpur.[130]

There seem to be some independent grounds which support this overarching picture of Ibn Maʿsum's movements, such as an epigram which he composed about Berar, including the following line, which makes a pun on the region's name:[131]

وقد كانت منازلنا قصوراً * ونحن اليوم ننزل في براري

We once lived in castles * Now we settle in the open countryside (*barari*).

This at least suggests that he visited the area. The dates also match up: if Ibn Maʿsum escaped Golkonda in Shaʿban 1092/August 1681, he would have arrived in Burhanpur in time for an audience with Awrangzib, who was there in early 1682.[132] Then there is the evidence of manuscript colophons: a subscription note appended to a copy of Ibn Maʿsum's *urjuza* on friendship, *Naghmat al-Aghani fi ʿIshrat al-Ikhwani* (*The Melody of Songs, on Companionship with Friends*), states that the author completed the text in Burhanpur.[133] Intriguingly, there are some indications that Ibn Maʿsum's connection to this town may have predated his removal from the court of the Qutbshahs, since the Cambridge manuscript of *Sulafat al-'Asr* was made there by an émigré Iraqi copyist, Muhammad Shafi' b. Qasim 'Ali al-Najafi, in Jumada al-Thani 1082/October 1671, two months after the text's composition.[134] At a minimum, this suggests that there was a ready market for the consumption of Ibn Ma'sum's Arabic texts in India outside the confines of Nizam al-Din Ahmad's entourage.

One might have imagined that Ibn Ma'sum's appointment to a *mansab* would make him feature in lists of Mughal officials or narrative histories of Awrangzib's reign, which concentrate heavily on the military bureaucracy as a class. Identifying a possible candidate is not an easy task, particularly as 'Ali is a common name, and one should not necessarily expect Mughal historians writing in Persian to use Arabic onomastics. Yet even so, no likely candidates stand out in the lists of Mughal aristocrats who held *mansabs* under Awrangzib.[135] Indeed, the whole issue of whether Ibn Ma'sum was even granted a *mansab* by the Mughals is actually brought into question by the Iranian biographer and poet Hazin Lahiji (d. 1180/1766), who seemingly met Ibn Ma'sum in 1117/1705–6, when the latter arrived in Isfahan. According to Hazin, Ibn Ma'sum's title of *khan* was bestowed on him while he was still in Golkonda.[136]

Two possibilities emerge from these conflicting narratives: that Ibn Ma'sum received some support from the Mughals and was posted to Burhanpur as a provincial bureaucrat; or that he received no honours at all and moved to Burhanpur because of some pre-existing association with the town. Even if he was appointed to the rank of 1,500, this was not an overly distinguished position for a man who had once been a member of a royal family, and it would probably reflect the fact that Ibn Ma'sum had been left with no political authority or landholdings in India after the regime change in which his father was killed. Awrangzib bestowed far higher ranks on a good number of the Qutbshahi *amirs* at the dynasty's collapse, as a way of ensuring continuity in the administration of the Deccan.[137]

The significant break with his former life precipitated by Ibn Ma'sum's relocation to the Mughal domains also affected the character of his literary output. Although he evidently worked to finalize *Anwar al-Rabi'* as soon as he was free from confinement, we have seen that the manuscript evidence shows it was really an intellectual product of his time in Golkonda. The first major new text which he published under the Mughals was *Naghmat al-Aghani*, a guide to friendship which uses several stories drawn from sources including *Kalila wa-Dimna* as exempla. He completed this text in 1104/1692–3, more than ten years after his release from prison. The poem is an *urjuza muzdawija*, making it easy to memorize, as the poet himself says, and it is linguistically much simpler than most of his earlier work.[138] As it adopts the tone of an ethical guide, advising the listener what the basic tenets of friendship are, remarking on how to behave with one's friends, how to treat them and which kinds of men one should avoid befriending, it is difficult not to see this text as an accessible introduction to Arabic *adab* for Indian audiences in Ibn Ma'sum's immediate surroundings. The fact that *muzdawija* verse is formally similar to the Persian *masnavi* (both consist of rhyming couplets), and that the narrative episodes in the poem which are derived from *Kalila wa-Dimna* were circulating in Persian and Indic sources too, may have made this text even more accessible to local audiences.[139] This kind of literary work is a reminder of Carl Ernst's call for us 'to consider Indo-Arabic literature in its inter-textual connections both with Indo-Persian and with the relevant Indic equivalents'.[140] Some of the versified episodes in the narrative are only to be found in Persian versions of *Kalila wa-Dimna*, such as the tale of the bear who crushed a man's head with a rock, which otherwise only appears in Kashifi's (d. 910/1504–5) Persian *Anvar-i Suhayli* (*The Lights of the Canopus*).[141] This may suggest that Ibn Maʿsum was reading Persian sources himself.

A year or so later, in 1106/1694, Ibn Maʿsum released his *takhmis* (amplification) of al-Busiri's *Qasidat al-Burda* (*Mantle Ode*), which he dedicated to Awrangzib.[142] The subject matter of this work, in praise of the Prophet, would have had a universal appeal to the Muslim community, and so it too can be seen as part of a process of adaptation which Ibn Maʿsum went through in the Mughal domains, in order to make his Arabic texts engaging for two groups at once: those trained in the high culture of literary Arabic; and a less literarily minded audience who had initially learned the language for religious purposes. It is possible that the urban environment of Burhanpur, with its numerous Islamic religious institutions, including shrines and a Friday Mosque, may have acted as a meeting-point for these two kinds of communities.[143]

Even when he was based in provincial settings in the 1680s and 1690s, Ibn Maʿsum continued to write Arabic *qasaʾid*. These poems are preserved in his *diwan*, one recension of which includes pieces dated up to 1119/1707–8, and which therefore seems to have been edited in Iran after his death.[144] Some of them can be construed as personal, and they do not necessarily have to have been written for an audience. They include an elegy for one of Ibn Maʿsum's sons, Abu Ismaʿil Ibrahim, who died in Rabiʿ al-Thani 1101/February 1690.[145] Ibn Maʿsum also seems to have composed more panegyrics to the Prophet during this time, such as a *qasida* dated 1098/1686–7, in which he writes:[146]

يدعوك عبد إليك يعزى * فهل له إذ دعا قبول
فؤاده بالأسى جريح * وجسمه بالضنى عليل
قد عاث صرف الزمان فيه * وخانه صبره الجميل
أصبح بالهند في انفراد * فلا عشير ولا قبيل
ليس به في الورى حفي * ولا له منهم كفيل

Your servant who longs for you calls out to you * Do you accept him when he calls?
His heart is wounded by grief * And his body is sickened by exhaustion.
The passage of time has ravaged him * And his once graceful patience has betrayed him.
He has become isolated in India * Without companions and relatives.
The people do not welcome him warmly * And he does not have a protector among them.

Poems such as these can be read as personal pieces which Ibn Maʿsum composed for himself, but as with *Takhmis Qasidat al-Burda*, it is possible that they may have been written for the larger Muslim community in the author's immediate surroundings. As they cultivate a mood in which praise of the Prophet consoles and actively protects the speaker in his isolation, marking the conclusion of a 'supplicatory panegyric pact', they do not have to be read in an excessively biographical way.[147]

A small corpus of Ibn Maʿsum's poems dating from his time spent under Mughal rule indicates that he continued to participate in scholarly networks, both in India and transregionally, albeit in a more limited fashion than before, and in correspondence rather than through sociable gatherings.[148] The character of a number of these pieces differs from the *qasaʾid* that he had composed in Golkonda, because their imagery is more explicitly transactional, implying that Ibn Maʿsum was seeking financial support from his addressees. Motifs such as the munificent hand of the correspondent, which showers gifts on the poet, occur more frequently in these poems, as do evocations of generosity, benefaction and favour.[149] The addressees of these poems tend to be other Twelver scholars who were also Arabic speakers with Iranian connections, showing how Arabic literary production could operate within a broader cultural environment that is now often characterized in scholarship as Persianate. They include the previously unidentified Sayyid ʿAli Karbalaʾi, who was possibly a jurist and theologian, once in the employ of the Qutbshahs, and the author of works such as *Hadiya-yi Qutbshahi dar Istikhraj-i Ayat-i Ilahi* (*The Qutbshahi Gift, on the Interpretation of Qurʾanic Verses*).[150] Ibn Maʿsum's most frequent addressee from this period is Husayn b. Sharaf al-Din al-Najafi, who is known in later works of biography only through these poems.[151] Ibn Maʿsum calls him a *sayyid*, a *sadr* and a *wizir*, but he was obviously a scholar as well, and he seems to have been active in both India and Iran. Whether he was a relative of ʿIsa b. Husayn b. Shujaʿ al-Najafi, a member of the Golkonda circle, is unclear.

One *qasida* in the *diwan* typifies the trend of forming bilingual, monocultural Arabic-Persian environments.[152] It is a poem which Ibn Maʿsum sent to Mukhlis Khan, whom I identify as *mir bakhshi* (paymaster general) under Awrangzib, a significant role within the administration of the empire which included managing the branding of horses and the compilation of muster roles.[153] If Ibn Maʿsum did indeed receive a *mansab*, then Mukhlis Khan would have been responsible for distributing his income. Mukhlis Khan features in biographical anthologies as a Persian poet, and as a patron of literature and scholarship, but there has previously been no assumption that he sponsored multilingual literary production.[154] We cannot know whether he actively encouraged Ibn Maʿsum to compose for him in Arabic, or whether Ibn Maʿsum decided that Arabic was the most appropriate vehicle to express his own artistic ingenuity, but as with the panegyrics that Nizam al-Din Ahmad addressed to Sultan ʿAbd Allah, the very fact of this poem's existence suggests that Arabic was deemed to be one of many languages appropriate for literary production within early modern Indian systems of patronage. Just like the Mughal noblemen who patronized the production of Sanskrit literature independently, Mukhlis Khan may have sought to sponsor the composition of Arabic texts in a private capacity, outside of his official post and duties.[155] Ibn Maʿsum's *qasida* has a carefully considered aesthetic, which would have resonated with readers who frequently consumed texts in Persian. It is bipartite, consisting of a lyric section describing wine-drinking in springtime, and a panegyric section which eulogizes Mukhlis Khan, and so formally it is in dialogue with many Persian praise poems that were written for Indian patrons in the seventeenth century. In terms of imagery and rhetoric, too, there are points of continuity between this and the contemporary corpus of Persian praise poetry that circulated in India, as the section describing the wine in the glass demonstrates:[156]

حمراء تسطع في زجاجتها * فكأنها لو لم تذب جمر
وكأنما إبريقها سحراً * إذ قهقهت لحمامة وكر
جليت على خطابها فحكت * عذراء ما عن وصلها عذر
يسعى بها ساقٍ لواحظه * سكرى وصفو رضابه خمر
حلو الهوى عذب مقبله * لكن مذاق مطاله مر

Red wine, shining in the glass * An ember, were it not liquid.
It is as though the gurgle of the jug at dawn * Were a cooing dove's nest.
She arises to meet her suitors, resembling * A maiden to whom you must
make love, without excuses.
A cupbearer serves her, his glances * Drunken, his fresh saliva intoxicating.
His fresh kisses are the sweetness of love * But the taste of his objections is bitter.

These lines manage to be in dialogue with both the Arabic corpus and the coeval Persian corpus.[157] The image of the wine as a bride and the drinkers as her suitors is also found in verses by Persian poets such as Talib Amuli (d. 1036/1626-7), laureate to the emperor Jahangir.[158] The *tibaq* (antithesis) between bitter and sweet is developed in verses on wine by poets such as Saʾib (d. 1086-7/1676).[159] The latter also likens rosy wine leaving the ewer to the sun rising at dawn, an image which shares a logical basis with Ibn Maʿsum's terser line comparing the ewer to dawn.[160] These points of continuity are unlikely to be the accidental, and may indicate the assumed presence of Persian as a literary frame of reference in the dedicatee's mind.[161] They suggest a cross-fertilization of imagery and rhetoric which can occur when texts are composed in multilingual environments, and which is specifically designed to appeal to audiences who are steeped in more than one literature. A comparable kind of Arabic poetic text composed in South Asia – albeit one produced within a different and modern context – has been studied by Tahera Qutbuddin, who examines the text's form and the multilingual environment in which it is performed.[162] Yet even as they were made comprehensible for local audiences, the poems that were composed within Ibn Maʿsum's network in India still constituted part of a consciously international, high culture of classicizing Arabic letters in their form, style and linguistic content, which could have simultaneously been understood by listeners in Golkonda, Sanʿaʾ and Mecca.

Conclusion

Together, Ibn Maʿsum and Nizam al-Din Ahmad constructed a new world of Arabic letters in the Deccan, attracting a large cohort of Arabic poets to the court of the Qutbshahs. Although the scale of their enterprise and its preservation within the historical record may be unusual, the existence of such an Arabic network in early modern India should not be seen as an historical anomaly. We have seen that the texts which this network produced not only fed into a transoceanic system of Arabic literary production, connecting authors in India with writers in the Arabian Peninsula and Iran, but that they also linked the Deccan with the Mughal north, making Arabic a localized literary language as well. Although there are other instances of Arabic becoming a vernacular literary idiom in early modern South Asia, meaning that in more general terms we should think of several different registers of the language, the most remarkable aspect of Ibn Maʿsum's circle is its use of a classicizing idiom to bridge both the international and the local. This was an idiom malleable enough to address Indian patrons such as Sultan ʿAbd Allah the Qutbshah and Mukhlis Khan the bureaucrat through panegyrics, to embrace the entire Muslim community through praise of the Prophet, and to construct an intellectual and emotional filiation with poets living across the sea.

Chapter 3

SAN'A'

AL-SARIM AL-HINDI

Over 2,000 miles west of Golkonda Fort, as the crow flies, is the port city of Mukha in Yemen. Ibn Ma'sum had spent fourteen months there in 1066–7/1656–7, during his passage from Mecca to the Deccan, while waiting to hear the outcome of an attempt on the life of Sultan 'Abd Allah.[1] During this time, he attended the assemblies arranged by Mukha's governor, Zayd b. 'Ali al-Jahhaf, and mined the manuscripts that were in circulation in the town for information about contemporary literary life in south Arabia.[2] To journey via the ports of Yemen – including Mukha, al-Luhayya, al-Hudayda, Aden and al-Mukalla – was a natural choice for any seventeenth-century traveller going between Mecca and India, and the shipping route that passed along the southern coast of Yemen and through Bab al-Mandab, the narrow strait dividing Yemen and the Horn of Africa, was a significant conduit for goods heading westwards towards the Mediterranean from South Asia.[3] This meant that the port cities of Yemen were significant entrepots in the international trade in commodities such as coffee, spices and textiles.[4] As the overland route from Iran to Mecca and Medina through Iraq was deliberately not maintained by the Ottomans, Yemen's coastal cities also attracted many travellers from the Safavid domains, who often journeyed by ship, making for Jidda via the Persian Gulf and the Arabian Sea.[5] Seventeenth-century Yemen was therefore closely connected to Iran and India, both in terms of circulation and in terms of diplomacy.[6]

These links shaped contemporary literary life in Yemen too. Alongside Ibn Ma'sum, many writers from Egypt, Syria, North Arabia, Iran and India spent some time there on their migrations, often being obliged to stay for longer than they had intended on account of the seasonal patterns of the monsoon winds. They brought with them the texts that they had memorized and copies of literary works. At least one manuscript of *Sulafat al-'Asr* arrived there while Ibn Ma'sum was still alive, testifying both to the interest of readers in Yemen in near-contemporary writing from elsewhere and to Yemen's links with global literary production.[7] The manuscript evidence also shows that other geographically oriented anthologies, including al-Maqqari's (d. 1041/1632) *Nafh al-Tib*, which surveys the literary history of the Maghrib and al-Andalus, were in circulation in Yemen during the seventeenth century, as were copies of canonical collections of poetry, including Abu Tammam's (d. 231/845 or 232/846) *Hamasa* and the epigram anthologies of al-Safadi (d. 764/1363).[8] These kinds of anthologies presented aspiring poets in Yemen with surveys of the Arabic corpus, supporting the production of classicizing poetry that sustained a transregional literary dialogue.

Despite this remarkable connectivity, early modern Yemen is sometimes characterized as a land apart in modern scholarship. There is some justification for this view. The interior was ruled by the Qasimi Imams, Zaydi Shi'i leaders who had taken control of San'a' in 1038/1629, expelling the Ottoman-appointed governors who had ruled Yemen since the mid-sixteenth century, and proceeding to cultivate a religious and political ideology which distinguished them as the righteous rulers of the Islamic *umma*.[9] It has often been inferred that Yemen's difference played out in the field of literature too. Modern scholarly discussions of Arabic poetry in early modern Yemen have largely focused on the kind of strophic verse called the *humayni*.[10] The *humayni* shares many technical characteristics with kinds of vernacular (*zajal*) poetry produced in places such as Egypt, Syria and Andalusia, but it is generally regarded as a quintessentially Yemeni type of poetry, and so the extent of its transregional circulation remains little discussed. The *humayni* did, however, travel internationally, contradicting the idea that seemingly 'popular' forms of verse have a more restricted potential for global circulation than types of poetry which are traditionally thought to belong to the realm of high culture, such as the classical Arabic ode (*qasida*).[11]

A particularly important and still unpublished work which provides evidence for the globalization of the *humayni* is *al-Madh al-Munaqqah min Fann al-Muwashshah* (*Polished Praise of the Muwashshah Type*), a collection of strophic eulogies dedicated to 'Abd al-Qadir al-'Aydarus (d. 1038/1628), a Sufi shaykh who was born in Gujarat to a Yemeni father and an Indian mother.[12] The eulogies were composed by a poet of Mecca named Ahmad b. Radi al-Din al-Qazani al-Makki, who had spent time in Yemen, meeting the *washshah* (poet of strophic verse) al-Hatim al-Ahdal (d. 1013/1604) – whom I mentioned in Chapter 2 as one of Ibn Ma'sum's models – and then emigrating to India to study with the 'Aydarus family. The poems in his collection are all highly intertextual, emulating a mixture of verses which the author terms *muwashshah*, *humayni* and *muqamma'*, by eminent poets of Yemen, such as 'Abd al-Hadi al-Sudi (d. 932/1525), and his predecessors 'Abd al-Rahman al-'Alawi (d. beginning of the sixteenth century), Abu Bakr al-Mazzah (d. after 1030/1427) and Ibn Fulayta (d. 731/1331).[13] Poets such as al-'Alawi and al-Mazzah were also used as models by Ibn Ma'sum, who wrote his own *muwashshah* verse in India, and who belonged to a social formation that was highly distinct from the Sufis of the 'Aydarus lineage.[14] Hence, non-classical literary forms could be used to forge a transnational literary idiom, which was produced and consumed in circles that transcended a single social and intellectual group.

Types of classicizing Arabic poetry, such as the *qasida*, the *qit'a*, the *muzdawija* and the *maqtu'*, were also composed in south Arabia during the seventeenth century, and they too connected into a system of transregional circulation. There is, however, a distinct dearth of published research on the use of such classical forms in early modern Yemen, which is partly conditioned by the arguments of early modern literary historiography.[15] Writing in the late seventeenth century, the literary biographer Yusuf b. Yahya al-Hasani (d. 1121/1709–10) made some pointed remarks about a poet of Sanʿaʾ called Ibrahim b. Salih al-Hindi (d. 1101/1689–90) and the state of literary life in Yemen at the time. Al-Hasani wrote that al-Hindi had cannibalized a *muzdawija* (poem in rhyming couplets) by the Mamluk poet Jamal al-Din b. Nubata (d. 768/1366), borrowing most of Ibn Nubataʾs phrasing and imagery and using it to write his own dispute poem.[16] Preliminary indications suggest that there may be some justification for this contention.[17] Al-Hasani maintained that when the plagiarism went unnoticed, al-Hindi:

> recognised the peopleʾs level of understanding and their memory for poetry, and so he put his feet up [lit. ʿstretched out his legs and his armsʾ] and relaxed. He was not incompetent, but Yemen has had no market for poetry since the days of the Ismaili missionaries, the clans of Zurayʿ [r. 473–569/1080–1173] and Sabaʾ [b. Ahmad, second husband to the Sulayhid queen Arwa in the late eleventh century]. For they were kings who were also poets, and so they attached importance to it and critiqued it. But our Zaydi Imams have paid it little heed, although the Imam al-Mansur bi-Llah al-Qasim b. Muhammad [d. 1029/1619–20] was a poet of many verses with an innate ability and abundant resources. The others have permitted affectation, with no criticism and no preference for the beautiful over the poorly crafted. Hence, poetry has become spoiled and its market is depressed.[18]

This chapter teases out a series of questions which are raised in al-Hasaniʾs discussion, focusing on the poet at the centre of the controversy, Ibrahim b. Salih al-Hindi, otherwise known by his pen name, al-Sarim al-Hindi.[19] Al-Sarim was the son of a migrant. His father purportedly belonged to the Banya, the caste of Hindu and Jain brokers who acted as middle men in the trading system of the Indian Ocean.[20] Unlike many other members of his community, who maintained their religious faith but occupied a marginal position in Yemeni society, al-Sarimʾs father converted to Islam, adopting the name Salih al-Muhtadi, literally ʿDevout, the Rightly Guidedʾ (or, ʿthe Convertʾ). Al-Sarim was born after his fatherʾs conversion, and grew up in Yemen as a Muslim. He has an entry in Ibn Maʿsumʾs *Sulafat al-ʿAsr*, originally as one of the poets whom Ibn Maʿsum appended to the text in his additions (*mulhaqat*), suggesting that he came to the anthologistʾs attention late in the composition process.[21] There is no indication that the two men ever met, so it is likely that an intermediary made Ibn Maʿsum aware of him. The two men seem to have a common contact in the form of Zayd b. ʿAli al-Jahhaf, Ibn Maʿsumʾs host during his stay in Mukha.[22]

Al-Sarim was trained in Arabic literary culture from a young age, making him another representative of a historical trend in which participation in Arabic textual production allowed non-Muslims and new converts to communicate with the majority.[23] He composed a number of *humayni* poems, but the greater share of his output consists of lyric and occasional *qita'*, chronograms, and *qasa'id* in praise of his patrons, the Qasimi Imams. Al-Sarim's unpublished *diwan*, of which two catalogued manuscript copies survive, indicates that he found his most consistent employment with the Qasimi Imam Ahmad al-Mahdi (d. 1092/1681).[24] He was also afforded patronage by al-Mahdi's son, 'Izz al-Islam Muhammad, and by al-Mahdi's uncle, the Imam Isma'il al-Mutawakkil (d. 1087/1676). The Qasimi Imams were famous for their scholarship – indeed, their political theology posited them as the most learned members of their society – and many of them were distinguished poets themselves, hence they constituted a literate audience.[25]

Al-Sarim seems to have been active as a poet from the early 1060s/1650s, and spent most of his career in Yemen. He is recorded as having left south Arabia only once, when he did *hajj* to Mecca.[26] Even when in Yemen, however, he was in constant motion between his hometown of San'a', pleasure-grounds such as al-Rawda (just north of San'a'), and the mountain fortresses used by his patrons, such as al-Damigh near Jabal al-Azad in the far north; al-Ghiras, north-west of San'a, which the Imam Ahmad al-Mahdi chose as his capital; and Shahara, an isolated citadel about a hundred kilometres north-west of San'a' which had previously been the seat of the Qasimi *da'wa*.[27] The fact that al-Sarim travelled to these fortresses and performed in them points to his inclusion in the entourage of his patrons. He was obliged to adopt their patterns in mobility as they moved around their domains.

My first point of enquiry here concerns the supposed parochialism of the literary scene in seventeenth-century Yemen. Al-Hasani's comments imply that the country was a backwater on the map of literary production, a place which lacked thoughtful patronage, well-read audiences and truly excellent poets, and which was not sufficiently linked to metropolitan centres elsewhere to attract a flow of figures who could inform literary taste. Yet his anecdote revolves around a poet whose father had migrated to Yemen from India, and the story is located in a biographical entry about another poet of San'a' called Haydar Aǧa, who came from an Ottoman military family. The background of these two men immediately suggests to the reader that seventeenth-century Yemen may have been a more worldly and well-connected place than al-Hasani admits. And indeed it was. Al-Haymi al-Kawkabani's (d. 1151/1738–39) biographical anthology of seventeenth-century Yemeni poets, *Tib al-Samar fi Awqat al-Sahar* (*Delicious Conversations Held at Dawn*) testifies to the quantity and quality of the literature produced by the author's contemporaries, as well as to its connections with poetry produced in other lands.[28] *Tib al-Samar* itself borrows the geographical format of anthologies such as al-Khafaji's *Rayhanat al-Alibba'*, the model for *Sulafat al-'Asr*, involving Yemen in a transregional metadiscourse about Arabic literary production.

My second point of enquiry in this chapter concerns the identity which al-Sarim cultivated in his poetry, particularly in his *qasa'id*. This is a question both of his own identity as a second-generation migrant, and of his literary identity, in terms of the poets whom he used as models. Even al-Sarim's pen name, meaning 'the trenchant

Indian', is highly intertextual, distinguishing him for his father's Indian origins, but simultaneously evoking a long history of trade and entanglement between India and south Arabia. The name is a pun with a literary lineage, referencing the swords of Indian steel (sing. *muhannad*) which feature in the corpus of Arabic poetry from as early as the *muʿallaqa* of ʿAntara b. Shaddad (lived sixth century CE).[29] The name also calls to mind verses such as a line by the fourteenth-century poet Ibrahim al-Miʿmar (d. 749/1348–9):[30]

أقول لصحبي حين يرنو بلحظه * خذوا حذركم قد سل صارمه الهندي

'When he looks my way, I say to my companions * "Be on your guard:
he has drawn his trenchant Indian blade (*sārimahu l-hindī*)"'.

Here, the metaphor posits the beloved's glances or eyelashes as cutting swords that wound the onlooker. Writing of the Mamluk era was an important point of emulative intertextual reference for poets in seventeenth-century Yemen, and while it is very unlikely that the pen name al-Sarim al-Hindi was conceived as a direct quotation from al-Miʿmar, the line testifies that it raised a series of associations within the corpus.

Personal identity is articulated within a broader complex of social identities. Al-Sarim's poetry suggests that his father may have converted to Zaydi Shiʿism, the faith of the Qasimi Imams, which tells us something of the tactical choices which he faced when considering how to progress socially in Yemeni society.[31] After the Qasimis had captured Sanʿaʾ from the Ottomans, they set about consolidating their control south of the city, westwards over the coast of the Tihama and eastwards towards Hadramawt.[32] In so doing, they were forced to negotiate their way with the other Muslim communities of Yemen, including the Sunni Kathiri dynasty.[33] The authority of the Imams was often contested throughout their domains for reasons that ranged from the sectarian to the tribal and the pragmatic. In a world of such factional political loyalties, *qasida* poetry which made the intellectual and emotional cases for the Qasimis as the justified rulers of Yemen – or which, perhaps more accurately, could have been understood by an audience of courtly onlookers as having fulfilled this function – was a significant political tool, and this is the genre of poetry in which al-Sarim would go on to specialize.[34] His praise poems often trace a complex dynamic of power, simultaneously eulogizing the Imams, encouraging the listener to accept their authority and their cause, and provoking the Imams themselves to political action.

Al-Sarim was a professional poet and a court scribe (*katib*), not a proselytizer or a political agent, but his praise poetry often made claims to seeking change in the real world. In several *qasaʾid* he encourages *jihad*, in this case meaning combat against the political enemies of the Imams. His poems of this type exhibit dynamic intertextuality, purposefully evoking panegyrics by poets such as al-Mutanabbi (d. 354/965), who had praised the military campaigns carried out against the Christian Byzantines by his most famous patron, Sayf al-Dawla al-Hamdani (d. 356/967);[35] and, perhaps more significantly, Ibn Haniʾ al-Andalusi (d. *c.* 362/973), who praised the Fatimid caliph al-Muʿizz li-Din Allah (d. 365/975), another case in which religious and political authority were intertwined.[36] That al-Sarim, the son of a convert, should have penned such poems, reflects the fact that the networks which were established through intertextuality were supranational and ideologically oriented.

San ʿa ʾ as a crossroads

Al-Sarim was a close friend of the father of Yemen's most prominent literary biographer in the late seventeenth and early eighteenth centuries, al-Haymi al-Kawkabani (d. 1151/1738–9), the author of *Tib al-Samar*.[37] This anthology is divided into just over 270 biographical entries which are grouped according to the geographical regions with which the subjects were associated. The territory that the anthology covers largely falls within the borders of modern Yemen. There are sections on the mountain fortress of Kawkaban, the author's hometown, which had also acted as the refuge of the Qasimi Imams during Ottoman rule; Sanʿaʾ, Yemen's most populous city; the territory stretching west from Sanʿaʾ to Mukha on the coast; and the north from Kawkaban up to Saʿda. An appendix contains entries on writers of significance from outside Yemen, including Ibn Maʿsum, Nizam al-Din Ahmad and al-Hurr al-ʿAmili (on whom, see Chapter 4), showing Yemen's involvement in an international network of literary historiography.

Thanks to *Tib al-Samar*, we know that al-Sarim was by no means exceptional among his peers in Sanʿaʾ's literary world in belonging to a family with a migratory background. The poet and jurist Muhammad b. ʿAli b. Lutf Allah al-Khwaja al-Shirazi was descended from a prominent family of merchants who, as his *nisba* indicates, had come from Shiraz, while the copyist Zayni is described simply as *ʿajami*, in this context meaning 'Persian'.[38] Turks whose families had settled in Sanʿaʾ during the period of Ottoman rule are also to be found among al-Sarim's contemporaries. They include the doctor (*hakim*) Shaʿban Salim Hasiki, and the prominent professional poet Haydar Ağa, a close associate of al-Sarim.[39] Nor should we forget Arab poets whose families had emigrated to Sanʿaʾ, such as Ismaʿil b. Muhammad Faʾi, who was of Syrian stock.[40] Sanʿaʾ's cosmopolitanism is reflected in the erotic epigrams produced in the city, where the beloved is sometimes figured as a non-Arab or a member of a minority community. Haydar Ağa has a *maqtuʿ* about a young man called Rama, a member of al-Sarim's patrilineal community, the Banya, who is depicted as having donned a belt interwoven with silver thread (a *barim*):[41]

بليت ببانيانٍ راق حسناً * تظل الشمس عاكفة أمامه
كأن بريمه لما تبدى * بريق الغور في أكناف رامه

I suffered in my love for a Banya of fine looks * Before whom the sun bows.
When his belt appears, it is like * Lighting flashing in the Jordan Valley,
around Rama.

Rama is both the name of the beloved in the poem and a town in the Jordan Valley (*al-Ghawr*).

Al-Sarim himself has an epigram in which the beloved speaks Persian. This motif is found in the work of earlier poets such as Ibn Sukkara al-Hashimi (d. 385/995) and Ibn al-Hajjaj (d. 391/1000), so we should be cautious about interpreting this piece as an insight into the social make-up of San 'a'.[42] Nevertheless, for the pun to be understood, the reader must know basic Persian greetings, which gives some indication of al-Sarim's expectations of his peers and may suggest that trade fostered awareness of tongues apart from Arabic in certain contexts in Yemen, particularly in urban, mercantile environments:[43]

أفدي الذي قد أذاب قلبي * وجار إذ واصل الجوارا
وقال إذ جاء شب بخير * لكن في القلب شب نارا

I would ransom myself for the one who tortured my heart * And who persecuted me when he had affairs with my neighbours.
When he arrived, he said 'good evening' * But he kindled a fire in my heart.

The trick in this piece derives from play on a non-Arabic word, here *shab* ('night' in Persian), which is visually identical to *shabba* ('he kindled' in Arabic).

In contrast to the poets of Hyderabad, who were first-generation migrants, most of the migrant poets of San 'a' were of a second generation, meaning that their parents had settled in Yemen. We may therefore ask whether their backgrounds are in any way relevant to their artistic identities. Al-Haymi al-Kawkabani dissociates the background of a poet from the body of their work when he writes of Haydar Ağa: 'he was born in San 'a', not knowing Anatolian Turks, and his poetic nature was whetted by mixing with the nobleman [in the city].'[44] In this representation, the way in which an author writes is shaped by the community in which they find themselves, particularly during childhood. At the root of this question is the issue of cosmopolitanisms, and the extent to which it is to be expected that when people have been set in 'transnational motion . . . many of them and their descendants will show signs of hybrid identity'.[45] The identity which writers cultivate in their work is necessarily performative, and it does not have to reflect the complex of loyalties which define their choices in their actual lives. Yet a link with an international network can in certain instances give a migrant writer access to concepts and materials which are less readily available to their peers.

Al-Haymi al-Kawkabani's discussions of manuscripts and intertextuality point to broad patterns in the circulation of texts, and to smaller communities of readers and writers. He shows us, for example, that he and members of his circle had access to works such as al-Tha'alibi's (d. 429/1038) *Yatimat al-Dahr* (*The Orphan Pearl of the Age*), a survey of the Arabic poetry produced in an area extending from Central Asia to Spain (but notably excluding the Arabian Peninsula) in the tenth and early eleventh centuries, and al-Khafaji's (d. 1069/1659) *Rayhanat al-Alibba'* (*The Sweet Basil of the Learned*), a survey of Arabic poetry focused on writers active in Egypt and Syria in the late sixteenth and early seventeenth centuries.[46] In fact, al-Haymi al-Kawkabani tells us that the first manuscript of *Rayhanat al-Alibba'* to arrive in Yemen had been copied for a nobleman who was visiting Mecca, and that al-Sarim read this codex soon after the aristocrat brought it back.[47] We can therefore assume that many poets active in urban centres in Yemen would have found access to a common corpus of Arabic texts. The fact that al-Haymi al-Kawkabani actively quotes from anthologies such as *Rayhanat al-Alibba'* and 'Imad al-Isfahani's (d. 597/1201) *Kharidat al-Qasr* (*The Maiden of the Castle*) when giving comparanda for lines by his contemporaries shows the extent to which these common source texts were internalized by both writers and critical readers in Yemen.[48]

Against this backdrop, communities were formed in which poets picked up, discussed and played with the imagery and rhetoric of the corpus together. As in Hyderabad, poetic gatherings (*majalis*) were one of the main conduits through which these communities took shape, the other being long-distance correspondence. Al-Haymi al-Kawkabani recalls a gathering that occurred one day when he, his friend al-Sayyid Ahmad b. 'Abd al-Rahim Ibn Yahya, and al-Sarim, met to discuss poetry.[49] The conversation passed from one topic to the other, by turns serious and comic, until the three began to speak of images connected to bowmen, and each began to quote epigrams linked by theme and device. That they used semantics and rhetoric as categories for analysing connections between poems underscores the importance of both to how they understood and practised intertextuality. Al-Sayyid Ahmad began by introducing an unattributed poem which is also quoted by al-Ibshihi (d. *c.* 850/1446), and hence probably dates to the Mamluk era:[50]

وأهيف القد ذي دلالٍ * طائر قلبي عليه واجب
كالشمس في كفه هلالٌ * يرمي إلى البدر بالكواكب

A flirt with a slender frame * My flighty heart ticks to his beat.
Like the sun, lune in hand, * He fires constellations at the full moon.

Al-Sarim responded by quoting a piece by another Mamluk poet, Ibn Qurnas (d. 671/1272–3), also representing a male beloved stepping forward to shoot. The quotation adds in a level of rhetorical complexity by introducing the element of *tawriya* (double entendre):[51]

أتى إليَّ مائساً * والردف قد أقلقه
يرشق ثم ينثني * لله ما أرشقه

He came towards me swaying, * Exhausted by riding on the croup.
He shoots, then turns away * By God, there is no-one more graceful.

Al-Haymi then joined in with a third piece of his own composition, about a huntsman who fires a fine shot with his bow:[52]

ولم أنس صياداً يصيب لقوسه * رنين عجيب عند إرسال نبله

كأني بها للصيد أنت توجعاً * وقد قطعت قبل الوقوع بقتله

I shall not forget a hunter who struck a marvellous sound * With his bow
when he unleashed his arrow.
As though in the moment of the shot I had groaned in pain for the game *
And stopped short before it was killed.

Al-Haymi reports that al-Sayyid Ahmad and al-Sarim responded to this epigram
with a great deal of excitement, proclaiming it a 'wonderful' (ʿajib) and 'new'
(mubtakar) image.[53] The reason for their pleasure lies in the fact that al-Haymi's
piece continues in the same broad field of imagery as the Mamluk era poems which
they themselves had quoted, but it focuses on a previously unheard-of element:
the sound of the arrow as it leaves the bow. Al-Haymi develops a form of fantastic
aetiology (husn al-taʿlil), figuring the whistle of the arrow as the narrator's sharp
intake of breath in pity for the game.[54] This employment of figurative expression
is arguably a more developed and complex use of rhetoric than we see in the
previous two pieces. The second line of the first poem in the chain depends on an
extended simile (tashbih), in which the sun stands for the beloved, the crescent
is the bow, the full moon is the target and the constellations are the arrows. In
the poem by Ibn Qurnas, we have a form of jinas on the root r-sh-q, in which
two senses of the word are used ('to shoot' and 'to be graceful'). Neither piece
approaches the ingenuity of al-Haymi in drawing together the first and second
lines of the poem.

Although al-Haymi's representation of this exchange is a polished, written
account, it nevertheless exposes the kinds of analytical discussion which
occurred at literary gatherings and the modes of thinking used to conceive of
intertextuality. A concern for the manipulation of images and rhetorical devices
may appear to us today to represent a narrow kind of formalism, yet there are
important elements here which anticipate modern critical understandings of
intertextuality. Many twentieth-century critics have emphasized the notion of
literary production as the tessellation of an 'impersonal field of crossing texts'.[55]
There is a sense in which al-Haymi and his colleagues agree with this idea, since
their conversation recognizes that there is an unending web of allusions behind
every act of authorship. Their understanding of intertextuality is also broader
than direct quotation or emulation, since the poems quoted above have a masked
relationship with one another – they do not share the same wording. At the same
time, al-Haymi's is an inherently interpersonal model of literary production, to the
extent that he conceives of texts as being genealogically bound together through
filiations whose significance can be tracked. In his estimation, the authorship
of any poem is both about responding to textual models and about engaging
with the temperament, qualities and ideas of other men. There is, therefore, a
social, even openly political, element to the act of writing, which anticipates
late-twentieth-century criticism's return to focus on questions of identity and
ideology in discourse.

A second, longer string of poems which al-Haymi presents later on in *Tib al-Samar* highlights this social function of intertextuality among al-Sarim's contemporaries. Al-Haymi gives an extract from a poem by al-Sarim which acted as the trigger:[56]

يا طيبها من ليلة أزهارها * تحكي الكواكب في سماء زبرجد
من زنبق غض ترى أغصانه * ما بين مياد وبين معربد
فكأنه قنديل فضة مخلص * قد أشعلت فيه ذبالة عسجد

How beautiful it was on a night when the flowers there * Resembled
constellations in a chrysolite sky.
Fresh lilies, whose stalks you see * Now swaying, now drunkenly brawling.
Like silver lamps, * Their golden wicks alight.

The anthologist is careful to point out that al-Sarim was far from the first poet to produce a simile on lily blossoms, giving an antecedent by the sixteenth-century Syrian Badr al-Din al-Ghazzi:[57]

وزهرة من زنبق * أنوارها وهاجة
صفراء في مبيضة * كالراح في زجاجة

A lily, * Its blossoms white-hot.
Yellow in white, * Like wine in a cup.

Even though this general theme may have been in circulation, al-Haymi shows that eight of al-Sarim's acquaintances picked up on his specific comparison likening the white lily flower with its golden stamens to a silver lamp containing candles. The basis of the image is a visual correspondence: when lilies flower, their peeled-back petals can bunch into the bulbous shape of a mosque lamp. Hierarchies are created here as a result of how each poet either refines or debases the image, and in accordance with the political prominence of the poet. Al-Haymi begins with al-Hasan b. al-Mutahhar al-Jurmuzi, a governor of Mukha, whom al-Sarim mourned in an elegy.[58] Al-Jurmuzi largely imitates al-Sarim, simply converting the lamps into candlesticks. It could be argued that his response is an act of homage, which does not attempt to break free of the model, but his political importance makes his advocacy of al-Sarim's image significant:[59]

انظر إلى الزنبق الأنيق وقد * أبدع في شكله وفي نمطه
كمثل قنديل فضة غرزت * شموع تبر تضيء في جسده

See the elegant lily, * With its marvellous form and shape.
Like a silver lamp planted in the ground, * With golden candles lit inside.

Next comes al-Husayn b. ʿAbd al-Qadir b. ʿAbd al-Rabb, a member of the ruling family of Kawkaban. Al-Sarim spent time in Kawkaban, and he praised other members of al-Husayn's family, so there may be a close interpersonal link here. Al-Haymi tells us that al-Husayn took al-Jurmuzi's poem and improved upon it, 'casting it well and correcting its foundation'.[60] Al-Husayn strengthens the comparison, figuring the bloom of the lily and the release of its scent as the lighting of the candle. Al-Husayn develops the image to the extent that it now functions independently of al-Sarim's poem:[61]

أتانا زنبق قد راق شكلًا * بعرف كاد ينشر كل ميت
كقنديل من البلور فيه * فتائل أسرجت من غير زيت

We were brought lily flowers, delicate in form * Releasing a scent that almost resurrected the dead.
Like a crystal lamp topped by * Wicks that were lit without oil.

Staying in Kawkaban, the jurist Ahmad b. Muhammad al-Zurayqi maintains the same point of focus (the contrast between the flower's petals and the stamens) but introduces a new object of comparison in the form of pointed arrows in a bulbous quiver:[62]

انظر إلى الزنبق لما أتى * مبتسماً عن الشنب القطر
كتركش قد صيغ من فضة * نباله ثقف بالتبر

See the lily as it comes towards us * Smiling through dewy white teeth.
Like a quiver fashioned from silver * Its arrows pointed with gold.

At this juncture, al-Haymi makes a comment which casts light on what he regards as the border between the inventive use of imagery and active plagiarism, citing another two-liner by another poet of Kawkaban, al-Sayyid Muhammad Ibn al-Husayn Ibn Yahya al-Himzi al-Kawkabani, which he deems to mark an act of poetic theft. The second line is almost a verbatim copy of al-Zurayqi's simile on the quiver, with the rhyme word changed.[63] This failure to push the image in a new direction stands in contrast to the achievement of the jurist Yusuf b. 'Ali, one of al-Haymi's acquaintances, in transforming the image. Yusuf b. 'Ali's poem runs as follows:[64]

انظر إلى الزنبق في أول ما * يظهر فض ختمه ترى العجب
كأنه مكاحل صيغت من البـ * ـلور في شكل بديع لم يعب
قد ضمنت مراوداً من فضة * قد جعلت حروفها من الذهب

Regard the lily as it first * Flowers. If you open its seal, you will see a wonder.
It is as though it were a vial for kohl, made of crystal, * A marvellous shape, beyond reproach,
Fused with silver kohl wands, * Their points fashioned from gold.

We can see a pattern emerging here. The poets for whom al-Haymi has time are the ones who introduce a new object of comparison for imagining the contrast between the petals and stamens of the lily. The particularly successful ones choose an object of comparison which strengthens the image, such as al-Husayn b. ʿAbd al-Qadir b. ʿAbd al-Rabb's introduction of the element of scent, or Yusuf b. ʿAli's comparison of the flower to gold-tipped kohl wands inside a vial, which implicitly observes the difference in colour between the filaments of the stamens (the kohl wands) and the anthers – the latter appear gold-tipped because they are covered in pollen. Al-Haymi criticizes the following piece by Shaʿban b. Salim al-Hasiki, another poet of Sanʿaʾ, saying that although it develops a fine comparison by likening the lily flower to hands clutching golden sticks, it fails to attend to Yusuf b. ʿAli's detailed observation of the anatomy of the flower:[65]

يا حسنة من زنبق * من فوق غصن أملد

كأنامل من فضة * ضمت مطارق عسجد

> What a beautiful lily flower, * Tender atop a branch.
> Like silver fingers * Clutching golden sticks.

Al-Haymi then shows how he himself would build on and extend Shaʿban b. Salim al-Hasiki's image to include the distinction between the anthers and stamens:[66]

أرى زنبقاً في الروض مثل أنامل * تمد من البلور لله ما أذكى

أنامل قد ضمت مطارق عسجد * هراوتها من فضة سبكت سبكا

> I see the lily in the meadow, like crystal fingers * Outstretched – by God,
> what could be more fragrant?
> Fingers clutching golden sticks * Their tips cast from silver.

Finally, al-Haymi introduces additional techniques into the response poems: *tadmin* (direct quotation) from earlier poets, and Qurʾanic allusion (*iqtibas*). These poems therefore have a whole field of intertexts in mind, following the filiation of the theme back to al-Sarim, but also making direct, formal reference to texts outside this chain. Al-Haymi's first example is by Shaʿban Ibn Salim al-Hasiki, quoting al-Maʿarri (d. 449/1058) in the second half of the second line. Al-Hasiki transposes al-Maʿarri's image, which refers to the dawning day, into a new context, describing the lily as it flowers and then withers. The evocation of the white-haired flower dyeing its hair with saffron is a figurative expression for the withering blossom shedding pollen over its petals:[67]

زنبق الروض قد تحير لما * لاح خد الشقيق أحمر قاني

واستحى حين شاب من أن يوافيه * فغطى المشيب بالزعفران

> The lily of the meadow blanched when * The cheek of its brother, the anemone,
> appeared, blood red.
> As it aged, it grew embarrassed to bear it company * And it covered its
> white hair with saffron.

The very last example that al-Haymi supplies is by al-Sarim's associate, Haydar Ağa, who picks up on the personification of the lily seen in al-Hasiki's poem, but introduces the element of *iqtibas*, citing Qur'an 48:1 ('Verily we have granted you a clear victory', lit. 'verily we have opened . . .') as a reference to the moment when the flower blooms:[68]

وزنبق مجلس بين الندامى * كشيخ حاز لطفاً في وقار
يريك إذا تلا (إنا فتحنا) * عمود الصبح في وسط النهار

The lily amid his boon companions at the gathering * Is like an old man,
graceful in his gravity.
When the verse 'Verily we have opened' is pronounced, it seems to you *
The glimmer of dawn in the middle of the day.

The most significant theme which arises from this string of quotations concerns poetic invention. The point which al-Haymi makes is that a text which bears no filiation has no purpose, because it and its author exist in isolation. Creativity is about developing elements which are latent in other people's work and making them known, or explaining an idea with greater clarity than one's predecessors. While it may ostensibly seem that the ten poems given above are all derivative variations of one another, the only thing that connects many of them is their broad topic. The real subject of each piece is the comparison, which differs markedly from poem to poem – sometimes the lily is like a candlestick, sometimes like a quiver full of arrows, a vessel in which kohl wands have been planted, fingers clutching golden sticks, or a venerable old man. Community is sustained as long as the poets approach the same object of enquiry from a subjective point of view.

Civic community: Al-Sarim's occasional poetry

One of the most interesting performance pieces in al-Sarim's *diwan* is a *qasida* in praise of the Qasimi Imam Isma'il al-Mutawakkil 'ala Allah (r. 1054/1644–1087/1676), which demonstrates the kinds of human and textual entanglements that linked seventeenth-century Yemen to the rest of the world. The rubrication introducing the poem states that it was composed in 1081/1670–1, when an army of 'Europeans' (*ifranj*) was infringing on the port of Mukha. The historical incident to which the poem responds is described in some detail in the chronicle *Tabaq al-Halwa wa-Sihaf al-Mann wa-l-Salwa* (*The Dish of Sweetmeats and the Bowls of Manna and Honey*), where it is written that a band consisting of Portuguese, English, French and Dutch corsairs descended on Mukha and threatened the governor, Hasan b. al-Mutahhar [al-Jurmuzi], accusing him of disloyalty to them.[69] Al-Jurmuzi attempted to buy time from the pirates, but they scaled the Fadli fortress with ladders and tortured the soldiers who were guarding it to death. The Yemenis responded with an onslaught on the fort, recapturing it, imprisoning about twenty of the Europeans and putting the remaining corsairs to sea. While the Europeans inflicted sporadic damage on the town with their cannons over the course of the following months, news of their presence travelled to Sanʿaʾ. The Imam Ismaʿil al-Mutawakkil's nephew, Sidi Safi al-Islam Ahmad, and Ahmad's son, ʿIzz al-Islam Muhammad, were already on their way to Mukha from Aden, most probably because the pirates had sunk one of Safi al-Islam's galliots, but al-Mutawakkil nevertheless dispatched one of his own sons, ʿAli, to aid his allies on the coast. When the armies finally arrived, there seems to have been little left to do, as the Europeans had become frustrated and sailed off.

This attack was not an isolated occurrence. By the late seventeenth century, Europeans had long since established themselves around the littoral of the Indian Ocean through settlements and factories, and they had come to be a major presence in the maritime economy of the region.[70] Indeed, when many of the Muslim figures who are discussed in this book travelled by sea, they did so on ships run by European crews.[71] Piracy went hand in hand with this kind of economic activity.[72] Al-Jurmuzi, the governor of Mukha who was threatened in the attack of 1670, chronicled the presence of European corsairs and the damage that they inflicted in the local area over the course of many years, from as early as 1060/1650.[73] The attack of 1670 does not appear to have been unusual in its violence. Nevertheless, as an occasion, it offered al-Sarim the opportunity to explore the grand theme of rectitude, and to articulate Qasimi identity in the face of a concrete and identifiable foe. His representation of the facts of the attack recasts events which had no concrete resolution as an ideological triumph, in a not dissimilar way to how al-Mutanabbi had once taken a prematurely halted raid into Byzantine territory as an occasion for reflection on Sayf al-Dawla's military prowess.[74]

The two copies of al-Sarim's complete works each provide a different frame for the poem: according to the Gotha manuscript, al-Sarim performed the *qasida* as a rallying cry for his patron to fight, when Safi al-Islam Ahmad and ʿIzz al-Islam Muhammad – both of whom also acted as patrons to al-Sarim – had already committed to war.[75] The Rampur manuscript adopts a slightly different emphasis, foregrounding the dynamic between Ismaʿil, his nephew, and his nephew's son, by stating that the two younger men had called on Ismaʿil to take up arms.[76] Given the impression that these rubrics evoke – a moment of crisis, a leader who is uncertain, or even cowardly, and who needs to be shaken into action – we may expect al-Sarim to model his poem on a classic of political theatre, and indeed he does, choosing a *qasida* by Ibn Haniʾ al-Andalusi (d. *c.* 362/973) in praise of the Hamdunid Jaʿfar b. ʿAli, governor of al-Zab (in modern-day Algeria).[77] Jaʿfar, who was purportedly of Yemeni descent, initially ruled al-Zab on behalf of the Fatimids, and he welcomed Ibn Haniʾ to his court as the artistic voice capable of expressing his political ambition, hence this poem is freighted with associations of military prowess and support for the propagation of a politico-religious ideal.[78] According to some narrative anecdotes, Ibn Haniʾ first performed his

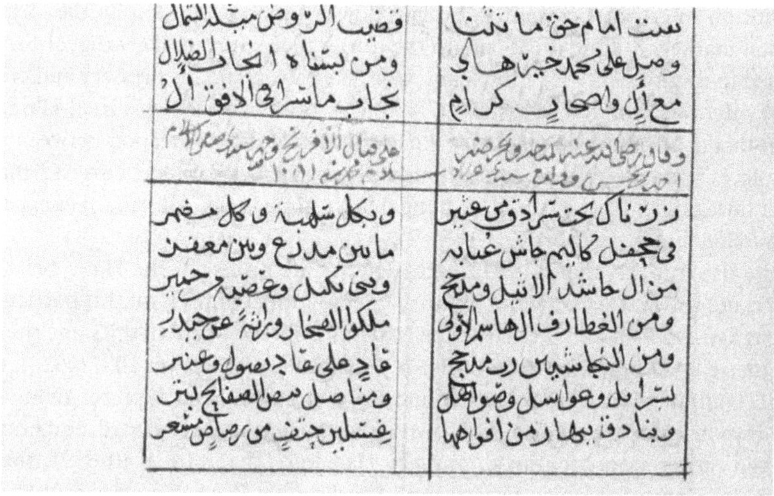

Figure 3 *Diwan al-Sarim al-Hindi.* Forschungsbibliothek Gotha der Universität Erfurt, MS. Orient A 2330, f. 13a. CC BY-SA 4.0.

ode before Ja'far's assembled men, who dismounted from their horses as one, leaving the patron the only man astride his steed, when the poet called out the line:[79]

من منكم الملك المطاع كأنه * تحت السوابغ تبع في حمير

Who among you is the intractable king, who seems to * Be Tubba' in Himyar
beneath his armour?

As with the other examples of emulative intertextuality discussed in this book, al-Sarim adopts the formal features of Ibn Hani''s *qasida*, reproducing and redistributing much of the imagery, and borrowing the rhyme and the metre, *al-kamil*, which was characterized by the theorist al-Qartajanni (d. 684/1285) as 'pure and grave'.[80] As *al-kamil* was the 'leading metre' of medieval, courtly Andalusian poetry, its use may have triggered a series of associations in learned listeners quite independently of the poem's rhetoric and imagery.[81]

The debt that al-Sarim's *qasida* owes to Ibn Hani' is not marked in the manuscripts of al-Sarim's *diwan*, and this particular poem is not quoted in other sources, which means that the reader must know the earlier piece in order to make the link and to understand al-Sarim's creative process. There is nothing inherently exceptional about this, as dynamic intertextuality is usually done practically within the Arabic corpus, and is not signalled through paratextual markers. It was normally only in pedagogical works, such as biographical anthologies or commentaries on *dawawin*, that the pre-modern philologists felt it necessary to remark on intertextuality and to explain how it functioned. Despite the lack of explicit markers linking this poem to the earlier piece, it is unlikely that al-Sarim wanted to disguise his use of Ibn Hani' from his patron and his primary audience, as we might be tempted to assume if we place too much credence in al-Hasani's claim that al-Sarim was a plagiarist. An awareness of the connection between the two pieces strengthens the poem's thesis and constructs a parallel between Isma'il al-Mutawakkil and Ja'far b. 'Ali, arguing that the time is ripe for Isma'il to expand his mission and his authority.

It is also unlikely that al-Sarim intended to hide his use of Ibn Hani' because he was not the first seventeenth-century poet to model himself on this particular ode, as *Sulafat al-'Asr* makes clear. Ibn Ma'sum quotes a poem in the same rhyme and metre by 'Abd al-Rahman b. 'Isa b. Murshid al-'Umari (d. 1037/1628), the grand *mufti* of Mecca, tracing its connections with Ibn Hani''s piece, giving his own response poem in praise of his own father, Nizam al-Din Ahmad, and noting an even earlier antecedent in a *qasida* by Hassan b. Thabit (d. *c.* 40/659), one of the most prominent poets to surround the Prophet.[82] Al-'Umari was a Sunni and a Hanafite, but he nevertheless evidently felt that Ibn Hani''s *qasida* was a suitable archetype to use when praising the military achievements of the *sharif* (ruler) of Mecca, Hasan b. Abi Numayy b. Barakat, and his son, Abu Talib, and when congratulating them on their victory over the population of the Shammar Mountains in Najd. All three poems – Ibn Hani''s model and the responses by al-'Umari and al-Sarim – are therefore about the imposition of the patron's authority on a recalcitrant and unbelieving enemy. The pieces by al-'Umari and al-Sarim are also thematically linked because they celebrate the patron's heir as his equal. Since al-'Umari died at the beginning of the seventeenth century and al-Sarim at its end, and since al-Sarim visited Mecca on pilgrimage, it is plausible to imagine that he was exposed to al-'Umari's poem before he wrote his own response to Ibn Hani'. This supposition is supported by a formal comparison between the three pieces, which demonstrates that eight rhyme words (little intertextual keystones around which the imagery of a line can be constructed) which are not found in Ibn Hani''s *qasida* are shared between al-'Umari and al-Sarim. While it is probable that yet more seventeenth-century responses to Ibn Hani''s *qasida* exist, it seems reasonable to assert that al-Sarim's engagement with Ibn Hani' was mediated through al-'Umari. The use of two antecedents, one classical and one contemporary, creates two sets of historical models for the poet-patron relationship between al-Sarim and al-Mutawakkil, each with its own resonances.

The three poems are of differing lengths, and accordingly they adopt contrasting rhetorical strategies. Ibn Hani' and al-'Umari begin with an ironic inversion of the conventionally erotic introit (*nasib*), making claims such as: 'The ring of swords unsheathed, and their bite / Into skulls, are more sonorous to us than a singing girl / The gleam of blades glinting in the dust / Is more glamorous and august to us than a resplendent face.'[83] For his part, al-Sarim cuts straight to the *rahil* – a convention of victory poems[84] – depicting the arrival of a delegation of warriors at the court of the Imam, and addressing the patron directly. The poem begins with the words 'we came to you', a pointed summation of the dynamic of the entire piece. As the syntax of the opening lines unfolds, we are slowly given more and more details of the delegation that has arrived at the court of the Imam:[85]

زرناك تحت سرادق من عثير * وبكل سلهبة[86] وكل مضمر

في جحفل كاليم جاش عبابه * ما بين مدرع وبين مغفر

من آل حاشد الأثيل ومذحج * وبني بكيل وعصبة من حمير

ومن الغطارف آل هاشم الأولى * ملكوا الفخار وراثة عن حيدر

ومن النجاشيين رب مدجج * عاد على عاد يصول وعنتر

بسرابل وعواسل وصواهل * ومناصل بيض الصفائح بتر

وبنادق ينهار من أفواهها * غسلين حتف من رصاص مشعر

We came to you beneath canopies of dust * And on every kind of hulking
warhorse and lean charger.
In a host like a frothing sea * Of armoured and crested men,
Warriors of ancient Hashid[87] and Madhhij,[88] * The clan of Bakil and parties
from Himyar,
Nobles descended from the Hashimites * Who have inherited glory
from Haydar,
And the Najashi family,[89] how many a one armed to the teeth, * Who attack
the unjust, and the clan of 'Antar,[90]
[Clad in] armour, with quivering spears, whinnying steeds * Cutting swords
of bright blade,
And muskets from whose barrels pours forth * The suppurating pus of death,
streaming from the wounds of bullets.

This strophe forms a coherent unit, hinged on l.7, which contains a Qur'anic reference to the pus (*ghisilin*) that pours from the bodies of the denizens of Hell (Q 69:36). This line foreshadows the reference that we will find in the closing sections of the poem to the ichor of the decapitated Christians. Al-Sarim builds up to the clausula through the repeated use of *wa-min* ('and from among') in ll. 3–5, a listing device which enumerates the different representatives of families local to al-Mutawakkil's capital at Duran who have come to his court, ready to defend the Qasimi kingdom; and, in l.6, the cadence with isocola of quadriliteral nouns which lays bare the rhythm of the poem. Importantly, the names are not random: they represent North Yemen's two major tribal confederations, and the Hashimites (descendants of the Prophet), arguing that the country is politically united behind the Imam. The intertextual connections with al-'Umari's poem are fairly clear here: references to dust (l. 1), the crests on the men's helmets (l. 2), and the whinny of the steeds (l. 6) are all a direct engagement with the *nasib* of the earlier piece (al-'Umari's ll. 1; 5–6). Al-Sarim goes on, marking a change in direction with a *fa-* (but, therefore), and another Qur'anic allusion, echoing Q15:94, 'So proclaim what you have been commanded, and turn away from the polytheists', the reference foreshadowing the appearance of the non-Muslim enemy in the poem:[91]

فاصدع أمير المؤمنين بما تشاء * منا ومر فلأنت خير مؤمر
فلقد يجرد أحمد بعزيمة * عظمت وسطوه قاسمي قسور
وسرى وجد إلى ذراك بهمة * قعساء تشمخ فوق هام المشتري
وتلاه عز إلال نجلك واثبأ * بالعزم يفترس افتراس غضنفر
قوم أقول إذا شممت أريحهم * فتكت لكم ريح الجلاد بعنبر
وإذا رأيت سيوفهم ناديتهم * وأمدكم فلق الصباح المسفر
فافخر أمير المؤمنين بهم فهم * بك يفخرون وأنت أعظم مفخر

'Therefore proclaim thou', Commander of the Faithful, what you wish *
Among us, and go, since you are the best authority.
For Ahmad led a detachment of men with imposing * Determination.
His assault was Qasimite, leonine.
He returned by night and strode into your ambit with a firm * Ambition that
towers over Jupiter's crown.
In his wake comes the glory of your progeny's lances, shimmering *
With a resolution which grasps with the grip of a lion.
A people of whom I said, when I caught their scent on the breeze, * 'The gale
of battle has assailed you with ambergris'.
And when I saw their swords, I called out to them: * 'The break of shining
dawn has sent you reinforcements'.
Take pride in them, Commander of the Faithful, for they * Take pride in you
when you are the most illustrious point of pride.

In this section, the poet has to contend with the fact that the addressee of the poem, al-Mutawakkil, is not the military hero who has gone out to face the unbelievers, a problem which does not confront Ibn Hani' and al-'Umari. Al-Sarim negotiates this issue by increasing his tempo through the use of *jinas* in l. 9 (*'azimatin 'azimat . . . qasimi qaswar*) and l. 11 (*yaftarisu iftirasa*) – a technique borrowed from al-'Umari's ll. 9 and 12 – and then engaging in rubato through quotation (*tadmin*) from Ibn Hani''s poem in ll. 12–13, framing it as direct speech. The concealment of these 'textual interpretants' reminds us that in the reading and recitation of poetry, 'there is an initiatory period and a delay in realizing what a given text is actually about'.[92] Continuing, in ll. 9 and 11, references to lions (*qaswar . . . ghadanfar*) recall the lion-like patrons of Ibn Hani''s and al-'Umari's poems, but also look forward to the lion-like lord of l.36, and bring us back to Haydar ('the lion'), 'Ali b. Abi Talib. In logical terms, l.14 presents a *takhallus* (transition) into praise of the Imam, emphasizing the mutual bonds of loyalty between al-Mutawakkil and the army which supports him. We now move firmly into the section of praise (*madh*):[93]

أنت الذي جددت شرع محمد * وأقلته عن عثرة المتعثر
وأرحت دين البغاء عن مراءاة * حتى أنار بصبح وجه أزهر
بالقائم المتوكل اتضح الهدى * وبدت أشعته بنور مطهر
هذا إمام العصر ذو الكرم الندي * ما زال يهزأ بالغمام ويزدري

إن جئت تسأل علمه ونواله * مدت سؤالك منه سبعة أبحر
صفو المحاجة من منير الوحي بل * كنه الحقيقة في الخفي المضمر
شرفت عمامته الكريمة رفعة * ما تاج هامة تبع في حمير
تتفاخر الخيل الجياد بحمله * وباسمه يرتاح صدر المنبر
وإذا تلوت لمنبر ألقابه * خضعت لهيبتها أسرة قيصر
ذي السؤدد الوضاح والجود الذي * تهمي أنامله بصوب كنهور
ملك إذا هملت يداه يغد عن * ماء الحيا وجوفه المثعنجر
أياك تسأل بعد ربك غيره * إلا الصفي فباله من عبقر
دع عنك عن سود الغمام فكفه الـ * بيضاء تزرع بالنضار الأحمر
رد بحر نائله ودع نهر الأولى * تخلوا فسائل جوده لم ينهر
أخلاق أحمد روضة بل جنة * حقاً وفيض نواله كالكوثر
ومحمد نجل الخليفة لذ به * تحمد فهو أخو الجنات الأخضر
ناهيك من بر وبحر لم يزل * فياض جود لم يكن لمكدر

You who renewed the Prophet's path * And raised it away it from the
stumbler's slip.
You recovered the faith of those who seek the truth from hypocrisy *
So that it shone with the dawn of a radiant countenance.
Leadership took form in al-Mutawakkil, vicar of God, * And news of
him became purified in light.
This is the Imam of the age, possessing abundant nobility, * Continually
mocking the clouds and jeering at them.
If you came to inquire of his knowledge and gifts * Your questions of
him would span seven seas.
The purity of the proof is of shining, divine inspiration, but * The essence
of truth is shrouded in secrecy.
His noble turban has risen as high * As the crown atop the head of
Tubbaʿ in Himyar.
Noble horses vaunt his attack * And the preacher on the *minbar* delights
in his name.
When you pronounce his titles from the pulpit * Caesar's face falls in terror
Of the one possessed of evident lordship and generosity, from whose *
Fingertips flows the downpour of dense, towering nimbi.
A king who, when his hands rain gently, produces * the water of life and its
copious abundance.
Take care not to ask who can be your lord after him * If not the pure one,
al-Safi, who has the mind of a chief.
Leave talk of dark mists, for his fair * Palm sows blossoms of pure gold.
Resort to the sea of his favour and leave the river * Of those are drained, for
'the one who begs for his generosity will not be chided'.
In truth, [Sidi Safi al-Islam] Ahmad's character is a meadow, rather, Paradise, *
And the torrent of his favour is like Kawthar.
And he took delight in Muhammad, the progeny of the caliphate. * Praise him
for he dwells in verdant gardens,
To say nothing of the land and sea, which permanently * Overflow with a
bounty which has never been sullied.

One could break this strophe (ll. 15–31) down into further subsections, as ll. 24–31 largely depend on an extended metaphor which figures the generosity of the poet's patrons, Isma'il al-Mutawakkil and Sidi Safi al-Islam Ahmad, as abundant rain. These images reflect commonplaces of the classical Arabic corpus in general, as well as praise poetry produced in late medieval and early modern Yemen in particular. One might compare these lines with poems by a sixteenth-century Yemeni court poet named Jarrah b. Shajir b. al-Hasan, who composed a number of panegyrics in praise of Jamal al-Din al-Mahdi b. Ahmad, the *amir* of Jazan. Jarrah likens his patron to a foaming sea, and writes that he nourishes the people in the manner of the ocean shoals.[94] Similarly, al-Sarim's direct contemporary Ahmad b. Ahmad al-Anisi composed and performed a *qasida* for al-Mutawakkil's son, the Imam al-Mu'ayyad Billah Muhammad (r. 1092/1681–1097/1686) in 1094/1682–3, in which he describes his patron as a sea of knowledge, who rains down a generosity which cannot be gauged onto those who seek his favour.[95]

In his own poem, al-Sarim builds on conventional images like these, and weaves them together to create something new. Antithesis (*tibaq*) features prominently as a structuring principle here, reflecting the theme of conflict between good and evil: faith is contrasted with infidelity (ll. 15–16); the fire with water (l. 16); light with dark (ll. 17; 20; 25; 27); the manifest with the hidden (l. 20); the pure with the sullied (ll. 20; 26; 31); the eminent with the abased (ll. 21; 23). Al-Sarim also contrasts addressees, maintaining two conversations at once. Sometimes he calls out to al-Mutawakkil (ll. 15–16; 31), and sometimes to the universal auditor (ll. 19; 26–27). The constant movement between points of view connects the patron with the audience, making both active participants in the spectacle and eliding their perspectives. In l. 27 the poet promises to move on from describing the patron's generosity, but hyperbolically he cannot, such is its magnitude, returning to it in the next line with the added emphasis of another Qur'anic allusion (to Q 93:10, 'Do not repulse the beggar'), which comes near to equating the Imam's beneficence with God's. The theme of generosity forms part of a complex of ideas, all linked through the theme of water, which seep through the poem: the Imam is a sea, as is his army, and it is on the sea that the corsairs' ships will founder. In intertextual terms, al-Sarim transposes the imagery of his interlocutors into a new context here: the images of thunderstorms, which describe the flashing swords of the victors, the whinnying of the horses, and the torrent of the enemy's blood in Ibn Hani' and al-'Umari, are transferred to the generosity of the Imam.

خذها أمير المؤمنين خريدة * نقلت مديحك عن صحاح الجوهر
شيبت حماستها برقة لفظة * وجبتك بالبشرى إذاً فاستبشر

Accept it, Commander of the Faithful, as a maiden, untouched, * Who has
brought praise for you made from unbored pearls.
Her ardour has cooled with the delicacy of speech * And she has come
to you with good news, so celebrate.

These two lines could be seen as a mechanical attempt to incorporate the imagery of al-'Umari, who devotes a full fourteen lines to an extended metaphor on the craft of his *qasida*, comparing it to a beautiful maiden clad in the finery of eloquence.[96] However, like ll. 27–28, they have an important structural function as a type of aside, a moment of self-reflection in which al-Sarim pretends to take the auditor outside the world of the poem, before launching into the final strophe. They represent another juncture of rubato, slowing the tempo of the *qasida* down and marking a shift before the poet delivers his message: that the Europeans have been defeated.

قد دمر الله البغاة بكفرهم * وأخو الضلالة ضارع لم ينصر

ما تصنع النينات مع أسد الشرى * هيهات ما يبغون غير مقدر

ذو الكفر والإشراك في أمواجه * قد صيد في أشراك رب غضنفر

بغية جنود الحق يبرق بغيهم * وله خفوق قلوبهم في المحشر

وتجذذت أعناقهم وصبيبها * أضحى صليب إهانة للمزدر

وكبيرهم فرقاً يفرق جسمه * وغدا بأشفار المخافة ينفري

رغموا به قصداً أريق نجيعه * منه وذلك رمي ذي زند وري

وقضى وخلف ربه في أسره * أرأيت رباً في إسار مصغر

ولهم على ما يزعمون جراءة * في البحر نافذة ولما تجأر

ومدافع لم يدفعوا عنهم بها * أمراً ورب البغي غير مضفر

وغدت مطايا سفنهم مبحورة * رمياً وظنوا أنها لم تخسر

لمضاء شرك يا إمام تبددوا * شذراً وبالماضي الحسام الأبتر

قطعت دوابرهم وسيفك قاطع * فاحمد إله الناس ربك واشكر

واسلم ودم للدين تحمي شرحه * لمطهم ومشطب وبسمهر

وبقيت في جيش الخلافة والعلا * وعلى الخلافة منك ثوب سنور

God has destroyed the unbelievers in their infidelity * The misled, lost,
were unaided.

What can babes[97] do with lions of the thicket? * How wrong was their
impotent desire.

Men of unbelief and polytheism amid the waves [of his sea] * Who were
hunted down in the nets of the lion-lord.

What the soldiers of Truth seek confounds their outrage * The fluttering of their
hearts will become frenzied on the Day of Judgement.

Their necks were slit, and their ichor * Was a greasy sacrifice, an insult
to the contemning.

Their leader's body was cut to pieces * As he was minced on the blades of fear.

They abased him, setting out to shed his lifeblood * And their shot was
fired from a lit firebrand.

He died and his lord left him in chains * Have you ever seen a lord belittled
in shackles?

They were insolent in what they claimed * As they sailed onto the sea and
did not supplicate God.

Their cannons did not carry out their orders * Since the lord of the infidel
provides no help.

Their ships were sunk with a single shot * Yet they believed that they could
not be broken.
Imam, they splintered themselves on the blades of traps * And on the
cutting sword.
Their rear-guard has been cut to pieces, as your sword is trenchant *
So praise your Lord, the God of the people, and give thanks.
Live well and long for the faith whose exposition you protect * With a
noble horse, a ridged dagger, and a tall spear.
May you remain in the army of the caliphate and eminence. * Because of you,
the Caliphate is decked in a cloak of mail.

Until this point in the *qasida*, al-Sarim has referred to the occasion of its
composition only in oblique terms. From a narrative perspective, it could be
argued that the listener is waiting to hear what has happened, and that this delay
therefore creates a sense of tension and expectation. But from the perspective of
the poet's logic, the defeat of the Europeans is known and has been implicit since
the opening verse, because the Imam rules with divine support. Therefore, the
final strophe does not exactly offer a resolution to the poem, but rather acts as a
kind of chiasm, an inversion and restatement of what has gone before. Ll. 34–6, for
example, can be seen as a parallel to ll. 8–10, demonstrating that while the armies
of the Imam march with firm ambition, the unbelievers are lost at sea. The failure
of the Christian enemy to measure up to its delusional estimation of its own power
is something that echoes representations found in earlier *qasa'id*, including not
only those of al-Mutanabbi and Abu Tammam;[98] but also those of al-Sarim's direct
contemporaries, such as Ahmad b. Ahmad al-Anisi, who writes of the banners on
the battlefield fluttering like the hearts of the pagan enemy.[99] Al-Sarim strengthens
our sense of chiasm rhetorically, through the continuing use of *jinas*. In l. 36, for
example, the root *sh-r-k* is repeated to contrapose the polytheism (*ishrāk*) of the
Christians and the metaphorical nets (*ashrāk*) in which the Imam has snared
them; and in l. 37 we have the root *b-gh-y* used in opposing senses, referring to the
thing sought (*bighya*) by the soldiers of truth and the outrage (*baghy*) committed
by the unbelievers. The technique is characteristic of the oppositional structure
of this *qasida*, and appears again in ll. 39; 41–43; 46 and 48. We also find chiastic
restatements of imagery from the first half of the poem, such as the horse, dagger
and spear of the penultimate line (l. 47), which are a reformulation of images
found in l. 6.

The final two and a half lines of the poem (ll. 46b–48) are marked by a strong
sense of closure through the *du'a*, or prayer for the patron. The very last line figures
the patron both as the embodiment of the caliphate and as the armour which
protects it. This is a similar image to ones that we find in *qasa'id* composed in
Yemen in a slightly earlier period. The aforementioned Jarrah b. Shajir b. al-Hasan,
for example, figures his patron as a 'cutting sword in the hand of God / Whose only
sheath is the caliphate'.[100] Reference to this family of images reinforces the feeling of
mutual loyalty that the poet has tried to stoke between the Imam and the listener,
a feeling on which the success of the poem would have hinged.[101] Structurally

this achieves an effect quite different from al-ʿUmari's poem, which ends with a prayer for the *sharif* of Mecca and his family, extending back to the Prophet, and then closes with a verbatim repetition of the poem's very first hemistich, a form of consummate circularity. Ibn Hani''s original carries a strong feeling of evolution, in that it starts with images of earthly spring – the breeze of war, the shining dawn, the fresh flowers of battle plucked from the furled stem of the sword – and ends with a heavenly garden – the clouds of divine mercy, the courts of Paradise, and the stream of generosity. From this ideological point of view, al-Sarim achieves something radically different from his models.

How might the connections which link al-Sarim's poem to the pieces by Ibn Hani' and al-ʿUmari create a sense of a community operating across space and time? My analysis of the *qasida* suggests the idea of al-Sarim's individuating authority, his deliberate and pointed engagement with earlier poets and the Qur'an. Yet, on one level, his close readings are only significant if his primary audience recognized them. While we have no direct evidence to inform us of the *qasida*'s reception, and therefore no proof that its primary audience was familiar with the pieces by Ibn Hani' or al-ʿUmari, it is worth repeating the fact that the Qasimi Imams were not only rulers but also, theoretically, the most eminent scholars in their society, and they famously composed and critiqued verse.[102] *Sulafat al-ʿAsr* contains entries on members of the ruling family whom Ibn Maʿsum regarded as excellent poets.[103] Therefore, we should not think of them as patrons who simply supported al-Sarim because the production of panegyric verse was regarded as one of the hallmarks of a flourishing court, but rather consider them as readers who may have recognized the filiation between al-Sarim's poem and its antecedents.

On the one hand, al-Sarim's emulative engagement with his models is not simply a form of homage, a recognition of the value of Ibn Hani' and al-ʿUmari, but also a deliberate attempt to fashion parallels over the course of history, arguing that he and the Qasimi Imams are the local, modern equivalents of Ibn Hani' and Jaʿfar b. ʿAli, and al-ʿUmari and the *sharif* Hasan b. Abi Numayy b. Barakat. This is an act of 'metaphorical[ly] projecting . . . the past onto the present', and using an historicized idiom to ally current events with antique ones.[104] Al-Sarim forces us to rethink our experience of events, so that our perception of time becomes non-linear, with moments looping back to similar occasions in the past. This feeds into the concept of response poems as 'commentaries, interpretations, and retractions of each other',[105] which seek to refine an idea in relative terms.

And yet, even as the poem's classical mould was familiar and contoured in such a way that an audience may well have known what to feel even before the poet's words were out of his mouth, this very familiarity may have imbued the *qasida* with a knowing and almost parodic feeling, reflecting Linda Hutcheon's conception of parody as repetition with critical distance.[106] Comparable examples of emulation have been studied by Beatrice Gruendler, who speaks of the 'silent overwriting' that was conducted by the Andalusian poet Ibn Darraj al-Qastalli (d. 421/1030), when he applied the rhyme words, metre and imagery of a *qasida* by al-Mutanabbi to a new theme.[107] Technically, there is a point in common between this kind of dislocation and the poetics of the Persian 'fresh style' (*shiva-yi taza*). This is a sort of modernism predicated not on a break with the forms of the past, but on the redeployment of known images and techniques in an unfamiliar way.

Conclusion

The poetry composed by al-Sarim al-Hindi and his circle indicates that seventeenth-century Yemen was not isolated from the global production of Arabic letters but, rather, fully integrated into a transregional system of classicizing literary production. Just as in India, we have to think of multiple literary registers of Arabic, and the language and forms of vernacular poetry like the *humayni* are a part of this broader corpus. However, in San'a', Mukha and Kawkaban, a diverse group of poets came together to compose lyric pieces (the lily poems), which were marked by a high degree of intertextuality with verse from Mamluk and Ottoman Syria and Egypt. Through a process of continual refinement, these authors collectively sought to invent a new expressive idiom for capturing the image that lay behind their pieces, linking them to each other and to writers of previous centuries. Al-Sarim also composed large performance works for his patrons which were characterized by intertextual dialogue with the historical corpus. As specific and occasional as his *qasida* on the European assault on Mukha is, it is marked by a cosmopolitan sensibility. This is not a form of cosmopolitanism predicated on 'openness to other religious traditions', but rather one based on a worldly collation of the Arabic literary corpus, which linked Yemen to North Africa, India and Mecca, across time.[108]

Chapter 4

MASHHAD

AL-HURR AL-'AMILI

Of all the networks of writers who are discussed in this book, the scholars of Jabal 'Amil are perhaps the most often recognized as a historically durative community, constituted through religious confession, kinship and an education rooted in shared approaches to philology, rhetoric and literary criticism. As a toponym, Jabal 'Amil refers to a rural, mountainous area in the south of modern Lebanon, and by extension the name is associated with the families of Twelver Shi'i scholars who historically populated the area. Since these families were first discussed in modern scholarship, there has grown to be a large body of research on the part which they played in the religious and intellectual history of the early modern period, as they rose to prominence in places far beyond the geographical confines of greater Syria.[1] Their migration to Iran and their role in helping to formulate the religious policies of the Safavid state in the sixteenth century have been analysed in detail.[2] It has also been demonstrated that 'Amilis travelled more widely, to places such as Cairo, the pilgrimage cities of Arabia, Bahrain, Iraq and India, settling and having children who broadened and complicated their networks.[3] Indeed, two members of the Arabic literary circle of Nizam al-Din Ahmad, examined in Chapter 2, were 'Amilis who had been educated in Isfahan.[4] Their presence in Hyderabad was connected to their occupations as jurists and theologians, reflecting the inclusion of Qutbshahi Golconda in the itineraries of Arabic-speaking Twelver Shi'i scholars during the seventeenth century.

While the historical spread of 'Amili scholars and their authorship of texts on the religious sciences are well-appreciated phenomena, their participation in the high culture of Arabic poetry has not been investigated in much detail by historians of literature.[5] Baha' al-Din al-'Amili (d. 1030/1621), the leading jurisconsult of Safavid Iran during the reign of Shah 'Abbas I (r. 996/1588–1038/1629), is the best-known 'Amili author of literary texts, famous for his *Kashkul* (lit. *Begging-Bowl*), a multilingual (Arabic-Persian-Turkic) miscellany which tessellates together extracts of verse and prose gathered from the classical, medieval and early modern corpora.[6] The *Kashkul* advances an encyclopaedic take on literary culture, navigating points of continuity between poetry, literary prose, mathematics, astronomy and the religious sciences, which makes the work into an exploration of knowledge as a whole.[7] Baha' al-Din also composed his own verse, including didactic *masnavi* poems in Persian, and lyric, narrative and funerary poetry in Arabic.[8]

Yet the importance of poetry to philological practices in both Arabic and Persian scholarly culture ensured that many other 'Amilis whose literary work has not been afforded the same recognition composed verse. Sometimes the poetry that they wrote reflected their professional and intellectual activities, consisting of *ikhwaniyyat* (poems of brotherly love), which served to demarcate and consolidate scholarly networks, or *qasa'id* in praise of the Prophet and the Twelver Imams, which connected into a much broader complex of religious praise poetry that was produced and consumed across classes and professions in the seventeenth century. Many 'Amilis also composed lyric poems. Although such lyrics would not have been acceptable as 'probative quotations' (*shawahid*), it is likely that their authors composed them to exemplify rhetorical devices, which were important within the context of philology.[9] It is therefore possible that these pieces are more connected to the scholarly work of their authors than we might assume if we see them out of context. Nevertheless, they point to a sustained engagement with the historical conventions of verse composition, and invite us to examine the 'Amilis as serious poets.[10] As I have implied, the importance of poetry as a philological tool in the early modern period means that we should be wary of viewing these figures through a modern lens which decouples literary activity and religious (or legal) scholarship from one another. In fact, these fields were constantly brought into dialogue: one may point to the medieval lyric poems that deliberately reframe direct quotations from versified works on Arabic grammar in an erotic context;[11] and to legal riddles that 'blur the boundaries of entertainment, edification, and display'.[12]

The purpose of the present chapter is to sketch out the formal and generic contours of the Arabic poetry composed by 'Amili scholars in Iran during the second half of the seventeenth century, and thereby to examine how Arabic literary activity in Iran connected into transnational scholarly networks that extended south-west to Mecca, and east to India. The figure on whom I have chosen to focus is al-Hurr al-'Amili (d. 1104/1693), a jurisconsult, scholar of *hadith* and biographer who grew up in the village of Mashghara in Jabal 'Amil, performed pilgrimage to Mecca and the Shi'i shrines of Iraq, and eventually moved to Iran, where he then based himself, becoming *Shaykh al-islam* at the shrine of the Imam Riza in Mashhad.[13] Al-Hurr composed a *diwan* of Arabic poetry, which survives. Surprisingly, even though he is much esteemed in Twelver circles, the *diwan* remains in manuscript.[14]

Al-Hurr is best known to scholars today for his very large work on canonical *hadith* entitled *Tafsil Wasa'il al-Shi'a ila Ahkam al-Shar'ia* (*An Elaboration of the Recourse of the Shi'a to the Provisions of Religious Law*), as well as a biographical dictionary about the scholars of Jabal 'Amil entitled *Amal al-Amil fi Dhikr 'Ulama' Jabal 'Amil* (*The Hope of the Hopeful, Recalling the Religious Scholars of Jabal 'Amil*). The latter is frequently mined for biographical data about the constitution of the 'Amili community by historians of religion and politics, but it is in itself a rich source of poetry, and it allows us to reconstruct al-Hurr's literary network, in the same way that we can use *Sulafat al-'Asr* and *Tib al-Samar* to show how local and transnational circles of poets were connected in the second half of the seventeenth century. *Amal al-Amil*'s temporal and geographical scope are actually far broader than the title might be taken to imply, and al-Hurr includes a number of famous poets of history, some of whom, such as Abu Tammam (d. 231/845 or 232/846) and Safi al-Din al-Hilli (d. 749/1348), had only a passing connection to southern Lebanon. The presence of such poets of the distant past seems designed to emphasize the stylistic models whom al-Hurr and his compatriots within his network valued. The literary-critical qualities of *Amal al-Amil* are also bolstered by al-Hurr's frequent citations from Ibn Ma'sum's *Sulafat al-'Asr*, even in his entries on himself, and on figures whom he knew personally, such as his paternal uncle and teacher, Muhammad b. 'Ali al-Hurr (d. 1081/1670-1).[15] Al-Hurr's use of *Sulafat al-'Asr* a matter of years after its completion in 1082/1671 may have been enabled by the fact that he and Ibn Ma'sum were linked through figures such as Husayn b. Shihab al-Din al-'Amili al-Karaki (d. 1076/1665-6), one of the members of the Arabic literary circle of Golkonda, who had lived in Iran for a time, and holograph copies of whose poems al-Hurr possessed.[16] In addition to underscoring the social connections between the two authors, the references also emphasize that they were linked through textual circulation. As with the writers of San'a', studied in Chapter 3, who read anthologies such as *Rayhanat al-Alibba'*, we can demonstrate that al-Hurr and his fellow 'Amili poets in Iran not only had access to a common corpus of contemporary poetry that was transmitted around the littoral of the Arabian Sea, but were also socially connected to authors in Arabia and India.

The fact that al-Hurr arrived in Iran when he had already grown into middle age may appear to be the most obvious reason why he composed poetry in Arabic rather than in Persian. In autobiographical statements in *Amal al-Amil*, he reports that he had spent the first forty years of his life in the Jabal, and while it is far from impossible that he learned Persian during this time, his comments about his teachers and his education show that Arabic was his primary language of high culture and his first vernacular too.[17] However, any multilingual examination of the literary culture of early modern Iran needs to make a nuanced account of the differing factors which encouraged authors to write in their language or languages of choice, and al-Hurr's professional occupation as a jurisconsult provides another compelling reason for his decision to compose in Arabic. Just as the patronage of an Arabic literary circle allowed Nizam al-Din Ahmad to reinforce the émigré Arabic-speaking community in Golkonda and to refine local understanding of the Arabic language through the performance and discussion of poetry, so too al-Hurr's continued use of Arabic in the diaspora allowed him to build a network with other legal scholars in Iran, Bahrain, Mecca and the Deccan, and to promote the study of philology and semantics.

We can compare al-Hurr with another, slightly younger 'Amili poet, Muhri (d. c. 1130/1717-18), who also spent many years living in Mashhad.[18] Unlike al-Hurr, Muhri was a second-generation migrant, who grew up in Isfahan, surrounded by Persian literary culture.[19] Muhri's poetry, including a Persian *masnavi* entitled

Sarapa (*Head to Foot*), is unpublished and in manuscript.[20] His collected works are primarily written in Persian, and the bulk of them consist of lyric *ghazal* poems, alongside a number of panegyrics in praise of the Imams and a *mustazad* eulogizing the Safavid Sultan Husayn (r. 1105/1694–1135/1722). Arabic does feature in Muhri's *qasa'id*, but its use is mostly restricted to a few remarkable poems at the end of the *divan*. These pieces are macaronic, interweaving Arabic and Persian into the same linguistic structures, as the opening lines of one of them illustrate:[21]

لي دلبر آب الحيوة خرام سرو روانه * نار الخليل عذاره والخط بوى دخانه
الجشم آهوى الختن والخال نافه مشكه * والچهره گلزار الارم والطره من ريحانه
درج العقيق الپر من الناسفته مرواريد تر * يروي حديثاً صح عن لبها وعن دندانه
مشكين سلاسل زلفه لما يريسها الصبا * فترى گذشته سنبل وا كرده في دامانه

> I have a sweetheart who is the water of life, a walking, strutting cypress *
> The down on his cheeks is the fire into which Abraham was cast, and his beard is smoke.
> His eyes are those of a musk deer, and his beauty spot is its navel * His face is the meadow of Iram and his ringlets are made of sweet basil.
> A box of carnelians, full of glistening, unbored pearls * Relates a correct *hadith* (or: tells a story that is unmarred) through his lips and teeth.
> When the east wind plucks a hair from his musky locks * You can see a hyacinth flowering on the hem of his skirt.

These lines represent a form of 'rhizomatic thinking',[22] going beyond the traditional form of Arabic-Persian *mulamma'at* (macaronic poems), in which one line is generally written in one language, and the next in the other.[23] While there are some precedents in the corpus, such as a poem by a twelfth-century judge of Amul, pieces that integrate Arabic and Persian grammar in this way are not common.[24] Here, although the grammatical structures can generally be interpreted as Arabic, it is necessary to read the lines with Persian pronunciation and without Arabic case endings to make them scan. Sometimes the grammar becomes a curious mixture of Arabic and Persian, as in the first hemistich of l. 2, where the Persian *izafa* and Arabic *idafa* are used simultaneously; and in the first hemistich of l.3, an extended metaphor comparing the beloved's lips and teeth to (red) carnelians and (white) pearls, where we have the Arabic definite article modifying the purely Persian words *pur* ('full') and *nasufta* ('unbored', or 'unstrung'), and one must insert a Persian *izafa* between the words *murvarid* ('pearls') and *tar* ('wet', by extension, 'glistening'). The letter *-h* at the end of each line can sometimes be read as part of the Persian adverbial form in *-ana*, and sometimes as the Arabic masculine singular possessive enclitic. The experience of reading the poem is strange – undoubtedly intentionally so – as one shifts between languages and grammatical systems, constantly reassessing the text.

We can see pieces such as these at either end of the spectrum of usage, from the artificial to the vernacular: they may have been contrived philological jokes, and equally they may play on the daily linguistic life of ʿAmilis in Iran, in which code-switching may have been quite common. The copy of Muhri's *divan* now held in the library of the University of Tehran appears to have been made for a son of the theologian Muhammad Baqir Majlisi (d. 1110/1698–9), indicating that its readership was probably a scholarly one, bilingual and philologically minded.[25] But even if Muhri's macaronic poetry was designed with bilingual audiences in mind, it does not actively demand that all of its readers be bilingual, since it can more or less be understood by a monolingual speaker of Persian, and Muhri's association with the court of Sultan Husayn places him in a social context where Persian and Turkic were the dominant languages. Al-Hurr, by contrast, worked in a religious and legal setting, both environments in which Arabic was preeminent in Safavid Iran. I argue that this difference between the communities in which the two men found themselves is a more decisive factor in determining the languages in which they chose to write than the difference in experience between being a first-generation and a second-generation migrant. The fact that there is a strong lyric element in the poetry of both al-Hurr and Muhri demonstrates that this is not a question of different languages being used to compose particular genres of verse, but rather an issue linked to the poets' interlocutors.

Al-Hurr's network

Amal al-Amil shows that al-Hurr had a little short of twenty interlocutors in Iran who composed poetry in Arabic.[26] Almost all of these men were religious scholars, and the majority of them were ʿAmilis, including some of al-Hurr's family – his father, his paternal uncles, his brother[27] – and some of his teachers.[28] A minority of them were concentrated in Isfahan, which was a significant centre of religious instruction on account of its many *madrasas*.[29] In the opening decades of the seventeenth century, it had been the centre of the network of Baha' al-Din al-ʿAmili, who still figured prominently in the intellectual landscape of al-Hurr and his contemporaries through connections of family and pupillage. An important ʿAmili figure of Isfahan who was young enough for al-Hurr to actually meet was the *shaykh* Muhammad b. ʿAli b. Ahmad al-Harfushi al-Hariri al-ʿAmili al-Karaki, who was appointed *ra'is al-ʿulama'* in Isfahan by Shah ʿAbbas, where he taught Ibn Maʿsum's teachers.[30] Al-Hurr had first encountered al-Harfushi while he was still in the Jabal.[31]

The majority of the poets of Arabic in al-Hurr's Iranian network lived in the town of Tus, near the shrine of the Imam Riza at Mashhad, where al-Hurr himself settled.[32] They included members of his family and his students, but also men such as the *shaykh* Ibrahim b. Ibrahim b. Fakhr al-Din al-ʿAmili al-Bazuri, who had studied with Baha' al-Din al-ʿAmili and al-Shahid al-Thani, and then moved to Khurasan.[33] Al-Hurr did not meet al-Bazuri, but purchased a number of the books that he had owned after his death, including holograph copies of his Arabic *diwan* and travelogue.[34] Another resident of Tus was Muhammad b. ʿAli b. Muhyi al-Din al-Musawi al-ʿAmili, chief judge of Mashhad, who composed a little poetry in Arabic to which al-Hurr did not have access.[35]

Outside of these two centres, members of al-Hurr's network included a poet of Arabic who lived in Gilan,[36] and another who made a home in Shiraz.[37] Three of al-Hurr's fellow poets of Arabic were not ʿAmilis, but rather Shiʿi scholars from the town of Huwayza in Khuzistan,[38] and then there are two Iranian divines, one of whom appears to have a pupil of al-Hurr, and another of whom transmitted texts to him.[39]

Mobility was a key aspect of the careers of many of al-Hurr's fellow religious scholars, and we can speak of his participation in a broader, international network, consisting of a further seven or so poet-divines who lived outside Iran.[40] Al-Hurr connected with these figures at different points in his life, from his childhood in Lebanon to his pilgrimage journeys. When he did *hajj* for the third time, travelling on the sea route from Iran to Bahrain and Mecca, he made the acquaintance of local men of learning throughout the trip, establishing ongoing correspondence with them and exchanging verse endorsements.[41] Linkages with Golkonda stemmed from both Isfahan and Mecca. While he was in Mecca on pilgrimage, al-Hurr had met Jaʿfar b. Kamal al-Din al-Bahrani, a member of the circle of Nizam al-Din Ahmad.[42]

Meetings such as these prompted the composition of highly intertextual poems that proclaimed the intellectual filiation of ʿAmili scholars with one another. A good example of this kind of emulative intertextuality emerges through a comparison of *Amal al-Amil* and *Sulafat al-ʿAsr*. The former contains a brief entry on Jamal al-Din b. al-Sayyid Nur al-Din ʿAli, with whom al-Hurr had studied.[43] After leaving Jabal ʿAmil, Jamal al-Din had travelled on to Mecca, Mashhad and lastly Hyderabad, where he was appointed to a leading position as a scholar. One of the poems which al-Hurr transmits from Jamal al-Din runs as follows:[44]

قد نالني فرط التعب * وحالتي من العجب
فمن أليم الوجد في * جوانحي نار تشب
ودمع عيني قد جرى * على الخدود وانسكب
وبان عن عيني الحمى * وحكمت يد النوب
ياليت شعري هل ترى * يعود ما كان ذهب
يفدي فؤادي شادناً * مهفهفاً عذب الشنب
بقامة كأسمر * بها النفوس قد سلب
ووجنة كأنها * جمر الغضا إذا التهب

A great burden overwhelms me * My state is a surprise
For a fire is alight within me * Lit by the pains of longing.
Tears flow from my eyes * Welling over my cheeks.
My eyes are fevered * And the hand of misfortune has sentenced me.
If only I knew whether you can see * If what has gone will return.
My heart is the victim of a slender * Fawn, of sweet mouth,
As upright as a tawny lance * With which he has robbed men of life;
With a cheek like * The ember of the euphorbia when it blazes.

This poem appears to be a simple love lyric, in which the narrative persona presents itself as exhausted by longing for the beloved. However, its real purpose is to mark a connection with another scholar. *Sulafat al-ʿAsr* contains the following piece in the same rhyme and metre by Hasan b. al-Shahid al-Thani (d. 1011/1602), the son of one of the most prominent Twelver jurists of the sixteenth century:[45]

أبهضني حمل النصب * ونالني فرط التعب
إذ مر حالات النوى * على دهري قد كتب
لا تعجبوا من سقمي * إن حيوتي لعجب
عاندني الدهر فما * يود لي إلا العطب
وما بقاء المرء في * بحر هموم وكرب
لله أشكو زمناً * في طرقي الختر نصب
فلست أغدو طالباً * إلا و بعينني التعب
لو كنت أدري علة * توجب هذا أوسبب
كأنه يحسبني * في سلك أصحاب الأدب
أخطأت يا دهر فلا * بلغت في الدنيا أدب
كم تألف الغدر ولا * تخاف سوء المنقلب
غادرتني مطرحاً * بين الرزايا والنوب
من بعد ما ألبستني * ثوب عناء ووصب
في غربة صماء إن * دعوت فيها لم أجب
وحاكم الوجد على * جميل صبري قد غلب
ومؤلم الشوق له * قلبي المعنى قد وجب
ففي فؤادي حرقة * منها الحشا قد التهب
وكل أحبابي وقد * أودعتهم وسط الترب
فلا يلمني لائم * إن سال دمعي وانسكب
واليوم نائي أجلي * من لوعتي قد اقترب
إذ بان عني وطني * وعيل صبري وانسلب
ولم يدع لي الدهر من * راحلتي سوى القتب
لم ترض يا دهر بما * صرفك متى قد نهب
لم يبق عندي فضة * أنفقها ولا ذهب
واسترجع الصفو الذي * من قبل كان قد وهب
تبت بذاك مثلما * تبت يدا أبي لهب

Distress has worn me down * A great burden overwhelms me
When distance became bitter * Fate decreed against me.
Do not be surprised at my sickness * For my life is surprising.
Fate has taken against me and * Desires nothing but my perdition.
A man cannot remain still * In a sea of worries and cares.
I complain to God of an illness * Laid out for me on the paths of deception.
I cannot seek anything without * Weariness afflicting my eye.
If only I knew the malady * That requires or causes this,
As though it counted me * Among the people of learning.
You are mistaken, fate, for I * Have learned nothing in the world.
How accustomed you are to treachery * You do not fear a reversal of fortune.
You have left me slack * Amid disasters and misfortunes,

Having dressed me in the * Garb of toil and hardship,
In a deathly exile, where I cannot * Answer if you call me.
The arbiter of longing has * Overcome my graceful patience.
And my wracked heart has judged in favour * Of the one tortured by longing.
So a brand is in my heart * Which has set my entrails on fire.
And I have bid farewell to my loved ones * Amid the earth.
No critic can censure me * If my tears flow and well.
Today my torment * Has brought my distant fate near.
When my homeland disappeared from my sight * And my patience ran out
and was wrested away.
My fate left nothing of my riding camel * For me but the hump.
Fate, you were not satisfied by what * You made me expend when it
had been plundered.
I have no silver left * To spend, nor gold.
And the purity which had been given to me * Before has been taken back.
Thus have I been destroyed, just as * 'The hand of Abu Lahab may be
destroyed' [Q 111:1].

Unlike Jamal al-Din's love lyric, this piece belongs to the genre of *shakwa* (complaint against fate). It could be read as a lament on suffering in general, or as a more specific meditation on the persecution which the author and his family suffered at the hands of the Ottoman authorities in the Levant, since al-Shahid al-Thani, the poet's father, was by some accounts killed on his way to trial in Istanbul, accused of heresy.[46] Jamal al-Din's response does not directly emulate the contents of the poem. Rather, it refracts or even distorts the imagery, while maintaining the same rhyme and metre, allowing us to perceive an echo of the model. It goes beyond parody and pastiche, instead acting more like a cap or amplification of the earlier poem. This reduces any sense of competition between the two poets, something which we may speculate Jamal al-Din would have wanted to avoid out of respect for the son of al-Shahid al-Thani.

Al-Hurr's poetry: Literary composition as a philological practice

It stands to reason that the ways in which seventeenth-century poets approached their craft would have varied according to their training. The starkest difference in method would lie between a poet who had learned to compose intuitively, through immersion in an environment where verse was recited and bandied about, and a poet who had received extensive academic instruction in the science variously called 'semantics and rhetoric', or 'imagery and rhetoric' (*'ilm al-ma 'ani wa-l-bayan*), which went hand-in-hand with a religious education at a *madrasa*, and complemented the study of the Arabic language and Qur'anic hermeneutics.[47] Nasrabadi tells of a man of Isfahan, a dervish called Mast 'Ali Isfahani, who began to compose after wandering around the bazar and repeating the poems that he heard there.[48] By contrast, al-Hurr belonged to a class of poets who were educated in how to read poems analytically and think about rhetoric and imagery as a system. His academic approach to poetry is revealed in one of his other unpublished works, a didactic *urjuza* (poem in *rajaz* verse) on semantics and rhetoric.[49] In the section on the science of rhetoric (*'ilm al-badi'*) in this piece, al-Hurr essentially lists devices used for structuring and analysing poetry, such as *tajnis* (homophony), *tibaq* (antithesis) and *ibham* (amphiboly).[50] While it is possible for individuals to compartmentalize their thinking when inhabiting differing professional personas, this *urjuza* provides further evidence that al-Hurr had a scholarly approach to composition.

The importance of rhetoric and semantics to al-Hurr's professional work as an interpreter of religious law would have given him an interest in their application across genres of Arabic poetry, and his *diwan* contains a wide array of types of verse, contradicting his own claim in his autobiography that 'most of [my *diwan*] is in praise of the Prophet' (*wa-aktharuhu fi madh al-nabi*).[51] While it is true that *qasa'id* devoted to the Prophet, the people of the Prophet's house (*ahl al-bayt*) and the Twelver Imams abound in his collected works, al-Hurr composed a significant number of short lyric pieces, riddles and chronograms. Indeed, the carefully curated representations of him and his work that are preserved in anthologies such as al-Muhibbi's *Nafhat al-Rayhana* give the impression of a lyric poet.[52] It is also important to remember that *qasida* verse is polythematic, and that there is considerable overlap between the erotic introits to al-Hurr's religious panegyrics and other forms of lyric verse, such as the epigram and the *qit'a*. Al-Hurr's lyric pieces are not just designed to amuse or to delight, and they should be considered an integral aspect of his intellectual work, particularly because lyric poetry has a heightened potential for semantic play.

One further group of al-Hurr's poems shows a blend of philological, juridical and lyrical thinking. The pieces in this corpus include the following:[53]

دع أخا الحسن والجمال إذا ما * ضن بالوصل أو ثناه الصدود
ليس عيد الأضحى لدي بعيد * كل يوم نلت المنى فيه عيد
فقبيح يجود بالوصل خير * من مليح بوصله لا يجود
فإذا ما تعذر الحج فالعمرة * جلبتني فإنني مصدود

Abandon a fine and handsome man whenever he * Does not give himself
to you or turns away.
The Festival of Sacrifice is no holiday in my eyes * But every day on which
I attain my desire is a celebration.
For an ugly man who gives freely of himself is better * Than a comely man
who is reticent.
Whenever the greater pilgrimage is impossible, then the lesser * Attracts me,
for I am prevented from prosperity.

وذات خال خدها مشرق * نوراً كركن الحجر الأسود
كعبة حسن ولها برقع * من الحرير المحض والعسجد
قد أكسبت كل امرئ فتنة * حتى إمام الحي والمسجد
كم هام إذ شاهدها جاهل * بل هام فيها عالم المشهد

A woman with a beauty spot, whose cheek * Is the point at which light dawns,
   like the corner of the black stone.
A Ka'ba of beauty, in a veil * Of pure silk and gold.
She has subjected every man to a trial of faith * Even the Imam of the
   quarter of the mosque.
How many ignorant men have been bewildered when they glanced at her * And
   even 'he who knoweth that which ye make known' is bewildered at her.

ستر ت محاسنها الحسان بلؤلؤ * وبجوهر وبفضة وبمسجد
هيهات ذاك الستر أظهر حسنها * حتى لقد فتنت إمام المسجد

The beautiful women covered their charms with pearls * Jewels, silver and gold.
That veil revealed their beauty * Until they subjected even the Imam of the
   mosque to a trial of faith.

These three epigrams follow on from one another consecutively in the *diwan*,
forming a logical progression in image and rhetorical device. The first begins
in a largely conventional way, as an arch parody of an advice poem on how to
handle relationships with men, and proceeding according to Adam Talib's formula
of 'premise, exposition, resolution'.[54] Rhetorically, it is dense: there is *radd al-'ajz
'ala al-sadr* (anticipation of the rhyme word) in l.2; and *tajnis* (homophony) and
tibaq (antithesis) in l.3. The fourth and final *bayt* is the punchline, introducing
an *istikhdam*, a form of double entendre in which more than one meaning of a
word is invoked. The first meaning is assumed because it is more obvious, but
grammar forces the reader to re-evaluate the line with the second meaning in
mind.[55] The set-up occurs in l.2, where the speaker proposes that every day on
which he attains his desires is equivalent to *'id al-adha*, the festival of the sacrifice
coinciding each year with the end of the *hajj*, which can only be made between
the eighth and tenth days in the month of Dhu l-Hijja. In l.4, a relationship with
a willing but unattractive man is figured as a consolation prize that is inferior to
a relationship with a handsome man, just as *'umra*, the lesser pilgrimage which
can be undertaken at any time of year, is inferior to *hajj*. The *istikhdam* is on the
word *masdud*, which means both 'rejected', in the sense that the handsome beloved
has declined the speaker's advances, and, in a technical sense, 'turned away from
pilgrimage' because enemy activity has blocked the caravan route.
   Pilgrimage takes us to the Sanctuary in Mecca, and the second poem
adumbrates the ways in which the beloved resembles the Ka'ba, figuring her as
the object of the lover's worship. Like the Ka'ba, she is draped in fabric. Again,
we have a form of *istikhdam* in l.3 on the word *fitna*, which can mean 'temptation'
in a general sense, or 'a trial of faith' in a more specific, theological context. The
idea that the beloved brings men's religious faith into doubt is reinforced in the
second hemistich of l.2, where the description of her headscarf as being fashioned
from pure silk and gold thread brings to mind debates in *hadith* literature as to
whether either material should be considered licit. Finally, the *tibaq* (antithesis) in
l.4 contrasts the man of ignorance (*jahil*) with 'he who knows outward appearance'

(ʿālim al-mashhad), which can be construed as a loose intertextual reference to the numerous passages in the Qurʾan where God is described as ʿālim al-ghayb wa-l-shahda, 'he who knoweth what is hidden and what ye make apparent'. The third poem offers a variation on the second, with the concept of *fitna* appearing again, and the presence of a *tibaq* between the concealed and the apparent (*al-situ azhara*). There is some rhetorical movement away from Poem Two in the presence of a *jinas* on the root *h-s-n* in l.1.

I would prefer to assert that al-Hurr composed pieces such as these, with their play on theological terms, less because he was a lawyer, and more because his training had instilled in him practices akin to what el-Rouayheb terms 'deep reading' (*mutalaʿa*), and an interest in how the meanings of words can be stretched or re-interpreted.[56] In fact, in the larger corpus of poems composed by seventeenth-century ʿAmilis, we can see an attempt to use lyricism to explore language and hermeneutics. The following extract from a longer wine poem by Muhammad b. ʿAli b. Mahmud b. Yusuf b. Muhammad b. Ibrahim al-Shami al-ʿAmili, Ibn Maʿsum's instructor in *adab*, who had studied in Isfahan and is the subject of an entry in *Amal al-Amil*, could be seen as a sophisticated exploration of the difference between perception and reality:[57]

خلعت ثوبها على التفاح * وترامت على خدود الملاح
كل ريحانة أرق من الرا * ح جلا لي شقيقة الأرواح
وردة فوق خده وقروحاً * بين جنبي داميات الجراح
حبذا ميعة الشباب وعيش * قد قطعناه في ظلال الرماح
زارني زورة الخيال وولى * في كرى النوم مزعجاً بالصباح
لست أقوى على الجفون المواضي * ويح نفسي من المراض الصحاح
سامح الله من دمي وجنتيه * وعفا عن بنانه الوضاح
لا تؤاخذ جفونه بفؤادي * يا إلهي كلاهما غير صاح

[The wine] bestowed its hue on apples * And flung itself onto the cheeks
of pretty women
Every sweet-smelling basil which was more delicate than wine * Appeared
to me as a kindred spirit.
A rose on his cheek, and wounds * Between my sides, suppurating with blood.
How fine is the prime of youth and pleasure * Which we have cut short
in the shade of spears.
He visited me in my imagination and lay with me * In my sleep, troubling
me in the morning.
I cannot hold out against cutting eyelashes * Woe to me from real illnesses.
May God endow his cheeks with my blood * And pardon his shining fingertips.
My God, do not retribute his eyelashes * With my heart – both are intoxicated.

The logical foundation of this section of al-Shami al-ʿAmili's poem lies in a form of *husn al-taʿlil* (fantastic aetiology), where the poet argues that the ruddiness of the beloved's cheeks is the blood of the lover, shed by the beloved's eyelashes, which, like miniature swords, have cut into the lover's body.[58] Even though the cause of the speaker's suffering is imagined, the physical effects of love sickness are not, as ll. 5–6 make clear: the spectre of the beloved has visited the lover at night, but despite the fact that he has been present only in the speaker's mind, the emotional impact that he has exerted on the speaker is real. Similarly, the desire that the sight of the beloved has excited in the speaker has caused 'real maladies'. The fanciful basis of the aetiology is unpacked and exposed, but this only serves to reinforce the weight of the poet's argument, which concerns the physical effects exerted by our estimative faculties.

Al-Hurr's pilgrimage narrative

The forms of community building studied in this book vary from the deliberate use of the same metre, rhyme, imagery and rhetoric as another poet, to looser engagements with the same *gharad* (general theme) or rhetorical device. The former approach allowed writers to construct deliberate parallels with their peers, and to lay out the ways in which they shared their ideas and their characters, because response poetry is rooted in comparison and close reading: it invites the reader to examine the answer alongside its model, and to find meaning in slight variations in argument, tone and mood. This inherently comparative quality makes the response poem a highly sociable form of verse when it is practised among direct contemporaries, one that says as much about social relationships as it does about art. More diffuse engagements with a general theme ostensibly demand less knowledge of the corpus on the part of the reader, but they can be more astute in their cultural literacy than response poems, as their use of intertextuality is less explicit.

One broad theme which was relatively common in both Arabic and Persian poetry around the littoral of the Arabian Sea during the seventeenth century was description of the pilgrimage to Mecca. Such poems, which can either be narrative pieces in rhyming couplets or long *qasa'id*, have some obvious overlap with the prose or prosimetric *rihla* (travel account), a type of writing that flourished in this era. Perhaps because poets were attempting to deliberate on a theme that was of universal importance to the Muslim community when they composed versified pilgrimage accounts, these poems are often marked by diffuse forms of intertextuality. We can also bear in mind the potential crossover between these forms of verse narrative and the manipulation of cognate motifs in coeval praise poetry. Fath Allah Ibn al-Nahhas al-Halabi (d. 1052/1642–3), for example, describes his journey over the abyss of the ocean, but figures his patron, not Mecca, as the object of his journey.[59]

Baha' al-Din al-'Amili wrote a versified pilgrimage account called *Sawanih Safar al-Hijaz fi l-Taraqqi ila al-Haqiqa min al-Majaz* (*Thoughts on a Journey to the Hijaz, on Ascension to Reality by Way of Figurative Expression*), which seems to have been composed in a mixture of Arabic and Persian. The text does not survive as a single piece; Baha' al-Din scatters fragments from it at various points in his *Kashkul*, making one wonder whether a complete edition of it ever was in circulation. The extracts that have come down to us suggest that, if an overarching narrative existed, it was written in rhyming couplets (*masnavi* for the Persian; *urjuza muzdawija* for the Arabic), and that it was interspersed with lyric interludes. Formally, this would place the work in dialogue with classical Persian *masnavi* poems such as Rumi's *Masnavi-yi Ma'navi* (*The Essential Masnavī*) and 'Attar's *Mantiq al-Tayr* (*The Conference of the Birds*), where the narrative is often punctuated by lyric analogies. Only three Arabic fragments from the *Sawanih* are given in Hijazi's modern reconstitution of the *diwan* of Baha' al-Din: two are lyric calls to the cupbearer, kinds of passage which are often used to break up Persian *masnavi* poems such as Nizami Ganjavi's *Sharafnama* (*The Book of Nobility*), and one is a story about a Kurdish man who could not bear to consider his mother's concupiscence, and so killed her.[60] Again, this kind of anecdote, which was written with the intention of being humorous, is in dialogue with exempla found in Rumi and 'Attar.

Although most of Baha' al-Din's text is now lost, we can speculate that his importance within the émigré 'Amili community may have encouraged al-Hurr to consider the *Sawanih* when composing his own pilgrimage poem. Al-Hurr's piece is a long *qasida*, and it survives in full in his *diwan*. Unlike the *Sawanih*, it does not consist of discrete vignettes, but it does combine narrative with non-narrative elements, much like a series of coeval, versified Persian travel accounts.[61] As with the *Sawanih* – consider its full title, with its equation of the approach to Mecca with the approach to an essential truth – there is an implication that the physical journey in space is the premise for a more profound journey in time towards Judgement Day. Much of the poem recounts the voyage by ship around the coast of Arabia, figuring the sea as an abyss of darkness and fear, the antithesis of brilliant Mecca. There is an almost eschatological element to the depiction of the sea journey, which may play into the idea of Judgement Day as the moment at which humanity is both annihilated and gives account of the divine instruction that it has received.[62] On a rhetorical level, *tibaq* (antithesis) plays an important role in structuring these sections of the *qasida*. The following extract, for example, constructs an antithesis in light, between the darkness of the night journey and shining Mecca, and in height, between the mountainous waves and the depths of the sea. *Jinas* (homophony) is equally important, appearing in ll. 3–4:[63]

ركبنا متون البحر في لجة الإسراء * ليروى صدى الأشواق من مكة الغراء
فقابلتنا أطواد موج محيطه * بنا بين أعلى الجو واللجة الخضراء
وكم قد نظرنا في الجهات فلم نجد * سوى فلك يجري وفلك لها مجرى
وقد كانت الغبراء قدماً تقلنا * فقد طالت الأشواق منا إلى الغبراء

We sailed on ships in the abyss of the night * To quench the thirst of our longing for noble Mecca.
And so the mountains of the waves in the surrounding sea reared up before us, * Appearing between the heights of the sky and the green depths.
How long we gazed around and saw * Only the heavens coursing by and the course of the boat.
The earth had once carried us * And now we longed for dry land.

These rhetorical structures parallel certain Qur'anic passages which al-Hurr would have undoubtedly known well. In Q 24:40, for example, the actions of those who do not believe are likened to:

ظلمات في بحر لجي يغشاه موج من فوقه موج من فوقه سحاب ظلمات بعضها فوق بعض

the darkness in the abyss of the sea, covered by wave upon wave, above which lie dark clouds heaped upon one another.

The same Qur'anic verse also includes a rhetorical device which al-Hurr replicates in this section of his poem - *jinas*. In terms of vocabulary, a more obvious parallel is the story of Noah in Q11, where Noah's ark is referred to using the word *fulk*, the word for embarkation is *irkab*, paralleling al-Hurr's *rakabnā*, and there are various references to the *majrā*, the course of the ark. The effect of this allusion is simple: through word association, al-Hurr leads his primary audience to think about the pilgrimage journey as a salvific one, a counter-example to the fates of the unbelievers and Noah's son.

The whole premise of al-Hurr's description of the sea in his *qasida* depends on a personification of the waves, which leads us into lyric imagery. In l.2 of the following extract, we have an example of *tatbi'* (metonymy), or an extended metaphor in which the plunging peaks of the waves are figured as a mouth leaning into a kiss. This then leads into lines rich in *tadbij*, or metonymy based on colour comparison:[64]

وقد شق قلب الموج والهول صدرها * فما تركت قلباً ولا تركت صدرا
وتعطف أحياناً على الماء ثغرها * كذي ظماء أهوى لكي يلثم الثغرا

The heart of the wave is torn and terror is its crest * It spares no heart and no breast.
Sometimes the wave inclines its mouth towards the water * As though thirsting, desiring to kiss its mouth.

* * *

ومن يركب الأهوال يبلغ بها المنى * ومن خاض لج البحر يلتقط الدرا
نسينا وصال البيض والسمر والهوى * لأهوال بحر تكسر البيض والسمراء
إذا ما رأينا خضرة الموج أقبلت * نرى للمنايا السود ألوية حمراء
متى رفعوا المرساة والريح عاصف * تظن جبال الأرض قد سيرت تبرى
وقد يرفع الملاح فضل شراعها * فتسبق طير الجو في السير والمسرى

Whoever masters their fears reaches their desire through them * And whoever dives into the depths of the sea catches pearls.
We forgot union with fair and dark women, and love, * In our terror of the sea which breaks blades and tawny lances.
When we saw the green waves approaching * We glimpsed the red banners of black death.

When they weighed anchor and the wind raged * You would think that the
mountains of the earth were being created.
The mariner raised the sails * And she overtook the birds of the sky in her
course at day and night.

Devices such as *tatbi* did not just feature in treatises on literary theory in the
seventeenth century. The Safavid *vaqi'a-nivis* (court historiographer) in the
reign of Sultan Sulayman, Muhammad Tahir Vahid (d. 1112/1701) wrote an
Arabic work on the *shawahid* ('probative quotations') in al-Tabrisi's (d. 548/1154)
Qur'anic commentary *Majma' al-Bayan* (*The Meeting Point of Expression*),
in which he discusses similar lyric lines by poets such as al-Akhtal (d. before
92/710).[65] Discussions in Qur'anic commentaries concerning verses which use
these techniques remind us that the frames of reference which al-Hurr had in
mind when composing his poetry encompassed both literary theory and exegesis.

As we would expect, intertextual connections with other poems are also present
in these lines. One could even search for links as far back as a *qasida* by the pre-
Islamic poet Bishr b. Abi Khazim, which contains a representation of a stormy sea
voyage.[66] In the seventeenth century, Ibn Ma'sum meditated on his own, real-life
experiences of the terror of sea travel in his prosimetric *rihla*, *Salwat al-Gharib*,
which he composed in 1074/1663–4. There, he quotes several pieces which are
structured in a similar way to the extracts by al-Hurr which I cited earlier. In the
following quotation by the grammarian Abu Hayyan al-Gharnati (d. 745/1344),
we have a comparable use of personification, antithesis and metonymy:[67]

لقد ذكرتك والبحر الخضم طغت * أمواجه والورى منه على السفر
في ليلة أسدلت جلباب ظلمتها * وغار كوكبها في أعين البشر
والماء تحت وفوق المزن واكفه * والبرق يستل أسيافاً من الشرر

I remembered you as the waves of the vast sea * Churned and swept the
people on.
On a night which let the skirts of its darkness trail * And whose constellations
were swallowed up in men's eyes.
Water lay below us and dripped from above the clouds * And lightning
unsheathed swords of sparks.

Ibn Ma'sum also quotes a line by Ibn Rashiq (d. *c.* 463/1070–1), the author of the
rhetorical treatise *al-'Umda* (*The Buttress*), who uses a transferred epithet when
describing a night-time storm:[68]

والجو يهطل والرياح عواصف * والليل مسود الذوائب داج

The sky rained in torrents, the winds raged * And black-locked night was dark.

Like these earlier grammarian-poets, al-Hurr stretches the meaning of words and
then builds on the figurative ideas that he has created. Having likened the waves to

mouths thirsting for kisses, he then develops the idea that the ship and the sea are like two doomed lovers at length in the passages that follow:[69]

تميس كما ماست عروس بديعة * منعمة هيفاً غانية عذراء

حكى صدها صد العروس مرارة * وإقبالها إقبال طلعتها الزهراء

تريك سكونا دائما في تحرك * سريع عجيب لا يحس ولا يدري

[The ship] sways like a bride ornamented in finery * Blessed with prosperity, slender, sufficed by her beauty, a maiden.
At times its course resembles the profile of the bride * And the east wind is the beauty of her shining countenance.
It departs, constantly silent as it moves * Quick and marvellous, it neither senses nor knows.

He then applies a similar technique of *tashbih* (simile) to describe the sails of the ship:[70]

تميل بأهلها غروراً وتنثني * فتحسبها رقاصة قد ثنت خصرا

كغانية ملفوفة في إزارها * تمايل سراً في المناهل أو جهرا

تحركنا كالطفل في المهد للكرى * ويمنعنا طيب الكرى أن نرى الذعرا

نعانق ألواح السفينة جهدنا * عناق غوان لا نطيق لها هجرا

نخوض ظلام الغم والبحر والدجى * ولسنا نرى شمساً ولسنا نرى بدرا

* * *

They incline to their mates in their pride and turn * So you would imagine them dancing girls, bending at the waist.
Like a young woman wrapped in a dress * Swaying by a spring, in secret or openly.
Rocking us to sleep like an infant in a cradle * [So that] the bliss of slumber prevented us from feeling fear.
We cling to the planks of the ship, pretending that they are * The necks of maidens whom we cannot bear to leave.
We plunge into the darkness of sorrow, the sea and the gloom * Without seeing the sun and the moon.

* * *

وألواحها السود استقرت قلوبنا * كنبل العيون السود إن رشقت تترى

وتلك الحبال المرسلات كأنها * فروع طوال زان محبوبة بكرا

وذاك العمود المستطيل كقامة * منعمة ممشوقة أطلعت بدرا

وذاك الشراع المشرق اللون مشبه * صباح وصال يطرد الليل والهجرا

The black planks calmed our hearts * Like graceful noble women glancing with black eyes.
And the flowing ropes are like * Long locks adorning a maiden beloved.
And the towering masts are like an extended, * Figure, blessed with prosperity, that has risen as the full moon.
And the sails, the colour of dawn, resemble * The morning of union, driving away the night and separation.

Al-Hurr manages to weave into these passages an eroticism that plays on his rhetorical use of *jinas*, which features heavily here. In the different lines we have examples of homophony such as *falak* (heavens) and *fulk* (ship), *sadr* in the sense of 'chest' and 'prow', and *iqbāl* in the senses of 'good fortune' and 'a favourable east wind'. This exploitation of the common and technical, or immediate and remote, senses of words derived from the same roots allows al-Hurr to build comparisons which cast love for the safety of the ship as desire for beautiful women, allaying the terror of the voyage through eroticism. In so doing, he constructs a masked intertextual relationship with the earlier poets quoted by Ibn Maʿsum. These connections are also evident if we compare al-Hurr's piece with a *qasida* which Ibn Maʿsum himself composed on his return journey from India to the Arabian Peninsula at the very end of the seventeenth century. In l.2 of the following extract, Ibn Maʿsum's phrasing and ideas closely correspond with those of al-Hurr in his description of the abyss of the ocean:[71]

إذا ما امتطيت الفلك مقتحم البحر * ووليت ظهري الهند منشرح الصدر

When I boarded the ship, diving into the sea * And turned my back to
India with a broad chest.

وأركبني فلك النجاة فأصبحت * على ثبج الداماء سابحة تجري

He put me in the ship of success and I became * A glider coursing over the
middle of the sea.

كأني بفلكي حين مدت جناحها * وطارت مطار النسر حلق عن وكر

As though I in my boat, when it spread its wings * And flew the course of an
eagle soaring from its nest . . .

The simile used in this last line, likening the boat to a bird as it courses over the waves, displays a distinct similarity with al-Hurr's description of the same phenomenon, suggesting that these poets shared a defined list of concepts which they wanted to address in their narratives:[72]

سرت كسهام أرسلت عن قسيها * تسابق رجع الطرف سيراً إذا مرا
تزيد بها الأعمار للقوم إن نجوا * وقد تنقص الآمال بل تقطع العمرا
ولما قطعنا ظلمة البحر والسرى * أضاءت لنا الأنوار من مكة الغرا
فقد أشرقت أبصارنا وقلوبنا * بها وأرتوت إذ ذاك أكبادنا الحرا
وقد قابلتنا طبعة الكعبة التي * قطعنا إليها بالسرى البر والبحرا

It went like an arrow shot from a bow * Outpacing the course of the eye
as it passed.
If they succeeded, the passengers' lives would be lengthened * But the journey
might have diminished their hopes or cut short their existence.
When we cut through the darkness of the sea and our nocturnal journey *
The lights of splendid Mecca shone for us.

Our sight and our hearts dawned in * Them, and at that moment our feverish
livers were refreshed.
And the impression of the Ka'ba, towards which we * Crossed land and sea,
received us.

It is almost as though Ibn Ma'sum could be capping al-Hurr when he too comes
to describe the emotional relief of arriving on dry land:[73]

أسفت على المرسى بشاطء جدة * فجددت الأفراح لي طلعة البر
وهب نسيم القرب من نحو مكة * ولاح سنى البيت المحرم والحجر
وسارت ركابي لا تمل من السرى * إلى موطن التقوى ومنتجع البر

It blew to its anchorage by the shore of Jidda * And the ascent onto land
renewed my delight.
The breeze of imminence blew from Mecca * And the resplendence of
the sacred house and the stone became apparent.
My mount travelled on through the night, unwearyingly, * Towards the
homeland of faith and the locus of piety.

It is possible that Ibn Ma'sum had actually read al-Hurr's poem: we have the
evidence of *Sulafat al-'Asr* and *Amal al-Amil* to show that the two men knew
of one another's work. However, his *qasida* is not designed to establish a direct
dialogue with al-Hurr. It is simply that the transnational professional community
of scholars in which the two men participated shared the same cultural literacy,
had a common canon and operated with the same literary competence. This was
a Shi'i educational community, connected in part by the migration of 'Amili
scholars on the Iran-Mecca-Hyderabad axis.

Conclusion

This chapter has identified a distinct approach to the composition of Arabic poetry
in seventeenth-century Iran, focusing on the imbrication of literary production
within philological scholarship as a whole. We have seen that poets such as al-Hurr
did have a strong interest in composing lyric poetry, and while opinions may differ
as to the taxonomies that we should use for describing the forms of *adab* produced
by members of the *'ulama'*, I would argue that modern literary scholars should
not discount the verse of poet-divines in the belief that it lies beyond our remit.
However, it does seem to me that this poetry should be studied with due regard
for its authors' fields of reference. The lyric poems composed by al-Hurr and the
community of 'Amili scholars in Mashhad and Isfahan not only connected their
authors locally through the use of forms and themes, and bound the diasporic
'Amili community together, but also functioned as sites for playing with semantics
and rhetoric, and potentially opened up debates about knowledge and cognition
that would have resonated within study circles. The 'Amili community in Iran may

therefore have used Arabic poetry in a more obviously scholastic way than many of their contemporaries in the Arabian Peninsula, even as writers like al-Hurr consulted a corpus of Arabic texts, like *Sulafat al-ʿAsr*, which were also accessible to his contemporaries in places such as Yemen. Yet, when he came to compose his versified pilgrimage narrative, al-Hurr evoked a body of images that feature in the work of his contemporaries across the Arabian Sea, once again connecting his local environment with a transoceanic high culture.

Chapter 5

HYDERABAD

FARAJ ALLAH AL-SHUSHTARI AND SALIK YAZDI

Salik Yazdi and Faraj Allah al-Shushtari: A collective biography

The contemporaries Salik Yazdi and Faraj Allah al-Shushtari should both be considered major poets of the mid-seventeenth century. If they are virtually unknown today, it is because their works remain unpublished and in manuscript.[1] Both men are likely to have been born in the final decade of the sixteenth century, both pursued intersecting itineraries, and the evidence suggests that they encountered one another in the Deccan. Faraj Allah's family came from Shushtar, in Khuzistan, south-west Iran. As we shall see, he evidently spent some time in Baghdad, Shiraz and Isfahan, before he migrated to Golkonda, where he attained great prominence as a secretary and a poet of Persian under Sultan 'Abd Allah the Qutbshah. As shown in Chapter 2, he was also patronized as a poet of Arabic by Sultan 'Abd Allah's chief minister, Nizam al-Din Ahmad. The sources suggest that he died in Golkonda towards the end of the seventeenth century.

Born in Yazd, Salik spent time in Shiraz, Isfahan, Baghdad and Basra, before leaving for India, where he first tried – perhaps without much success – to carve out a place for himself as a poet at the Mughal court. He subsequently found favour in Golkonda, where he was present alongside Faraj Allah in the middle of the century. He then left the Deccan for North India once more, entering the service of the Mughal emperor Shah Jahan in 1066/1655–6. He is known to have died, impoverished, in Delhi in 1081/1670–1.

This chapter develops a picture of the two poets' lives, their migrations and their literary networks. It also offers a comparative reading of their careers, exploring how they used their poetry to connect with their audiences. It is necessary to establish the contexts in which the two men operated if we are even to categorize them as migrant poets, as this basic research has not yet been done.

Faraj Allah al-Shushtari

Faraj Allah features in a work about Shushtar and its famous sons by his contemporary and fellow townsman 'Ala al-Mulk Shushtari Mar'ashi (date of death unknown). ʿAla al-Mulk was the son of the jurist and scholar Nur Allah, an émigré to India who was made chief judge of Lahore in the late sixteenth century, and who is today remembered as a Shiʿi martyr, flogged to death on the orders of the Mughal emperor Jahangir in 1019/1610.[2] The existence of ʿAla al-Mulk's work, which is entitled simply *Firdaws* (*Paradise*), points to the importance of networks of sectarian and civic allegiance on the international stage, since it testifies to the transregional spread of scholars and poets far beyond the town of Shushtar, and to their continuing contact with, and loyalty to, one another. These networks were evidently durative, and when one citizen of a particular town forged a career in a distant land, it opened up opportunities for his compatriots. Such may well have been the case with the poet Khalqi (d. 1047/1637–8), another scion of Shushtar who emigrated to the Deccan, where he taught at the royal hospital (*Dar al-Shifa ʾ*) in Hyderabad and was employed to edit several books for Sultan ʿAbd Allah.[3] ʿAla al-Mulk's *Firdaws* makes it clear that Khalqi and Faraj Allah shared the same teacher, another reason which encourages us to speculate that Faraj Allah may have been prompted to travel to the Deccan because of his fellow townsman's success there.[4]

Writing from the perspective of a contemporary, ʿAla al-Mulk describes Faraj Allah as a student of the theologian Mir Taqi al-Din Nassaba of Shiraz (d. 1019/1610–11).[5] This indicates that Faraj Allah spent time in Shiraz during his youth, and gives us a terminus ante quem for his birth; if he received instruction from Nassaba, it is likely that he was born at a point between 1590 and 1595. This supposition is supported by Ibn Maʿsum's statement that Faraj Allah was upwards of seventy years old when he encountered him in the *majlis* of Nizam al-Din Ahmad.[6] As Faraj Allah was one of Nassaba's students, we can also locate him within a network of religious scholars who were trained in Shiraz and who attained prominence in India.[7] In addition to giving this piece of information, ʿAla al-Mulk describes Faraj Allah as a 'learned man, poet, secretary and composer of riddles' (*fāzil u shāʿir u munshī u muʿammāʾī*), which would tend to confirm what the facts of his education suggest: that Faraj Allah may have been a professional poet, but that poetry was not the only way in which he earned his living.[8] Nasrabadi's *tazkira* emphasizes that Faraj Allah attained 'limitless property and wealth' in the service of Sultan ʿAbd Allah.[9] It may have been through practising a series of complementary professions at the court of Golkonda, including the composition of lyric and panegyric poetry, secretarial work and scholarship, that Faraj Allah met with such success. However, it is clear that he was celebrated as a poet in his own time, as Saʾib (d. 1086–7/1676) responded to one of his *ghazals*.[10]

The only other concrete date to hand concerning the life of Faraj Allah can be deduced from an indirect quotation ascribed to the literary biographer Taqi Awhadi (d. after 1042/1632–3), who purportedly met the poet at the port of Cambay in Gujarat.[11] We know that that Awhadi was in Gujarat from *c.* 1015–21/1606–13, and if this statement is true it would therefore suggest that Faraj Allah made straight for India after the conclusion of his studies.[12] The literary biographer Qudrat Allah Gupamavi (d. 1281/1864–5) states that Faraj Allah died towards the end of the seventeenth century.[13]

Turning away from the narrative sources, we can look to Faraj Allah's own poetry for information about his life. Substantial caveats are required, because the statements which he makes in his lyric verse are not intended to be positive. Nevertheless, he does make some suggestive references, such as the remark:[14]

عبارتم عربی گو معانیم عجمی * کلام من عجمی مغز استخوان عربیست

My style is Arabic, my images Persian * My discourse is Persian, my flesh
and blood are Arab.

Comments such as this are often made by poets writing in an adopted idiom of high culture.[15] In this case, they cast Faraj Allah as an Arab whose approach to writing mingled the imagery and rhetoric of Arabic verse with those of Persian. It may seem to us reductive that a poet who so obviously inhabited cosmopolitan spaces would create such an antithesis between lineage and culture. Nevertheless, these remarks point to a recognition of the idea that identity could be constructed in different ways. Faraj Allah is suggesting his participation in a shared artistic idiom of Persian high culture and his embrace of a way of being common to Safavid men of learning trained in the Islamic religious sciences.

We also find allusions to cities in Faraj's Persian verse. The poet's evocation of Baghdad and Isfahan would have acquired a heightened significance if he did actually spend time in them, marking nostalgia for both a textually constructed ideal and a real, remembered past. Baghdad and the Tigris are the home of his idealized beloved, a Yusuf of beauty,[16] while he speaks of Isfahan in the following terms:[17]

عشرت آبادی فرج چون اصفهان افتاده است * کس چرا باشد به این حسرت درین غربت سرا

Why would anyone be so distraught, in this house of strangers * As Faraj
when he arrived in Isfahan, the abode of pleasure?

He also refers to Shiraz, where we have located him in his youth, and he balances Iran against India in representing his former and current existence:[18]

نیست با آب و هوای هند طبعم سازکار * آب شیراز و هوای اصفهان می‌سازدم

My nature can find no harmony with the land of India * The waters of
Shiraz and the air of Isfahan suit me.

And:[19]

رشک ایران شد دکن در عهد عبد الله شاه * هرچه خواهی هست اما بادهٔ شیراز نیست

The Deccan has become the envy of Iran in the age of King ʿAbd Allah * It is
whatever you may wish it to be, but there is no wine of Shiraz.

While it may superficially appear that lines such as these are designed to vaunt Iran over India, a more nuanced interpretation is required. Faraj's references to the cities of Iran evoke the qualities for which they were renowned in the historical corpus of poetry: Isfahan was famous for its equitable climate, while Shiraz was known for its wine, and for the canals, most particularly the Ruknabad, which watered the city.[20] Faraj's comparisons do not denigrate the Deccan. Instead, they are purposefully designed to imply that, at the time when he was writing, there was not the same historical weight of literary representations of the Deccan as an idyll in Persian which already framed understandings of cities like Shiraz and Isfahan. We find further images which seem designed to re-orient the Deccan and to place it on the map of Persian poetry, such as:[21]

در دکن بنشین گل از کشمیر و از کابل بچین

'Settle in the Deccan and pick flowers from Kashmir and Kabul', an allusion to the corpus of poems in which Kashmir is depicted as the garden of India, and the tulips of Kabul are celebrated. Another seemingly complimentary image plays with the story of Khaqani's (d. between 582 and 595/1186 and 1199) imprisonment in Shirvan:[22]

چند آزار زبونان فرج الله کشم * من نه خاقانیم و ملک دکن شروان نیست

For how long should I, Faraj Allah, bear the cruelty of the contemptible? * I am not Khaqani, and the realm of the Deccan is not Shirvan.

Salik Yazdi

While our understanding of Faraj Allah's travels must remain fragmentary in some respects, a fuller picture is available for his slightly younger contemporary, Salik Yazdi. To begin, Nasrabadi offers the following information on the poet: Salik started his career in Shiraz, and then travelled to Isfahan in the guise of a dervish.[23] He subsequently emigrated to Golkonda, where he became affiliated with the court of Sultan ʿAbd Allah.[24] Nasrabadi then states that 'when they expelled the Mughals from the Deccan, he went to Shahjahanabad [Delhi]'.[25] This is an ambiguous turn of phrase, but, as suggested herein, Salik's poems, most particularly his chronograms and his odes, may indicate that Nasrabadi is referring here to the defection of the *Mir Jumla* Muhammad Saʿid Ardistani from the side of the Qutbshahs to that of the Mughals in 1066/1655. Further support for this thesis is available in the biographical anthology of Kishan Chand Ikhlas (d. after 1160/1747), *Hamisha Bahar* (*Forever Spring* or *The Oxeye Daisy*), where it is reported that Salik entered the service of Shah Jahan in 1066/1655–6, the same year as the defection.[26]

Nasrabadi continues to state that after Salik's arrival in Delhi, Danishmand Khan (d. 1081/1670), a poet-patron also known by the pen name Shafiʿa Yazdi, showed him particular favour, on account of the fact that the two men were both from Yazd.[27] Salik became impoverished when his property was stolen from him, and he died in Delhi, sometime prior to the completion of the first draft of *Tazkira-yi Nasrabadi* (1086/1676).[28] The dating can be refined from other sources, according to whom Salik died in 1081/1670–1.[29]

Considerably more detail, which invites us to rethink the statements of Nasrabadi and the other biographers, can be found in Salik's *divan*. It is clear that his travels were more convoluted than the anthologies suggest. One poem, which must date among his earliest, describes the house of Mirza Hakim, the *kalantar* (mayor) of Yazd, his hometown, indicating that he may have been supported as a poet from a young age.[30] As one would expect of a budding poet, he evidently progressed from Yazd to the more competitive environment of Shiraz, because he composed three poems in praise of Mu'in al-Din Muhammad, 'the Asaf of the Age', who became vizier of Fars in 1018/1610.[31] In one of these poems, a eulogy, he writes that he has praised Mu'in al-Din Muhammad 'for some time'.[32] Taken together, this information suggests that Salik may have spent an extended period in Shiraz during the second or third decade of the seventeenth century, enjoying a form of patronage that was not royal but aristocratic. Aristocrats and high-ranking bureaucrats would continue to support him throughout his career.

A small number of Salik's occasional and commemorative poems support the biographers' claims that he continued from Shiraz to Isfahan. It is worth bearing in mind that the majority of his output consisted of *ghazals*, and if he met with success in the Safavid capital he probably achieved it through composing lyric, rather than panegyric poetry. Part of his audience may have consisted, not of an elite, but of a more middle-class reading public. Nevertheless, he did dedicate a *tarkib-band* to the *sadr* Mirza Habib Allah, one of the highest officials in the land;[33] and he wrote another *tarkib-band* in praise of Amir Khan, the *qurchi-bashi*, head of the Safavid royal guard from 1041/1632 to 1046/1637, during the reign of Shah Safi (r. 1038/1629–1052/1642).[34] The only piece preserved in the extant manuscripts which he wrote in praise of a Safavid monarch is a short *qasida* composed when a falcon which Shah Safi had lost was recovered.[35] It is most probable that these three poems do not locate Salik within the Safavid royal entourage; instead, they may mark his attempts to gain a foothold within larger networks that expanded out from the palace. A poem dedicated, after all, is not automatically a poem accepted.

It was probably at this point, in around 1635, that Salik decided to emigrate to India. We can trace his path from Isfahan to Iraq. A short *masnavi* in praise of Baghdad and the bathhouse constructed by its Safavid governor, the Georgian Biktash Khan, locates him there at some point between 1040/1631–1047/1638.[36] It seems that he then travelled south, towards the Persian Gulf. In a *tarkib-band*, he describes a ship which he saw at Basra, and praises its governor, 'Ali Padishah, who was in power from 1033/1624 to 1055/1645.[37] We are left to speculate about how exactly Salik reached India, but the port of Basra was a major hub of connectivity with Sind, Gujarat, Malabar and Kerala in the 1630s, and his description of a ship in his poem to the city's governor is suggestive.[38]

It is from the early 1640s onwards that we can begin to speak of Salik's movements with precision, because his chronograms from this time are recorded in the manuscripts. The evidence indicates that Salik made serious attempts to gain the favour of the Mughals before he headed south. In a chronogram, he celebrates the birth of a son of Prince Dara Shukuh (d. 1069/1659) in 1053/1643–4.[39] He also dedicated an undated eulogy to a certain Asaf Khan, who is likely to be the illustrious *khan-i saman*, one-time governor of Bengal and the Punjab, and commander of the Mughal armies in the Deccan.[40] As this Asaf Khan died in 1051/1641, the existence of these poems would give us a terminus ante quem for Salik's arrival in north India that is consistent with the view that he left Iraq by 1638 at the latest.

The year 1053/1643–4 may have been the year in which Salik travelled to the Deccan, because, in addition to the chronogram on the birth of Dara Shukuh's son, he also has another chronogram dated to this year, celebrating the birth of a boy to a certain Janbaz Khan.[41] The only likely candidate who bears this name is an Iranian émigré with the proper name Ahmad Husayni Mazandarani, who is mentioned in the commonplace of Nizam al-Din Ahmad Gilani, the doctor of Sultan ʿAbd Allah the Qutbshah.[42]

Salik obviously hoped to make an entrance in Golkonda, as one of his panegyrics to Sultan ʿAbd Allah is introduced by a rubric stating that it was composed when the author was travelling from Akbarabad (Agra) to Hyderabad.[43] The quantity of his poems dedicated to the elite of the Qutbshahi sultanate suggests that it was in the Deccan, finally, where he found a consistent source of royal and aristocratic support. By arriving in Hyderabad, he joined the ranks of a number of émigré poets from Iran who clearly formed an elastic network in the Qutbshahi sultanate, including not only Faraj Allah al-Shushtari, but also Amani of Kirman (fl. *c.* 1070/1659–60), who wrote panegyrics in praise of Sultan ʿAbd Allah. Like Salik, Amani had eulogized Mirza Habib Allah in Isfahan.[44] Another poet who formed part of this network is Mir Kazim Husayni of Najaf, known as Karim, who composed a long ethical work for Sultan ʿAbd Allah which reformulates narratives taken from Mirrors for Princes, including Nizami's *Haft Paykar*.[45]

Salik's chronograms from Golkonda cover the period between 1055/1646 and 1064/1654, indicating that he stayed there for around a decade. One of his major patrons appears to have been Sultan ʿAbd Allah himself, to whom he addressed eleven *qasaʾid* and dated pieces. Some of these are eulogies, but others are occasional poems which speak to the ways in which he interacted with the sultan. He memorialized ʿAbd Allah's construction of a bridge at the port of Masulipatnam in 1057/1648;[46] an orchard in 1063/1653–1064/1654;[47] a house of mirrors in 1063/1653[48] and celebrated the renovation of a palace in 1055/1645.[49] Poems such as these have the air of officially sanctioned performance pieces, designed to chronicle the king's building programme. Like Kalim Kashani's poems on the architectural patronage of the Mughal emperor Shah Jahan, 'poem and building [are] united as projections of royal dominion across time and space' in these texts.[50]

Salik did not just write for Sultan ʿAbd Allah. His extant poems locate him in a network of émigré Iranian scholars, bureaucrats and military leaders who were responsible for much of Golkonda's political direction. He composed three poems in praise of the *pishwa* Muhammad ibn al-Khatun al-ʿAmili (d. 1050s/1640s), who was one of the most eminent political figures and scholars in the first half of ʿAbd Allah's reign, and an exegete, a scholar of logic and philosophy, a prose stylist, and a patron in the fields of lexicography, historiography, the religious sciences and poetry.[51] Salik's major patrons, however, to whom he dedicated a combined total of twelve poems, were Ibn al-Khatun's successor, Mir Muhammad Saʿid Ardistani, *Mir Jumla* of Golkonda, and Mir Muhammad Saʿid's son, Muhammad Amin. Like the poems which he composed for the sultan, the pieces that Salik wrote for these two men range from straightforward encomia to commemorations of their constructions. Mir Muhammad Saʿid was a diamond merchant and a shipping magnate in addition to acting as prime minister of the Qutbshahi state, and so it is perhaps unsurprising that Salik's poems to him include a celebration of a ship that he had launched in 1057/1647.[52] The date in this poem is given through the words ʿA ship on the way to the eternal Kaʿbaʾ, a reminder of the transregional system of connectivity in which Salik and his patrons consciously participated.[53]

Salik also memorialized Mir Muhammad Saʿid Ardistani's military campaigns against the rajas of the Carnatic, commemorating the capture of fortresses at Guti in 1056/1646 and Gandikota in 1060/1650.[54] These campaigns were conducted with the support of the sultan, but Mir Muhammad Saʿid's autonomy was evidently a source of some worry for ʿAbd Allah, and Salik's composition of these pieces may, to an extent, mark the poet's increasing support for, and reliance on, the family of Mir Muhammad Saʿid. Salik would go on to write a chronogram in 1061/1650-1, celebrating the construction of a mansion for Muhammad Amin.[55] As we saw in Chapter 2, similar poems were composed in Arabic for Ibn Maʿsum and his father when they took up residence in new homes in Hyderabad. Salik's Persian piece attempts to tread something of a political tightrope, expressing loyalty to the family of the *Mir Jumla* while also offering a degree of praise to the Sultan.

Since Salik had thrown his lot in with the family of Mir Muhammad Saʿid Ardistani, the events of 1066/1656 had an inevitable effect on the poet's career. That year, Mir Muhammad Saʿid collaborated with the future Mughal emperor Awrangzib (d. 1118/1707), at this point responsible for Shah Jahan's Deccan campaign, in the co-ordination of the Mughal attack on Golkonda.[56] Sultan ʿAbd Allah had Muhammad Amin temporarily arrested and incarcerated. In early 1066/1655, Mir Muhammad Saʿid was formally welcomed by the Mughals and began the journey north to Delhi.[57] Muhammad Amin followed in his wake. While it remains a matter for speculation, it seems likely that this is the moment of ʿexpulsionʾ which Nasrabadi describes in his biography of Salik.

Regardless of the exact trigger for his move north, Salik's praise poems indicate that he returned to Delhi in around 1655, and began to eulogize a new series of patrons. There is only one poem dedicated to Shah Jahan.[58] A further two are addressed to Zafar Khan Ahsan (d. 1073/1662-3), the governor of Kabul and Kashmir who is discussed in more detail in Chapter 6.[59] Another praises Shayasta

Khan (d. 1105/1694), the son of one of Salik's dedicatees from his first stay in the north, Asaf Khan.[60] Shayasta Khan was close to Awrangzib and had been heavily involved in the Mughal campaign against Golkonda, and so Salik's connection to him may be indicative of the partisan circles in which he found himself in Delhi. Curiously, there is not a single poem by Salik in either of the Tehran and Hyderabad manuscripts which is dedicated to his supposed patron in Delhi, Danishmand Khan. As we saw for his sojourn in Isfahan, this absence opens up the likelihood that it was through short, lyric *ghazals*, not long, formal pieces, that Salik forged his most important literary relationships in Delhi.

A cross-reading of the biographies of Faraj Allah and Salik and the kinds of poetry which they wrote raises a series of interesting problems. Both men covered an expansive geographical area, and their itineraries are marked by affinities, such as their stays in Iraq, which highlight the importance of hubs of connectivity like the port city of Basra to literary production in the Safavid-Ottoman borderlands. Thanks to his eulogies, we know a lot more about Salik's movements and the mostly aristocratic, or aristocratic-bureaucratic, contexts in which he tried to find success, than we do about Faraj Allah and his migrations. We may speculate that Faraj Allah enjoyed greater security than Salik, partly because he was not just a professional poet, but a secretary and a scholar too, and partly because his bilingualism with Arabic gave him a second set of interlocutors in India. However, I would like to hold off from interpreting the evidence in this way. At the heart of this issue lies the question of why individuals such as Salik and Faraj Allah travelled. Did they journey to India because they were unsuccessful in Iran and Iraq, or did they regard circulation positively, as the key to a greater exposure to the world, as a way to generate more income and to forge connections, and as a means to improve their writing? The evidence overwhelmingly suggests that figures like Salik and Faraj Allah thought in a networked way: travel was an inherent aspect of a literary career.

Salik's Khusraw u Shirin: A dialogue with the corpus

The manuscript of Salik's collected works which is now housed at the University of Tehran contains a short *masnavi* poem entitled *Dastan-i Khusraw u Shirin az Tab'-i Salik Yazdi* (*The Story of Khusraw and Shirin [Re-Told] from the Temperament of Salik Yazdi*). The most famous version of this romance, which tells the story of the affair between the Sasanian king Khusraw Parviz (r. 590–628 CE) and the princess Shirin, forms part of the *Khamsa* (*Five Works*) of Nizami Ganjavi (d. 613/1217 or earlier). In the centuries after Nizami's death, poets authored responses to his narratives, and in time these responses became models for imitation themselves.[61] The game, if we are to call it that, became increasingly complex over time, as each imitation drew on its forebears and developed links with more and more versions of the story.[62] By the beginning of the seventeenth century, at least eleven poets had written *masnavis* entitled *Khusraw u Shirin* or a variant thereof, and many further narrative poems had engaged with elements of the *Khusraw u Shirin* corpus, from plot devices, to imagery, to the cultivation of a similar emotional tone in representing an ideal of romance.[63] An evolving tendency to shift from focusing on the relationship between Khusraw and Shirin to concentrating on the relationship between Shirin and Farhad may reflect a desire to emphasize Farhad's more self-sacrificing code of love at the expense of Khusraw's 'concupiscent passion'.[64]

On the basis of the titles alone, it may be tempting to imagine that the later versions of the narrative are conservative in their approach to storytelling, in their depiction of the protagonists, and in their use of imagery, but in fact they each possess a unique voice. A connected group of poets who lived in Timurid Herat, including Jami (d. 898/1492), ʿAli Shir Navaʾi (d. 906/1501) and Hatifi (d. 927/1521), may have been the first set of prominent contemporaries to publish responses to *Khusraw u Shirin* which were in dialogue with one another, each designed to distinguish the author from his interlocutors but to acknowledge the chain in which he found himself.[65] Navaʾi's response was composed in Chaghatai Turkic, developing a multilingual aspect to the reception of the story which would be amplified throughout the early modern period.[66] Because of dynastic connections and the circulation of cultural capital, Herat was an equal source of inspiration to authors active in Safavid Iran, the Toqay-Timurid Khanate of Central Asia, Mughal India and the Deccan sultanates, and poets active in these polities during the sixteenth and seventeenth centuries set about creating their own networks of *Khusraw u Shirin* texts, which re-articulated the geographical locus of literary authority in the Persianate world.

The recorded number of Persian versions of *Khusraw u Shirin* composed during the seventeenth century is at least nine, almost as many as were written during the preceding four centuries since Nizami's death, and so it seems that this period witnessed a vogue for re-fashioning the story.[67] References to the love triangle between Khusraw, Shirin and Farhad were ubiquitous. They were commonly alluded to in contemporary lyric poetry – including the lyrics of Faraj Allah:[68]

گر شود شیرین ز فوت کوهکن غمگین چه سود * ماتم فرهاد را در بیستون باید گرفت

What benefit is there if the death of the man who levelled mountains saddens Shirin? * Farhad must be mourned at Bisutun.

Narrative sources relate that murals depicting the protagonists of Nizami's romances were also to be found in the mansions of Hyderabad during the seventeenth century, including images of Khusraw spying Shirin bathing, and manuscript copies of all the pre-existing versions of *Khusraw u Shirin* were circulated and read at this time.[69] Furthermore, re-imaginings of Nizami's romances formed a significant part of the landscape of Dakhni literature which was also being produced during the seventeenth century under Qutbshahi patronage.[70] The popularity of the story and common understandings of how it should be depicted would have meant that any seventeenth-century poet embarking on a rewriting of *Khusraw u Shirin* faced a considerable test of their creative powers, since engaging with the same material, the same metre and the same fields of imagery as their predecessors exposed them to greater critical scrutiny and actively encouraged comparison between them and other poets. That readers thought in this comparative way is clear from remarks made by the anthologist Nasrabadi, who writes of Mirza Jaʿfar Qazvini (d. 1021/1612): 'In the imperfect opinion of the present writer, nobody after Shaykh Nizami told the story of *Khusraw u Shirin* better than he did.'[71] However, a cross-reading of the many different seventeenth-century recensions of the story suggests that we should step back from considering them a uniform mode or genre of writing. When one actually sits down to compare them, the differences between them are palpable.[72] The *Farhad u Shirin* of Mir ʿAqil Kawsari of Hamadan, for example, is both far longer and far more plot-driven than many of the other seventeenth-century rewritings, and the characters of the nurse and Mahin Banu, who both play an important role in Nizami's original, figure prominently.[73] The version by Mashriqi of Herat, by contrast, is far more lyrical, and concentrates on theorizing love and passion.[74]

When Salik Yazdi came to write his version of the story in Golkonda, sometime around 1060/1650, he considered the other recensions which had been composed in Iran and India. The introduction to his poem includes a catalogue of past poets whom he regarded as models, including Vahshi Bafqi (d. 991/1583), who spent most of his life in Salik's hometown of Yazd and the nearby palace complex at Taft in Iran;[75] and one of Vahshi's correspondents, ʿUrfi Shirazi (d. 999/1591), who emigrated to India and was supported by ministers of the Mughal emperor Akbar (d. 1014/1605).[76]

Three of Salik's contemporaries whose versions of the story we should also consider when thinking about his rewriting are: the aforementioned Jaʿfar Qazvini, who rose to prominence under the Mughal emperor Jahangir (r. 1014/1605–1038/1627); Adham (d. 1060/1650), who spent time at the court of Shah Jahan (r. 1037/1628–1068/1657) at a similar time to Salik's first visit;[77] and Mirza Muhammad Amin Shahristani (d. 1047/1637) who pursued careers in Iran, Mughal north India and the Deccan, serving for a time as prime minister of Golkonda under Sultan Muhammad Quli (d. 1020/1612).[78] Using the pen name Ruh al-Amin, Shahristani wrote not just a version of *Khusraw u Shirin* but also a complete set of responses to the other four poems of Nizami's *Khamsa*.[79] His employment at the court of the Qutbshahs makes it likely that Salik read his version of the story too.

The recension of Salik's *Khusraw u Shirin* as it survives in the Tehran manuscript is incomplete, and it is therefore impossible to know for sure whether the poet had intended it as a full-length romance or as a representation in miniature, but the way in which the extant text treats the narrative suggest that the complete story may have been short, a maximum of about forty pages. Salik's approach is marked by a pronounced lyricism, to the extent that points of narrative action famous from Nizami's version are largely absent from his poem. The rubricated headings of the sections of the poem show how Salik works out the narrative:

482 – *The Story of Khusraw and Shirin [Re-Told] from the Temperament of Salik Yazdi*

483 – On the feats of the king of men and the lion of heaven ['Ali ibn Abi Talib].

485 – In praise of the pivot of princes, king 'Abd Allah [the Qutbshah].

487 – The reason for the book's composition, and praise of 'Inayat Allah, the doctor.

489 – A parable [on alchemy, alluding to the difficulty of inventing images which Nizami had not, leading into a discussion of poetic creativity and the corpus].

493 – In praise of speech.

494 – The beginning of the story.

495 – A definition of passion.

497 – Shirin's arrival at the garden and Khusraw's observation of her approach.

501 – Khusraw goes hunting.

503 – Khusraw arrives at the garden.

508 – Farhad goes to Bisutun.

509 – Shirin goes to see Bisutun.

511 – The text breaks off.

As these subtitles imply, Salik's version of the romance consists of a series of scenes, rather than a continuous story. Like Nizami and many of the later authors, Salik begins the text with encomia to speech (*sukhan*) and passion (*'ishq*), but then he takes the narrative in a different direction. The events which drive the action forward are flattened out, and focus is instead given to linking descriptions of the natural world with the interior, emotional landscape of the protagonists. The only four characters to receive any attention are Khusraw, Shirin, Farhad (the master builder who acts as Khusraw's antithesis) and Shapur, Khusraw's right-hand man who brings the lovers together. While Salik was able to strip out much of the narrative because the plot of the story would have been familiar to his readers, it was his deliberate choice to pare down the action in this way. In general, his approach contrasts strongly with that of his near-contemporary Ruh al-Amin, who displays a clear concern for exploring the motivation of the characters and plotting, and who retains additional characters present in Nizami's original, including Khusraw's father, Hurmuz; Shirin's mother, Mahin Banu; and Shirin's horse, Shabdiz. Salik's diminished focus on narrative, in contrast, is much more closely connected to the version of 'Urfi, another incomplete work, in which the story is confined to the two locations of an isolated garden and Mount Bisutun. 'Urfi even states that he has minimal interest in the characters, and is instead motivated to explore the nature of love, which points towards a re-evaluation of the function of the romance, away from narrativity and towards lyricism.[80]

A close reading of the ways in which the poets treat the same imagery serves to show how Salik constructed his own textual network. Salik begins the first main section of his narrative, 'Shirin's arrival at the garden and Khusraw's observation of her approach', in the following way:[81]

صباحی خنده زن بر صبح نوروز * که دلها را بود غم عشرت آموز

شفق پیرایه بر آفاق می‌بست * چو بنّای خورنق طاق می‌بست

هوا چون شاهدان در غاره کاری * بسر می‌زد گل از ابر بهاری

One daybreak, smiling over new year's morn * When the sorrow that afflicts
hearts turns to joy,
Rosy dawn decorated the horizon * Erecting an arch like the architect
of Khawarnaq.
The sky poured droplets from the spring clouds onto the roses * Like beauties
when they drink wine in the morning.

As the day dawns, we come across the intoxicated Shirin, asleep. The breeze,
personified, wends its way towards her:[82]

صبا ترسان و لرزان بر قفا رفت * که می‌داند که بر جانش چها رفت
بپرسید از صبا شیرین طناز * که ای نامحرم خلوتگه راز
مگر از هستی خود سیر گشتی * که در خلوت سرایم چیر گشتی
صبا افتاد بر خاک و دعا گفت * دعایی در خور زلف دو تا گفت
که چون پرسیدی از من کز کجایم * نیم بیگانه یار آشنایم
غلام طره است نامم نسیم است * مرا با سنبلت عهد قدیم است

Trembling and afraid, the east wind touched the nape of her neck * Who can
know the thoughts that passed through its soul?
The playful Shirin asked the breeze: * 'Trespasser upon my secret place
of solitude',
'Surely you have had enough of your existence * That you boldly enter my
chamber?'
The east wind fell to the earth and let out a prayer * A prayer for the life of
her two long tresses.
Saying: 'Why do you ask me where I am from? * I am no stranger, but
well-known to you'.
'This is the slave of your ringlets, my name is 'Zephyr' * I am an old lover
of your hyacinthine locks'.

We can think of the connections between these lines and the rest of the *Khusraw
u Shirin* corpus in terms of a series of linkages, some of which are made strong
and overt, and others of which are present but de-emphasized. Like the other
responses to Nizami discussed here, Salik's poem is in the same metre as Nizami's
original *Khusraw and Shirin, hazaj-i musaddas-i mahzuf*, providing a rhythmic
ground that is primarily associated with the story.[83] The relationship with Nizami's
text also extends to rhetoric and imagery. On the level of the plot, the closest
passage in Nizami's romance concerns the arrival of Shapur at the meadow where
Shirin and her companions come to entertain themselves.[84] The zephyr in Salik's
version, another emissary, acts as a distant echo of Shapur. Nizami describes
Shirin's entourage of maidens as being in a place that is 'forbidden' (*mahram*),
whereas the breeze in Salik's rendition is an uninvited trespasser (*nā-mahram*,
using the same word).[85] In another parallel, Nizami states that the women 'brought
roses and sprinkled them with wine', an image which Salik echoes in the line: 'The
sky poured droplets from the spring clouds onto the roses / Like beauties when

they drink wine in the morning.'[86] These similarities, which are not particularly noticeable to the casual reader, nevertheless suggest that Salik's engagement with Nizami was deliberate and sustained. He bore Nizami's text in mind even when he tried to achieve a completely different effect, transposing his predecessor's images and rhetoric into new settings.

If Salik acknowledges Nizami, he creates a far more obvious connection to 'Urfi, borrowing from him the scene in which the breeze wakes Shirin. 'Urfi depicts the scene as follows:[87]

نسیم باغ گفتی در دماغش * مقیمم تا برم در صحن باغش

گلی در گلشن آرم مست و چالاک * که هر گل صد گریبان را زند چاک

ز بوی گل در آمد عطر در تاب * به یک عطسه تهی شد چشمش از خواب

بیاض چشم گلگون چهره پر نور * سراپا همچو چشم خویش مخمور

ز نرگس دور کرد آشفته سنبل * هوای ابر دید و نکهت گل

*   *   *

بدل گفتا که هنگام صبوح است * نسیم باغ و می معجون روح است

The breeze said in her mind: * 'I will persevere until I carry [the scent of roses] throughout the garden'.
'I will make a rose in the rose-bed drunken and fleet * So that each flower will tear its collar a hundred times'.
The perfume of roses enveloped her locks * And in that instant her eyes emptied of sleep.
The whites of her eyes were roseate, her face filled with light * From head to toe she was as intoxicated as her eye.
She moved her dishevelled hyacinths away from her narcissi * Spying the cloudy sky and the fragrance of the roses.

*   *   *

She said to herself: 'It is time for the morning draft * The garden's breeze and wine are an electuary for my soul'.

Due to their shape, hyacinths are used to symbolize tresses of hair, while narcissi are used as symbols for eyes because the shape of their flowers seems to mimic the pupil set inside the iris, inside the white.

When we compare this passage with the extract from Salik which is quoted above, we can observe the different strategies that the two poets use to describe how the breeze wakes Shirin. In 'Urfi's story, the breeze is endowed with a voice and agency, but it is not personified to the extent that it is in Salik's version. Salik develops a single line from 'Urfi's version, depicting the breeze wending its way among Shirin's hair, and builds on the eroticism latent in this image by likening the brush of the breeze against Shirin's neck to the touch of a lover. Salik uses the following dialogue between Shirin and the servile breeze to represent Shirin as a stronger and more eroticized character than she appears in 'Urfi's version.

Just as Salik constructed a dialogue with Nizami and ʿUrfi, so too Ruh al-Amin practised a similar kind of close reading of his predecessors' imagery while exercising considerable latitude with plotting. In Ruh al-Amin's version of the story, the points of continuity in imagery that I have discussed here are to be found in the section of the narrative which relates how Khusraw sets off for the hunt. Nizami uses a highly distinctive image to describe the dawn:[88]

چو شد دوران سنجابی و شق دوز * سمور شب نهفت از قاقم روز

When the spheres clad themselves in grey squirrel fur and sewed up the rents in their garments * The sable of the night hid from the ermine of the day.

Ruh al-Amin provides a nod to this line in his description of dusk settling on the mountain tops:[89]

فگنده کوه قاقم از بر خویش * زده گلهای رنگین بر سر خویش

The mountain threw off the ermine cloak from its chest * And set colourful roses upon its head.

He continues with his metaphor for the onset of dusk, describing the creep of the setting sun over the landscape:[90]

شقائق کوه را پیرایه گشته * چمن را چشم بلبل دایه گشته
گرفته جام بر کف لالۀ مست * فشانده ارغوان بر یاسمین دست

Poppies ornamented the mountain * Black-eyed peas kept watch over the meadow.
The drunken tulip took a goblet of wine in its palm * And the Judas tree danced with the jasmine.

Ruh al-Amin's approach to metaphor in these lines can be compared with that of Salik. Both poets use the word *pīrāya* ('ornament') when describing the rosy glow of the crepuscle, but Salik's image is altogether simpler, since he names the red dawn (*shafaq*) explicitly and writes that it ornaments the horizon. Ruh al-Amin, on the other hand, employs the same field of imagery to build a compound metaphor: the spread of red poppies over the mountainside is a circumlocution for the russet glow of the sun as it sinks lower over the ridges. These kinds of transpositions expose how the poets developed pre-existing images until the objects of their comparisons became almost unrecognizable.

The seventeenth century has been characterized as a period in which poets expounded an aesthetic of 'fresh-speak' (*taza-guyi*), ultimately meaning the creation of new poetic images (*maʿni-afarini*) by the rhetorical transformation of familiar tropes.[91] Lines which provoked surprise in the reader, emerging from the texture of a poem, were often valued most highly by those critics who embraced the movement.[92] A cross-reading of *Khusraw u Shirin* texts invites us to think about the development of images as a longer dialogue between each poet and corpus, rather than a radical break with the past. Indeed, when poets and theorists of the seventeenth century spoke of new meanings, they were not advocating that the corpus be ignored, rather the opposite.[93] In the introduction to his *Khusraw u Shirin*, Salik describes Nizami using the discourse of *taza-guyi*, writing:[94]

نظامی آنکه آن افسانه پرداخت * هزاران معنیی بیگانه پرداخت
عروسان معانی بکر بودند * سرای عقد و مهر فکر بودند

Nizami, the one who related that tale * Used a thousand unknown images.
The brides of his imagery were previously untouched * They were the
palace of intricacy and the seal of thought.

Furthermore, Salik writes that Nizami's *Khusraw u Shirin* consists of speech that is 'fresh (*tar*) and colourful (*rangīn*)', both words which feature in seventeenth-century critical treatises.[95] Salik also highlights the individual voices of the authors of the *Khusraw u Shirin* corpus, saying: 'the sound of those who have gone still reverberates / Each re-telling has a fresh (*tāza*) melody'.[96] Finally, he emphasizes that 'The sea of poetic images has no shore / The bubbles [on its surface] are the seal on a vast treasure'.[97] In addition to casting Nizami as a great poetic innovator, Salik's remarks can be seen as a manifesto for what he practices in his writing: a form of creativity based on a close reading of other poets' works, down to the individual line.

A panegyric ghazal by Faraj Allah

Salik's transposition of a narrative romance into a primarily lyrical setting draws our attention to the problem of how he and other émigré poets in Golkonda employed poetic genres. In his introduction to his *Khusraw u Shirin*, he states that he was prompted to compose the poem when he heard an acquaintance, the doctor 'Inayat Allah, recite some *ghazal*s which alluded to the characters of the two lovers.[98] This reminds us that textual genres cross-pollinated one another. We find similar transformations with praise poetry. Even though the *qasida* was still used as a vehicle for praise during the seventeenth century, it had long since ceased to be the only verse form harnessed for eulogy. As we saw when surveying Salik's itinerary, many of the poems that he addressed to named dedicatees were not *qasa'id*, but rather *tarkib-band*s or comparatively short *qita'*. An equally important type of poetry that could be used for praise was the *ghazal*. The brevity, lyricism and polysemy of the *ghazal* form had been exploited for centuries. Hafiz (d. 792/1390) is one of the most widely imitated poets in later periods whose descriptions of idealized beloveds could often assume a double significance as references to real courtly figures who attended the gatherings in which his poems were first performed, where an added dimension of visual interaction between performers and spectators would have brought out layers of meaning that are sometimes only hinted at in his texts themselves.[99] Such levels of significance may be present in a *ghazal* which Faraj Allah dedicated to Sultan ʿAbd Allah. Like many early modern *ghazals*, the poem largely rejects eroticism in favour of a profoundly melancholic air:[100]

نوبهار از کیسهٔ ما رفت و گلشن باز نیست * از بهار آوازه و از بلبل آن آواز نیست
غنچه دلگیر است با منقار بلبل بسته است * سرو غمناکست با قانون قمری ساز نیست
باغ افتاد از شکفتن عندلیبان را چه شد * سوخت گل صد شمع و یک پروانه در پرواز نیست
راز مستان بر زبان نعــرهٔ مستانه است * سینهٔ بی طاقتان آرامگاه راز نیست
کبک ما با چنگل شهباز بازی میکند * نیست در صحرائی مرغی که شاهین باز نیست
زاغ در گلزار ما فریاد بلبل میکند * صعوه اینجا کمتر از مرغ سخن پرداز نیست
اینکه ما از وصل او دوریم از تقصیر ماست * کوتهی از ماست تقصیر[101] از کمند ناز نیست
سوز ما از تاب برق حسن عالم سوز اوست * رو بانجامی ندارد هرچه را آغاز نیست
چون ستایم عشق را چون گوش بی پرواگرست * چون نمایم حسن را چون چشم بینش باز نیست
رشک ایران شد دکن در عهد عبد الله شاه * هرچه خواهی هست اما بادهٔ شیراز نیست
جستحوی او فرج از آب و آتش میکند * جلوه میجوید دلش پروانه آتشباز نیست[102]

> The first days of spring have left our purse, but the rose garden has not bloomed *
> There is no sign of spring and no song of its nightingale.
> The rose-bud is melancholy, closed like the nightingale's beak * The cypress
> mourns – it is not in tune with the crescent harp of the turtle dove.
> The garden has failed to bloom, what has happened to the nightingales? *
> A hundred candles burnt the roses and not a single moth is in flight.
> Drunkards cry out their secrets with a fuddled slip of the tongue * The chests
> of the helpless are no burial ground for confidences.
> Our partridge plays with the hawk's claws * No bird is on the plain, for the
> royal falcon has not returned.
> In our meadow the crow mimics the nightingale * A finch is not inferior to a
> song bird here.
> That we cannot reach him is our fault * We fall short – the fault is not in the
> trap that coquetry sets.
> The lightning of his beauty, which ignites the world, is what burns us *
> Whatever has no beginning cannot end.
> How can I praise love when my ear overhears? * How can I show love when
> my eyes are not open to see?
> The Deccan has become the envy of Iran in the age of King ʿAbd Allah *
> It is whatever you may wish it, but there is no wine of Shiraz here.
> Faraj tries to find it with fire and water * His heart looks for its appearance,
> but the moth will not immolate itself.

The mood of the poem evokes the absence of the patron, and it might encourage readers to speculate that Faraj Allah is using lyricism to draw Sultan ʿAbd Allah back to court after a period away from it. The piece is also a deliberate attempt to make new meaning out of familiar topoi, marking dissonance and the poet's dislocation from Iran. In this respect, it is wholly in tune with the historical corpus of poems produced by writers active in locations such as Anatolia, who often played with the geopoetics of their spatial distance from Fars.[103] It is built around the absence of what ought to be present: the rose and the nightingale, the royal falcon – an emblem for the king himself – the beloved, and the wine of Shiraz. Spring has arrived, but the traditional symbols of its advent are nowhere to be found. This is partly a metaphor, an attribution to nature of the feeling of desolation experienced by the narrator in the absence of the beloved-patron, but it is also a statement that poetic tropes are not universally mimetic, a reflection of the fact that at Nawruz, when the gardens of Iran blossom, the Deccan is coming into summer. The impossibility of bridging the gap between expectation and reality is strengthened as the poem continues. Crows, which do not warble, unsuccessfully mimic the nightingale, because the beloved is out of reach.[104] The final two lines of the poem make explicit the thesis that has been developed throughout: the Deccan's physical distance from Iran, its climactic and cultural differences, force a re-interpretation of familiar imagery. The poet cannot imbibe the wine of Shiraz in India. The *ghazal*'s pessimism, and its intellectualism, offer evidence that poetry produced under patronage, for named dedicatees, was not always expected to be flattering. As with Nizam al-Din Ahmad's *qasida* in praise of Sultan ʿAbd Allah, which I studied in Chapter 2, Faraj Allah's poem is freighted with expectation about the listener's familiarity with the corpus.

Shared audiences: A dialogue between Faraj Allah and Salik

Thanks to Ibn Maʿsum, we know that Faraj Allah was still alive and in Golkonda after 1068/1657. It therefore seems plausible to infer that he was in the city during the previous decade, and that his path crossed with that of Salik. The fact that Faraj Allah inscribed the *jung* of Fayyaz in Hyderabad in 1054/1644–5 and Salik Yazdi autographed the same volume in Hyderabad just one year later provides firmer evidence that both poets were in the city at the same time, and mixed in similar circles.[105] My comparison of the two poets' *ghazals* in manuscript strengthens this hypothesis, because there are examples of emulative connections between their work.[106] Two poems in particular allow us to explore how Faraj Allah and Salik constructed a literary connection with one another. More generally, these poems also provide an insight into concepts of creativity in the seventeenth century, casting light on how poets thought about imitation. We can be certain that these pieces represent a deliberate exchange, because Salik ends his poem with a direct quotation (*tazmin*): 'as Faraj says: "One cannot take a dispute from this house to the next"'.

The two pieces are lyric poems, sharing the same, rare rhyme and *radif* in -*ana niza*ʿ, and the same metre, distinctive formal elements which bind them together.

Faraj Allah evidently wrote his first, because he is quoted by Salik. His poem runs as follows:[107]

کی کنم با فلک سفله درین خانه نزاع * هیچ عاقل ننموداست بدیوانه نزاع
چشم بر دست ز بونتر ز خودی مارا نیست * بر سر گنج نداریم بویرانه نزاع
سینه‌ای فربه و پهلوی پری میخواهد * باز با کبک ندارد بسر دانه نزاع
بر سر سرو و گل و شمع درین باغ مرا * نیست با فاخته و بلبل و پروانه نزاع
ما چو مو کاسهٔ زان موی میانیم نه زلف * نیست ما را بسر زلف تو با شانه نزاع
ما بآن چشم زبان فهم سخنها داریم * نیست ما را بمی و ساغر و پیمانه نزاع
زخم بحث و جدل و برو حرم مأسور است * همه جایست همین نیست بمیخانه نزاع
بحث یاران همه افسانه حقیقت دیگر است * از دو دانا نسزد بر سر افسانه نزاع
آشنایست کزو کینه فرج میخیزد * هیچ بیگانه نکردست به بیگانه نزاع

How can I can dispute with ignoble fortune in this house? * No sane person disputes with a madman.
We do not rely on anyone more helpless than ourselves * We cannot dispute with ruins over the treasure.
Whoever has a stout chest wants the torso of an angel * The hawk does not dispute with the partridge over grain.
I have no dispute with the ring-dove, the nightingale and the moth * Over the cedar, the rose, and the candle in this garden.
We are not like a tress of hair, but like a brush amid that hair * We have no dispute with the brush over your tresses.
We speak to those understanding eyes * We have no dispute over the wine, the cup and the goblet.
Arguments and controversies strike and the sanctuary is prey to them * Everywhere is the same, but there is no dispute at the tavern.
It is fantasy to argue with lovers – reality is different * Two wise men do not dispute over a fairy tale.
The one who has caused Faraj's rancour is known to us * No stranger disputes with a stranger.

Like the panegyric *ghazal* discussed above, this poem is shot through with melancholy. A first reading may suggest that it is a love poem, but the central idea of 'dispute' (*niza*'), which features as the repeated *radif*, may engage on some level with the concept of dialectic, which would have been important within scholarly *majalis*. The motif is developed into complementary ideas: the impossibility of contradicting what fortune has in store, a lovers' quarrel, the irascibility of the drunkard, and philosophical debate over truth. Its themes are echoed in a second poem by Faraj Allah about the separation of lovers, which begins:[108]

خط پاکی بستان از همه هنگام وداع * نتوان برد ازین خانه بان خانه نزاع

At the moment of parting, draw a clean line under everything * One cannot take a dispute from this house to the next.

Salik responded to the poem which I have given in full, but he chose the opening line of Faraj Allah's second *ghazal* for direct citation in his emulation. This opens up the possibility that Salik's emulative, intertextual use of Faraj Allah's collected work was designed to construct a sustained and complex dialogue with his fellow poet. His full response runs:[109]

صلح کیشان بسیارند بجانانه نزاع * آشنا یانه گذارند به بیگانه نزاع[110]
با جدل چشم تو از زلف دلم میخواهد * همچو مستی که کند بر سر پیمانه نزاع
آه را شانه کش طرهٔ شمشاد کنم * که دلم راست درین سلسله با شانه نزاع
چشم بیگانه نگاه که بگردش آمد * که درین بزم کند شمع بپروانه نزاع
تنگ چشمست فلک چشم باشکم دارد * مور[111] در خرمن و دارد بسر دانه نزاع
ای فلک از من مجنون[112] بسلامت بگذر * میکند کودک بیباک بدیوانه نزاع
جلوهٔ خانه برانداز دل و دینی گو * که برانداز ازین کعبه و بتخانه نزاع
رفتم از خانهٔ زنجیر که مجنون باشد * چند تا چند توان کرد بدیوانه نزاع
میکنم صلح بسالک چو فرج میگوید * نتوان برد ازین خانه بآن خانه نزاع

> Men of peace dispute much over my darling * Familiar or not, they dispute with strangers.
> Your eyes quarrel with your tresses for my heart * Like a drunkard trying to keep hold of a wine goblet.
> I will turn my moans into the hand-maid of the box-tree's locks * For my heart disputes with the brush over those ringlets.
> See the stranger's eyes as they begin to turn * For at this feast the candle disputes over the moth.
> Fate is covetous, with eyes in its belly. * The ants are in the harvest, disputing over the grain.
> Fate, greet me, the madman, as you pass * It is a fearless child who disputes with a man possessed.
> Overturn the splendour of this house, proclaim a heart and creed * Which can banish dispute from this Ka'ba and idol temple.
> I left the chain that binds the man possessed * From time to time one can dispute with a madman.
> I make peace with Salik when Faraj says: * 'One cannot take a dispute from this house to the next'.

Each line in Salik's *ghazal* finds a clear antecedent in Faraj Allah's work, so that Salik's ll. 1–9 correspond, in order, to Faraj Allah's ll. 9, 6, 5, 4, 3, 1, 8, 1 and 1 (of *ghazal* No. 2). There is a clear method to this progression: Salik begins with the end of Faraj Allah's poem, moving backwards, and then ends with a twist by referencing a different *ghazal*. Three lines from the original do not find responses in the imitation. Salik's engagement with Faraj Allah's imagery is designed to construct meaning out of his predecessor's work, and in this sense his technique is almost exegetical. We can see this in Salik's l.2, corresponding with Faraj Allah's l.6, where Faraj Allah merely suggests the lover's drunken gaze at the beloved, but Salik builds a far more explicit, and arguably far more vivid, image, of the beloved's eyes and hair fighting for the narrator's attention like peevish drunkards trying to gain control of a goblet. At the same time, Salik exercises enough latitude to make his images definitively his own, and transforms Faraj Allah's piece into a text more easily recognisable as a love lyric. He achieves this through different strategies of rhetoric and imagery. In l.5, for example, he responds to Faraj Allah's antithesis (*tibaq*) between men of 'stout chest' and angels with narrow waists by speaking of the corpulent belly and narrow eyes of fate. In so doing he retains a rhetorical device but changes the imagery. Salik also inverts some of the images, as in his l.8, where he contradicts Faraj Allah's argument that it is not possible to dispute with the mentally unwell. This is not simply a technical move. It also cultivates a different emotional tone, representing the poet's narrative persona as less constrained by the malevolence of fate.

Conclusion

The dialogues discussed in this chapter demonstrate that Iranian migrant poets in Golkonda were engaged in two activities which might seem contradictory but were, in fact, complementary: the close reading of the corpus and a process of dislocation to fit the new, local context in which they found themselves. Like their peers active in Golkonda in Arabic, Salik and Faraj Allah used intertextuality as a way to build connections with each other, their contemporaries elsewhere, and their predecessors. Salik Yazdi's rewriting of *Khusraw u Shirin* acknowledged Nizami Ganjavi as one of the first great 'modernists', but sought to refashion his story with a more lyrical sensibility, so as to do in the Deccan what 'Urfi had done in Iran. This deliberately overwrote the work of poets like Ruh al-Amin, who did not adopt so much latitude in his own reimagining of the story. But dislocation was not confined to narrative poetry: Faraj Allah's lament for the absence of his patron-beloved becomes a metapoetic exploration of how conventional images rooted in a sense of place, such as evocations of the wine of Shiraz, become untethered symbols that are more closely allied with a mood and with a weight of literary associations than they are with an extratextual reality. Finally, we saw how Faraj Allah and Salik, having played with convention, came together to rewrite one another's work. In so doing, they marked their connection to one another and the shared, new intellectual world that they were forging together in the Deccan.

Chapter 6

KABUL AND NORTH INDIA

SA'IB, ILAHI, AHSAN AND ASHNA

Sa'ib as a node in a network

Widely read and appreciated today, Sa'ib Tabrizi (*c.* 1000/1592–1086–7/1676) is recognized as one of the greatest poets of Persian of any historical period. He is frequently discussed in isolation, as a solitary genius, and there are some aspects of his life which provide evidence for such a reading.[1] For one, he spent most of his career outside obvious structures of patronage. Born in Isfahan, into a wealthy family of Tabrizi merchants, he was already a man of independent means when he set out for India in 1034/1624–5.[2] His stay in the Mughal Empire was relatively short, lasting only seven years, but during this time he developed a close association with courtiers such as Zafar Khan Ahsan (d. 1073/1662–3), governor of Kabul and then later Kashmir, whom he served as a professional poet.[3] Sa'ib returned to Iran in 1042/1632, to a life of self-sufficiency.[4] He spent most of his remaining forty-five years in Isfahan, acting as a host of literary gatherings, teaching the occasional pupil, disseminating his poetry in manuscript to the capital's reading public, and addressing a relatively small corpus of praise poems to the Safavid monarchs Shah 'Abbas II (r. 1052/1642–1077/1666) and Shah Sulayman (r. 1076/1666–1105/1694).[5] The fact that he had no particular need to participate in structures of patronage after his return to Iran makes it tempting – although inaccurate – to assume that he stood outside networks.[6]

A second reason why Sa'ib is often viewed as a man who stood apart from his contemporaries is the quantity of his output. The overwhelming majority of his poetry consists of *ghazals*, of which Muhammad Qahraman's edition counts 7,015 in Persian (as well as a handful in Turkic, which Sa'ib would have spoken with his parents), far in excess of what many canonical poets produced.[7] To give a contrasting example, editions of the *divan* of Hafiz (*c.* 715/1315–792/1390) typically consist of just under 500 *ghazals*. The presence of a private scriptorium in Sa'ib's house in Isfahan may have helped to ensure that his poems were disseminated in manuscript as he composed them, rather than that he lived with them and edited them down, but regardless, it is an extraordinarily voluminous body of work.[8] The ostensibly lyrical quality of this corpus, and the relative paucity of occasional poems in Sa'ib's *divan*, both make the process of mapping his entire web of interlocutors a complex one, and lead, again, to the impression that his character and his verse were marked by individuality and strength of feeling, rather than by sociability. As the poet himself claims, projecting himself as a man who cannot be understood by his fellows:[9]

صائب از قحط سخندان چه به من میگذرد * به سخنکش نشود هیچ سخنور محتاج

Sa'ib, what matters it to me that men of literary taste are nowhere to be found? *
No eloquent poet needs an auditor.

Yet, Sa'ib did function as an important node within literary networks in Mughal India, in Safavid Iran, and between the two states. He was a source for Nasrabadi, who had a close friendship with him, and he transmitted information about émigré poets who had gone from Iran to India to the anthologist, contributing to the circulation of knowledge about the state of literary production in the Mughal Empire.[10] Nasrabadi reports that he visited Sa'ib at his house in Isfahan, where he met other men of letters;[11] and that he saw and read numerous manuscripts which the famous poet had in his library, including copies of the ten *divan*s of Hakim Rukna-yi Kashi (d. 1066/1655–6), who may have had quite an influence on Sa'ib's formative years.[12] Nasrabadi, who was well regarded by his contemporaries as a prose stylist, also co-wrote letters with Sa'ib that they addressed to Mulla Mustafid Chakdilaki, a poet of Balkh who worked for the Toqay-Timurid Khanate of Central Asia.[13] The *tazkira* gives some impression of the ways in which Sa'ib made his presence felt more broadly in Isfahan's literary world too. He chose a pen name for Mirza 'Ala al-Din Muhammad, a grandson of Shah 'Abbas I;[14] and he recommended junior poets for employment with state officials, indicating how literary prestige and political structures were intertwined.[15] Significantly, we find similar stories concerning Sa'ib's activities in Mughal India, making him part of a select group of otherwise mostly political figures who not only achieved success, but who were also regarded as authorities, within more than one state. To give an example, Sa'ib chose a pen name for Mirza Amin, a high-ranking Mughal functionary who served in Bengal.[16]

Sa'ib fell in with Zafar Khan Ahsan when he arrived in Kabul, his first stop after he entered the Mughal territories overland. There he encountered another poet of a similar age, who was already attached to the governor's retinue: Ilahi Hamadani (d. *c.* 1063/1653). While Sa'ib's name is still feted today, Ilahi lies forgotten, and both his *divan*, and a *tazkira* which he wrote, entitled *Khizana-yi Ganj-i Ilahi* (*The Vault of the Divine Treasure*), remain in manuscript.[17] A *sayyid*, Ilahi had left his native town of Asadabad in western Iran in order to carve out a career for himself. Initially, he followed a similar itinerary to Faraj Allah al-Shushtari and Salik Yazdi, moving to Shiraz in order to attend a *madrasa* in 1010/1601–2, and then migrating on to the Safavid capital at Isfahan.[18] It seems that Ilahi decided to depart Iran for India in 1018/1609–10, and that he spent several years in Qandahar en route, before arriving in the then Mughal capital at Agra.[19] The biographer Taqi Awhadi met him there in 1022/1613–14, by which time Ilahi had managed to enter the circle of Mahabat Khan (d. 1044/1634), at this point a trusted courtier of the emperor Jahangir.[20] Evidently, Ilahi established a broader courtly network, as he had attached himself to Zafar Khan Ahsan by the time that the latter was appointed governor of Kabul in 1033/1623–4, and he accompanied him there.[21] Like Sa'ib, he was highly mobile while he was in the service of Zafar Khan, following him wherever he travelled. Zafar Khan's appointment as governor of Kashmir in 1042/1632 coincided with Sa'ib's return to Iran, but Ilahi remained loyal to his patron, and he settled in Kashmir for good, eventually dying there in around 1653.[22] He famously had his own garden constructed in Kashmir, which became a gathering place for poets and was memorialized in poems by Zafar Khan Ahsan and Qudsi.[23]

As is the case with the other literary circles discussed in this book, for us even to be able to speak of a connection between Sa'ib and Ilahi requires a detailed investigation of poems and biographical anecdotes, many of which remain in manuscript. Since the collected works of Sa'ib are published and can be accessed with facility, and the works of Ilahi cannot be studied so simply, there is an inequality in the evidence which makes it easier to assume that Sa'ib was the major poet and Ilahi the minor. Yet there are indications that Ilahi and Sa'ib were treated with equal respect within Zafar Khan's entourage. This is all the more comprehensible since Sa'ib was still a young man who was gaining a reputation for himself when he arrived in Kabul. Ilahi had been canonized by the essayist Mulla Tughra, who names him as one of the best writers of the era;[24] and by the poet Salik Qazvini, who devotes a section of his topographic *masnavi*, *Muhit-i Kawnayn* (*The Sphere of the Two Worlds*), to him.[25] Ahsan also lists Ilahi and Sa'ib as equals in his poem *Maykhana-yi Raz* (*The Tavern of Mystery*), stating that both men helped him to develop his own poetic temperament:[26]

شکفته به کابل چو شد طبع من * فزون شد مرا شوق فکر سخن

*

سر آمد ز یاران آن انجمن * الهی و صائب ز اهل سخن

When my poetic temperament blossomed in Kabul * My desire to think through speech increased.

*

Ilahi and Sa'ib were the most eminent poets * Among the friends at that gathering.

Zafar Khan's discussion of his own poetic temperament (*tab '*) brings us onto one of this chapter's key concerns: how patronage and poetic talent created two hierarchies which often undermined one another. Even though Ahsan was the social superior of Sa'ib and Ilahi within the political structures of Mughal India, he was their inferior in verse, a dilettante in a field where they were professionals. Poetry brought Ahsan socially closer to Sa'ib and Ilahi in other ways, too: like them, he wrote his own panegyrics in praise of the Mughal emperor Shah Jahan (r. 1037/1628–1068/1657), making him, on some level, just another eulogist in the orbit of the imperial court. We find a parallel set of fluid hierarchies in the connection between Ahsan's son, 'Inayat Khan Ashna (d. 1082/1671), and the professional poets whom he knew and supported, including Kalim Kashani (d. 1061/1651).[27] Ashna is best known today for his summary chronicle of the life of Shah Jahan, compiled during his brief stint as superintendent of the imperial Mughal library, but he was also an accomplished poet whose *divan* survives in manuscript.[28]

This chapter brings Sa'ib, Ilahi, Ahsan and Ashna together by asking how their engagement with a shared set of themes made them participants in a literary community which transcended rigid social structures, even as it took shape within a formal system of patronage. While Ahsan and Ashna supported the professional poets financially, they also drew on their work when writing their own verse. A distinct approach to intertextual practice emerges here, in which authorship becomes a way of integrating hierarchies with one another, melding subject matter borrowed from a political superior together with techniques practised by the best professional poets.

In praise of Kabul and its governor

Sa'ib and Ilahi both cemented their connection to Ahsan by composing pieces in celebration of him and the city which he governed, Kabul.[29] Sa'ib's *qasida* is particularly interesting because it seems to make a punning reference to Ilahi in its very last line:[30]

الهی تا جهان آرا و شهر آرا به جا باشد * جهان آرایی و آرایش کشور بود کارش

As Ilahi's name means 'my God' or 'divine', the line can potentially be understood as an amphibology. One possible sense is:

My God, for as long as the Jahan-Ara meadow and Shahr-Ara garden stand *
His business is to support the world and this country.

Or, the line can be read to mean:

Ilahi, for as long as the Jahan-Ara meadow and Shahr-Ara garden stand *
His business is to support the world and this country.

While it would be unusual to draw reference to another poet in the closing line of a *qasida*, the kind of ambiguity that we see here should be considered within the primary context of the poem's performance. If Sa'ib recited the poem within the presence of both Ahsan and Ilahi – which he may well have done at a *majlis* – then his call to the other major poet in Ahsan's retinue would have created the impression that eloquence as a whole was endorsing Ahsan's power, reflecting my broader contention here that these poems establish competing hierarchies. Read in this way, the line would argue that Ahsan derived his authority from the consensus of the poets. On another level, reference to Ilahi's name could signal the presence of emulative intertextuality with his poetry.

Discussions of aspects of the text as it worked in performance must necessarily remain speculative, but as we shall see, Sa'ib's panegyric is connected with Ilahi's piece about Ahsan and Kabul on a textual level. In one strophe of his poem, Sa'ib describes the citadel of Kabul, evoking its eminence and its impenetrability to potential enemies. Just as another one of his poems focuses on the *pul-i shahi* (the royal bridge, or the Hasanabad Bridge) over the Zayanda Rud in Isfahan, casting Shah 'Abbas II as a metaphorical conduit that unites the city, so too does this piece equate the patron with a symbolic topography.[31] Kabul had a political significance, both as a potentially vulnerable city close to the borders of Safavid Iran and the Toqay-Timurid Khanate, and as the most northerly major conurbation of the Mughal Empire, a potential base for the expansion of the empire's dependencies into Central Asia, which was the homeland of the royal family's Turkic ancestors. Texts composed for Mughal patrons in other languages, including Sanskrit, also celebrated the imposition of order on the empire's northernmost fringe, figuring the road between Kabul and Delhi as a highway of prosperity.[32] The significance of the city would not have been lost on Sa'ib and Ilahi, as migrants from neighbouring Iran who were trying to adapt to the political landscape of the Mughal realm. Both poets devote energy to describing Ahsan's martial prowess and his ability to defend Kabul, as well as his administrative skill and just rule, which justify his control over the city.[33] In so doing, they engage with an expansive body of seventeenth-century Persian poetry about place which often functioned as a textual space for poets and their patrons to experiment with ideas about the shape of urban society.[34] Sa'ib evokes the fort in the following terms:[35]

اگر در رفعت برج فلک سایش نمیبیند * چرا خورشید را از طرف سر افتاده دستارش
حصار مارپیچش اژدهای گنج را ماند * ولی ارزد به گنج شایگان هر خشت دیوارش
نظرگاه تماشاییست در وی هر گذرگاهی * همیشه کاروان مصر میآید به بازارش
حساب مه جبینان لب بامش که میداند * دو صد خورشید رو افتاده در هر پای دیوارش
به صبح عید میخندد گل رخساره صبحش * به شام قدر پهلو میزند زلف شب تارش

If it does not touch the heights of the tower of the firmament * Then why has the sun's turban fallen askew?
The serpentine fort resembles a dragon twisted around treasure * Yet every brick in its wall is worth a princely fortune.
Whenever the caravan from Egypt arrives in the bazar there * Every alley is transformed into a spectacle.
Who knows how many luminous beauties strut along the ramparts? * Two hundred suns shine along every foot of the wall.
The rosy face of its iron gate smiles on the morning of 'Id * The tresses of the dark rival it on the Night of Power.

There are several images here which are echoed in different contexts later on in the same poem, emphasizing how Kabul has moulded itself around Ahsan: the height of the citadel, which finds an equivalent in the height of Ahsan's ambition; the serpentine (*mārpīch*) fort, an evocation of the staggered defensive walls of the citadel, which is mirrored by the serpentine writhing of those who envy Ahsan's calligraphic hand; and the turban of the sun, later matched by the turban of Ahsan himself, implying that Ahsan is, like many dedicatees, its peer. The parallels not only imply that Ahsan has impressed himself on the landscape of the city, but also tie the military and bureaucratic administration of Kabul together; the fluid motion of Ahsan's hand across the page is a metonymy for his oversight of chancellery documents:[36]

نوای جغد چون آوازۀ عنقا به گوش آید * خوشا ملکی که باشد شحنه عدل تو معمارش
فلک از آفتاب آیینه داری پیشه میسازد * که گرم حرف گردد طوطی کلک شکربارش
چو از هند دوات آید برون طاوس کلک او * خورد صد مارپیچ رشک کبک از طرز رفتارش
نباشد حاجت سرمایۀ بال هما او را * سعادت همچو گل میروید از اطراف دستارش
بلند اقبالی دارد که گر بر آسمان تازد * به زور بازوی قدرت کند با خاک هموارش
ز بس در عهد او دزدی برافتاده است از عالم * نیارد خصم دزدیدن سر از شمشیر خونبارش
رباید تیزی از الماس و سرخی از لب مرجان * نماید جوهر خود را چو شمشیر گهربارش
خدنگش را مگو بهرچه سرخی در دهن دارد * ز خون دشمنان پان میخورد لبهای سوفارش

I can hear the owl screeching as loud as the ʿAnqa * Happy is the kingdom
built by your just oversight.
The heavens make the sun their mirror-bearer * As the sugar-cracking
parrot of his pen begins to chatter.
When the peacock of his pen leaves the India of his ink-well * The partridge
writhes in jealousy of its graceful movements.
He has no need for the profit that the royal eagle's protection bestows *
Good fortune grows on his turban like the flowers on its fabric.
So lofty are his auspices that were he to launch an assault on heaven *
The strength of his forearm would level it to earth.
In his time, theft has disappeared from the world to such an extent * That
the thieving enemy cannot retract its head from his bloody sword.
He robs the diamond of its keenness and coral lips of their crimson *
His brilliance sparkles like his bejewelled sword.
Do not even speak of his arrows, the lips of whose notches * Chew the betel
of the enemy's blood, so much crimson is in their mouths.

Like many panegyrics of the period, such as a regnal ode which Kalim produced to mark the coincidence of Shah Jahan's lunar birthday with the anniversary of his accession, aspects of this poem celebrate the state's expansion of its borders and the regulation of its imperial subjects.[37] The swift punishment for theft, for example, is a common theme, as is the force of the patron's enmity towards insurrection. These poems are not just concerned with praising the patron as an isolated figure, but also with showing how the patron imposes order on the nation. Saʾib's image in the final line given earlier is particularly striking, likening the tiny notches on Ahsan's arrows, fired into the bodies of the enemy and caked in their blood, as mouths chewing on the stimulant preparation paan (a mixture of betel and areca nut), which causes the user to produce copious amounts of red spittle. The image depends on a play with scale and perspective, magnifying the notches to many times their size, and figuring them as living and moving to make them seem more animate, more predatory. The effect is unsettling and highly memorable, transforming the conventional argument that the patron makes bloodshed licit into something distinctive.[38]

As arresting as Sa'ib's imagery is, we find a number of continuities between his *qasida* in praise of Ahsan and Ilahi's *tarkib-band* on the same broad topic. As a stanzaic poem, in which each strophe addresses a distinct theme, Ilahi's piece manages to connect lyric and bacchanalian images of spring and wine-drinking with praise of Ahsan. In the verses reproduced hereafter, there are several examples of masked intertextuality that mirror tropes found in Sa'ib's poem. Shared motifs include the image of Ahsan as the 'forearm' (*bāzū*) of the caliphate, and the idea that he silences the enemies of the imperial state with his weaponry. These pieces show how specific images passed between Sa'ib and Ahsan and were

Figure 4 © The British Library Board: *Divan* of Ilahi, British Library, Add. MS. 25330, f. 63a.

altered in circulation, and how both poets were working with a similar set of raw materials. This particular literary community operated through transforming the same common root images across genres.[39]

ما را ز بهار کابل آمد * یاد همدان و کوه الوند

از هر مویم بهاری افشاند * اندیشه مدحت خداوند

آن خواجه که در نظام و آرام * ملک است ز کلک او برومند[40]

آن خواجه که در حساب جودش * اندک باشد هزار چون اند

بازوی خلافه جمله الملک * دستور شهنشه عدوبند

حیدر دل ابو الحسن که دستش * از خیر آرزو در افکند

تیغ خلقش بود گلوگیر * بر جان مخالفان چو سوگند

Spring in Kabul brings to mind * Recollections of Hamadan and Mount Alvand.

Spring has made my every hair thrill * With thoughts of praise for my lord.

The master, thanks to whose pen, the kingdom * Prospers in order and peace.

The master, in the enumeration of whose generosity * A thousand paeans are as few as three.

The forearm of the caliphate, the prime minister * The emperor's vanquishing councillor.

Abu l-Hasan, the lionheart, whose hand * Puts the best of hopes to shame.

The sword of his nature suffocates * The souls of the enemy, as does his oath.

As Ilahi moves into a lyric description of the cupbearer, we can begin to see the instability of the images that are present in Sa'ib's poem and how they are shaped in other contexts. Both pieces evoke the act of writing and conjure images of serpentine movement using the word *pīch* ('twist') within the space of a line, but whereas in Sa'ib's *qasida* it is Ahsan who writes, the partridge that writhes in envy of his calligraphy, and the crenelations of the fortress that coil, in Ilahi's poem it is the cupbearer who writes and his crooked locks of hair which curl. Ilahi's imagery is almost cartographic, figuring the hair of the beloved as a tortuous valley into which the heart of the lover travels. The effect of the image is to emphasize the ardour of the narrative voice's desire for the beloved. As the poem is spatially anchored in Kabul, it is not hard to see the image as an evocation of the mountainous landscape which surrounds the city, relating the human subject matter of the poem to a topography of place in the same way as Sa'ib's poem does.[41] Rooted in the depiction of the same form of movement, the line figuring the beloved's hair as a twisting valley acts as an analogue to Sa'ib's evocation of the serpentine fort of Kabul.[42]

ساقی بنشین حمایل[43] دست * با گردن شیشه کن حمایل

کین نامه خط شکسته خویش * با زلف تو میکند مقابل

در وادی پیچ پیچ زلفت * هرگز نرسید دل بمنزل

تو شاهد خامه راست خطی * با حسن جمال[44] خان عادل

کز هر جعدش امید پیمود * در وادی منزلت مراحل

خانی که کشیده دست جودش * دلهای شکسته در سلاسل

خوش سلسله‌ای که هیکل آمد * آزادان را بگردن دل
دیباچه عقل و دین مظفر 45 * احسن لقب و حسن شمایل

Server, take off your sword-belts * And hang the wine-jug from your neck.
For the curled hand of your letter * Rivals your locks.
My heart can never reach the bottom * Of the twisting valley of your tresses.
You are a witness to the unwavering brush * With the beauty of the just lord,
From whose every ringlet hope has set out * On a journey into the valley.
A lord whose munificent hand has bound * Broken hearts in chains.
Beautiful chains shaped like * The heart strings of noblemen.
The overture of the intellect and the victorious faith * The one known as
Ahsan, of splendid character.

As we do not have a chronology to indicate whether Sa'ib's *qasida* or Ilahi's *tarkib-band* came first, we cannot know which of these two pieces is the antecedent. However, we can talk about an 'allusive field' of images that are shared between them.[46] This shared body of images includes the two poets' descriptions of Ahsan's accoutrements. While Sa'ib speaks of the flowers 'growing' from the sides of Ahsan's turban – a reference to the brocade flowers sewn onto the fabric *of* his turban – Ilahi imagines hyacinth flowers growing from the water or 'spring' of Ahsan's sword (*chashma-yi tigh*), the water of the sword being the watered steel from which the blade is made. It is possible that the image of flowers growing from this water is not a fantastic aetiology, but a reference to the hilt of the sword, whose engraved surface may have been set with jewels or glass cut into floral patterns. Just as images of curling and twisting featured earlier on in the two texts, here both poets are making finely observed descriptions which connect the patron's trappings with the growth of flowers. Ilahi develops his conceit further:[47]

در ملک ز نوبهار عدلت * از چشمهٔ تیغ رسته سنبل
آزادی طبع دهر وقتست * کز گردن جمری افکند غل
بر دست صبا نهی سلاسل * گر با لب گل کند تطاول
دیوان مرا ز وصف خلقت * هر صفحه چو دامنست پر گل
در دامن دولت تو گویی * از مادر زاد بخت کابل
نشستم و دل دهم وفا را * شهر آرایی کنم ثنا را

During the spring of your justice, hyacinths have grown * Throughout the
land in the water of your sword.
The nature of the age is liberty * For the fetters fall from the necks of the helpless.
You would tie the hands of the east wind with chains * If it dallied on the
lips of the rose.
My descriptions of your character make each leaf * Of my collected works a
flower-filled skirt.
You might say that in the bosom of your rule, * Kabul was born under a lucky star.
I have settled down, devoting myself to loyalty * I sing the praises of the
Shahr Ara Garden.

The kind of emulative intertextual links that connect Saʾibʾs piece with Ilahiʾs would tend to suggest that the two poets read one anotherʾs work very closely, and that they composed poems which could be cross-read harmoniously as ideologically complimentary pieces. However, part of the skill of being a distinguished professional poet was the ability to produce a text that could be read independently. In choosing different poetic forms for their dialogue, Saʾib and Ilahi emphasized their individuality and refused to place themselves in a hierarchy. We turn now to a series of poems which create a stronger sense of authority and pupillage.

Slipping hierarchies in the saqinamas

The *saqinama*, or bacchanalian poem, is generally arranged around repeated calls for the cupbearer to pour wine for the speaker, to ease his worldly cares.[48] It enjoyed enormous popularity during the sixteenth and seventeenth centuries, so much so that the storyteller and poet ʿAbd al-Nabi Qazvini (d. after 1041/1631–2) put together an anthology devoted exclusively to the genre, which is weighted towards examples contemporary with the compiler.[49] One of the most famous – and longest – *saqinama*s is by Zuhuri Turshizi (d. 1025/1616), who rose to prominence as a court poet in the Deccan, firstly in the sultanate of Ahmadnagar, and later at Bijapur. Zuhuriʾs *saqinama* engages very clearly with themes of place, describing the city of Ahmadnagar, its public spaces and the palace of the poetʾs patron in detail.[50] As poems which can involve lyric, panegyric and narrative modes, *saqinama*s constitute a potentially open genre with a wide range of possible intertextual references. This malleability is compounded by the fact that they can be written in different forms. Often, the *masnavi* (consisting of rhyming couplets) is used, but strophic *saqinama*s in the *tarkib-band* and *tarjiʿ-band* forms are found too.

No *saqinama*s by Saʾib survive, although the theme of wine-drinking and lyrical descriptions of the cupbearer constitute an important part of his *ghazal* and *qasida* poems. On the other hand, Ilahi, Ahsan and Ashna all did compose *saqinama*s, and additional pieces which are in connected forms and genres. There is a certain amount of crossover between these poems and the work of other professional poets who were patronized by Ahsan, including the *saqinama* of a certain Asad.[51] In composing their pieces, Ilahi, Ahsan and Ashna all consciously developed a textual network which strengthened their connection to each other and distinguished them from the authors of *saqinama*s with whom they did not wish to bind themselves, like Hakim Rukna-yi Kashi (d. 1066/1655–6);[52] Mirza Nizam Dast-i Ghayb (d. 1029/1620);[53] and Fawji (d. before 1086/1676).[54] The authors of *saqinama*s who were active in the same spaces as Ilahi, Ashna and Ahsan, but at a slightly later date, incorporated masked references to their poems into their own compositions, thereby engaging in a similar practice of acknowledging the local corpus but not emphasizing their dependence on it.[55] Emulative links were cultivated with poets with whom one wanted to ally oneself.

In Ahsan's *masnavi, Maykhana-yi Raz* (*The Tavern of Mysteries*), the poet cites Zuhuri's *saqinama* as one of his models, and he also incorporates the Deccan into his narrative, discussing his journey there and drawing reference to a famine which affected the region.[56] The marked textual connection to Zuhuri and the involvement of the south here could be seen through a 'geopoetical' lens – by travelling to the Deccan, Ahsan links himself with texts that were composed there, including Zuhuri's *saqinama*, emulating its style and themes in his writing. This idea has to be balanced against Ahsan's use of the historical corpus of Persian poetry – one of the most distinctive features of *Maykhana-yi Raz* is the repeated use of the phrase *biyā sāqī* ('come, cupbearer!'), which is a direct quotation from the *saqinama* of Hafiz, a canonical poet – but nevertheless, as the setting of the poem shifts to different locations, so might we expect Ahsan to emulate the work of his contemporaries who were local to those places, creating a poetic geography of the Mughal Empire.[57] It is not the case that Ahsan had to choose between diachronic intertextuality with the work of poets such as Hafiz and synchronic intertextuality with the work of his contemporaries. Diachronic intertextuality with canonical authors is a mark of most literary activity. Synchronic intertextuality is more idiosyncratic, depending as it does on the corpus of contemporary writers to which an author is exposed.

As we have already seen, when the spatial focus of *Maykhana-yi Raz* shifts from the Deccan to Kabul, Ahsan describes his gatherings with poets in the city's gardens, picking out Ilahi and Sa'ib by name. In invoking the two poets, Ahsan signals his emulative engagement with their work on a textual level. In order to unpack some of these links, we can begin by turning to lines from a *saqinama* by Ilahi. Here, the poet describes the advent of spring:[58]

چو صوفی بجوش اندر آمد چمن * ز نوسبز شد خرقهٔ نارون
خروشند مرغان تسبیح خوان * پی ذکر در مسجد آشیان
شکفتن ز هر غنچه آغاز شد * گره بستهٔ شاخ گل باز شد
بهارست و هر گل برقص اندر است * در و بام آبستان زیور است
جمال چمن بس که دارد صفا * غبار ورخ سبزه گردد هوا
ز شوق چمن موج با صد شتاب * پرد همچو مرغابی از روی آب

The meadow has burst into a frenzy, like a Sufi, * And the elm has
donned a belt of flowers.
The birds cry out, reciting their prayers, * Chanting the name of God in
the nest's mosque.
Every bud has begun to blossom * And the fast knots on the rose stems
have loosened.
It is spring. Every flower has begun to dance * And the houses are pregnant
with new life.
As pure as the beauty of the meadow may be * It is the air that transforms
misty mires into greenery.
Waves skit over the water like ducks * In their passionate rush towards
the meadow.

As life in the garden begins to blossom, the season of merry-making arrives, and the narrative shifts to an inn. Ilahi begins to transpose imagery of the natural world into a new setting, showing how the features of the meadow find their equivalents in the human environment of the tavern. The vessel-shaped buds in the garden are visually analogous to vats of wine, the zephyrs find their counterpart in the whisperings of the clientele, the moon on a bright night glints like a set of keys, the light flickers on the surface of the wine in the cups, making them look like flickering candles, and the whole inn takes on the feeling of a paradisical garden, seemingly more real than heaven because it is tangible. One of the most distinctive images here is the transferred epithet of the 'duck of the wine' (*batt-i bāda*), which refers to a swan-necked ewer. Although it is found in the work of earlier poets such as Hafiz, it seems to have been exploited by Sa'ib and his contemporaries in particular for the way in which it is able to connect the natural world with the human setting of the tavern.[59] Representations of the swan-necked ewer singing or swooping low are metaphors for the act of tipping and pouring the wine-jug.[60]

گل از بس که دارد تمنای مل * لبالب ز ملء روید از شاخ گل
چنان گشته هر طبع میخانه جوی * که میخانه دارد[61] بمیخانه روی
چه میخانه گلزار اهل نیاز * زخمها درو غنچها نیم باز
نسیمش نفسهای مستان او * بط باده مرغ خوش الحان او
حریمش برفعت چو قصر خیال * کلیدش دهد روشنی چون هلال
بحدی درو تاب می گشته جمع * که بی شعله در وی فروزند شمع
در آن عشرت آباد جنت سرشت * نگنجد الم چون گنه در بهشت

Since the flowering rose longs for wine * Its buds overflow the stem in full bloom.
Every heart seeks out a tavern * So that one hostelry faces another.
What taverns! The prairies of the thirsting, * With caskets for newly opened buds.
The breeze that whispers through them is the exhalation of the drunk *
And the swan-necked ewer is their melodious songbird.
Their walls stand as high as the fortress of the imagination * And their keys
shine like the crescent moon.
There, so many cups of wine glimmer * That flameless candles seem to burn.
There is no room for suffering in these empyrean pastures * Just as heaven will
admit no sin.

Cognate images appear in a *saqinama* by 'Inayat Khan Ashna, the son of Zafar Khan Ahsan. Like Ilahi, Ashna connects the meadow with the tavern, picking out the advent of spring as the moment when thoughts turn to merry-making:[62]

بیا ساقیا ساغر می بیار * که می خوش بود خاصه فصل بهار
ز وصل خودم چون رساندی بکام * از آن باده خواهم که ریزی بجام

Come here, server, and bring a cup of wine * For the delights of wine
increase in spring.
I want the wine that you pour into the goblet * When you satisfy my desires.

Just as Ilahi engages with physiology by remarking that one's nature (*tab*ʿ) inclines to the tavern in spring, Ashna identifies a medical justification for drinking wine – it helps to thicken the blood, which has thinned with the changing seasons. The poet then develops images connected to the swan-necked ewer, describing it as the '"peacock" of the tavern', which 'has dived upon its prey more than a hawk' since it has been filled with wine:[63]

بیا ساقی غمگساران[64] بیا * بیا شمع شب زنده داران بیا

بهارست و در هر تنی خون فزود * رگ شیشه باده باید گشود

ولی خون بیحد نشاید گرفت * به اندازهٔ طرف باید گرفت

{بآگاهی ساقی آن ماه روس * نماید بط باده کار خروس[65]}

گل و سبزه مینا و پیمانه بس * بط باده طاوس میخانه بس

دهد باده از راز بالا خبر * بلی چشم میناست بر فرق سر

{بود روی ساغر درخشان از می * شود شیشه لعل بدخشان از می[66]}

بجز شیشه‌ای باده[67] خوشگوار * ندیدست در چشمه کس آتشبار

از آن دم که با باده دمساز شد * بط می شکاری تر از باز شد

بمیخانه چو آمد زاهد درون * چو طنبور شد در رگش خشک خون

Come here, server of the sorrowing * Come here, candle of the night walkers.
It is spring, and our blood has quickened * We must open the wine-vat's veins.
Yet we should not bleed it dry * We must take enough for the whites of our
     eyes to redden.
{Under the care of the cupbearer, a Russian moon, * The swan-necked ewer
     crows like a cockerel.}
The roses, verdure and cup suffice * The swan-necked ewer, peacock of the
     tavern, is enough.
The wine tells the world above our secrets * Heaven's eyes are on the crowns
     of our heads.
{The chalice's face shines at the sight of wine, * Which turns the bottle into
     a ruby of Badakhshan.}
The only time that anyone has seen fire mixed in water * Is in a glass of
     mellow liquor.
Since it has become one with the wine * The swan-necked ewer has dived
     upon its prey more than the hawk.
And since the puritan has entered the tavern * The dry blood in his veins
     thrums like the lute.

Ilahi and Ashna would not be participants in a community if all that they shared was the usage of an isolated motif. The point at which the relationship between the two poets crosses over into emulative intertextuality is when they manipulate the same images within overlapping formal and generic contexts. The motif of the swan-necked ewer – on which I concentrate because of its rarity – is found, albeit only occasionally, in the broader corpus of the period, for example twice in the *ghazal*s of Bidil (d. 1133/1721), and once in the collected works of Jalal Asir (d. 1049/1639), neither of whom was associated with Ilahi or Ashna.[68] Jalal

Asir uses the motif to different effect in an incomplete *ghazal*, joking that the heat of the lover's desire has roasted the swan-necked ewer.[69] Bidil, for his part, employs the image as a philosophical exemplum, comparing himself to a hollow swan-necked ewer, and saying that, like it, he has 'wings made of wine'.[70] Although the same object is being represented in these lines, there is no obvious, emulative connection between Bidil's application of the image and Ashna's usage of it. On the other hand, I argue that Ashna is deliberately forming a textual link with Ilahi by employing the same image within a web of motifs that are shared between their poems: springtime, gardens, merry-making, blossoming flowers, songbirds and taverns.

Another good example of this kind of emulation, which shows just how a poem can act as a nexus of sociability, comes in Ashna's repeated uses of the formula *biyā sāqī*. As we have already seen, the ultimate root of this formula within the generic context of the *saqinama* is Hafiz, whose famous poem begins with this phrase, but Ashna builds an even closer connection to his own father's bacchanalian poem through his choice of wording. His line:[71]

بيا ساقى غمگساران بيا * بيا شمع شب زنده داران بيا

Come here, server of the sorrowing, * Come here, candle of the night walkers,

has an obvious formal connection to Ahsan's *Maykhana-yi Raz*, where instead of *biyā sāqī-yi ghamgusārān biyā*, we find *biyā sāqī-yi maygusāram biyā*, of which it is a very strong echo. More generally, Ahsan's repeated calls to the cupbearer in the following lines of *Maykhana-yi Raz* anticipate Ashna's development of the imagery. In l.4 of the following extract, the similes likening red wine to pigeon's blood and a hangover to a hawk both point forward to Ashna's metaphor comparing the act of draining the vat to a sacrificial blood-letting, and foreshadow his evocation of the swan-necked ewer through their references to birds:[72]

بيا ساقى ميگسارم بيا * بيا اى دواى خمارم بيا
بيک جام بشکن خمار مرا * بمى تازه کن نوبهار مرا
بهارست اى ساقى مى پرست * بيک جام صد توبه بايد شکست
ميى همچو خون کبوتر بيار * باين خون بود تشنه باز خمار
بهارست اى ساقى نو نهال * بذوق گل و لاله بر خود ببال
نظر ميکشان را بانعام تست * گل و لاله را چشم بر جام تست

Come here my server, you who pour and sip, * Come here, antidote to
my hangover.
Cure my headache with another goblet * Start my spring once again with wine.
It is spring, cupbearer, you worshipper of wine * You must break a hundred
penances with a single cup.
Bring a wine as crimson as dove's blood * For which the hawk of my
hangover thirsts.
It is spring, cupbearer, my sapling * Stand tall, like the lily and the tulip.

Drinkers gaze only with your favour * The lily and the tulip stare at the cup of
your countenance.

As Ahsan develops his theme in *Maykhana-yi Raz*, he depicts recurring bouts
of drinking, using structural elements, like recapitulation, to mimic the sensory
experience of repeatedly raising the goblet and experiencing the cognitive
dissonance of inebriation. We find similar repetitions in the poems by Ilahi and
Ashna. Ahsan borrows elements of Ilahi's approach to rhetoric and imagery here,
for example by using the *isti ʿara* 'wet-nosed' (*tar-damāgh*) to describe the closed
buds of the roses covered in dew. This metaphor, which is based on the idea that
the bud of the rose is pointed, elongated and therefore visually analogous to a nose,
is comparable with Ilahi's analogy likening the furled buds to casks of wine: both
find a bacchanalian point of comparison to describe the closed flower. Similarly,
Ahsan's idea of converting night into day through joy finds an antecedent in Ilahi's
description of the nocturnal tavern, where the cups of wine stand in for candles.
Both images are about the transformation of darkness into light through wine:[73]

بهارست و گلشن پر از بوی گل * توان کرد عشرت ز پهلوی گل

ز فیض بهارست گل تر دماغ * دو بالا شود نشاه می بباغ

بهارست در روز باید طرب * بخور می بکوتاهی عمر شب

چراغ طرب را بر سحر بر فروز * نشاط شبت را بدل کن بروز

بهارست و گلها بود رنگ بست * چو بلبل بهر گل شدم می پرست

It is spring and the scent of roses floats throughout the garden * We can delight
ourselves alongside the flowers.
The spring showers leave the roses wet-nosed * Wine leaves us twice as drunk
in the garden.
It is spring – we must dance for joy in the daylight * And drink wine
throughout the brief night.
Light the lamp of joy at dawn * Glee is for the night, which you must
change to day.
It is spring, and the colour has settled on the roses * I worship wine as
the nightingale lusts after the rose.

Further on in *Maykhana-yi Raz*, Ahsan evokes the mountains, writing that their
slopes (*kamar*, lit. 'belt') have been hidden in greenery. This description parallels
Ilahi's representation of the elm tree, quoted earlier, in which the poet writes that
the tree has donned a belt of greenery. Such transpositions of conceits into new
contexts are paralleled by both poets' use of techniques including *mura ʿat al-nazir*
('observance of the similar', or compound metaphor). Ilahi builds a metaphor
in which he likens the birds to men reciting the five daily prayers, and he then
compounds it by comparing their nest to the mosque. Similarly, Ahsan likens
the mountainside to an emerald mine and then compounds it by describing the
wine as 'ruby-red'. In both cases, the poets introduce a field of imagery in the first
hemistich and extend it associatively in the second:[74]

بهارست و پرگل شده دشت و در * نهان کوه در سبزه شد تا کمر

چو کان زمرد شده کوهسار * بود باده لعلگون خوشگوار

کند خون توبه علاج صداع * ورع را نمودیم دیگر وداع

بهارست و گل در چمن خود نماست * اگر بشکفد طبع بلبل بجاست

چو بلبل نیم عاشق رنگ و بو * بباغم گل رو بود آرزو

چو وصل بتان آرزو میکنم * ز حسن بتی گفت و گو میکنم

It is spring, and the plains and vales are full of flowers * The mountain is
hidden up to its waist in greenery.
The hillside has become like an emerald mine * And ruby wine is easy on
the tongue.
The blood of repentance eases our headache * We have bidden farewell
to temperance.
It is spring and the rose in the meadow flaunts itself * If it blooms, the
nightingale's passion will be justified.
I am not like a nightingale, enamoured of bright colours and fragrant scents, *
I long for a rosy face in the garden.
And since I yearn to be with my idols * I speak of the beauty of idols.

The use of overlapping images and techniques in the *saqinama*s of Ilahi, Ashna
and Ahsan is part of their creation of a shared idiom of representation that is partly
emotive and partly ethical. When analysing poems such as *saqinama*s, we have to
move beyond the limitations that our expectations of a genre and its conventions
impose and instead investigate the particular world view that authors are espousing.
Ilahi, Ashna and Ahsan construct a dialogue with one another which celebrates
intoxication (both literal and figurative) and argues that it can liberate the intellect.
We see this idea in Ilahi's description of the blood thrumming in the veins of the
ascetic, or in the following passage, where Ashna speaks of a wine 'that could keep
house with Plato', developing an image that is found in the *saqinama* of Zuhuri:[75]

بیا ساقی غمگسارم بیا * بیا شمع شبهای تارم بیا

زمینای گردون کش بر ستیز * بجامم زروی عنایت بریز

شرابی که از فرط فرزانگیش * فلاطون بنازد به همخانگیش

{شرابی که چون چشم غلمان و حور * از او چشم داغست لبریز نور[76]}

{شرابی که آرام دلها از اوست * شرابی که سرسبز مینا از اوست[77]}

چه بیهوده خواهی ز دستش ایاغ[78] * مزن دم که ساقی ندارد دماغ

{ز بس بوسه زد بر لب جام زر * دهانش بتنگ آمده چون شکر[79]}

بمی اینچنان گشته بی التفات * که بد میبرد نام آب حیات

مرا ذوق ساغر دلا میکشد * طلب می کنم گر مرا میکشد

بیا ساقی آن زاده تاک را * که باشد ازو آبرو خاک را

شرابی که جامست ازو سرخ رو * کدو نیز سرسبز باشد ازو

بمن ده که پایم بسنگ آمده است * دلم پر ز هستی بتنگ آمده است

Come here, server of the sorrowing, * Come here, lamp of my dark nights.
Rail this once against Heaven * And favour my goblet

With a wine so old * It could have kept house with Plato.
A wine that brightens the eye and makes it overflow with light * Like the
eyes of young men and the women of Paradise.
A wine which consoles the heart * And refreshes the cup.
How vain to ask for the cup from his hands * Do not waste your breath –
the cupbearer is giddy.
He has kissed the golden chalice so often * That his mouth is now as small
as a grain of sugar.
His mind has wandered so much with wine * That he curses the water of life.
Longing for the goblet drags me in its wake * I will seek it even if it kills me.
Come cupbearer, bring me the child of the vine * In which the earth takes
so much pride.
A wine which leaves the wine-cup flushed * And makes the goblet bloom.
Give it to me, for my feet have turned to stone * And my once vital heart flutters.

While all three poets figure wine as an agent of intellectual liberation, the key to
the philosophical symposium of the *majlis*, and as a herald of joy, which prepares
the way for romantic encounters, they also exhibit a distinct anxiety about the
transgressive nature of wine consumption and associate it with addiction and
mortality. As Ashna says, 'I will seek it even if it kills me.' The equation between wine
and blood is a very old image which appears in Persian as far back as the Rudaki's (d.
329/940–1 or later) *Madar-i May*, and it is associated with a complex of motifs that
figure the grape as the 'daughter of the vine' (*dukhtar-i raz*), the sacrificial victim
of the vintner.[80] This makes the idea of imbibing disquieting, but the poets imply
that they are caught in an existential trap for which wine consumption is the only
solution. Ahsan and Ashna discuss the idea of 'repentance' (*tawba*), a Qur'anic
word, and the impossibility of keeping their vows of abstention, which leads to
the apprehension of divine judgement that Ahsan describes in the following piece,
part of a longer *saqinama*:[81]

سرگرمی ما باده کشان از می ناب است * بی نشاء می کاسهٔ سر جام حبابست
بی باده مغنی گر از آهنگ فتادست * بی نغمهٔ تر دختر رز نیز کبابست
روزی که دهد ساقی ما جام شماره * آن روز بما باده کشان روز حسابست
از شیشه می دل نفسی دور نگردد * پروانهٔ پر سوختهٔ شمع شرابست
در جلوه در آرید دگر دختر رز را * کز دوری می کار من خسته خرابست
در دام شرابیم نداریم گریزی * ساقی پی دن بردن ما این چه شتابست
ما باده کشان جمعه و شنبه نشناسیم * بی قید از اینم که ایام شبابست
در میکده صد توبه بیک جام شکستیم * کردیم اگر توبه سحر شام شکستیم

We tipplers delight in undiluted wine * Even without its intoxicating scent,
the goblet's head is our beloved.
If the singer is deprived of wine, he loses his melody * Without a succulent tune,
the daughter of the vine becomes parched.
For us drinkers, the Day of Reckoning is when * Our cupbearer counts how
many times he has passed around the goblet.

Our hearts are constant to the glass * They are the moths singed in
wine's candle.
Bring the daughter of the vine into the light again * For my separation from the
wine has left me forlorn.
We are in wine's snare with no escape * Why do you rush after us, cupbearer,
to carry off the vat?
We boozers do not know Friday from Saturday * I have no ties, for I am in
my youth.
In the tavern, we broke a hundred penances with a single cup * If we recanted
at dawn, we sinned by dusk.

Of the three poets, Ilahi is the most explicit in representing intoxication as a
snare for the unwary, making the cadences of his *saqinama* – with its repeated
elements implying that the narrative persona is being propelled ineluctably
towards his doom – stronger. He has quite a developed excursus on the divine
punishment that awaits those who consume alcohol, writing that hypocrites
have a prior sense of Inferno, and saying that those who imbibe wine cannot
drink the water of piety.[82] These warnings allow him to pivot his discourse into a
discussion of 'Ali b. Abi Talib as a salvific figure, the 'emperor of those gathered
at the assembly of generosity' (*shahinshāh-i mahfil-nishīnān-i jūd*).[83] This may
strike readers as a curious realignment in a poem that otherwise celebrates wine
as an agent of self-knowledge, but, like the characters projected by Ahsan and
Ashna in their poems, Ilahi's persona is fully aware of the paradox which his
poem seeks to explore: that wine both liberates and entraps. We see this idea
clearly in his metaphorical reading of the desire for wine as the flood of Noah,
which has already swept him away:[84]

بیا ساقی آن می که آشوب روح * ازو گشت پیدا چو طوفان نوح
بمن ده که دارد امیدم گرو * بمیخانه‌ها کشتی ماه نو
ز طوفان حذر آن زمان داشتم * که سودای ساحل بجان داشتم
کنون پیش چشمم چه دریا چه دشت * که تا دوش آب از سرم بر آمدست[85]

Cupbearer, bring the wine which disturbs * My soul like Noah's flood.
Give it to me, for ark of the new moon * Has sailed away with my hopes in
the taverns.
At that moment I feared the flood * My soul had a dark longing for the shore.
Now sea and plain are the same to me * For the waters have risen to my neck.

Conclusion

In this chapter, I have identified Sa'ib within a network of his contemporaries,
whose interactions both supported extratextual social hierarchies through
panegyric poetry and undermined them by making professional poets the source
of literary authority. I have also described how the principal inspiration for

Ahsan and Ashna's *saqinama*s was not the famous Sa'ib, but rather Ilahi. The fact that Ilahi is all but forgotten today is a reminder that canonical hierarchies change over the centuries, and that we need to reconstruct the dynamics that persisted within defined settings such as courts if we want to understand which writers were regarded as models in their own time. My reading of the materials suggests that the emulative relationship between Sa'ib and Ilahi is mature, in the sense that each poet really transposes the imagery and techniques of his peer across forms and genres, rather than simply copying them. Latitude of interpretation is the main aesthetic of this form of imitation, which establishes the two poets as independent equals, invested in a common project.[86] Ahsan and Ashna are more emulative of, and hence dependent on, the work of Ilahi, with Ashna being particularly dependent on his father. This does not necessarily have to be a sign that Ashna was a weak poet; rather, it is the mark of an attempt to ally himself politically and ideologically with Ahsan, creating a literary network which followed the contours of the political structures of the Mughal state.

Chapter 7

ISFAHAN

SALIM, DARVISH YUSUF AND AKBAR

The exodus of poets from Iran to India during the seventeenth century is such a well-documented social phenomenon that it is not hard to rattle off a list of the most famous migrants (Kalim, Salim Tihrani, Talib Amuli, Qudsi, Sa'ib), or to pick out the most common destinations of their journeys (Agra, Shahjahanabad, Kashmir). Yet if we turn our focus in the opposite direction and try to come up with a list of poets who migrated from India to Iran, we might struggle to name a single one, since there are no instantly recognizable authors who were born in the Mughal Empire or in the Deccan Sultanates and who sought patronage with the Safavids. Some readers may even go so far as to assume that no poet born in India would have even entertained the idea of travelling to Iran during the seventeenth century, since the state of the literary market in South Asia was so robust, and the vast wealth of the Mughal aristocracy, provincial governors and rulers of smaller kingdoms ensured that there were many potential centres of patronage in addition to the imperial Mughal court, many of which attracted émigré poets quite independently.[1] An Indian poet of Persian would have been able to spend his life circulating from patron to patron without ever needing to risk his life and his livelihood by setting sail for Iran on the Arabian Sea.

Yet a number of poets who were raised in India did actually make the journey to Iran. They are almost entirely forgotten today, but I argue that they are particularly significant because an examination of their work can help us to complicate the assumption that seventeenth-century literature in Persian was born from a marriage of convenience between Iranian talent and Indian money. Those figures who travelled against the current and journeyed from India to Iran invite us to interrogate not only the idea that the 'Indian Style' (*sabk-i hindi*) was solely forged through the tastes of Indian patrons, but also the very concept that seventeenth-century poetry can be reduced to a single manner and mode of expression. By examining how Indian authors integrated into literary circles in Iran at the same time as more famous groupings of émigré Iranian poets were formed in India, we can chart the extent to which early modern literary aesthetics evolved stochastically, creating cliques of writers and readers in different cities, and how they were modified in tandem through the widespread circulation of a common corpus of materials.

It is all the more remarkable that scholars have not sought to study the presence of Indian writers in early modern Iran because the Indian community was consistently identified as one of the largest and most visible immigrant groups in the Safavid domains.[2] European observers who visited Isfahan throughout the seventeenth century routinely estimated that 10,000 émigré Indians, who were primarily involved in the businesses of moneylending and long-distance trade, were permanent residents of the Safavid capital.[3] Little precise demographic data is available regarding the background of these émigrés, but they were clearly a diverse group. Some, like al-Sarim al-Hindi's father in Yemen, were Banya;[4] others were Afghan and Panjabi subjects of the Mughal Empire.[5] Citizens of Indian polities also had an established presence in Iran's port towns – both on the Persian Gulf littoral and on the Caspian coast – and in major cities such as Shiraz, where a bazar and a caravansary capable of accommodating 200 people were organized and run by Indian traders, many of whom were textile merchants.[6] As Stephen Dale puts it, the émigré Indian community appears 'to have exerted a pervasive economic influence in [seventeenth-century Iran]; dominating the foreign trade between India and Iran, operating as influential merchants within Iran and supplying capital to a chronically capital-starved Iranian economy'.[7] This internationalism was also reflected in Persian literary texts produced in seventeenth-century Isfahan: the Safavid court historiographer Muhammad Tahir Vahid (d. 1112/1701), for example, composed a narrative poem which relates the adventures of two lovers who journey from India to Isfahan.[8] As migration between Iran and India was bidirectional in the fields of business and trade, it is logical to enquire whether poets too formed part of the inward flow of people to the Safavid domains.

Three protagonists

As the three men whom I have chosen to study in this chapter did not form part of Iran's resident community of Indian merchants, their stories serve to broaden our understanding of the variety of ways in which the Safavid and Mughal empires were connected. The first, Darvish Yusuf Kashmiri, is listed in Nasrabadi's chapter on religious scholars and learned men.[9] His name indicates that he was a Sufi from Kashmir. Nasrabadi tells us that he came to Isfahan with the intention of settling down and marrying, demonstrating the transregional links that familial alliances created.[10] For a while he rented a room in the *madrasa* of the calligraphers, which was located by the Haruniyya Mosque in central Isfahan.[11] He then put together enough money for a house, with the help of the *vaqi'a-nivis* (i.e. the court historiographer, Muhammad Tahir Vahid), who patronized him for an extended period of time.[12] Nasrabadi tells us that Darvish Yusuf was not only very learned, but also a talented party-organizer and a great wit.[13] The narrative that he creates is one of Darvish Yusuf's successful integration into the life of the Safavid capital: he married, he secured the patronage of a high-ranking politician, and he played host to *majalis* at his house. Nasrabadi is obviously admiring of him and makes no comment which might suggest that Isfahani society either considered the presence of Persian speakers from outside the Safavid domains to be unusual or looked down on Darvish Yusuf because he was not a local. Participation in a shared system of learning and social behaviours – exemplified in Nasrabadi's account by the institution of the *majlis* – gave Darvish Yusuf a way into the literary life of Safavid Isfahan.

Elsewhere in his anthology, Nasrabadi devotes an entry to a second poet who came from India to Iran, Mir Lutf Allah, known by his pen name, 'Salim' (سليم).[14] The son of Mir Sayyid 'Ali of Kashmir, and evidently a Twelver Shi'i, Mir Lutf Allah Salim was motivated to travel west in order to study with religious scholars and to visit the pilgrimage sites of Iraq, but he ended up making many exchanges with Iranian poets, and the anthologist classes him as a professional poet, not as a divine. Nasrabadi tells us that the overland route from Kashmir to Iran was blocked by the Afghans at the time when Salim was setting out, so he went to Shahjahanabad, and from there to the port of Surat, where he waited four months for the monsoon to arrive.[15] He took a ship to Bandar 'Abbas and then travelled inland to Shiraz, where he began to spend time with local writers.[16] The choice of this route and the timing of the journey correspond with common practice at the time: sailing with the northeast monsoon in late autumn or early winter allowed passenger ships to cross the Arabian Sea to Bandar 'Abbas in two to three weeks.[17]

After a short time in Shiraz, Salim journeyed on to Isfahan, where he debated religious topics with the scholar Muhammad Baqir Khurasani (d. 1090/1679) and then went to Najaf and Karbala to perform pilgrimage.[18] On his return to Iran, he was patronized by the *vizir* of Kirmanshahan, and travelled to Hamadan, Qum, and back to Isfahan.[19] Nasrabadi's good friend, the prominent poet and bureaucrat Mir Najat (d. *c.* 1126/1714), was at that time setting out for Mashhad, and so Salim joined him on the journey.[20] Having visited the shrine of the Imam Riza, Salim went on to Herat, where he spent time with Mir Sa'd al-Din Muhammad Raqim (d. 1100/1688-9), the local governor and himself an author.[21] He then returned to Mashhad, where he bumped into another influential poet, Mirza Muhsin Ta'sir of Tabriz (d. 1129/1716-17), who was on his way to Mazandaran.[22] Salim was struck by a sudden desire to see the Caspian region, perhaps because it was often represented as the Iranian homologue of Kashmir.[23] The more famous Salim (سليم) Tihrani had re-labelled his poem describing Lahijan, in Gilan, as a work about Kashmir when he was transplanted to India.[24] Ta'sir and Mir Lutf Allah Salim therefore set off west together, stopping in Astarabad and spending some time there with the *vizir* Mir Muhammad Rahim.[25] Salim then returned to Isfahan, where he was still living, according to Nasrabadi, in 1089/1678-9.[26] Like Darvish Yusuf Kashmiri, Salim appears to have been fully integrated into Safavid networks after his arrival in Iran: Najat and Ta'sir were two of the country's most prominent writers in the 1670s, and Raqim was one of the most significant poet-patrons in Khurasan; he is best known today for his support for Shawkat Bukhari (d. 1107/1695-6).[27] We have previously encountered Raqim as one of the authors who inscribed the *jung* of Fayyaz.

The third protagonist of this chapter is known to us in a great amount of detail, thanks to a text entitled *Tarikh-i Kishikkhana-yi Humayun* (*The History of the Royal Guard House*), which was completed in Isfahan in 1110/1698 by the poet Nur al-Din Muhammad Sharif Kashani (d. 1123/1711–12), known by his *takhallus*, Najib. Najib himself features in *Tazkira-yi Nasrabadi* as a young man, the son of a draper from Kashan, who had arrived in Isfahan several years before the compilation of the anthology and set himself up in the capital's Kashan Caravansary.[28] He also appears in Maliha's *Muzakkir al-Ashab* as a prickly and arrogant protégé of the governor of Yerevan.[29] His *History* is a remarkable account of Najib's interactions with the Mughal prince Jalal al-Din Akbar (d. 1119/1707), the third son of the emperor Awrangzib (d. 1118/1707), who should not be confused with his forebear, the third Mughal emperor Akbar the Great (d. 1014/1605). For a time, Prince Akbar acted as governor of Kashmir, and it was there that he first encountered Najib, who had emigrated to India and entered Akbar's service as a court poet in around 1676–7.[30] In 1090/1679, Akbar attempted to stage a coup against Awrangzib, but the plot failed, and Akbar was forced to flee to the border town of Qandahar, which the Safavids had wrested from Mughal control in 1058/1648.[31]

Akbar's matrilineal kinship with the Safavids made Iran the obvious destination in which to seek asylum from his father's acrimony, but it was only in 1099/1687–8, after about nine years on the periphery of the empire, that the Safavid Shah Sulayman allowed him to come to Isfahan.[32] There, three courtiers who had a prior association with Akbar – Najib, Mulla Muhammad Amin Sa'd Allah Khani and Mulla Baha' al-Din Fazil Hindi – were appointed to attend the prince in watches (*kishik*s) on alternate days of the week, keeping him company but also collecting information on him.[33] Najib, who must have spent a total of about 800 watches with Akbar over the course of the prince's eight years in the Safavid capital, recorded the discussions that they had in his history, which was written for the grand *vizir* and former court historiographer, Muhammad Tahir Vahid (the patron of Darvish Yusuf Kashmiri).[34] The narratives of the watches follow the daily life of Akbar and his entourage in Isfahan, as they move through spaces ranging from Akbar's lodgings to the gardens of Iranians who had returned from India. Najib's account provides us with a closely observed, psychologically nuanced portrait of his charge, as the two men discuss history, politics, philosophy and poetry.

Tarikh-i Kishikkhana-yi Humayun is full of moments which speak to how a transregional Persian culture was both maintained and constantly undermined, as Akbar and his interlocutor muse on contrasting dreams of power, consider sectarian differences, and use humour to both connect with and distinguish themselves from each other. In one episode, Akbar goes with his entourage to the house of Mirza Ahmad, a Safavid courtier from an eminent Mughal family, and the party relaxes by fishing in a stream running through Mirza Ahmad's garden.[35] The exiled pretender to the Mughal throne catches several fish, which he lays out, gasping, on the edge of the stream. He then asks his companions what the fish are 'saying' as their mouths convulse, promising the haul to the winner of the contest. The first guesses are pedestrian: one follower imagines that they are greeting Akbar, the emperor; another pretends that they are predicting how they will sate the party's hunger. Akbar himself jokes that they are asking why he has forsaken sea fishing to dredge a narrow channel, a comment on his diminished circumstances. Najib, picking up on this, retorts: 'no, they are saying something else: that sea fishing has its season, but it requires the aid of Noah's ark (*safina-yi nūh*).' 'Noah's ark' is conventionally understood as a reference to the 'ship' of Shi'ism, and so his implication is that if Akbar wants to launch an assault on the Mughal Empire he should first convert to the Safavid state religion. Akbar is noticeably discomfited by this comment, and the other courtiers tell Najib to be 'sincere'. He tries again: they are asking for water. One of the courtiers complains that his own guess was far more astute, and Najib delivers his punchline: 'Just so. A leech knows the tongue of a fish better than anyone.' Akbar collapses with laughter and rewards Najib with the fish.

As seemingly innocuous and bucolic as a fishing trip may be, the interactions between Akbar, his entourage and Najib are predicated on a complicated mixture of mutual distrust and a shared way of being. Akbar's dreams of following in his ancestor Humayun's footsteps and returning to India with a conquering army must have seemed delirious to critical audiences in Isfahan, and there is a sense in which Najib's initial remarks are slightly cutting: his veiled comment on Shi'ism, dismissed as 'sarcasm' (*ramz*) by the others, implies that Akbar should realize how dependent he is on Safavid support. At the same time, Najib is present at the gathering as Akbar's boon-companion, and there is an expectation, formed through a cultural convention, that he discharge the role of resident wit and make the pretender laugh. When he does this, Akbar tells him that he has done his job (*kār-i khud kardī*).[36]

Globalizing culture and political borders

While Darvish Yusuf, Akbar and Salim came from contrasting backgrounds and each of them found themselves in Safavid Iran for different reasons, their stories are united by their use of textual production and literary criticism as a way of exploring shared identities with Iranians. These shared identities are part of a globalizing culture of ethics conducted in Persian, which inevitably rubs up against the boundaries instituted by early modern political dispensations. Darvish Yusuf's participation in the cultural life of Isfahan is attested by a series of letters that he wrote, which were selected for inclusion in manuscript albums and commonplaces, where they both served as emulable models of good style and documented the connections between members of the literary elite. Such albums have recently been studied by Kathryn Babayan, who describes how they preserve "networks of the texts and intersecting lives that mattered" to their compilers.[37] In an album that is now in the collections of the University of Isfahan, one of Darvish Yusuf's letters is surrounded by correspondence between his patron, Muhammad Tahir Vahid, and the heirs of the poet Hakim Rukna-yi Kashi, as well as an epistle by the writer Nasira-yi Hamadani, showing how the compiler of the volume quite literally imbricated Darvish Yusuf into the fabric of Safavid literary culture.[38]

Darvish Yusuf's missive is intriguing because it acts as a meeting point for a series of interests. It is addressed to an unnamed merchant, and the end makes it clear that it is essentially an apology for a perceived slight. Darvish Yusuf couches the apology in an extended metaphor which plays off both the addressee's background in commerce, and the author's professional work as a religious adept, all in richly rhymed prose (*saj ʿ*). Using the language of transnational trade, Darvish Yusuf opens the letter by likening conception and birth to a maritime journey:

مخفی نماند که ساکنان عدم آباد بعد از مدت مدید و عهد بعید متاع اضداد اربعه را بحال خریداری
نموده‌اند و از خطهٔ شهر مذکور متوجه دار الظهور حضرت وجود گردیده‌اند و چون به بندر بحرین
صلب و رحم ابوین رسیده‌اند چند روزی باندازِ بخرج بهاء اللؤلؤ والمرجان از جهت بعضی تکمیلات
صوری و معنوی مکث کرده‌اند و از آنجا بدار الشواغل دنیا نزول اجلال ارزانی داشته‌اند.

It should not be kept hidden that, after a lengthy period of time, the inhabitants of the land of non-existence decided to purchase the goods of the four elements, and set off from the aforementioned place towards the domain of Presence. When they reached the port of the two seas of their parents' loins and womb, they paused for several days, as they sought to buy pearls and coral so as to acquire extrinsic and intrinsic perfection, and then bestowed themselves on the abode of earthly cares in a disembarkation of glory.

The letter is undoubtedly intended to be abstruse and to contain layers of meaning that bear repeated reading. In composing it, Darvish Yusuf draws his addressee towards him by creating a marriage of their interests, between his own background in theology and philosophy and his interlocutor's mercantile activity. This is a rapprochement through an elision of their world views. In this sense, it contributes to a globalizing culture.

As we have seen with the tale of the fishing trip, Najib's encounters with Prince Akbar were not always so smooth. Akbar was evidently vocal in sharing his hopes for rule with members of his entourage, and even in his diminished circumstances, he adhered to ceremonial as best he could, as though he were the future emperor of Mughal India. The patronage of courtly poetry formed part of his practices, and Najib's *Tarikh-i Kishikkhana-yi Humayun* contains numerous *qasaʾid* which the poet composed and performed himself for the exiled prince. Given the anecdotal tone of Najib's history, the work provides a relatively rare insight into how panegyric verse could be received, and of the criticisms which could be levelled against it. There is one particular episode in which Najib performs a *qasida* in celebration of the Persian New Year (*nawruz*) for the prince. He sets the scene by saying that he was the third of Akbar's entourage to be admitted into his presence that New Year's Day, and that Akbar had lined up boxes full of *ashrafis* (gold presentation coins) as gifts for his followers. Najib's box contained ten gold coins. He performed his panegyric, but Akbar was angered by the imagery of the poem and refused to present him with his gift. Instead, he demanded that Najib explain and justify the thesis of the poem.

The reason for Akbar's vexation was fairly simple: he criticized Najib for using similes of darkness and shadow when referring to Akbar and India in his poem.[39] Najib indicates that Akbar perceived the scheme of imagery as a personal slight, designed to denigrate India as a land in the shade of Iran's brilliance. It might seem to us that debates such as these are rather inert reflections on the frail egos of rulers, or a blunt form of geopoetics in which Iran is being pitted against India. However, a comparison between this *qasida* and others that were in circulation shows how Akbar had a set of expectations for how he should be represented, and that Najib was attempting to walk a political tightrope. The poem begins as follows:[40]

نوشته بر قدح مه به زعفران خورشید * همین دعا که مبارک بود الهی عید
توان به گرد چنین سال گردشی گشتن * که بر مراد تو گردیده همچو گردش عید
گشوده بیدق اقبال پرچم اجلال * دمیده صبح سعادت ز مشرق امید
به شب زیادتی روز بعد از این رمزی ست * که روزگار ز ایران سپه به هند کشید
چو شب که از اثر آفتاب گردد روز * زمین سایهٔ هند آفتاب رو گردید
به هند داد تسلط تو را شهنشه دین * چنان که روز مسلط به شب شد از خورشید
ستاره نیست به شب جلوه گر که روز است * فلک به نام تو در هند زر زد و پاشید
اگر نه قبله مردم تویی به هند چرا * چو روی تافتی از خلق قبله هم گردید
ز شوق آنکه شود بر سر تو سایه فکن * همای سلطنت هند از آشیانه پرید
نخواست تا به غلط سایه افکند بر غیر * چو مرغ قبله نما سایه را به پر دزدید

The sun has inscribed in saffron on the goblet of the moon * This very prayer: 'May divine 'Id be blessed'.
One can celebrate the end of a year like this, in which your accession coincides with the new year * For 'Id has turned on your wishes, as though revolving around them.
Fortune's pawn has unfurled the flag of might * And the dawn of joy has broken from the eastern sky of hope.
The lengthening days to follow are a mark * That fate has drawn its army from Iran to India.
For when the influence of the sun turns night to day * The shadowy land of India becomes bright-faced.
Faith handed absolute power to you, emperor, in India, * Just as the day was given control over the night through the sun.
The stars do not shine in the night sky, because it is day. * The heavens minted coins and scattered them in your name over India.
If the people of India do not direct their prayer to you * Then why does the place to which you have turned from them become the focus of their prayers as well?
The regal bird of India has flown the nest * Longing to cast its shadow over your head.
It did not want to err by casting its shadow on another. * Like a weathercock, it stole the shade with its wing.

* * *

چراغ دولت هند از تو گشت روشن باز * چنان که آینهٔ شب ز پرتو خورشید

The lamp of the Indian state burns brightly again because of you * Like the
beam of the sun in the mirror of the night.

Akbar was evidently familiar with the poetry that was being produced and
consumed at the Safavid court, as he compared the poem just cited with another
qasida by Najib which the poet had written for Sultan Sulayman. This *qasida* has
the refrain 'sun' (*āftāb*), which is used in a number of other seventeenth-century
panegyrics, including, perhaps significantly, one in praise of the Prophet that
was composed by Mir Damad (d. 1041/1631);[41] as well as a number of *ghazals* by
Sa'ib.[42] The main difference between Najib's pieces in praise of Prince Akbar and
Sultan Sulayman is not that Najib represents Iran as a kingdom of light and India
as a land of darkness, but rather that Najib explicitly describes Sultan Sulayman
as the sun – a source of warmth, power and beauty. He writes: 'There is no king
but you on land and sea / Only one sun shines over every country.'[43] We find the
implication that Akbar is like the sun in the *qasida* that Najib composed for him,
but we have to reach this conclusion through induction, as when Najib builds a
parallel between the bestowal of power on Akbar and the bestowal of light on
India. By way of contrast, there is no doubt in the panegyric to Sultan Sulayman
that the Safavid king is the centre of the universe:[44]

ای در نقاب ماه رخت مضمر آفتاب * آیینهٔ جمال تو را در بر آفتاب

از برق تیغ حسن تو هر کس شهید شد * در قطره قطره خون بودش مضمر آفتاب

من با کدام دیده چو خفاش بینمت * ای ذره ذره حسن تو را در بر آفتاب

روی توام ز کعبه و بتخانه بازداشت * آدم پرست کرد مرا کافر آفتاب

چون یوسف از نقاب برون آ که عمر هاست * بر کف گرفته تیغ و ترنج زر آفتاب

انگشت حیرتش به دهان مانده از شعاع * تا دیده روی ماه تو در خاور آفتاب

یک ذره اش قبول نباشد به چشم خلق * تشریف حسن اگر تو نپوشی بر آفتاب

خوابانده ابروان تو شمشیر بر هلال * افکنده چشمت از مژه خنجر بر آفتاب

در رخنه های شانهٔ زلفت شده نهان * از تاب مهر روی تو چون شهپر آفتاب

از دانه دانه خال تو مه مردمک به چشم * وز حلقه حلقه زلف تو در منظر آفتاب

پایش نمیرسد به زمین گویی از غرور * سر برگرفته با تو ز یک بستر آفتاب

واجب شد آفتاب پرستی به کاینات * روزی که گشت حسن تو را مظهر آفتاب

گفتم به ماه روی تو دارد شباهتی * خود را سجود کرد ز هی کافر آفتاب

من آن نیم که بی تو برم التجا به ماه * من آن نیم که سجده نمایم بر آفتاب

The moon of your cheek in your veil outshines the sun * The sun is reflected in
the mirror of your beauty.
Mankind is martyred in the glint of your beauty's sword * The trickle of
blood that it sheds obscures the sun.
Like a bat [brought into the light], how can I gaze on you, * Each mote of
whose beauty is an equal to the sun?
Your face turned me away from the Ka'ba and the temple * The sun, the
idolator, made me worship man as God.

Discard your veil, like Joseph, for it is an age * Since the sun took the blade
and the golden orange in hand.

When the sun saw the moon of your face in the east * It held a finger of
beams to its lips in astonishment.

The eyes of the people would not accept even one of its motes * If you did
not garb the sun in beauty.

Your brows rain swords at the crescent moon * Your eyes cast daggers at
the sun.

Like downy hair, the sun hid from the heat of your face's beauty * In the flat
of your tresses.

The pupil of the moon's eye comes from your beauty spot * And I have a
sun before my gaze in the ringlets of your tresses.

You may say that it is pride which forbids the tip [of your hair] to touch the
ground * The sun has lifted its head from the same pillow as you.

On the day when your beauty made the sun apparent * Creation was
enjoined to worship the sun.

I said that your face resembled the moon * It was right that the idolotrous
sun bowed before it.

I cannot take refuge in the moon without you * Nor can I bow before
the sun.

Here, in the introit to the *qasida*, the sultan is depicted in an eroticized fashion, with the famously veiled prophet Joseph acting as his alter ego. The sun is compared to the ladies of Potiphar's household, who were so distracted when they saw Joseph that they sliced into their hands rather than cutting open the oranges which they were holding. The poet's approach here, which places the patron-beloved at the centre of the matrix of images, contrasts strongly with his technique in the *qasida* addressed to Akbar, where the pretender is essentially divested of agency: fortune, fate and the heavens have awarded Akbar with power, but he is not represented as bringing his dreams to bear in the world. Najib continues in this vein, again mounting an overtly ideological challenge to Akbar to convert to Shi'ism, and ending the poem with the assertion that Akbar is the beneficiary of fate:[45]

تو کار خود به علی و اجاق او بگذار * که روشن است از این نور مشعل خورشید
به رنگ ماه رخ از نور آفتاب متاب * که صبح طالعت از مشرق امید دمید
شکفته شو که گل خرمی دمید به باغ * بهار شو که خزان رفت و نوبهار رسید
سریر شاه جهانیت جاودان باشد * به خرمی و جهانگیریت مبارک عید
زمانه کرد در این سال نو به تو تحویل * سریر هند و کلید خزاین امید

Leave your affairs to 'Ali and his family * For the torch of the sun is bright
thanks to their light.

Do not turn your cheek, as pale as the moon, from the light of the sun *
For the dawn of your ascendent fortune has broken from the eastern sky
of hope.

Blossom, since the rose of joy has bloomed in the garden * And turn to
spring, for autumn has disappeared and the equinox is here.
May your throne, the throne of the king of the world, be eternal * And may
your ʿId be blessed with delight and empire.
This new year, Fate handed you * The throne of India and the keys to the
treasury of hope.

We also have to bear in mind that Akbar's expectations of how he ought to have
been represented in panegyric poems would have been shaped by the eulogies
performed at the Mughal court. When we compare such pieces with Najib's *nawruz
qasida*, Najib's deviation from convention becomes clearer. In the following extract
from a panegyric by Talib Amuli in praise of Jahangir – itself seemingly a response
to a poem by Fayzi (d. 1004/1595) in praise of Akbar – the emperor is depicted as
an emissary of light.[46] It is not that the sun has illuminated India, but rather that
the emperor is the source of illumination, 'the divine ray of light':[47]

رسيد مژده که اينک جهان جاه رسيد * طراز کشور و آرايش سپاه رسيد
رسيد مژده که اينک ز پيش طاق جلال * فروغ چتر سليمان ببارگاه رسيد
رسيد مژده که اينک ز چين طرۀ شاه * علم علم اثر نور صبحگاه رسيد
رسيد موکب اقبال شاه و بر اثرش * حشم حشم سپه نصرت اله رسيد
بآستان جلالش ز شوق گردون را * نخست ديده رسيد آنگهی نگاه رسيد

Good news has come – behold, the orb of majesty * The ornament of the land
and the adornment of the army.
Good news has come – behold, the splendour of Solomon's parasol has
come from the * Portico of grandeur to the hall of audience.
Good news has come – behold, from the curl of the king's lock * The
banner of dawn light, which bears the mark of a prince, has arrived.
The cavalcade of the king's good fortune is here, and in its wake *
The mighty mass of the army, divinely victorious, has arrived.
First, heaven longed its eye to the threshold * Of his majesty, then held
its gaze.

*   *   *

بکنج غمکده حيران نشسته بودم دوش * که لمعۀ بدلم در شب سياه رسيد
بگوش ناگهم از هفتمين رواق سپهر * ندا رسيد که شاه ملک سپاه رسيد
ز فيض پرتو اين مژده در سياهی شب * ز روزنم تتق نور تا بماه رسيد
ز شاديانه خروشم نوای غم شد زار * چنانکه گه نرسيدم گه بگوش و گاه رسيد
بگفتم از چه شبستان هند شد پر نور * زمانه گفت ببين پرتو اله رسيد

Last night, I sat bewildered in a doleful corner * When a flash of light
touched my heart in the dark.
A voice called to my unsuspecting ear from the seventh heaven, *
Saying: 'the king, the commander of the army, is here'.

In the darkness of the night, the flood of this beam of good news * Made a
blanket of light reach the moon from my window.
Sorrow's lament grew faint at my joyful cry * So that I could not hear it as
dawn arrived.
I said: 'What has made benighted India radiant?' * Fate replied: 'See,
the divine ray of light has arrived'.

A comparison between the three panegyrics discussed in this section indicates
that the poems in praise of Jahangir and Sultan Sulayman expound a shared view
of the ruler, whereas Najib's piece to Akbar deliberately reduces the agency of the
prince. This only becomes clear when we read across the poems, as Najib's *qasida*
seems at first glance to consist of unadulterated eulogy. Ironically, perhaps, Akbar
was only able to perceive Najib's slight because he had a thorough grounding in
the conventions of the corpus. Once again, poetics are sustained by a transregional
culture, but the political field gives shape to literary community.

The limits of community: Poems ascribed to 'Salim'

Any literary historian who extends the purview of their research beyond materials
which have been published in modern critical editions becomes aware that our
entire impression of premodern authors' identities and their work is predicated on
the vagaries of manuscript culture. To quote Jean Bollack, 'it is impossible to build
an interpretation based on the raw material without going through the history
of interpretations'.[48] Not only can material aspects of the book, such as wormed
pages, missing folios and cacography, lead to mistaken attributions of poems to
the wrong poet, but the record itself is the accretive result of editorial choices
made by scribes. This is not a problem that pertains exclusively to seventeenth-
century Arabic and Persian literature by any means, but the issue is exacerbated by
the fact that only a minority of the collected works of the period have been print
published, and that those as yet unpublished seventeenth-century *diwans/divans*
which do survive are often limited to two or three manuscripts per poet, scattered
across collections globally.

The study of Mir Lutf Allah Salim's poetry presents a prime example of how
manuscript cultures shape our understanding of authors, because there appear
to have been two poets who both lived at the end of the seventeenth century,
who both came from Kashmir, and who were both called Salim (سالم). The
second was called Hajji Muhammad Aslam Salim, and he was the father of the
biographer Muhammad Aslah, who compiled a *tazkira* of poets of Kashmir.[49]
Aslam purportedly came from a family of Brahmins and converted to Islam
under Awrangzib, who appointed him to serve his son, Prince A'zamshah.[50] After
Awrangzib's death, A'zamshah very briefly became Mughal emperor for about
three months in 1707, before he was killed at the Battle of Jajau. During this time,
Aslam acted as one of A'zamshah's court poets, as his *khan-i saman*, and as the
superintendent of the imperial Mughal purchasing department.[51]

It is conceivable but unlikely that the two Salims were one and the same man, a recent convert who fabricated a Shi'i pedigree for himself when he visited the Safavid domains in his youth, and who later returned to India. Nasrabadi, who makes no mention of Hajji Muhammad Aslam, is our only source of information about Mir Lutf Allah, and his account forms the basis of subsequent discussions of this poet in the *tazkiras*.[52] Hajji Muhammad Aslam's son, Aslah, makes no identifiable mention of Mir Lutf Allah Salim in his own biographical anthology.[53] Potentially, therefore, we could simply be seeing a single life interpreted in different ways by two different biographers, writing decades apart. But it was common for a single *takhallus* to be shared by more than one poet, and on the balance of probability they were separate individuals.

Due to their shared pen name and the fact that they must have been direct contemporaries, it is not always immediately clear which manuscripts that are catalogued as the *divan* of 'Salim' represent the collected works of which poet. While I do not aim to underplay the likelihood of mistaken identities when attempting to find and study the poetry of Mir Lutf Allah, I judge the extant manuscripts of Salim's poetry now held in Oxford, Qum and Rampur to all be the work of Hajji Muhammad Aslam, primarily because none of the quotations from Mir Lutf Allah's work that are found in Nasrabadi's *tazkira* are featured in these volumes.[54] I therefore cast this as an opportunity to identify where the boundaries of community can be thought to lie. If the poetry that is ascribed to 'Salim' in the record engages with the work of Mir Lutf Allah's interlocutors in Iran but was actually composed by Aslam in India, it provides an occasion to explore how the intertextual connections between contemporaries who lived at different ends of the Persian zone of circulation differ from the dynamics of response poems shared between authors who settled in the same spaces.

Two *ghazals* which are found in the Rampur and Qum manuscripts of the *divan* of Hajji Muhammad Aslam help to elucidate this problem. Every line in these poems ends in *imshab* ('tonight'), a *radif* which had been popular since the twelfth century and remained so in the long seventeenth century.[55] Among the print published poets of the seventeenth century, Bidil;[56] Jalal Asir;[57] Mir Razi Danish;[58] Nazim Haravi;[59] Naziri;[60] Sa'ib;[61] Sadiq Samit;[62] Salik Qazvini;[63] Saydi;[64] Shapur;[65] Shawkat;[66] Shifa'i[67] and Ta'sir[68] all composed *ghazals* with this refrain, as did 'Ali Naqi Kamra'i;[69] 'Abd Allah Amani;[70] the *amir* Amani;[71] Atashi;[72] Faraj Allah Shushtari;[73] Hadi;[74] Ilahi;[75] Najat;[76] Nawras Damavandi,[77] Qubad Bayg Gurji Kawkabi;[78] Raqim;[79] Riza;[80] Tahir Vahid[81] and Yatim Burujardi,[82] whose collected works all remain in manuscript.

These poems all bear a loose connection to one another through the use of common items of lexis and broad themes, but it is possible to distinguish more defined 'paraphrase networks' of texts within this group which exist in a closer, emulative relationship, based on the use of at least several shared images and a dialogue in emotion and argument. Examining the corpus of seventeenth-century *ghazals* ending in *imshab* becomes an experience of remembering and forgetting lines. A newly encountered, apposite turn of phrase effaces and overwrites the old ones, and seems to capture the core of the idea which the poets are collectively trying to bring across. The poems take on the quality of palimpsests, with layers of imagery developed by earlier members of the chain visible just beneath the surface of each text. The poem becomes 'the point of departure for its aesthetic affect'.[83] Salim's *ghazals* in *imshab* show the strongest connections to pieces by Saydi, Sa'ib, Shapur and Bidil, and looser links to the poems of Jalal Asir, Atashi, Hadi, Mir Razi Danish and Nazim. They clash quite jarringly with the pieces by poets such as Riza and Sadiq Samit, which suddenly seem overtly neoclassical when placed side by side with them. Salim's first poem runs as follows:[84]

چمن طوفانی فیض و تجلی بی نقاب امشب * نمک دارد شکست رنگ گل در ماهتاب امشب
که شد طاقت گذارم میطپید در استخوان جوهر * چو فانوس خیالم از هجوم اضطراب امشب
ز جوش انتظار کیست طوفان گذار من * نگاهم میچکد از دیده چون اشک کباب امشب
سیه مست خیالم نشاه هوشست در مغزم * چو مهتابم بود بیداری سرخوش خواب امشب
ز هر برگ گلی بوی کباب تازه می آید * که می آید بگلشن برق شوخی در رکاب امشب
حواس بیخودی جمعیت مدهوشی شکون دارد * قدح لبریز و مطرب مست و ساقی بی حجاب امشب
بحیرت همزبانم با خموشی گفت و گو دارم * صدای آید از هر سو که میگوید جواب امشب
شب هجر ست پنداری کباب وعدهام سالم * نشستم تا قیامت در کمین آفتاب امشب

The meadow is storm-tossed with divine bounty and glory is unveiled tonight *
The shattered colour of the roses in the moonlight seems graceful tonight.
For my forceful step electrifies the kernels of the elements * Like the magic
lantern of my imagination in the onslaught of tonight's commotion.
Why such stormy progress? For whom do I wait anxiously? * My tears spit
from my eyes like frying fat tonight.
Black-drunk fantasy spawns understanding in my mind * Too intoxicated
to sleep, my wakefulness is like a moonbeam tonight.
Every rose petal releases the smell of burning * For playful lightning has
accompanied me to the meadow tonight.
In oblivion, my astonished senses augur well * The goblet overflows, the
minstrel is drunk and the cupbearer is unveiled tonight.
I speak as one with bewilderment and communicate with silence * I hear
answering voices from all sides tonight.
It is the night of parting and you would think me, Salim, burnt by promises
* I have sat down here until the end of time, to ambush the sun tonight.

In its very first line, this *ghazal* signals a relatively strong connection with Sa'ib's piece in the same rhyme and refrain. Where Salim speaks of the meadow being 'unveiled', and of the 'shattering of the colour of the roses in the moonlight', Sa'ib writes of the rose being 'unveiled', and of the scent of the jasmine flowers being burnished in the moonlight.[85] On one level, then, this is essentially a series of transpositions, or even substitutions, where cognate images ('the rose' and 'the jasmine', 'the colour' and 'the scent') are plugged into comparable grammatical structures.[86] However, Salim does not simply change Sa'ib's phrasing. In describing the 'shattering' of the colour of the roses – a reference to the moonlight bleaching the colour of their petals – Salim's l.1 also manages to engage with the first half of

Sa'ib's l.5, 'the moonlight has made the daughter of the vine into mother's milk', a metaphor for the moonlight bleaching the colour of red wine in a cup.[87] He therefore develops emulative and masked connections with Sa'ib at the same time, allowing him to dispense with allusion to his predecessor's poem in a short space. Further lines in Salim's *ghazal* could be construed as indirect evocations of Sa'ib's imagery. In l.4, for example, when the poet likens his waking to a moonbeam, we might see a distant connection with Sa'ib's l.3, 'sleep burns in my gaze like the moth's wing tonight', the root idea behind both images being an equation between insomnia and bright light.[88] Beyond formal connections such as these, however, the two poems lack a more profound connection in what we might call ideology, argument and emotion. The idea of burning in expectation, and of being struck with sensory impairment, permeates Salim's *ghazal*, whereas Sa'ib's piece argues that the moonlight brightens the wine, the wine illuminates the night and, by extension, that intoxication heightens the senses. The two pieces make opposing claims.

A comparable reading can be made of a *ghazal* by Raqim that shares the same formal features as the pieces by Salim and Sa'ib. This poem also advances its own, individual argument:[89]

ز شوخیهای آن مژگان و چشم پر عتاب امشب * گدازد آب در شمشیر و مستی در شراب امشب

صفایی داشت بزم عشرتم از تاب رخساری * غبار خاطرم گردید گرد ماهتاب امشب

کجا شمعی زرشک آن گل رخسار میسوزد * که دارد بال و پر پروانه از موج گلاب امشب

مکن عرض تمنا کز سوال ما سبک مغزان * گرانی میکند بر آن لب نازک جواب امشب

ز پا ننشست ساقی تا بما ننمود زاهد را * بدستی سبحه و دست دگر جام شراب امشب

ز بس جوش طپید نهای دل بر داشت آرامم * چو شمع کشته دارم حسرت یک چشم خواب امشب

تغافلهای او را از خدا خواهم که جز راقم * ز ناکامی کس دیگر نباشد کامیاب امشب

As you bat your lashes and your eyes censor me, you * Have melted the water
　　　　of swords and the drunkenness of wine tonight.
A shining cheek cleansed the feast of my merriment * My dusty memories
　　　　became moonbeams tonight.
Where is the candle to burn in envy of those rosy cheeks? * For the moth's
　　　　wings are made of waves of rosewater tonight.
Do not tell of your desires, for the questions that we pose, giddy headed, *
　　　　Leaden those glib lips tonight.
The cupbearer did not sit to rest until he had shown us the ascetic * A
　　　　rosary in one hand, a wine-cup in the other tonight.
My heart beat so quickly in trepidation that it carried off my calm * I long
　　　　for a moment's sleep tonight, like an extinguished candle.
In response to his feigned negligence of me, I ask God that no one except
　　　　Raqim * Should turn their frustration into satisfaction tonight.

Although it is immediately obvious to the reader that this *ghazal* is connected to the pieces by Salim and Sa'ib through its rhyme and refrain, it becomes harder to identify a specific intellectual and emotional dialogue between Raqim and his fellow poets when we begin to take the poem apart. It is true that we find images repeated. For example, Raqim's l.3 refers to the moth, as does Sa'ib's l.3, but the use of the motif in both cases is different: Raqim imagines the moth beating wings of rosewater, whereas Sa'ib's l.3 uses the more conventional trope of the moth immolating itself in the flame. Similarly, Raqim's l.4, containing a *tibaq* between the light- or giddy-headed drunkards (*sabukmaghzān*) and the heavy or leaden lips of the beloved, might be compared with Salim's l.7, for the simple reason that both are on the broad theme of speech, but beyond this very general connection there does not seem to be an act of debate, or of community formation, of the kind that we saw in the dialogue between Salik Yazdi and Faraj Allah Shushtari in Chapter 5, and between Ilahi, Ashna and Ahsan in Chapter 6. Indeed, Raqim's poem makes the beloved the object of our gaze, whereas in the pieces by Salim and Sa'ib the beloved is essentially incidental to the narrative voice's exploration of its own consciousness.

A second set of poems with the refrain *imshab* by Raqim, Sa'ib, and Salim broaden and complicate our study of connections between the three poets, potentially introducing double the number of allusions, as lines in these *ghazals* could conceivably display intertextual links with the group rhyming in -*āb*. This kind of cross-pollination does in fact occur: in the following poem by Salim, l.8 finds a distant echo in l.5 of the *ghazal* by Raqim that is given above, as the poets evoke a censorious figure (Raqim's ascetic, Salim's preacher) who has become intoxicated. This image is a trope, but its appearance within the context of these pieces which share the same refrain and metre shows how a series of themes and variations that were commonly identified as belonging to this formal framework are divided up and modified by the poets. Families of images become associated with a particular *radif*.

Salim cultivates a different atmosphere in this poem than in his earlier piece. While the former is an exploration of the narrator's cognition, and is tinged with the feeling that his senses have been dimmed, the following *ghazal* explores the psychology of frustrated love. The two pieces might be likened to scenes of a play. They are complementary, and although they can be read as independent pieces, they might be thought of as linked in narrative terms, as two episodes in a story of embittered love, with one describing the separation of the lovers and the other elucidating the psychological impact of this separation. Their formal connection and their recycling of variant motifs reinforce the sense that they fit together in a sequence.[90]

مگر در خواب از وصل تو بوی می‌شنید امشب * که چون سیماب این چشم سفیدم می پرید امشب

بتمکینی ز سیر گلشن آیینه‌ای می آید * که پنداری نگاهش ناز را میآفرید امشب

خدا از چشم زخم صبح این شب را نگهدارد * چه میشد اندکی گر چرخ هم میآرمید امشب

چنان کز شعله گیرد کامل پروانه در مستی * لب لعل ترا در خواب چشمم می مکید امشب

چه سیری داشت انداز نگاه گوشه چشمش * که دامان تغافل دستها رس میکشید امشب

نفس در جستجوی دادرس میسوخت افغانم * بدرد کجکببها چون ببندم دل رسید امشب

چو موج بحر بود از ماهتاب فیض امدادم * ز جیب هر نفس صبح خیالی میدمید امشب

چه شوری داشت واعظ چون خم سرخوش از مستی * بگوشش نشاه سرشار بوی میکشید امشب

چنان در انتظارت زندگانی تلخ میدیدم * که چون مار دو سر بد نفس دل میگزید امشب

از فراقش بود شوری در سرم سالم * که شد خواب پریشان عضو عضوم میرمید امشب

Did I dream that we were together? * My unseeing eyes winced like
quicksilver tonight.

Our passage across the meadow afforded us a mirror * Into which you
would think a glance created beauty tonight.

May God preserve the eyes of this night from the blow of the dawn * What
would happen if the heavens were stilled tonight?

Just as the drunken moth attains its desire from the flame * My eyes bit
your ruby lips tonight.

How the corner of his eyes darted, chasing a course * Since hands grabbed
at the skirts of ignorance tonight.

My breath burnt my sighs as it sought redress * When the pain of vicious
jibes fettered my heart tonight.

Moonbeams of divine bounty gave me wave upon wave of succour, like the
sea. * A false dawn broke from my every breath tonight.

How confused the preacher was, overflowing as a full vat, * As the distant
hum of drunkenness reached his ears tonight.

Life tastes bitter to me as I wait for you * For tonight it bit my heart like a
livid, two-headed snake.

Salim, my head spun in separation from him * For when sleep fled, my eye
flickered tonight.

Raqim's second *ghazal* in *imshab* is also marked by a sense that it represents a
continuation of his first poem, and it is also stamped with formal allusions to other
pieces in the broader corpus of seventeenth-century poems in *imshab*. As in his
first piece, Raqim keeps the narrative within the setting of the gathering (*bazm,
anjuman*). It is as though we have moved further on in the story: the contrast
between speech and silence is extended here, so that not only the beloved's feigned
ignorance of the narrator but also the psychological impact on the narrator of
the beloved's temporizing are represented. The memory of the beloved's blazing
cheeks, which brightened the narrator's gaze in the previous poem, is now a source
of agitation, to the extent that the narrator interprets the petals of the flowers in the
garden as visual analogues for the beloved's face. This continuity in storytelling is
matched by allusions to images that are found in the work of other poets. In l.2 of
the following piece, for example, we have a reference to the 'magic lantern of the
imagination' (*fānūs-i khayāl*), which is also found in l.2 of Salim's first poem given
earlier. The imagery is linked, but the ideas are not:[91]

بآیینی که وا کرد است چاکر پرهن امشب * کند جان در تن مهتاب آن سیمین بدن امشب

که روشن کرده فانوس خیال یوسف ما را * که میآید ز خود شمع بوی پرهن امشب

خیال خواب راحت سخت شیرین گشته درچشمم * بس است افسانهٔ من سرگذشت کوهکن امشب

نمیدانم چه تعبیر است این خواب پریشان را * که آمد بر زبان در غربتم نام وطن امشب

چه شد گر نیست در بزم تو ما را رخصت حرفی * ز شوخیهای مژگان تو میریزد سخن امشب

ادب مهر لبم بس گر خموشیها اثر دارد * نیاید بر زبان یار غیر از حرف من امشب

خموشیهای آن لب کرده از بس تنگ عیشم را * نمیگردد زبان من بحرف آن دهن امشب

درین گلشن بیاد آن گل رخسار نالیدم * ز تاب چهرهٔ گلها چراغان شد چمن امشب

غضبناکی و خون میریزد از مژگان بیباکت * بغیر از شمع کو سرزنده در انجمن امشب

نمیدانم که خواهد شد چراغ خلوتم راقم * که چون پروانه میسوزم ز شوق سوختن امشب

In the rite in which your slave ripped open his shirt tonight * That silver chest put the spirit into the body of the moonbeams tonight.

The magic lantern of my imagination illuminated our Joseph * For the candle gives off the scent of his shirt tonight.

My dreams of easy sleep became sickly sweet in my eyes * My tale is the fate of Farhad tonight.

I have no interpretation for such a fractured dream * For the name of my homeland came to my lips in exile tonight.

What would happen if we were forbidden to speak at your feast? * The flutter of your lashes scatters words tonight.

The only seal that my lips need is civility, if silence takes effect. * My beloved will speak only my words tonight.

The silence of those lips has put my life in danger * My tongue will not speak of that mouth tonight.

I wept in this garden at the memory of those rosy cheeks * The heat of the faces of the flowers has filled the meadow with lamps tonight.

Loathing and blood weep from your fearless eyes * Apart from the candle, whose head is clear and bright in our assembly tonight?

I do not know, Raqim, what will happen to the lamp of my solitude * For I blaze like a moth in longing to burn tonight.

Figure 5 © The British Library Board: *Divan* of Raqim, British Library, MS. Or. 3487, f. 37b. By permission of the British Library.

These poems by Salim, Sa'ib and Raqim all display strong intertextual links with one another, testifying to the high degree of connectivity in the circulation of Persian literary texts between Iran and India in the seventeenth century, which meant that poets who did not know one another were often able to access each other's work.[92] It would be accurate to claim that they are evidence of a literary network, in the sense of a sophisticated system for disseminating contemporary poetry internationally. Yet despite their formal similarities, Salim, Sa'ib and Raqim each use circulating motifs to differing effect in their poems, building a separate argument and a contrasting emotional tone. I argue that these types of poems, which are comparable only at a formal level, should be distinguished from the nuanced debates over ideas that we find in the work of poets who inhabited the same spaces, who participated in the same political or social structures, and who corresponded with one another. The latter type of intertextual engagement is about the formation of a real community of shared interests.

Conclusion

Najib's representation of the experiences of émigré Indians in Iran, the actual literary artefacts that émigré writers like Darvish Yusuf Kashmiri produced, and poems that respond to a popular refrain, all have much to tell us about the globalizing quality of seventeenth-century Persian literary production. Najib's *History* provides a rare insight into the limits of literary community, showing how cosmopolitan tendencies were brought into question by political ideologies. Darvish Yusuf's missive also encourages us to pause and consider ways in which a transregional community of writers could be drawn together and forced apart. If the points of fracture which it exemplifies are not national, they are nevertheless based on collective identities: despite its elision of the author's perspective with that of his addressee, the letter is an apology for a social mistake, and therefore its existence is predicated on the author and the addressee *not* seeing eye to eye. Although the malleable and open quality of literary culture is often emphasized in scholarship on the Persianate, we need to bear in mind how the use of the same images and the same devices in two texts can often mark difference rather than promote similitude. We saw this in Najib's poems in praise of Akbar and Shah Sulayman, and in the *ghazals* of Hajji Muhammad Aslam Salim. Just as Najib uses the same images to compare and contrast his patrons, Salim also uses a common form and rhetorical fabric to distinguish himself from authors such as Sa'ib and Raqim.

CONCLUSION

Noi eravam lunghesso mare ancora,
come gente che pensa a suo cammino,
che va col cuore e col corpo dimora.

—Purgatorio II.[1]

There is an obvious reason why the works of seventeenth-century poets such as al-Sarim al-Hindi, al-Hurr al-ʿAmili, Faraj Allah al-Shushtari and Ilahi Hamadani have not been read or celebrated for over 300 years: they have been inaccessible. One could argue that this process of forgetting had already begun at the close of the seventeenth century, as some of the polities in which the poets had worked were subsumed into others. Manuscripts of their verse travelled far and wide, dispersing across the Arabian Sea through family networks and the book trade, leaving the communities in which the poets had established themselves, and preventing scribes from collating and re-issuing their texts. There are only two catalogued copies of the *diwan* of al-Sarim al-Hindi in existence, both of which were made by the same hand. One of these manuscripts seems to have left Yemen for India very soon after the poet's death, and ended up in the library of the nawab of Rampur. The situation became even more fragmented over the following centuries, as colonial regimes subsequently removed a significant body of this manuscript material to Europe, consigning it to an archive of Orientalist knowledge and effectively stripping it of its literariness.[2] Physical inaccessibility – the relegation of texts to the archive – was suddenly coupled with a form of intellectual inaccessibility: this material now belonged to history, and was not supposed to have a bearing on literature's present or its future, even as it may yet have done.

Modern nationalisms and monolingualism have also had their part to play in making these texts 'homeless', to use Mohamad Tavakoli-Targhi's formulation: early modern poets who were active in Arabic on the territory of modern Iran, in Persian on the territory of modern Saudi Arabia or in Arabic or Persian on the territory of the modern Republic of India do not fit comfortably into conceptualizations of national literary heritage.[3] Intellectual movements such as eighteenth- and nineteenth-century Iran's *Bazgasht-i Adabi* ('Literary Return') allied what was natural with what was (at least theoretically) autochthonous, making medieval Persian texts produced on the territory of a Greater Iran the ultimate source of literary authority, and rendering the estranged aesthetics of early modern literature actively alien. Ideas about good poetry became Romantic, paralleling

Wordsworth's definition of the composition of verse as 'the spontaneous overflow of powerful feelings',[4] an idea partly predicated on his fusion of the natural with the national.[5]

Into which model do these seventeenth-century poets therefore fit? The obvious paradigm is that of World Literature, in David Damrosch's sense of literature that circulates beyond national borders. Yet the archetype requires some modification if it is to encompass the early modern Arabian Sea. Contemporary scholarship has tended to see world literatures as the result of a 'cultural conflict between nations and national literatures to control the rhythms and outcomes of . . . "literary time".[6] However, the world which I have examined in this book did not consist of embattled monolingual states attempting to foist their own idioms onto one another, but rather polities which found what Sanjay Subrahmanyam calls 'important and creative intellectual tensions' in multilingualism.[7] We are therefore faced with what Emily Apter terms 'language worlds that bleed out of dichotomized generic categories'.[8] Multilingual environments, seen in nineteenth- and twentieth-century scholarship on early modern Arabic and Persian literature as a marker of instability and decline in the literary ecumene, are not phenomena that solely occur in cultures where aesthetic regimes are collapsing – sometimes they can be the dominant aesthetic itself.[9]

Within these spaces of creative tension, I argue, seventeenth-century poets produced texts which established their globalizing quality by responding to the corpus of classical poems and postclassical poems that observed classical convention. Engaging with this tradition allowed seventeenth-century poets to connect their local communities with a transnational 'high' culture in 'a conscious project of monumentalizing' that extended beyond the regional.[10] Consequently, from Hyderabad to Mecca and Tabriz, poets active in both Arabic and Persian adopted shared approaches to intertextuality which were based on the formation of emulative and masked links between new poems and the corpus. And yet, we have to introduce a distinction between the adoption of common methods and the embrace of a single style. As much as their methods depended on a globally accepted technique of reading and responding to the corpus, seventeenth-century poets did not ultimately attempt to form 'a stylistic unity out of the flotsam of literary history'.[11] Instead, they created communities which were often centred in a particular geographical location, growing to incorporate writers active in distant regions in – to use Homi Bhabha's phrasing – 'chiasmatic intersections of time and place'.[12] Many such communities existed, and therein lay the undoing of the system. The literary genealogies and chains of pupillage in which writers found themselves were not universal, but nor were they national. Instead, there was a multiplicity of aesthetics understood as 'historically local and consciously new'.[13] Subsequently, as the political systems which had encouraged the growth of this globalizing literature changed, poets reading this body of seventeenth-century work only a generation later were confronted with a 'temporality of estrangement'.[14]

Rabindranath Tagore's essay on the concept of World Literature, first delivered as a lecture in 1907, ends with a call for us to recognize 'a totality in each particular author's work'.[15] Tagore meant 'totality' in the sense of a timeless, universal feeling of humanity, but I would like to suggest a second, linked concept: totality as the 'pluralistic' poetic text which engages with the corpus as a whole.[16] I have shown here that the pluralistic poem, with its layers of intertextual references extending across time and geographical space, was, throughout the seventeenth century, a key mechanism through which people around the littoral of the Arabian Sea built links with one another. This material has as much to tell us about the construction of early modern societies, their self-representation and memorialization as documentary sources, narrative histories, works of intellectual history and material objects. However, the only means by which we can perceive the globality of this poetry is by reading it closely. And to do that, we must return to the manuscripts.

MANUSCRIPT SOURCES

SIGLA, BIBLIOGRAPHICAL REFERENCES AND DESCRIPTIONS

The following is a list of the most important manuscripts which are discussed in this book and the sigla ascribed to them.

A1 = *Album*, RP-T-00-3186 (the so-called 'Witsen Album'), Rijksmuseum, Amsterdam, the Netherlands. A collection of portraits, mostly representing seventeenth-century courtiers of the Deccan sultanates and the Mughal Empire, which was made in Golkonda in 1686. There is an entire series of other albums containing paintings that are based on these or common models, including Kupferstichkabinett Dresden, CA 112; Bibliothèque nationale de France, Département des Manuscrits, Smith-Lesouëf 233; and British Museum, London, United Kingdom, 1974,0617,0.2 (formerly British Library Add. MS. 5254).

A2 = Correspondence, Add. MS. 6600, British Library, London, United Kingdom. Ref: Rieu 1879-1883, 1:398b. Copies of letters composed by Hajji ʿAbd al-ʿAli Tabrizi, Nazir al-Mamalik of Golkonda, in the name of ʿAbd Allah Qutbshah, Nizam al-Din Ahmad, Hakim al-Mulk (i.e. Nizam al-Din Ahmad Gilani, the royal physician), and other courtiers.

A3 = *Tazkira-yi Nasrabadi*, MS. 3016, Majlis-i Shura-yi Milli, Tehran, Iran. Refs: Dirayati 2010, 2:1097, No. 58411; *TN, yik sad u panj*. An autograph copy of the text made by the copyist Sabz ʿAli Baba Ahmadi (who is also the copyist of A4) at the start of Dhu l-Hijja 1086/February 1676. The colophon is followed by a note in Nasrabadi's hand, dated Muharram 1089/February 1678, stating that he authenticated this manuscript, which was made for his friend Murshid Khan. This MS does not contain as many entries as Vaziri 2602. See *TN, yik sad u panj*.

A4 = *Tazkira-yi Nasrabadi*, MS. 2602, Vaziri Library, Yazd, Iran. Refs. Dirayati 2010, 2:1097, No. 58413; *TN, navad u du*; Nasrabadi 1378s, *chihil u panj*. An autograph copy of the text made by the copyist Sabz ʿAli Baba Ahmadi (who is also the copyist of A3) in 1091/1680. After the colophon there is a note in Nasrabadi's hand, dated Rajab 1091/July 1680, saying that he authenticated this manuscript, which was made for Mirza Rafiʿ. This figure may be Vaʿiz Qazvini

(*TN*, 245; cf. Vaʿiz Qazvini 1359s, 54, where he is stated to have died in 1088/1677 or 1090/1679). The MS also bears a seal marking Nasrabadi's approval of the text. The modern editors regard this MS as the final clean copy of the *tazkira*.

A5 = *Tazkira-yi Nasrabadi*, 'Supplément persan 1505', Bibliothèque nationale de France, Paris, France. Ref: Storey 1953, Vol. 1, Pt. 2: 820. This MS is mentioned as a possible holograph because a subscription note at the end states: 'the book was completed in the hand of its compiler in 1083' (*tamma al-kitāb bi-yad muʾallifihi al-faqīr fī sanat 1083 min al-hijra*). This statement is brought into question by the presence of the date 1089 in the biography of Mir Lutf Allah Salim in the MS. Palaeographical comparison between the hand used in the MS and Nasrabadi's hand in Majlis 3016 and Vaziri 2602 does not support the idea that Supp. Pers. 1505 is a holograph.

A6 = *Tazkira-yi Nazim Tabrizi*, MS. 1115/1, Majlis-i Shura-yi Milli, Tehran, Iran. Ref: Dirayati 2010, 2:1097, No. 58406. A copy of Nazim Tabrizi's anthology of Persian poetry, completed in Mecca in 1036/1626-27. Undated.

A7 = *Jung-i Fayyaz*, MS. 9707, University of Tehran Central Library, Tehran, Iran. Ref: Dirayati 2010, 3:984-987, No. 82079; Danishpazhuh 1358s. A commonplace book owned by Mirza Muhammad Fayyaz, the brother of Muhammad Baqir Sabzavari (d. 1090/1679). The MS was assembled between 1048/1638-9 and 1076/1665-6 by Fayyaz during his extensive travels around the Arabian Sea, and contains notes in the hands of upwards of thirty-seven poets and scholars of the period, including Faraj Allah al-Shushtari and Salik Yazdi.

A8 = *Anis al-Hujjaj*, MS. 8917/1, Majlis-i Shura-yi Milli, Tehran, Iran. Ref: Dirayati 2010, 2:274, No. 36392. A copy of Safi b. Vali Qazvini's guide for pilgrims. Undated.

B1 = *Kashkul ya Mikhlah*, 'MS. Ilahiyat 129', University of Tehran Central Library, Tehran, Iran. Ref: Dirayati 2010, 8:675, No. 227299. A commonplace book of extracts, mostly to do with the law, Qur'anic exegesis and medicine. The quoted texts do display an obvious connection to Ibn Maʿsum – they include pieces ascribed to Nizam al-Din Ahmad which he may have transmitted to his son – but it is unlikely that this is one of Ibn Maʿsum's compilations, because the text includes the sermon that Jaʿfar al-Bahrani pronounced at the wedding of Ibn Maʿsum, who is introduced in a rubric as 'our lord and master' (*sayyidna wa-makhdumna*). The contents of the MS need to be compared with Malik Museum MS 516, and Isfahan, Madrasa-yi Sadr-i Bazar MS 96, both of which are also purportedly copies of this compendium, before further conclusions can be drawn.

B2 = *Al-Hadaʾiq al-Nadiyya fī Sharh al-Fawaʾid al-Samadiyya*, MS. 1911, University of Tehran Central Library, Tehran, Iran. Ref: Dirayati 2010, 4:547, No. 100209. A holograph in the hand of Ibn Maʿsum, completed on 13th Jumada al-Akhira 1079/18th November 1668.

B3 = *Fihris Khalq al-Insan*, MS. 10136, Majlis-i Shura-yi Milli, Tehran, Iran. Ref: Dirayati 2010, 7:1243, No. 209271. A copy of Volume Two of Mahmud b. Abi l-Hasan al-Naysaburi's (d. ca. 1130 CE) *Khalq al-Insan*, containing a list of contents in the hand of Ibn Ma'sum, and a series of poems that he noted on the blank opening pages. He dates his own additions to Sha'ban 1077/January 1667 and Safar 1081/July 1670.

B4 = Anthology, MS. 8974, Majlis-i Shura-yi Milli, Tehran, Iran. Ref: Dirayati 2010, 2:6, No. 28975. An anthology of short works on grammar etc. copied for Ibn Ma'sum in late 1082/1672 by Sa'id b. Darwish b. 'Ali al-Kujarati (the scribe of B6; he also refers to himself as al-Ahmadabadi in this MS).

B5 = *Mawdi' al-Rashad fi Sharh al-Irshad*, MS. 6370, Mar'ashi Library, Qum, Iran. Ref: Dirayati 2010, 10:375, No. 280021. A copy of Ibn Ma'sum's commentary on Arabic grammar, made in Muharram 1070/September 1659, about two years after the author's arrival in India.

B6 = *Sulafat al-'Asr fi Mahasin A'yan al-'Asr*, 'Ragıp Paşa 1120', Süleymaniye Library, Istanbul, Turkey. Ref: Ragıp Paşa 1868, 47, cat. no. 1120. An autograph manuscript of the text, made by the copyist Sa'id b. Darwish b. 'Ali al-Kujarati (i.e. Gujarati) and approved by Ibn Ma'sum. According to the colophon, Ibn Ma'sum completed the composition of the text on Thursday, 7th Rabi' al-Thani 1082/13th August 1671. Al-Kujarati finished this draft on 28th Jumada al-Ula 1082/1st November 1671. Ibn Ma'sum's note states that he approved it in Dhu l-Qa'da 1082/March 1672. This MS appears to have eluded scholars. It is absent from Brockelmann, and it has not been used in modern print editions of *Sulafat al-'Asr*.

B7 = *Sulafat al-'Asr fi Mahasin A'yan al-'Asr*, MS. Or. 1427, Cambridge University Library, Cambridge, United Kingdom. Ref: Arberry 1952, 35, cat. no. 219 (a). A copy of the text completed in the town of Burhanpur on Saturday, 5th Jumada al-Thani (sic) 1082/9th October 1671 by Ibn Qasim 'Ali Muhammad Shafi' al-Najafi. If the colophon is accurate, this MS predates al-Kujarati's clean copy (B6) by a month. This MS is absent from Brockelmann, and it has not been used in modern print editions of *Sulafat al-'Asr*.

B8 = *Mulhaqat al-Sulafa*, MS. 7037, Majlis-i Shura-yi Milli, Tehran, Iran. Ref: Dirayati 2010, 6:171, No. 154020. A copy of the text completed in 1257/1841-42. Despite its late date, this MS is significant because it seems to be based on the author's draft, and contains a number of entries appended under the title *Mulhaqat Sulafat al-'Asr* (*Addenda to Sulafat al-'Asr*). These entries are all in the standard editions of the text, suggesting that *Mulhaqat Sulafat al-'Asr*, which commentators such as al-Jaza'iri considered to be a lost continuation of the anthology, may have in fact been incorporated into the final, standard recension of *Sulafat al-'Asr* (however, see al-Ka'bi 2009, 89).

B9 = *Anwar al-Rabi' fi Anwa' al-Badi'*, 'Ragıp Paşa 1074', Süleymaniye Library, Istanbul, Turkey. Ref: Ragıp Paşa 1868, 45, cat. no. 1074. An autograph copy of the work, which states that the 'original' manuscript on which it is based (*nuskhat al-asl*) was completed by Ibn Ma'sum in his own hand at noon on Thursday, 19th Dhu l-Qa'da 1093/19th November 1682. The colophon and autograph show that B9 was copied by Ahmad b. Muhammad b. 'Abd al-Sajjad al-Huwayzi (from Huwayza in Khuzistan) in 1104/1692–3, and that it was then checked and approved by Ibn Ma'sum over the course of several reading sessions, the last one of which occurred in Muharram 1106/August 1694. This MS appears to have eluded scholars. It is absent from Brockelmann, and it has not been used in modern print editions of *Anwar al-Rabi'*.

B10 = *Anwar al-Rabi' fi Anwa' al-Badi'*, MS. 1777/2, University of Tehran Central Library, Tehran, Iran. Ref: Dirayati 2010, 2:243, No. 35495. A partial draft holograph of about a third of *Anwar al-Rabi'*, dated 13th Muharram 1081/2nd June 1670. Ibn Ma'sum refers to his *badi'iyya* here by the title *al-Nass al-Jali 'ala Taqdim 'Ali (The Manifest Text, in 'Ali's Presentation)*. This MS appears to have eluded scholars. It is absent from Brockelmann, and it has not been used in modern print editions of *Anwar al-Rabi'*.

B11 = *Nafthat al-Masdur*, MS. 1777/1, University of Tehran Central Library, Tehran, Iran. Ref: Dirayati 2010, 10:754, No. 288666. A draft holograph of the opening sections of Ibn Ma'sum's anthology on migration and homesickness, *Nafthat al-Masdur*. Acephalous and incomplete. The work was previously thought unlocated (Lowry 2009, 179). Absent from Brockelmann.

B12 = *Anwar al-Rabi' fi Anwa' al-Badi'*, unnumbered MS., Madrasa-yi Mansuriyya, Shiraz, Iran. Ref: Dirayati 2010, 2:243, No. 35496; Hafiziyan 1383*s*, 50. Another holograph in the hand of Ibn Ma'sum. Undated. Absent from Brockelmann.

B13 = *Salwat al-Gharib wa-Uswat al-Arib*, unnumbered MS., Madrasa-yi Mansuriyya, Shiraz, Iran. Ref: Dirayati 2010, 6:190, No. 154519; Hafiziyan 1383*s*, 51. A copy of *Salwat al-Gharib* made in Dhu l-Qa'da 1082/March 1672. This MS appears to have eluded scholars. It is absent from Brockelmann, and it has not been used in modern print editions of the text.

B14 = *Naghmat al-Aghani fi 'Ishrat al-Ikhwani*, MS. 5086, Majlis-i Shura-yi Milli, Tehran, Iran. Ref: Dirayati 2010, 10:744, No. 288466. A copy of Ibn Ma'sum's *urjuza* on friendship. The colophon states that it was done from a copy of the text that was made in Ibn Ma'sum's hand in Burhanpur in Dhu l-Hijja 1104/August 1693.

C1 = *Al-Madh al-Munaqqah min Fann al-Muwashshah*, MS. 2019, University of Tehran Central Library, Tehran, Iran. Ref: Dirayati 2010, 9:320, No. 249477 (= microfilm of Dirayati 2010, 9:320, No. 249476). These two works are incorrectly labelled in Dirayati's survey. MS 2019 is a copy of *al-Madh al-Munaqqah min Fann al-Muwashshah* by Ahmad b. Radi al-Din al-Qazani al-Makki, a collection of strophic poems in praise of the Sufi scholar of Ahmadabad, Muhyi al-Din 'Abd al-Qadir b. al-Shaykh al-'Aydarus (d. 1038/1628). For this work, see Brockelmann 1938, 2:617.

C2 = *Al-'Urf al-Nadi min Shi'r Ibrahim ibn Salih al-Hindi*, 'MS. Orient A 2330', Universität Erfurt, Thuringia, Germany. Ref: Brockelmann 1902, 399. A copy of the *diwan* of al-Sarim al-Hindi, in the same hand as Rampur, Arabic MS. 5346. The preface is by the poet's son, who may also be the copyist. No colophon. A *terminus ante quem* for the production of the MS is provided by an owner's note dated Muharram 1114/June 1702.

C3 = *Al-'Urf al-Nadi min Shi'r Ibrahim ibn Salih al-Hindi*, 'Arabic MS. 5346', Raza Library, Rampur, India. Ref: Brockelmann 1938, 545. A copy of the *diwan* of al-Sarim al-Hindi, in the same hand as Gotha Orient A 2330. The preface is by the poet's son, who may also be the copyist. No colophon.

C4 = A commentary on *Lamiyyat al-'Ajam*, MS. Or. 3165, British Library, London, United Kingdom. Ref: Rieu 1894, 668, cat. no. 1056; Talib 2019, 132. This commentary was compiled by Muhammad b. 'Umar Bahraq al-Hadrami (d. 939/1533), a Yemeni scholar who made a career under the Muzaffarids of Gujarat. The MS is dated 1092/1681.

C5 = *Diwan Jarrah b. Shajir*, MS. Or. 408, British Library, London, United Kingdom. Ref: Cureton and Rieu 1846-71, 751. The collected works of a sixteenth-century Yemeni court poet named Jarrah b. Shajir b. al-Hasan, who composed a number of panegyrics in praise of Jamal al-Din al-Mahdi b. Ahmad, *amir* of Jazan. The MS may be of the eighteenth century or the nineteenth century.

C6 = *al-'Alam al-mufrad min shi'r al-muthanna Ahmad b. Ahmad*, MS. Or. 3859, British Library, London, United Kingdom. Ref: Rieu 1894, 690, cat. no. 1096. The collected poetry of Ahmad b. Ahmad al-Anisi, on whom see al-Haymi al-Kawkabani 2002, 2:220.

C7 = *Sulafat al-'asir*, MS. 3841, British Library, London, United Kingdom. Ref: Rieu 1894, 692, cat. no. 1099. A commentary by Ahmad b. Muhammad al-Haymi al-Kawkabani on Husayn b. 'Abd al-Qadir b. al-Nasir's *qasida* in praise of the Prophet. This MS is dated 1146/1734.

C8 = *Tib al-Samar fi Awqat al-Sahar*, MS. Glaser 85-86, Staatsbibliothek zu Berlin, Berlin, Germany. Ref: Ahlwardt 1887-1899, 6:504-505, cat. nos 7425-7426. A copy of al-Haymi al-Kawkabani's anthology *Tib al-Samar fi Awqat al-Sahar*. Volume 1 (Glaser 85) completed in 1160/1749; Volume 2 (Glaser 86) completed in 1213/1798.

D1 = *Diwan al-Hurr al-ʿAmili*, MS. 602, Malik Museum, Tehran, Iran. Ref: Dirayati 2010, 5:126, No. 122395. A holograph copy of the *diwan* of al-Hurr al-ʿAmili. Dated in his hand 1098/1686-87.

D2 = *Divan-i Muhri ʿAmili*, MS. 3217, University of Tehran Central Library, Tehran, Iran. Ref: Dirayati 2010, 5:402, No. 129482. A copy of the (largely) Persian *divan* of Muhri, copied in Shaʿban 1115/January 1704 by Asad b. Hasan Bayg Turbati (or Tabrizi).

D3 = *Sarapa*, MS. Elliott 252, ff. 140b-144bʾ, Bodleian Library, University of Oxford, Oxford, United Kingdom. Ref: Sachau and Éthé 1889, col. 712, cat. no. 1168. An undated copy of Muhri ʿAmiliʾs *masnavi* poem describing the human figure.

D4 = *Poetry by al-Shahid al-Thani*, MS. 4717, ff. 57a-59a, Majlis-i Shura-yi Milli, Tehran, Iran. Ref: Dirayati 2010, 5:234, No. 125110. Copied by Muhammad b. Rida al-Hurr, Dhu l-Qaʿda 1096/September 1685.

D5 = *Urjuza fi al-Maʿani wa-l-Bayan*, MS. 879, pp. 148-150, Majlis-i Shura-yi Milli, Tehran, Iran. Ref: Dirayati 2010, 9:829, No. 261693. 11th/17th century.

E1 = *Divan-i Faraj Allah Shushtari*, ʿH.L. 597ʾ, Khuda Bakhsh Oriental Public Library, Patna, India. Ref: ʿAbd al-Muqtadir 1912, cat. no. 288. A hastily written copy of the *ghazals* of Faraj Allah Shushtari, with several lacunae. This MS must have been copied before 1167/1754, the date mentioned in a note on the fly-leaf.

E2 = *Divan-i Faraj Allah Shushtari*, ʿStowe, Or. 15ʾ, British Library, London, United Kingdom. Ref: Rieu 1895, 207, No. 327. A copy of *ghazals* and *rubaʿiyyat* of Faraj Allah Shushtari. No colophon. Made before 1122/1710-11, the date of an ownerʾs note on the fly-leaf.

E3 = *Divan-i Salik Yazdi*, MS. 3287, University of Tehran Central Library, Tehran, Iran. Ref: Dirayati 2010), 5:179, No. 123586. The *qasaʾid, saqinama, masnavi* of *Khusraw u Shirin*, and *ghazals* of Salik. Undated. A palaeographical comparison between the hand in which this MS is copied and the holograph hand of Salik in the Jung of Fayyaz may suggest that this MS was made by the poet himself.

E4 = *Kulliyat-i Salik Yazdi*, ʿMS. Dawawin 404ʾ, Oriental Manuscripts Library and Research Institute, Hyderabad, India. Ref: Asafiyya 1914, 724, cat. no. 404. The occasional poems, *ghazals* and *rubaʿiyyat* of Salik. Undated.

E5 = A commonplace book owned and inscribed by Nizam al-Din Ahmad b. Taj al-Din ʿAli al-Ghaffari, physician to Sultan ʿAbd Allah the Qutbshah, MS. 9466, Majlis-i Shura-yi Milli, Tehran, Iran. Ref: Dirayati 2010, 9:892, cat. no. 263015 (N.B. the constituent texts of this commonplace are catalogued separately throughout DENA).

E6 = *Khusraw u Shirin-i Amin*, MS. 1120, Majlis-i Shura-yi Milli, Tehran, Iran. Ref: Dirayati 2010, 4:871, No. 108927. A copy of Ruh al-Amin's *Khusraw u Shirin*. Undated, but ostensibly of the seventeenth century.

E7 = *Divan-i Salik Yazdi*, MS. Or. 9752, ff. 245b-289a, British Library, London, United Kingdom. Ref: Meredith-Owens 1968, 58. A late-eighteenth or nineteenth-century collection of occasional and lyric poems, identified as the work of Salik Yazdi on the fly-leaf; comparison with E3 and E4 confirms that at least some of the poems given in this MS are indeed by Salik Yazdi. However, the *ghazals* from *zal* to *kaf* are missing, and only a few occasional poems are given. For these reasons, the MS. has not been used as a textual witness in this study.

E8 = *Farhad u Shirin*, MS. Or. 342, British Library, London, United Kingdom. Ref: Rieu 1879-1883, II: 673b. A copy of Mir 'Aqil Kawsari's recension of the story of Farhad and Shirin. The MS is dated 1250/1834. On Kawsari, see *TN*, 394.

E9 = *Divan-i Mashriqi*, Add. MS. 7800, British Library, London, United Kingdom. Ref: Rieu 1879-1883, II: 683a. The collected poetry of Mirza Malik Mashriqi, who served Hasan Khan in Harat. On the poet, see *TN*, 351. The MS appears to date to the seventeenth century.

E10 = The works of Karim, MS. Or. 305, British Library, London, United Kingdom. Ref: Rieu 1879-1883, II: 683b. The *ruba'iyyat* and ethical poems of Mir Kazim Husayni of Najaf, known as Karim, who found employment at the court of Golkonda in the reign of Sultan 'Abd Allah. The poet is not well known, and copies of his works appear to be very rare. For a letter addressed to him by *Mir Jumla* Muhammad Sa'id Ardistani, see A2, f. 82a.

E11 = *Divan-i Amani*, MS. I.O. Islamic 2694, British Library, London, United Kingdom. Ref: Ethé and Edwards 1903-, 1: col. 857, cat. no. 1571. The collected poems of Mulla 'Abd Allah Amani, on whom see *TN*, 439. Having grown up in Kirman, Amani emigrated to Hyderabad, where he found employment at the court of the Qutbshah 'Abd Allah, before returning to Isfahan. Manuscripts of his work are rare. This MS was copied at Hyderabad in 1070/1659–60; it is probably a holograph.

F1 = *Masnavi*s of Zafar Khan Ahsan, Royal Asiatic Society Persian MS. 310, University of Cambridge Library, Cambridge, United Kingdom. No catalogue. Ref: <https://www.fihrist.org.uk/catalog/manuscript_2870>; see also Sharma 2017, 144. A holograph copy of the *masnavis Jilva-yi Naz* and *Maykhana-yi Raz*, completed by Ahsan in Lahore on 26th Dhu l-Hijja 1073/1st August 1663.

F2 = *Divan-i Ashna*, MS. 7761, University of Tehran Central Library, Tehran, Iran. Ref: Dirayati 2010, 5:300, No. 126875. Undated. *Qasa'id, ghazals, masnavi*s and *ruba'iyyat*.

F3 = *Divan-i Ashna*, Persian MS. 3523, Raza Library, Rampur, India. Ref: Siddiqi 1997, 310. Undated. *Ghazals, fardiyyat, ruba'iyyat*, incomplete *ghazals, tarji'band* poems, *masnavis, matla'iyyat*, and *qasa'id*.

F4 = *Divan-i Ilahi*, Persian MS. 3487, Raza Library, Rampur, India. Ref: Siddiqi 1997, 301. An undated but early MS containing *qasa'id, ghazals, ruba'iyyat, muqatta'at*, and *masnavis*, mostly in alphabetical order.

F5 = *Divan-i Ilahi*, Add. MS. 25330, British Library, London, United Kingdom. Ref: Rieu 1879-1883, 2:687b. Dated 1042/1632, and hence within the life of the poet. Containing *qasa'id, tarkib-* and *tarji'-band* poems, *muqatta'at, masnavis, ghazals* and *ruba'iyyat*.

F6 = *Khizana-yi Ganj-i Ilahi*, MS. Sprenger 323, Staatsbibliothek zu Berlin, Berlin, Germany. Ref: Pertsch 1888, 609, cat. no. 646; Sprenger 1853, 66-87. The autograph draft of Ilahi's *tazkira*.

F7 = *Divan-i Asad*, MS. Or. 5437, British Library, London, United Kingdom. Ref: Meredith-Owens 1968, 50. A partial copy of the collected poems of Asad, a poet who praised the Mughal emperor Jahangir and Mahabat Khan. The MS may date to the eighteenth century.

F8 = *Masnavis* of Hakim Rukna Kashi, MS. Or. 475, British Library, London, United Kingdom. Ref: Rieu 1879-1883, II: 688b. A copy of three narrative poems by Hakim Rukna Kashi (d. 1066/1655–6), including his *saqinama*. The MS probably dates to the seventeenth century. On the poet, see *TN*, 312.

F9 = The prose compositions of Tughra Mashhadi, Add MS. 16852, British Library, London, United Kingdom. Ref: Rieu 1879–83, II: 742a-744b. Numerous prose compositions by Mulla Tughra, who made his career as a secretary under the Mughals and the Qutbshahs. The MS is dated 1141–7/1729–35. On Mulla Tughra, see *TN*, 482.

F10 = *Divan-i Nizam Dast-i Ghayb*, MS. Or. 2998, British Library, London, United Kingdom. Ref: Rieu 1895, 202, cat. no. 319. The collected poetry of Mirza Nizam (d. 1029/1620), one of the *sayyids* of Dast-i Ghayb, Shiraz. On the poet, see *TN*, 383. The MS appears to date from the seventeenth century.

F11 = *Kulliyat-i Binish*, 'MS. Egerton 705', British Library, London, United Kingdom. Ref: Rieu 1879-1883, II: 695a. The collected works of Binish (d. ca. 1100/1688-89), who settled in Kashmir and praised the Mughal emperor Awrangzib and Muhammad Qasim Kashani, the local comptroller. According to the *tazkira Hamisha Bahar*, Binish was from Iran. See Rashidi 1967-, 1:142. This would help to explain the number of poems which he composed describing

Kashan, Mazandaran and Isfahan. The MS appears to date from the eighteenth century.

F12 = *Divan-i Fawji*, MS. Or. 302, British Library, London, United Kingdom. Ref: Rieu 1879-1883, II: 690a. The collected poetry of Mir Muqima Fawji, on whom see *TN*, 449. Fawji was closely associated with Mirza Jan Bayg, a military commander stationed in Orissa. He travelled between Iran, India and Mecca, and met Nasrabadi. This MS appears to date to the late seventeenth century.

F13 = *Divan-i Ashna*, MS. I.O. Islamic 1982, British Library, London, United Kingdom. Ref: Ethé and Edwards 1903-, 1: col. 866, cat. no. 1584. An early copy of the collected poetry of Ashna, dated 1060/1650 (within the life of the poet).

G1 = *A Letter from Darvish Yusuf Kahsmiri to a Merchant*, MS. 892, University of Isfahan Central Library, Isfahan, Iran. Ref: Dirayati 2010, 10: 494, No. 282929 (with the classmark 124).

G2 = *Divan-i Salim*, Persian MS. 3637, Raza Library, Rampur, India. Ref: Siddiqi 1997, 329. Copied Shawwal 1133/August 1721, on the order of Mirza Muhammad Aslah, most probably the poet's son. *Ghazals* of Muhammad Aslam Salim.

G3 = *Divan-i Salim*, MS. 5768, Ma'sumiyya Library, Qum, Iran. Ref: Dirayati 2010, 5:179, No. 123592. Undated. *Kulliyat* of Muhammad Aslam Salim, including eulogies of the Mughal emperor Muhammad Shah A'zam (r. March–June 1707).

G4 = *Masnavis of Salim*, MS. Elliott 258, ff. 271b-294b; 303b-307, Bodleian Library, Oxford, United Kingdom. Ref: Sachau and Éthé 1889, cols 711-12, cat. nos 1166–1167. The *masnavis Ganj-i Ma'ani* and *Ta'rif-i Shah A'zam* by Muhammad Aslam Salim. *Ganj-i Ma'ani* was copied in 1097/1685–6.

G5 = *Muntakhab al-Ash'ar*, MS. Elliott 247, ff. 1-197, Bodleian Library, Oxford, United Kingdom. Ref: Sachau and Éthé 1889, cols 239-255. A biographical anthology of Persian poetry composed by Mubtala Mashhadi in 1161/1748.

G6 = *Makhzan al-Ghara'ib*, MS. Elliott 395, Bodleian Library, Oxford, United Kingdom. Ref: Sachau and Éthé 1889, cols 316-396. 'The largest biographical dictionary of Persian poets which was ever written', compiled in 1218/1803-4 by Ahmad 'Ali Khan Hashimi of Sandila. This MS was made in 1224/1809.

G7 = *Divan-i Raqim*, MS. Adabiyat 85-DA, University of Tehran Central Library, Tehran, Iran. Ref: Dirayati 2010, 5:165, No. 123240. Undated, but apparently of the seventeenth century.

G8 = *Divan-i Raqim*, MS. Or. 3487, British Library, London, United Kingdom. Ref: Rieu 1895, 209, cat. no. 332. An undated but early copy of the *divan*, consisting of lyric pieces only, with the preface by Muhammad Sadiq Mashhadi, who seems to have been one of Raqim's dependents.

G9 = *Divan-i Nawras*, MS. Or. 3644, British Library, London, United Kingdom. Ref: Rieu 1895, 210, cat. no. 333. The collected works of Nawras Damavandi, on whom see *TN*, 581. The poet found employment in Isfahan with the help of Sa'ib. The MS would appear to be a holograph.

G10 = *Divan-i Amani*, MS. Or. 2872, British Library, London, United Kingdom. Ref: Rieu 1895, 199, cat. no. 312. The collected works of Amani, a bilingual (Persian-Turkic) poet who died around 1016/1607-08. The MS appears to date from the seventeenth century.

G11 = *Divan-i Mirak*, MS. Or. 4912, British Library, London, United Kingdom. Ref: Rieu 1895, 204, cat. no. 322. The collected works of Mirak Naqqash, a poet of the time of Shah 'Abbas II. The MS is dated 1054/1644.

G12 = *Divan-i 'Ali Naqi Kamra'i*, MS. Or. 3505, British Library, London, United Kingdom. Ref: Rieu 1895, 203, cat. no. 320. The collected works of 'Ali Naqi Kamra'i, on whom see *TN*, 337. The MS. appears to date to the seventeenth century.

G13 = *Divan-i Riza*, MS. I.O. Islamic 1568, British Library, London, United Kingdom. Ref: Ethé and Edwards 1903-, 1: col. 840, cat. no. 1538. The collected works of a poet named Riza, most likely to be Mirza Muhammad Riza, vizir of Azarbayjan, on whom see *TN*, 103. Undated.

G14 = *Divan-i Atashi*, MS. I.O. Islamic 1685, British Library, London, United Kingdom. Ref: Ethé and Edwards 1903-, 1: col. 838, cat. no. 1536. The collected works of Muhammad Hakim Amin, with the pen name Atashi, who was a court poet to Muhammad 'Adilshah in Bijapur in the third decade of the seventeenth century. The MS, part of which was completed in 1034/1624, appears to be an autograph.

G15 = *Divan-i Hadi*, MS. I.O. Islamic 1889, British Library, London, United Kingdom. Ref: Ethé and Edwards 1903-, 1: col. 864, cat. no. 1581. The collected works of a seventeenth-century poet named Hadi, who may be the son of Mirza Rafi' Shahristani, the *sadr* (see *TN*, 139).

G16 = *Divan-i Tahir Vahid*, MS. I.O. Islamic 41, British Library, London, United Kingdom. Ref: Ethé and Edwards 1903-, 1: col. 900, cat. no. 1653. 'The largest collection extant' of the poems of Mirza Muhammad Tahir Vahid (on whom, see *TN*, 22), patron to Najib Kashani, and friend to Sa'ib. Undated.

G17 = *Divan-i Yatim Burujardi*, MS. 3635, University of Tehran Central Library, Tehran, Iran. Ref: Dirayati 2010, 5:455, cat. no. 130793. The collected poems of

Yatim Burujardi (on whom, see *TN*, 563). The MS. lacks a colophon, but most probably dates from the seventeenth century.

G18 = *Kulliyat-i Qubad Bayg Gurji Kawkabi*, MS. 6054, University of Tehran Central Library, Tehran, Iran. Ref: Dirayati 2010, 8:747. The collected works of Qubad Bayg Gurji Kawkabi (on whom, see *TN*, 444). The MS. was purportedly copied in 1054/1644.

G19 = *Divan-i Mir Najat*, MS. Elliott 89, Bodleian Library, Oxford, United Kingdom. Ref: Sachau and Éthé 1889, col. 710, cat. no. 1162. The collected poetry of Nasrabadi's friend Mir ʿAbd al-ʿAl Najat (on whom, see *TN*, 483). This MS. was copied in 1185/1771.

NOTES

Preface

1 Watt et al. 2012.
2 Watt et al. 2012.
3 Haykel 2003, 31.
4 Haykel 2003, 31.
5 Smith et al. 2012.
6 Matthee 2020.
7 De Planhol et al. 2020.
8 Matthee 2020.
9 Matthee 2020.
10 Matthee 2020.
11 Burton-Page et al. 2012.
12 Burton-Page et al. 2012.
13 Burton-Page et al. 2012.
14 *SA*, 1:42.
15 Saʿidi Shirazi 1961, 71.
16 *TN*, 75; 287.
17 *TN*, 79.
18 A8, f. 208b.
19 *SA*, 2:775; 781.
20 *TN*, 7.
21 *SA* 1: 42.
22 A8, f. 208a.
23 A8, f. 198b. SA, 62.

Introduction

1 A1.
2 Out of the large body of scholarship on this topic, see Subrahmanyam 2011, 90–103; Sherwani 1974, 482.
3 For multilingual literary production in Golkonda, see Wagoner 2011, 94; Sherwani 1974, 528–35; Sharma 2020.
4 Orsini 2015; Thornber 2009, 2.
5 I borrow the phrase 'cosmopolitan vernacular' from Sheldon Pollock. See Pollock 1998.
6 Sherwani 1974, 528–35; Sharma 2020.

7 Ricci 2011, 2.
8 Behl 2012, 18–20.
9 Pollock 2006, 569.
10 See D'Hubert 2018, 258.
11 See al-Musawi 2015, 14.
12 Truschke 2016, 7.
13 Busch 2011, 94.
14 See Asif 2020, 164.
15 Spivak 2003, 87.
16 Salati 1999a, 15.
17 Salati 1999a, 15. His descent from Gawhar Shad Baygum is confirmed in a letter by Nizam al-Din Ahmad: A2, f. 48b.
18 Salati 1999a, 14–15; 27.
19 Reichmuth 2009, 9; Alavi 2015, 93–4. For an overview of the role of *sayyid*s in Safavid Iran, see Newman 1999.
20 B6, f. 4b.
21 al-Makki 1967, 1:320.
22 Lowry 2009, 175; Salati 1999a, 19.
23 Lowry 2009, 176.
24 His biography and verse are given in *SA* 1:300–15.
25 Salati 1999a, 19–20.
26 Salati, 1999a, 28, n.9.
27 See Salati 1999a, 29.
28 See Salati 1999a, 30.
29 See Sarkar 1930, 4:395; Sherwani 1974, 443.
30 See Sherwani 1974, 586, n. 243, quoting Sa'idi Shirazi 1961, 234.
31 See Khan 1953, 4; 10–11; 14.
32 SA 2:746. See also Mu'id Khan 1963, 42–3.
33 See Sarkar 1930, 4:398–9.
34 Ibn Ma'sum 1988a, 301.
35 For summaries of the careers of Khalifa Sultan and Mirza Mahdi, see Newman 2009, 81–7.
36 A2, ff. 48b–49a.
37 A2, ff. 49a–51b. For the text of the *farman* granting Nizam al-Din Ahmad ownership of the *madrasa* and its holdings, see Fasa'i 1378s, 1:481–2.
38 Fasa'i 1378s, 1:481–2.
39 Ibn Ma'sum must have died after submitting court documents in Shiraz in Rabi' al-Awwal 1118/June 1706, but before his sons filed a complaint in Ramadan 1119/ November 1707, in which he is stated to be deceased. For the documents, see Ranjbar 1377s, 54. As his *diwan* contains a piece dated 1119, which began in April 1707, he is most likely to have died between April and November that year. See Ibn Ma'sum 1988a, 464.
40 See *SA* 1:240; 2:452; 2:504; 2:511; 2:796. Regarding the migration of seventeenth-century scholars to Mecca more generally, see el-Rouayheb 2015a, 153–70; 257–61.
41 See *SA* 2:536; 2:723; Ibn Ma'sum 1988b, 225. See also Salati 1999a, 23.
42 See Lowry 2009; Mu'id Khan 1963; Salati 1999a.
43 See Ibn Ma'sum 1962; Ibn Ma'sum 1994–95, 31–42.
44 See Fasa'i 1378s, 2:1045.

45 See al-Ka'bi 2008, 52. The text, which has been printed, is entitled *Nashwat al-Sulafa wa-Mahall al-Idafa*.
46 al-Ka'bi 2008, 52.
47 See Ranjbar 1377s, 52–4.
48 Ranjbar 1377s, 52–4.
49 On al-Tha'alibi as an anthologist, see Orfali 2016. On Bilgrami, see Toorawa 2008, 2009; and Ernst 2013.
50 B6.
51 Kia 2020, 109.
52 SA 1:34–5. On al-Khafaji, see van Gelder 2009.
53 SA 1:34–5. However, al-Khafaji's text begins with a member of the Manufi family. See al-Khafaji 1967, 1:8.
54 See Bray 2010, 245.
55 See Casanova 2004, 85–91; Bernard 2018, 44.
56 See Green 2018, 854–5; Green 2011, 6.
57 See Boehmer 2005, 236.
58 See Dimock 2008, 3.
59 For an introduction to Persian *tazkiras* as a type of text, see Losensky 2021b, 354–70. For the biographical anthology in Arabic, see Orfali 2016; and Kilpatrick 2003.
60 See A3 and B6. Sabz 'Ali also copied A4. Nasrabadi's date of death is unknown. See Nasrabadi 1378s, *bist u haft*; Gulchin Ma'ani 1969–71, 1: 400. A5 is not a holograph, as has been assumed.
61 *TN*, 666.
62 *TN*, 666.
63 *TN*, 667.
64 *TN*, 667; 669. See also Fotoohi 2020.
65 *TN*, 669.
66 *TN*, 669.
67 See Zakir al-Husayni 1393s.
68 *TN*, 672; Emami 2016, 201; Losensky 2021a, 452.
69 Anderson 2016, 6.
70 See Damrosch 2018, 4.
71 See Losensky 1998, 102.
72 On seventeenth-century editorial practices in Persian, see Alam 2015, 183–4; White 2021.
73 See Dhavan 2020, 461–2.
74 *TN*, 455.
75 *TN*, 455.
76 *TN*, 81.
77 Nancy 1991.
78 Binbaş 2018, 6.
79 al-Musawi 2015, 81.
80 Burke 2004, 6.
81 Webb 2017, 63–4.
82 On the postclassical city as a site for knowledge production, see Muhanna 2018, 19.
83 *SA*, 31.
84 *SA*, 36.
85 *SA*, 36.
86 *TN*, 5; 472; 669; 670; 672.

87   *TN*, 4.
88   *SA*, 37.
89   See Sing 2017; Busch 2011, 3–15.
90   Jayyusi 2006, 38.
91   See Schwartz 2020, 35–9; Losensky 1998, 1–5.
92   There is a significant body of scholarship on the term *sabk-i hindi*. Representative studies which mark changes in thinking over the past seventy years include: Bertel's 1956; Bausani 1958; Yarshater 1974; Faruqi 2004.
93   Zipoli 1981, 276.
94   Rypka 1968, 295; see also Losensky 1998, 201.
95   Faruqi 2004, 9.
96   Bausani and Pagliaro 1960, 487.
97   See Kinra 2007; Kim 2021; Losensky 2018, 583–593; Losensky 1998, 194–5.
98   Shibli Nu'mani 1948–55, 3:165–6; Sa'ib 1991, 1:304; 1:396; 2:1289; 3:1196; 5:2812. See also Losensky 1998, 305.
99   See Futuhi 2000, 311–15.
100 Futuhi 2000, 311–15; Losensky 1998, 5.
101 Basha 1989, 85.
102 See Losensky 1998, 4.
103 Guillory 1993, 270.
104 For a notable exception, see Losensky 1998, 15.
105 McLaughlin 1995, 264–5.
106 See Chen 2017, 94.
107 See Losensky 1998, 310.
108 Clayton and Rothstein 1991, 8.
109 See Kristeva 1969.
110 See Bloom 1997.
111 Green 2012, 213–14.
112 See Losensky 1998, 130–1.
113 See Barthes 1977, 160.
114 See Losensky 1998, 111; 205.
115 See 'Ali 2010, 192; Brookshaw 2003; Pfeifer 2022, 7–9.
116 See Zipoli 1993, 9; Losensky 1998, 107–8.
117 For more on the concept of emulation, see Losensky 1998, 110.
118 See Zipoli 1993, 12; Losensky 1998, 111.
119 Tomasello 1999, 60.
120 Tomasello 1999, 95.
121 Harb 2020, 94–5.
122 Kamens 1997, 36–7.
123 I borrow the term 'reference culture' from Denecke 2014, 22. For a discussion of classical Arabic canons, see van Gelder 2003, 48–54. For changing Persian canons, see Lewis 2018, 504–14; Sharma 2012b.
124 Even in Iran, Central Asia and India, basic literacy in Arabic was regarded as essential among Muslim communities for accessing the Qur'an. See Szuppe 2011, 67–72.
125 See Alam and Subrahmanyam 2004, 68–9; Kinra 2015, 63–5; Robinson 1997, 174–84.
126 See Miner 1990, 92.
127 Ho 2007, 349.

128 Culler 2015, 301.
129 Suleiman 1998, 2.
130 Dabashi 2012, 8.

Chapter 1

1 Gulchin Ma'ani 1369*s*.
2 See Calmard 2000, 355.
3 Andrés Neuman, quoted in Dehoux 2019, 31.
4 *SA*, 1:37.
5 *SA*, 2:684.
6 For a case from the seventeenth-century Malay Archipelago with certain points of continuity in this particular regard, see Wormser 2015.
7 See Walravens 2020; Bahl 2020b, 203–5.
8 See Ho 2006, 116–51; Khalidi 2004, 335–6.
9 See Balachandran 2015; Balachandran 2020a, 129–63.
10 See Prange 2018, 12–16.
11 Prange 2018, 171–2; Ho 2006, 152–3; Eaton 1978, 13.
12 See Alam and Subrahmanyam 2017; Flatt 2019, 120–64; Bahl 2020b, 218–20.
13 See Kugle 2021, 6–7.
14 Mortel 1997, 245–6.
15 See Eaton 2005, 105–28; Wink 2004, 146–7.
16 See, for example, Balachandran 2020b, 156–9.
17 See Bahl 2018a, 76–114; al-Musawi 2015, 97–100.
18 See Qutbuddin 2007, 330–1; Ahmad 1978, 194–203; 221–52.
19 See Muinuddin 1939, 1; 13–17; 63; 76. For al-Sa'igh, see Kilpatrick 2011a, 62.
20 Ahmed 2015, 303.
21 The literature on elite migration is extensive. See Haneda 1997; Subrahmanyam 1992; Fischel, 2020a; idem 2020b, 106–48; Szuppe 2004, 1010–17.
22 For the migration of subaltern figures, see Digby 1993, 255–60; for the migration of scholarly families, see Quinn 2021, 101–5.
23 Eaton 2020, 45–57; 195–239.
24 See Green (ed.) 2019, 17–18; Alam 2003, 135–42; Sharma 2000, 14–18.
25 See Wink 2004, 146–8; Eaton 1978, 14; 96; Siddiqi 2014, 176; 181; Peacock 2021, 172–4.
26 See Peacock 2020.
27 Islam 1970, 117; Sherwani 1974, 432.
28 On Ardistani, see Subrahmanyam 1988. On Niknam Khan, see Dayal 2020.
29 Shakeb 2017, 164–6.
30 See Floor and Javadi 2013, 569–72.
31 Floor and Javadi 2013, 570.
32 Floor and Javadi 2013, 573.
33 *TN*, 42; 61.
34 See Dirayati 2010, 5:1–456.
35 Premodern Iranian authors of Arabic texts on science and religious topics have been studied in more detail. See Al Qays 1984-.
36 Dirayati 2010, 352–3.
37 *SA*, 1:95; 1:109; 1:120; 1:129; 1:131.

38   *SA*, 1:132. 1:177; 1:188 ; 1:300; 1:323.

39   *SA*, 1:224 ; 1:455; 1:461.

40   *SA*, 1:282.

41   *SA*, 2:795.

42   *TN*, 367; 375; 585; 589; 615.

43   *TN*, 615.

44   *TN*, 615.

45   *TN*, 589.

46   A6, p. 4. See also Gulchin Maʿani 1969–71, 1:383.

47   Darabi 2012, 2:29.

48   Kia 2020, 171.

49   For an approach to Nasrabadi as a critic, see Nasrabadi 1378s, *panzdah - hijdah.*

50   For the parts of *Khulasat al-Ash ʿar* that have been published, see Kashani 2005-.

51   E.g. *TN*, 65; 89; 142; 171; 252; 392; 455; 513; 573. On the inclusion of female poets in early modern Persian literary historiography, see Sharma 2009.

52   *TN*, 77; 292; 441. For Hindu poets of Persian, see Pellò 2012.

53   Compare *TN*, 583; 585; 594; 625.

54   *TN*, 672.

55   *TN*, 90; 660; 662.

56   *TN*, 26; 40; 45; 48 (two entries); 51; 52; 58; 62; 74; 104; 108; 113; 126; 146; 148; 165; 167; 168; 175; 176 (two entries); 179; 197; 238; 242; 255; 258; 260; 274; 288; 296; 312; 378; 391; 398; 434; 445; 449; 450; 455; 456; 458; 464 (two entries); 467; 476; 477; 484; 492; 497; 513; 519; 522; 523; 525; 538; 548 (two entries); 551; 555; 564; 565; 574; 582; 600; 614; 617; 624; 632; 639; 652.

57   *TN*, 31; 81; 90; 127; 524; 527; 539; 634.

58   *TN*, 242.

59   *TN*, 249; 250; 251; 252; 264 (two entries); 267; 278; 280; 288; 397; 459; 497; 571.

60   *SA*, 1:78; 1:86; 1:240; 1:315; 1:331; 1:323; 1:369; 1:401; 2:427; 1:452; 2:504; 2:511; 2:533; 2:570; 2:722; 2:743; 2:781; 2:784; 2:796; 2:805; 2:816; 2:837–8; 2:877; 2:893; 2:895.

61   *SA*, 1:66; 1:118.

62   *SA*, 1:207.

63   *SA*, 2:740.

64   *SA*, 1:240; 1:323; 1:369; 1:452; 2:504; 2:511; 2:796.

65   For al-Maqqari as the source of most of the entries, see *SA*, 2:906; 2:919; 2:931; 2:943; 2:949; 2:951. The *nuniyya* given at *SA* 2:921–8 is quoted in al-Maqqari 1988, 5:23–9. The epigraphic poem given at *SA*, 2:928–9, is quoted in al-Maqqari 1983, 136–7.

66   For the presence of scholars from the Maghrib in seventeenth-century Mecca, see el-Rouayheb 2015a, 153–70.

67   *SA*, 2:485; 2:503; 2:511; 2:514; 2:589; 2:596; 2:614; 2:636; 2:654; 2:658; 2:668; 2:680.

68   Muʿid Khan associates more biographical subjects with the court of Golkonda than are named here. See Muʿid Khan 1963, 56 ff. Some of these identifications appear to be mistaken, including Kibrit al-Madani, whom Muʿid Khan links with the Golkonda circle because Ibn Maʿsum writes of him ʿ*anshadanī fī rihlatihī*ʾ. I interpret this phrase to mean ʿhe transmitted to me in his travelogueʾ, rather than ʿhe recited to me on his journeyʾ.

69   *SA*, 1:78; 1:86; 1:315; 1:331; 1:401; 2:427.

70   *SA*, 2:533; 2:570.

71 *SA*, 2:743.

72 *SA*, 2:781; 2:784.

73 *SA*, 2:805; 2:816; 2:837–8.

74 *SA*, 2:877; 2:893; 2:895.

75 The participation of one further figure is unlikely: Khalaf al-Badi notes that al-shaykh Jamal al-Din Muhammad b. Ahmad al-Shahid grew up in Damascus, emigrated to Mecca and lived next to the Haram, then went via Yemen to Hyderabad, where he died in 1098/1686 (*SA*, 1:363). This would appear to be a mistaken identification. The man to whom Khalaf al-Badi is referring is Jamal al-Din b. Nur al-Din ʿAli b. ʿAli b. Abi l-Hasan al-Musawi al-ʿAmili al-Jubaʿi, who flourished slightly later. He became a major religious figure in Hyderabad under Sultan ʿAbd Allah's successor, Abu l-Hasan. On him, see Salati 1999b, 618. Ibn Maʿsum provides nothing to suggest that Jamal al-Din Muhammad b. Ahmad al-Shahid, the actual subject of the entry, went to Golkonda.

76 *SA*, 1:170; 1:229; 1:244; 1:436; 1:451; 1:452; 2:511.

77 Floor 2021.

78 *TN*, 96; 129; 169; 173; 180; 181; 195; 197; 223; 285; 298–9; 396; 434; 440; 553; 555 (two entries); 559 (two entries); 560 (two entries); 589; 617.

79 *TN*, 35; 68; 93; 208; 457; 497; 597.

80 *TN*, 190; 204; 217; 227; 235; 261; 268; 367; 433; 487; 497; 549; 558; 588; 621; 652.

81 *TN*, 96; 192.

82 *TN*, 52; 69; 75; 79; 84; 85 (two entries); 86; 88; 90; 91; 94; 104; 119; 123; 137; 139 (two entries); 142; 147 (two entries); 160; 167; 170; 171; 174; 175; 180; 186; 188; 190 (two entries); 191; 192; 194; 195; 197; 199; 202; 204; 211; 212; 221; 228; 229; 242; 252; 258; 260 (two entries); 261; 265; 267; 272; 278; 281; 290; 298 (two entries); 312; 316; 322; 325; 327; 340; 344; 346; 348; 357; 360; 363; 365; 366; 367; 370; 379; 392; 397; 399; 404 (two entries); 406; 407; 408 (two entries); 411; 413; 429; 430; 434; 438 (two entries); 440; 441; 442; 445; 448; 449; 461; 463; 464; 467; 471; 472; 473; 476; 478; 479; 481; 482; 485; 492; 510; 520; 527; 537; 540; 543; 551; 552; 553 (two entries); 558 (two entries); 559; 560; 563; 566; 568; 569 (three entries); 570 (two entries); 571 (three entries); 572; 573; 574; 577; 583; 585; 588; 593; 600 (two entries); 603; 607; 608; 610; 615; 617; 620; 660; 662.

83 *TN*, 79; 105; 173; 190; 231; 291; 319; 356; 359; 383; 401; 403; 412; 416; 439; 443; 444; 464; 469; 475; 486.

84 *TN*, 79; 192; 194; 195; 197; 199; 204; 211; 212; 242; 258; 265; 272; 281; 312; 316; 319; 344; 357; 359; 365; 401; 404; 408; 434; 438; 439; 448; 449; 461; 471; 467; 476; 478; 479; 485; 486; 492; 527; 540; 551; 553; 558; 559; 560; 563; 569 (two entries); 570; 572; 588; 603.

85 *TN*, 340.

86 *TN*, 357.

87 *TN*, 113; 160; 172; 175 (two entries); 189; 197; 198; 199; 207; 228; 261; 290; 304; 325; 366; 367; 375; 381; 406; 429; 442; 450; 459; 463; 490; 491; 492; 501; 510; 544; 549; 558; 583; 585; 589; 594; 615; 617; 620; 648; 664.

88 *TN*, 160; 175; 197; 199; 228; 290; 325; 366; 367; 406; 429; 442; 463; 492; 510; 558; 583; 585; 615; 617; 620.

89 *TN*, 95; 96; 218; 228; 365.

90 *TN*, 379.

91 *TN*, 218.

92 *TN*, 560; 624; 639; 643.

93 *TN*, 624.
94 *TN*, 79; 92; 93; 159; 292; 652.
95 *TN*, 648.
96 *TN*, 623.
97 On Maliha's text, see McChesney 1990.
98 *SA*, 2:805.
99 A2, ff. 44a–45b.
100 *SA*, 2:806.
101 *SA*, 2:807.
102 See Green 2014, 561.
103 See, for example, al-Muhibbi 1967–69, 2:382; 3:178; 3:186; 4:178; 4:187 for references to Ibn Ma'sum and Nizam al-Din Ahmad. The text of al-Muhibbi 1967–69, 2:381 shows borrowed phrasings when compared with *SA*, 2:570; and al-Muhibbi 1967–69, 3:187–8, shows borrowed phrasings when compared with *SA*, 2:808. See also Beers 2020, 244.
104 Mutribi Samarqandi 2003, 277–8.
105 See Pellò 2015, 305.
106 See Shafieioun 2019, 159–60; Heinz 1973, 12; cf. Dadvar 1999, 203–4; for a critical rejoinder to this view, see Losensky 2021a, 448–51.
107 See Shafieioun 2019, 171–2.
108 *TN*, 413; 473; 478. For more examples, see Dadvar 1999, 204–5.
109 For relationships between poets and male coffee-waiters, who often engaged in prostitution, see *TN*, 67; 155; 237; 445; 472; 553; 605. For how a poet was punished for an affair with a servant of the royal household, see *TN*, 419. See also Babayan 2021, 23.
110 See Collot 2014, 66.
111 For Safavid Iran, see Floor 2000, 118–19.
112 *TN*, 582; SA 1:386–9. See also Salim 1349*s*, 507; 516; 523. For professional mendicancy in an earlier period, see Papoutsakis 2017, 64–9.
113 *TN*, 11.
114 See Gulchin Ma'ani 1369*s*, 1: *panj*; Ahmad 1976, 125.
115 *TN*, 637.
116 See Matthee, Floor and Clawson 2013, 31.
117 See Akopyan 2021.
118 *TN*, 624. This assumes that Nasrabadi is using the conversion rate of fifty 'abbasis to a *tuman*. For the conversion rate, see Avery, Fragner and Simmons 2020.
119 *TN*, 56.
120 *TN*, 327.
121 *TN*, 417.
122 *TN*, 539.
123 *TN*, 435.
124 *TN*, 593.
125 *TN*, 374.
126 *TN*, 573.
127 *TN*, 503.
128 Two hundred and fifty 'abbasis equate to 500 *mahmudi*s. A master bricklayer earned 75 *mahmudi*s per month. See Siebertz 2013, 215.
129 Six hundred 'abbasis per year equate to 1,200 *mahmudi*s, or 100 *mahmudi*s per month. An interpreter earned fifty *mahmudi*s per month. See Siebertz 2013, 215.

130 Eight hundred *ʿabbasi*s equate to 1,600 *mahmudi*s. A groom earned 45 *mahmudi*s per month (540 *mahmudi*s per year). See Siebertz 2013, 215.
131 *TN*, 371.
132 *TN*, 394.
133 *TN*, 402.
134 *TN*, 608. For the scarcity of wood, see Kaempfer 2018, 104.
135 *TN*, 396. On the role of *sadr*, see Ansari 2002, 73–9.
136 *TN*, 392.
137 *TN*, 392.
138 *TN*, 466.
139 Metre: *mutaqarib-i musamman-i mahzuf. TN*, 603. See also Matthee 2012, 91.
140 See ʿAli 1966, 7.
141 For further figures, see Dadvar 1999, 137–44.
142 *TN*, 160. For the salary, see Moosvi 2015, 214, Table 9.1.
143 *TN*, 191. For the salary, see Moosvi 2015, 214, Table 9.1.
144 *TN*, 566.
145 For the conversion rate, see Shakeb 2017, 156.
146 *TN*, 359.
147 *TN*, 359. The actual value of the stipend is given in A2, ff. 43a–44a.
148 A2, ff. 43a–44a.
149 See Matthee, Floor and Clawson 2013, 50; 120–30.
150 See Matthee 2012, 97–100; Floor 2000, 81; Newman 2009, 94–6.
151 For documented instances of upselling by long-distance merchants, see Aguletsʿi 2003, 196–7.
152 See Shakeb 2017, 155.
153 Metre: *rajaz-i musamman-i matvi va makhbun. TN*, 356.
154 See also *TN*, 325; *SA*, 1:386; 1:421. See also Floor 2000, 80; 83; 85; 187–90.
155 See Matthee 2012, 87.
156 See Matthee, Floor and Clawson 2013, 43.
157 See Floor 2000, 105.
158 *TN*, 429.
159 *TN*, 429.
160 *TN*, 429.
161 *TN*, 429.
162 *TN*, 551.
163 *TN*, 551.
164 *TN*, 466.
165 *TN*, 467.
166 Al-Bahrani 2008, 66.
167 A7; see Danishpazhuh 1358s.
168 See A2, f. 65a.
169 A7, ff. 143b; 162b–165a; 240b–241a.
170 The twelfth poet is Rafiʿ al-Din Muhammad Husayni. See A7, f. 39b; *TN*, 271.
171 A7, ff. 306b–307a; *TN*, 565.
172 A7, ff. 113b–114a; 227b; *TN*, 119.
173 A7, f. 345a.
174 A7, ff. 37b–38a; *TN*, 475.
175 A7, ff. 93a–99a; *TN*, 469.
176 A7, f. 143b; *TN*, 195.

177 A7, ff. 194b–196b; *TN*, 353.
178 A7, ff. 202b–206b; *TN*, 316.
179 A7, f. 225b; *TN*, 509; Thackston 2020.
180 A7, f. 307b; *TN*, 406.
181 A7, f. 65b; *TN*, 560.
182 A7, ff. 151b–152a; 226b–227a; *TN*, 553.
183 *TN*, 179; 80.
184 *TN*, 81; 319; 469; *SA*, 2:785. See also Chapter Five.
185 *TN*, 179.
186 A7, ff. 202b–206b.
187 A7, ff. 37b–38a.
188 *SA*, 2:785.
189 *SA*, 2:816.
190 *SA*, 2:828.
191 *TN*, 113.
192 *TN*, 464.
193 *TN*, 464. *SA*, 1:42.
194 *SA*, 2:796.
195 *TN*, 175.

Chapter 2

1   Lowry 2009, 176.
2   B1, unnumbered folios.
3   B2 f.1a.
4   Ibn Maʿsum 1988a, 477.
5   B3 f.1a.
6   See Ranjbar 1377*s*, 54.
7   See Salati 1999a; Alam and Subrahmanyam 1996, 139; Schimmel 1973, 8; Lowry 2009, 176–7.
8   Ibn Maʿsum 1988b, 169.
9   On him, see Abdesselem 2012.
10 Ibn Maʿsum 1988b, 172. The source for the poems is al-Thaʿalibi 2000, 3:269–77.
11 Metre: *kamil*. Ibn Maʿsum 1988b, 172.
12 Metre: *kamil*. Ibn Maʿsum 1988b, 173.
13 For parallel cases, see Bahl 2018a, 115–53; 193–234; Bahl 2018b.
14 B2, B3, B4, B5, B6, B9, B10, B11, B12, B13.
15 See the collected articles in Bauden and Franssen (eds.), 2020.
16 B3.
17 B3, unnumbered folios.
18 B4.
19 On these texts, see Stewart 2010; Stewart 2017.
20 B5.
21 See Lowry 2009, 177.
22 B11, seven unpaginated folios at the beginning of the MS.
23 al-Musawi 2015, 163. On the history of the *badiʿiyya* form, see Bauer 2006.
24 See Lowry 2009, 179–80.
25 B10.

26 B9.
27 Bilgrami 2015, 162.
28 *SA*, 1:42–8. An alternative translation of this poem is offered in Muʿid Khan 1963, 46–52.
29 al-Musawi 2015, 71.
30 For these structural elements, see Jacobi 1971, 74–85.
31 See Hussein 2011; Stetkevych 1993, 114.
32 Metre: *tawil*. Ibn al-Farid 1985, 98.
33 Dhu l-Ghada is a valley in Najd. See al-Zabidi 2001, 39:171.
34 Metre: *tawil. SA*, 1:43.
35 See Gruendler 2003, 231.
36 Metre: *tawil. SA,* 1:45.
37 Metre: *tawil. SA*, 1:46.
38 Metre: *tawil. SA*, 1:46.
39 See Balachandran 2020a, 147–8.
40 Metre: *tawil. SA*, 1:47.
41 *SA*, 1:48.
42 For surveys of literary production in these other languages at the court of Golkonda, see Wagoner 2011; Sharma 2020; Siddiqua 2011, 285–456.
43 See Peacock 2020.
44 *SA*, 2:893.
45 *SA*, 2:895.
46 *SA*, 2:878; 881.
47 See Bahl 2020a, 214–15.
48 See A2, f. 65a.
49 See al-Hurr al-ʿAmili 1966, 34.
50 See al-Musawi 2015, 159.
51 For a discussion of such gatherings in eighteenth-century north India, see Tabor 2019, 87.
52 *SA*, 1:84.
53 *SA*, 2:887.
54 *SA*, 2:427–8.
55 *SA*, 2:427.
56 *SA*, 2:428. See also Muʿid Khan 1963, 69.
57 On the concept of factionalism, see Fischel 2020b, 117–29.
58 *SA*, 1:78. See also Muʿid Khan 1963, 98.
59 Metre: *kamil*. SA 2:785–6. An alternative translation is offered in Muʿid Khan 1963, 84–5.
60 Metre: *mujtass-i musamman-i makhbun*. E1 f. 94b.
61 See Abu Nuwas 1958–2006, 4:150, No. 7; Hafiz 1362s, 1:506.
62 *SA*, 2:784–5.
63 The word *ʿuyūn* is being used here as an untranslatable pun, meaning both 'wellsprings' and 'eyes'. For the poet as shepherd or pastor, see Stetkevych 1993, 148.
64 See also *SA*, 2:782.
65 For a contrasting survey of the circle of Nizam al-Din Ahmad, see Muʿid Khan 1963, 56–95.
66 *SA*, 1:86; 315. See also Muʿid Khan 1963, 132–6.
67 *SA*, 1:316–18.
68 *SA*, 1:78.

69 For the letter, see *SA*, 1:241.
70 *SA*, 1:79–80.
71 Metre: *khafif. SA*, 1:82.
72 *SA*, 1:331.
73 See Ibn Maʿsum 1988b, 98; *SA*, 1:331.
74 See Ibn Maʿsum 1988b, 98.
75 See Ibn Maʿsum 1988b, 95; 121.
76 See *SA*, 1:335.
77 See *SA*, 2:816–29.
78 For an example of how poets could struggle to attract attention in the Mughal north, see Kaicker 2018, 338.
79 See Bauer 2014; Veseley 2003.
80 See *SA*, 1:351–2; 354; 356; 2:847; 2:853.
81 See *SA*, 1:334; 2:461; 2:661; 2:745.
82 Metre: *ramal.* SA 2:745.
83 *SA*, 2:746.
84 *SA*, 2:885.
85 *SA*, 2:887.
86 See Bauer 2014, 210–11.
87 *SA*, 2:895; emended on the basis of B6, f. 319b.
88 *SA*, 2:898.
89 See Talib 2018a, 83–6. For further lyric poems from Golkonda, see Muʿid Khan 1963, 124–5.
90 Manjak Basha 2009, 225–384.
91 *SA*, 1:57.
92 For similar poems, see Harb 2017, 136. The term is explained in more detail in al-Bahrani 1386s, 2:1102.
93 See *SA*, 1:107; 1:117; 1:126; 1:128; 1:330; 1:653.
94 See Papoutsakis 2022, 377–8.
95 *SA*, 1:57. For the lineage of the theme, see Richardson 2012, 42; 85. For an earlier period, see al-Thaʿalibi 2000, 5:21. For a contemporary epigram about a beloved with ophthalmia which was composed in Medina, see *SA*, 2:460.
96 See al-Haymi al-Kawkabani 2002, 2:516.
97 Metre: *ramal.* SA 2:784.
98 Metre: *munsarih.* SA 2:782.
99 On the city as a space for the short lyric poem, see Talib 2018b, 138–40; 142–9; 155–7. See also el-Rouayheb 2005, 63–5; Andrews and Kalpaklı 2005, 32–6.
100 Metre: *tawil. SA*, 2:676. Emended using B6, f. 238a.
101 Metre: *kamil. SA*, 1:344.
102 Metre: *basit. SA*, 1:346.
103 Metre: *tawil. SA*, 1:345.
104 See, for example *SA*, 1:245; 1:316.
105 In addition to the group of poems discussed in the following pages, further sets of response poems include: *SA*, 1:318–21, a dialogue between Ibn Maʿsum, his brother Shihab al-Din Ahmad, and the Mamluk poet al-Khiyami (not al-Khaʿthami, as garbled in the print edition); and *SA*, 95–8, a series of poems exchanged between Nizam al-Din Ahmad, al-Jawhari and ʿAli b. Hasan al-Marzuqi.
106 Metre: *tawil.*
107 *SA*, 2:424.

108   See Péri 2020, 234. For the Levantine echoes, see al-Taluwi 1983, 1:159–60.
109   On the Ahdal family, see Löfgren 2012; al-ʿAydarus 2001, 572–3.
110   Krenkow 1910, 4 [in the Arabic pagination].
111   See al-Isfahani 2010, 7:140–1.
112   *SA*, 2:424.
113   *SA*, 2:423.
114   *SA*, 2:423. B6 f. 143b.
115   Metre: *tawil. SA*, 2:718.
116   Metre: *tawil. SA*, 2:718.
117   Metre: *tawil. SA*, 2:425. Emended on the basis of B6, f. 144a.
118   Metre: *tawil. SA*, 2:425.
119   Metre: *tawil. SA*, 2:425.
120   Metre: *tawil. SA*, 2:426. For the theme of the beloved as a garden, see Schoeler 1974, 44.
121   Metre: *tawil. SA*, 2:426. Emended on the basis of B6, f. 144b.
122   See Bauer 1992, 1:205.
123   See Ricci 2011, 156–7, quoting ʿAlim 1993, 305.
124   For Shaykh Sadaqat Allah's poems, see ʿAlim 1993, 134.
125   Bilgrami 2015, 162.
126   Ibn Maʿsum 1988a, 301.
127   Bilgrami 2015, 162. For an alternative account, see Muʿid Khan 1963, 101.
128   Bilgrami 2015, 162.
129   Bilgrami 2015, 162. See also ʿAli 2012; Moosvi 2015, 205.
130   Bilgrami 2015, 162. See also al-Hasani 1978, 6:185–6.
131   Metre: *wafir*. Ibn Maʿsum 1988a, 228. See also Muʿid Khan 1963, 101.
132   See Bendrey and Verma 1934, 84.
133   B14 f.31a; see also al-Bahrani 1386s, 1:162.
134   B7 f. 328a.
135   See the appendices to ʿAli 1966; Ram 1985, 1–241.
136   Lahiji 1375s, 98.
137   See the appendices to ʿAli 1966.
138   Ibn Maʿsum 1988a, 538.
139   For comparisons, see Muʿid Khan 1963, 13.
140   Ernst 2011, 43.
141   Ibn Maʿsum 1988a, 568–9; Kashifi 1336s, 159–62.
142   Ibn Maʿsum 1363s.
143   For the significance of Burhanpur as a centre of Islamic learning, see Gordon 1988, 425–33; Bazmee Ansari 2012; Schimmel 1973, 5; Kugle 2021, 15–22.
144   See Ibn Maʿsum 1988a, 464.
145   Ibn Maʿsum 1988a, 477.
146   Metre: *basit*. Ibn Maʿsum 1988a, 337–8.
147   See Stetkevych 2010, 143.
148   Ibn Maʿsum 1988a, 55, 141, 190, 193, 198, 291, 319, 407, 415.
149   E.g. Ibn Maʿsum 1988a, 191–2; 194.
150   Ibn Maʿsum 1988a, 190; Dirayati 2010, 11:942.
151   Ibn Maʿsum 1988a, 55, 141, 193, 198, 291, 407. See also al-Amin 1979, 26:49.
152   Ibn Maʿsum 1988a, 200.
153   See ʿAli 2012.
154   Hasan 1878, 395.

155   See Truschke 2016, 8.

156   Metre: *kamil.*

157   For a discussion of comparisons between wine and the beloved in classical Arabic wine poetry, see Kennedy 1997, 14–17.

158   Talib Amuli 1967, 14.

159   Sa'ib 1985–91, 1:136.

160   Sa'ib 1985–91, 1:110. For earlier comparanda, see Lewis 2010, 269–70.

161   For a comparable, later case, see Leese 2021, 15.

162   See Qutbuddin 2021.

Chapter 3

1   Ibn Ma'sum 1988b, 93.

2   *SA*, 2:722; Ibn Ma'sum 1988b, 93–121.

3   See Um 2009, 28–32.

4   Um 2009, 28–32.

5   See Alam and Subrahmanyam 2007, 230; Shafir 2020, 17; and Chapter 4 here. It is clear that the overland route was still used, however. See Floor 2006, 506–7, and A8.

6   See Haykel 2003, 34–5; al-Hibshi 1986, 18–22.

7   See Rieu 1894, 461; al-Haymi al-Kawkabani 2002, 2:520.

8   See Rieu 1894, 452; 679; 702.

9   See Haykel 2003, 31–2.

10   See Dafari 1966; Dufour 2011; Wagner 2009.

11   For a discussion of a further group of non-classicizing texts that circulated internationally, see Kilpatrick 2011b; Özkan 2020a, 53–9.

12   C1.

13   On the term *taqmi'* (giving rise to *muqamma'*), see Dafari 1966, 164–5. For the lives and verse of the poets listed here, see Dafari 1966, 61–3; 56–9; 52–4; 6–7; al-Khafaji 1967, 2:460–1. On al-Mazzah and his predecessors, see Dufour 2011, 179–97.

14   See Ibn Ma'sum 1988a, 498–9; 503–4; 515–16.

15   Exceptionally, see al-Hibshi 1986, 219–56.

16   On Ibn Nubata, see Bauer 2008; on the poem in question, see Bauer 2007, 293.

17   Compare, for example, C2, f. 33b, l. 16 (*yā habbadhā mahniyatu l-awsāli / qāti'atu l-a'māri ka-l-hilāli*); and Ibn Nubata 1905, 586, l. 21.

18   Al-Husayni 2009, 2:82–3; Wagner 2009, 109.

19   On al-Sarim, see also al-Muhibbi 1967–69, 3:565–84; Shirwani 2017, 56; al-Shawkani 198-, 1:16–17; Zabara 1957, 1:69; al-Hibshi 1986, 399.

20   See Um 2009, 163–7.

21   See B8, p. 616.

22   See C2 f.112a.

23   *SA*, 2:756–7.

24   C2 and C3.

25   Haykel 2003, 36–8.

26   See C2, f.55b; C3, p. 114.

27   Haykel 2003, 34 n. 30.

28   al-Haymi al-Kawkabani 2002. This author has attracted little attention in modern scholarship, apart from in van Gelder 2013, 345–51; Talib 2018b, 142–6.

29   'Antara 2018, 12, l.62.

30 al-Mi'mar 2018, 122. Metre: *tawil*. The second *misra'* is given without an attribution in *SA*, 2:756.
31 Cf. al-Hibshi 1986, 399.
32 See Haykel 2003, 32; 40.
33 Haykel 2003, 40–1.
34 On interactions between urban and tribal poetic systems in modern Yemen, see Caton 1990, 46–8. The extent to which al-Sarim's poem would have genuinely brought about political change would have depended on a number of factors, including, most obviously, the composition of the group present at its recitation.
35 See Latham 1979; Hamori 1981; Hamori 1992.
36 See Smoor 1991; Qutbuddin 2005, 7–8; 16.
37 Texts by al-Sarim are also reproduced in al-Haymi al-Kawkabani 2020, 56–7; al-Haymi al-Kawkabani 1986, 99–100; 157.
38 Al-Haymi al-Kawkabani 2002, 1:467; 1:471.
39 Al-Haymi al-Kawkabani 2002, 1:567; 1:638.
40 Al-Haymi al-Kawkabani 2002, 1:582.
41 Metre: *mutaqarib*. Al-Haymi al-Kawkabani 2002, 1:645. See also C8, Volume 1, f. 287a.
42 See al-Tha'alibi 2000, 3:12; 3:106–7.
43 Metre: *basit*. C2, f.125a; C3, 233.
44 Al-Haymi al-Kawkabani 2002, 1:639.
45 Robbins, Horta and Appiah (eds.) 2018, 1.
46 Al-Haymi al-Kawkabani 2002, 1:219; 1:232; 1:294; 1:313; 2:519.
47 Al-Haymi al-Kawkabani 2002, 1:480.
48 See, for example, Al-Haymi al-Kawkabani 2002, 1:550; 1:661. See also C7, ff. 64a–66a.
49 Al-Haymi al-Kawkabani 2002, 1:73.
50 Metre: *basit*. See al-Ibshihi 1986, 2:435.
51 Metre: *rajaz*.
52 Metre: *tawil*.
53 Al-Haymi al-Kawkabani 2002, 1:73.
54 On this rhetorical figure, see van Gelder 2008.
55 Clayton and Rothstein 1991, 4.
56 Metre: *kamil*. Al-Haymi al-Kawkabani 2002, 2:236–8.
57 Metre: *rajaz*. For his life and work, see Pfeifer 2022.
58 C2, f.103a; C3, p. 198.
59 Metre: *munsarih*.
60 Al-Haymi al-Kawkabani 2002, 236.
61 Metre: *hazaj*. Text emended with reference to C8, Volume Two, f. 50a.
62 Metre: *sari'*.
63 For further such examples of *sariqa*, see Özkan 2020b, 89–91.
64 Metre: *rajaz*. Text emended with reference to C8, Volume Two, f. 50b.
65 Metre: *rajaz*.
66 Metre: *tawil*.
67 Metre: *khafif*.
68 Metre: *wafir*.
69 Wazir 1985, 267–9.
70 See Subrahmanyam 1988, 515–16; Subrahmanyam 2018, 219–20; Brouwer 2006, 75; 120–3; 152–6; 265; 277–87.

71 See also Subrahmanyam 1988, 515–16; Serjeant 1963, 120.

72 See Serjeant 1963, 122–9.

73 Serjeant 1963, 122–9.

74 Hamori 1992, 64–70.

75 C2, f. 13a.

76 C3, p. 23.

77 Yalaoui's edition of Ibn Hani''s *diwan* notes that this poem was most probably dedicated to another patron, Abu l-Faraj al-Shaybani. See Ibn Hani' al-Andalusi 1995, 149; Yalaoui 1976, 86.

78 See Yalaoui 1976, 74–8.

79 Metre: *kamil. SA*, 1:161.

80 See van Gelder 2012, 59.

81 See Frolov 1999, 247.

82 *SA*, 1:152–66.

83 *SA*, 1:153.

84 See Meisami 2003, 146.

85 Metre: *kamil*. For the notion of 'syntax time', see Key 2018, 217.

86 See Ibn Manzur 1999, صلهب.

87 See al-Maqhafi 2002, 1:389.

88 See al-Maqhafi 2002, 2:1472.

89 See al-Maqhafi 2002, 2:1719.

90 See al-Maqhafi 2002, 2:1129.

91 Metre: *kamil*.

92 Riffaterre 1978, 109.

93 Metre: *kamil*.

94 C5, f. 55b.

95 C6, f. 19a.

96 On this figure, see Stetkevych 2002, 280.

97 See Piamenta 1990–91, 2:502.

98 See Bray 2000, 58.

99 See C6, f. 18b.

100 C5, f. 9b.

101 See Gruendler 2008a, 329.

102 See Haykel 2003, 26.

103 *SA*, 2:687; 698; 704; 711.

104 Stetkevych 1991, 263.

105 Fakhreddine 2015, 199.

106 Hutcheon 1985, 6.

107 See Gruendler 2008b, 437.

108 See Feener and Gedacht 2018, 16.

Chapter 4

1 Winter 2010, 20–7.

2 Abisaab 2015, 147–74; Newman 1993; 416Stewart 1996a, 1996b, 2006.

3 See Salati 1999b.

4 *SA*, 533; 570.

5 For a notable exception, see Kilpatrick 2008, 71–4.

6   See Stewart 2009, 36–7; Bosworth 1989.
7   See al-ʿAmili 1961.
8   See ʿAmili 1361s; Hijazi 1999, 273–400.
9   For the history of 'probative quotations', see Gilliot 1996.
10 On the use of *shawahid* in premodern Arabic philology in general, see Baalbaki 2001.
    On seventeenth-century philological practice, see Bahl 2020a; el-Rouayheb 2015b.
11 See Orfali 2011, 450–1.
12 See Keegan 2020, 221.
13 See Newman 2010, 193–5; Abisaab 2015, 130–1; Scarcia 2012.
14 D1.
15 al-Hurr al-ʿAmili 1966, 1:145; 1:170.
16 al-Hurr al-ʿAmili 1966, 1:72.
17 al-Hurr al-ʿAmili 1966, 1:142.
18 Salati 1999b, 623–4; al-Sadr 1986, 326.
19 *TN*, 568.
20 D2–D3.
21 Metre: *rajaz-i musamman*. D2, p. 361.
22 I borrow the term 'rhizomatic thinking' from Bhatti 2015, 8.
23 For the history of the form, see Virani 2008.
24 See de Blois 2004, 285; Ibn Isfandiyar 1941, 1:132–5.
25 D2, p. 376.
26 al-Hurr al-ʿAmili 1966, 1:25; 1:42; 1:65; 1:69; 1:78; 1:84; 1:92; 1:98; 1:120; 1:155; 1:162;
    1:170; 1:175; 2:154 (two entries); 2:156; 2:223; 2:292.
27 al-Hurr al-ʿAmili 1966, 1:65; 1:78; 1:98; 1:170.
28 al-Hurr al-ʿAmili 1966, 1:92; 1:162; 2:223.
29 al-Hurr al-ʿAmili 1966, 1:69; 1:92; 1:120; 1:162; 2:154.
30 al-Hurr al-ʿAmili 1966, 1:162.
31 al-Hurr al-ʿAmili 1966, 1:162.
32 al-Hurr al-ʿAmili 1966, 1:25; 1:42; 1:65; 1:78; 1:98; 1:170; 1:175; 2:156; 2:223; 2:292.
33 al-Hurr al-ʿAmili 1966, 1:25.
34 al-Hurr al-ʿAmili 1966, 1:25.
35 al-Hurr al-ʿAmili 1966, 1:175.
36 al-Hurr al-ʿAmili 1966, 1:84.
37 al-Hurr al-ʿAmili 1966, 2:154.
38 al-Hurr al-ʿAmili 1966, 2:154 (two entries); 2:156.
39 al-Hurr al-ʿAmili 1966, 2:223; 2:292.
40 al-Hurr al-ʿAmili 1966, 1:45; 1:81; 1:124; 2:53; 2:57; 2:112; 2:146.
41 al-Hurr al-ʿAmili 1966, 1:81; 1:124; 2:53; 2:112; 2:128; 2:146.
42 al-Hurr al-ʿAmili 1966, 2:53; SA, 723.
43 al-Hurr al-ʿAmili 1966, 1:45.
44 Metre: *rajaz*. al-Hurr al-ʿAmili 1966, 1:45.
45 Metre: *rajaz*. Cf. *SA*, 507; 509–11. Hasan Zayn al-Din is a misprint for Hasan b.
    Zayn al-Din. See B6, f. 174a. I have emended the text of the poem on the basis of B6,
    ff. 175b–176a. Al-Shahid al-Thani's poetry seems to have been copied and read by
    al-Hurr's family in Iran. See D4.
46 Kohlberg 2012.
47 The phrasing 'semantics and rhetoric' is from el-Rouayheb 2015a, 29.
48 *TN*, 600.
49 D5.

50 D5, p. 150.
51 Al-Hurr al-ʿAmili 1966, 1:145.
52 See al-Muhibbi 1967–69, 2:337–45, ignoring the editor's conflation of him with his brother.
53 Metres: *khafif; sariʿ; kamil.* D1, p. 170.
54 Talib 2018a, 26.
55 For further discussion of *istikhdam*, see Talib 2019, 124–7.
56 See el-Rouayheb 2015b.
57 Metre: *khafif.* B6, f. 190a-b. *SA*, 548–9. See also al-Hurr al-ʿAmili 1966, 1:173.
58 For the root of this image, see Bauer 1998, 235.
59 Ibn al-Nahhas 2018, 215.
60 See Hijazi 1999, 354–5; 356–7; 394–5.
61 On these texts, see Ala Amjadi 2021, 293.
62 See Neuwirth 2014, 113.
63 Metre: *tawil.* D1, p. 288.
64 Metre: *tawil.* D1, p. 289; 290. For discussions of *tadbij*, see Ibn Maʿsum 1968, 6:118–22; C4, ff. 13b–14a.
65 Vahid 1338s, 174–5.
66 See Montgomery 2015, 169–71.
67 Metre: *basit.* Ibn Maʿsum 1988b, 54.
68 Metre: *kamil.* Ibn Maʿsum 1988b, 54.
69 Metre: *tawil.* D1, p. 289.
70 Metre: *tawil.* D1, p. 290–1.
71 Metre: *tawil.* Ibn Maʿsum 1988a, 171.
72 Metre: *tawil.* D1, p. 293.
73 Metre: *tawil.* Ibn Maʿsum 1988a, 172.

Chapter 5

1 On Faraj Allah, see Gulchin Maʿani 1369s 1:525–8; *SA*, 2:784–94; Beers 2020, 241–2. On Salik, see Gulchin Maʿani 1369s 2:1003–4; Dayal 2017, 565; Siddiqua 2011, 412–21; Devare 2018, 257.
2 See Hidayet Hosain 2012.
3 See Gulchin Maʿani 1369s 1:381–3; Shushtari 1973, 87.
4 Shushtari 1973, 70; 87.
5 Shushtari 1973, 70.
6 *SA*, 2:785.
7 See Lefèvre 2017, 328.
8 Shushtari 1973, 70.
9 *TN*, 475. See also Bilgrami 1918, 2:94.
10 See Bilgrami 1918 2:94. The *ghazal* is found on E1, f. 122a.
11 See Valih Daghistani 2006, 3:1604.
12 See Awhadi 2010, 1: *shast u shish.*
13 Gupamavi 1336s, 541.
14 Metre: *mujtass-i musamman-i makhbun-i mahzuf.* E1, f. 39b.
15 See also *SA*, 2:757.
16 E1, f. 94b.
17 Metre: *ramal-i musamman-i mahzuf.* E1, f. 10b.

18 Metre: *ramal-i musamman-i mahzuf.* E1, f. 117b.
19 Metre: *ramal-i musamman-i mahzuf.* E1, f. 47b.
20 See Razi 1999, 1:185; Brookshaw 2019, 24.
21 Metre: *ramal-i musamman-i mahzuf.* E1, f. 135b. For the tulips of Kabul, see Razi 1999, 2:611. For the meadows of Kashmir, see Razi 1999, 2:618.
22 Metre: *ramal-i musamman-i salim al-sadr va makhbun al-hashv va-l-zarb al-mahzuf.* E1, f. 33b. Khaqani may or may not have actually been imprisoned, but he represents Shirvan as a prison (*habsgah*) in his verse. See Beelaert 2020.
23 *TN* 469. See also Arzu 2006, 2:628; ʿAzimabadi 2012, 1:765.
24 *TN* 469.
25 *TN* 469.
26 Sprenger 1854, 124.
27 *TN*, 469. See also Dayal 2017, 565.
28 *TN*, 469. The comment that Salik was already dead is present in the first draft of the text: A3, f. 221b.
29 Sprenger 1854, 150.
30 E3, p. 556; E4, f. 22a. The defective MS. E7 is not used as a witness here.
31 For the dating, see Fasaʾi 1378*s*, 1:457. The three poems are: a description of the mansion of Muʿin al-Din Muhammad (E4, f. 29a); a polythematic *qasida* (E4, f. 16b; E3, p. 539); and a description a letter sent to Muʿin al-Din Muhammad (E4, f. 31a). For more on this figure, see Matthee 2012, 157.
32 E4, f. 17a.
33 E4, f. 9b; E3, p. 541. For Mirza Habib Allah, see Matthee 2012, 22.
34 E4, f. 17b; E3, p. 552. For the dating of Amir Khan's tenure, see Haneda 1989, 78. On the role of *qurchi-bashi*, see Ansari 2002, 103–7.
35 E4, f. 7a.
36 E4, f. 51b. This period corresponds to the governorship of Bektash Khan. See Maeda 2003, 253.
37 E4, f. 23b; E3, p. 559. For the governorship of ʿAli Padishah, see Matthee 2006, 60.
38 For Basra's maritime connections with India during this period, see Matthee 2009, 108; Floor 2006, 507.
39 E4, f. 58a.
40 E4, f. 12a; E3, p. 546. On Asaf Khan, see Lefèvre 2012.
41 E4, f. 59a.
42 See E5, p. 386. On Nizam al-Din Ahmad, Hakim al-Mulk, see Bandy 2021.
43 E4, f. 3a.
44 E11, ff. 60b–62a; ff. 62a–63b.
45 E10, ff. 312b–315a.
46 E4, f. 49b; E3, p. 580.
47 E4, f. 67b; E3, p. 590.
48 E4, f. 53b; E3, p. 589.
49 E4, f. 67a; E3, p. 589.
50 See Losensky 2015, 47.
51 E4, ff. 4a; 19b; 61b; E3, p. 533. On Ibn al-Khatun, see Sherwani 1974, 506.
52 E4, f.58b. On Mir Muhammad Saʿid, see Subrahmanyam 1988, 516–17.
53 E4, f.58b.
54 E4, ff. 55b; 59b; E3, p. 593. The existence of these poems is mentioned in Dayal 2017, 565. On the capture of these two fortresses, see Sarkar 1979, 49–51.
55 E4, f. 56b; E3, p. 595.

56 On the story of the defection, see Sarkar 1979, 118–21; Sherwani 1974, 483.
57 See Sarkar 1979, 118–21.
58 E4, f. 13a.
59 E4, ff. 15a; 26a; E3, pp. 537; 564.
60 E4, f. 14a.
61 See Orsatti 2020.
62 For a broad discussion of this theme, see Lewis 2018, 550. For the case of Amir Khusraw's rewritings, see Gabbay 2009, 686–92; Gabbay 2010, 41–65.
63 See Duda 1933, 116–17; and the titles listed in Dirayati 2010 under *Khusraw u Shirin*, *Shirin u Khusraw*, and *Farhad u Shirin*.
64 See Meisami 1987, 194.
65 On this circle, see Toutant 2016. Their contemporary Salimi Jaruni composed a version of the story in Shiraz in 880/1475–76. See Jaruni 1382*s*, *bist u du*.
66 For earlier Turkic recensions, see Zajączkowski 1958.
67 See Dirayati 2010 under *Khusraw u Shirin*, *Shirin u Khusraw*, and *Farhad u Shirin*.
68 Metre: *ramal-i musamman-i mahzuf*. See E1, f. 41a.
69 See Sardar 2010, 87. The source for this description is Sa'idi Shirazi 1961, 62.
70 See Sharma 2020, 404–5.
71 *TN*, 75.
72 See also Orsatti 2020.
73 See E8.
74 See E9, ff. 166a – 174b.
75 See Losensky 2020b.
76 See Losensky 2020c. On the two versions of the poem, see Duda 1933, 110–16.
77 See Thackston 2020.
78 For references to further influential re-writings of *Khusraw u Shirin*, see Losensky 1998, 204.
79 Two of Ruh al-Amin's romances have been published in facsimile. See Ruh al-Amin, 2012a and 2012b.
80 See Duda 1933, 115.
81 Metre: *hazaj-i musaddas-i mahzuf*. E3, p. 497.
82 Metre: *hazaj-i musaddas-i mahzuf*. E3, p. 498.
83 See Thiesen 1982, 124–5.
84 Nizami 1366*s*, 156–7.
85 Nizami 1366*s*, 157.
86 Nizami 1366*s*, 157.
87 Metre: *hazaj-i musaddas-i mahzuf*. 'Urfi 1378*s*, 3:130.
88 Metre: *hazaj-i musaddas-i mahzuf*. Nizami 1366*s*, 156.
89 Metre: *hazaj-i musaddas-i mahzuf*. E6, p. 102.
90 Metre: *hazaj-i musaddas-i mahzuf*. E6, p. 102.
91 For a theoretical overview of the problem, see Kinra 2007. A cross-reading of the theory against poetic practice is given in Losensky 1998, 195–202.
92 See Losensky 1998, 200–1.
93 See Losensky 1998, 203.
94 Metre: *hazaj-i musaddas-i mahzuf*. E3, p. 490.
95 E3, p. 491. One of the most interesting critical treatises is Lahuri 1977.
96 E3, p. 491: *hanūz az raftagān āvāza hast / bi-har gūyī navā-yi tāza hast.*
97 E3, p. 491: *ki daryā-yi ma'ānī bī-karān ast / habābash muhr-i ganj-i shāygān ast.*
98 E3, p. 488.

99   On such levels of polysemy, see Brookshaw 2019, 132–5.
100 Metre: *ramal-i musamman-i mahzuf.* E1, f. 47a-b; E2, f. 58a-b.
101 E2, f. 58a-b: *īnjā.*
102 E2, f. 58a-b: ll.10 and 11 are given in reverse order.
103 See Ingenito 2021, 217.
104 For the antithesis between crows and nightingales in Indo-Persian poetry of the
     late seventeenth and eighteenth centuries, and the significance of these images, see
     Mikkelson 2017, 525.
105 A7, ff. 37b–38a; 93a–99a.
106 In addition to the poems edited and analysed here, see also E1, f. 22b, and E3, p.19,
     ghazals in *-ā daryāb.*
107 Metre: *ramal-i musamman-i salim al-sadr va makhbun al-hashv va-l-zarb al-mahzuf.*
     E1, f. 107a; E2, f. 127a.
108 Metre: *ramal-i musamman-i makhbun-i mahzuf.* E1, f. 107a; E2, f. 127b.
109 Metre: *ramal-i musamman-i salim al-sadr va makhbun al-hashv va-l-zarb al-mahzuf.*
     E3, p. 306; E4 II, pp. 390–1.
110 E3, p. 306: line absent.
111 E3, p. 306: text wormed.
112 E4 II, p. 391: *man u majnūn.*

Chapter 6

1   See, for example, Browne 1924, 164.
2   *TN*, 316; Losensky 2020a.
3   *TN*, 316; Losensky 2020a. On Zafar Khan, see Sharma 2017, 143–66.
4   Losensky 2020a; cf. Safa 1364s, 1275.
5   Losensky 2020a. The praise poems are given in Saʾib 1991, 6: 3559; 3561; 3564; 3566;
     3567; 3571; 3573; 3574; 3576; 3580; 3582; 3586; 3590; 3592; 3595; 3597; 3599.
6   See Losensky 2020a; Gulchin Maʿani 1364s, *si u panj.*
7   Saʾib 1991; Losensky 2020a, 2021a, 463.
8   *TN*, 559; Losensky 2020a; Gulchin Maʿani 1364s, si u shish.
9   Metre: *ramal-i musamman-i salim al-sadr va makhbun al-hashv va-l-zarb al-mahzuf.*
     Saʾib 1991, 1110.
10   *TN*, 399.
11   *TN*, 179.
12   *TN*, 312; Losensky 2020a; Gulchin Maʿani 1364s, *si u nuh.*
13   *TN*, 634.
14   *TN*, 16.
15   *TN*, 581.
16   *TN*, 191.
17   F4, F5, F6. See also Naim-Siddiqi 2020.
18   See Pertsch 1888, 609.
19   Gulchin Maʿani 1369s, 1:95–6.
20   Gulchin Maʿani 1369s, 1:94–5.
21   Rieu 1883, II:687b.
22   Rieu 1883, II:687b.
23   Gulchin Maʿani 1359s, 1:99. F1, f. 18a; Qudsi 1996, 790.
24   See F9, f. 54b.

25 See Salik Qazvini 1994, 614–15. On this *masnavi*, see Sharma 2021, 319–21.
26 Metre: *mutaqarib-i musamman-i mahzuf.* Gulchin Maʿani 1369s, 1:99. F1, f. 83a. On this poem, see Sharma 2017, 150.
27 *TN*, 81.
28 See Popp 2018. For the summary chronicle, see ʿInayat Khan 1990.
29 In addition to the materials studied here, see Sharma 2017, 97.
30 Metre: *hazaj-i musamman-i salim.* Saʾib 1991, 3627.
31 See Losensky 2004, 205; and Sharma 2017, 97–8.
32 See Truschke 2021, 193.
33 Sharma 2017, 97–8.
34 See Sharma 2011.
35 Metre: *hazaj-i musamman-i salim.* Saʾib 1991, 3626.
36 Metre: *hazaj-i musamman-i salim.* Saʾib 1991, 3627.
37 See Kalim Kashani 1957, 45.
38 For more conventional images, see Fasihi Haravi 1383s, 26; 30.
39 Metre: *hazaj-i musamman-i akhrab-i maqbuz-i mahzuf.* F4, f. 233a; F5, f. 63a.
40 F4: line absent.
41 See Sharma 2017, 97.
42 Metre: *hazaj-i musamman-i akhrab-i maqbuz-i mahzuf.* F4, f. 233b; F5, f. 63b.
43 F5, f. 63b: *va haykil.*
44 F5, f. 63b: *sanā-yi.*
45 F5, f. 63b: *zafar khān.*
46 The phrase 'allusive field' is drawn from Losensky 1994.
47 Metre: *hazaj-i musamman-i akhrab-i maqbuz-i mahzuf.* F4, f. 234b; F5, f. 64b.
48 See Sharma 2002; Losensky 2014.
49 See Qazvini 1340s.
50 See Sharma 2012a; Sharma 2004, 74–5; for Zuhuri's time in Bijapur, see Zuhuri 2011, *shast u du – haftad u sih.*
51 See F7, f. 97b; f. 126b.
52 See F8, f. 63a.
53 See F10, f. 107b.
54 See F12, f. 163a; f. 165a.
55 See, for example, F11, ff. 77a–82b.
56 On this poem, see Sharma 2017, 150.
57 See Hafiz 1362s, 2:1052.
58 Metre: *mutaqarib-i musamman-i mahzuf.* F4, f. 193a; F5, f.96a–96b.
59 See Hafiz 1362s, 1:464.
60 Metre: *mutaqarib-i musamman-i mahzuf.* F4, f. 193b; F5, ff. 96b–97a.
61 F5, ff. 96b–97a: *ārad.*
62 Metre: *mutaqarib-i musamman-i mahzuf.* F2, f. 51b; F3, p. 155; F13, f. 45b.
63 Metre: *mutaqarib-i musamman-i mahzuf.* F2, ff. 52b–53a; F3, p. 157; F13, f. 46b.
64 F13, f. 46b: *maygusārān.*
65 F3, p. 157: line absent.
66 F3, p. 157: line absent.
67 F13, f. 46b: *shīsha u bāda.*
68 See also Ghani Kashmiri 1362s, 70.
69 Asir 2005, 497.
70 Bidil 1962–, 1:186.
71 Metre: *mutaqarib-i musamman-i mahzuf.*

72 Metre: *mutaqarib-i musamman-i mahzuf.* F1, f. 69a.
73 Metre: *mutaqarib-i musamman-i mahzuf.* F1, f. 69b.
74 Metre: *mutaqarib-i musamman-i mahzuf.* F1, f. 70a.
75 Metre: *mutaqarib-i musamman-i mahzuf.* F2, f. 50a-b; F3, p. 153; F13, f. 40a-b. For Zuhuri, see Qazvini 1340*s*, 367.
76 F3, p. 153: line absent.
77 F3, p. 153: line absent.
78 F2, f. 50a and F13, f. 40a: *dilā az kaf-i ū chih jūyī ayāgh.*
79 F3, p. 153: line absent.
80 See Rudaki 2012, 98–104; Brookshaw 2014.
81 Metre: *hazaj-i musamman-i akhrab-i makfuf-i mahzuf.* Ahsan 1976, 130. For a cognate representation, see Qudsi 1996, 836. For a contrasting one, see Razi Artimani (198–), 21.
82 F4, f. 191a.
83 F4, f. 192a.
84 Metre: *mutaqarib-i musamman-i mahzuf.* F4, f. 190b; F5, f. 98b.
85 F5. F. 98b: *ābrāham az sar guzasht.*
86 See Losensky 1994, 234.

Chapter 7

1   For one such case of a sub-imperial court attracting poets from abroad, see Lefèvre 2014, 104.
2   Levi 2002, 164.
3   Levi 2002, 165; Dale 1994, 64.
4   Dale 1994, 58.
5   Dale 1994, 61.
6   Levi 2002, 167; Dale 1994, 64.
7   Dale 1994, 67.
8   See Emami 2018, 163; Sharma 2017, 195.
9   *TN*, 292.
10 *TN*, 292.
11 *TN*, 292.
12 *TN*, 292.
13 *TN*, 292.
14 *TN*, 652.
15 *TN*, 653.
16 *TN*, 653.
17 Dale 1994, 46.
18 *TN*, 653.
19 *TN*, 653.
20 *TN*, 653.
21 *TN*, 653.
22 *TN*, 653.
23 See Kia 2020, 90.
24 *TN*, 327. See also Kia 2020, 80.
25 *TN*, 653.
26 *TN*, 653.

27   See *TN*, 643; Rahman 2012.
28   *TN*, 526.
29   Maliha-yi Samarqandi 1390s, 406–8.
30   See Losensky 2021a, 465–6.
31   Kashani 2015, *bist*.
32   Kashani 2015, *bist u yik*.
33   Kashani 2015, *bist u panj*.
34   Kashani 2015, 10.
35   Kashani 2015, 195–6.
36   Kashani 2015, 196.
37   Babayan 2021, 80.
38   G1, unnumbered folios.
39   Kashani 2015, 91. For comparable representations, see Dale 2003, 203.
40   Metre: *mujtass-i musamman-i makhbun-i aslam*. Kashani 2015, 89–90.
41   See Damad 1385s, 36–42.
42   See Saʾib 1991, 1:430–3; see also the work of less prominent poets, such as G11, f. 20a.
43   Kashani 2015, 91.
44   Metre: *muzariʿ-i musamman-i akhrab-i makfuf-i mahzuf*. Kashani 2003, 509.
45   Metre: *mujtass-i musamman-i makhbun-i aslam*. Kashani 2015, 90.
46   See Fayzi 1362s, 34–5.
47   Metre: *mujtass-i musamman-i makhbun-i mahzuf*. Talib Amuli 1967, 22–3.
48   Bollack 2016, 48.
49   See Aslah 1967.
50   G6, f. 190b; G5, f. 89b; Arzu 2006, 2:603; ʿAzimabadi 2012, 1:742.
51   G6, f. 190b; Aslah 1967, 116.
52   G6, f. 190b.
53   Aslah 1967, 115–16.
54   G2, G3, G4.
55   See Lewis 1994, 201, 2018, 468.
56   Bidil 1962-, 1:158.
57   Asir 2005, 63–4.
58   Danish 2000, 49.
59   Haravi 1374s, 51–2.
60   Naziri 1379s, 39.
61   Saʾib 1991, 1:437–8.
62   Samit 1393s, 22–3.
63   Salik Qazvini 1994, 42–3.
64   Saydi 1364s, 97.
65   Shapur 1382s, 173–6.
66   Shawkat 1382s, 146–8.
67   Shifaʾi 1983, 284–5.
68   Taʾsir 1373s, 299.
69   G12, f. 93a.
70   E11, f. 125b.
71   G10, f. 94a.
72   G14, f. 54b.
73   E1, f. 21b.
74   G15, f. 36b; f. 37b.

75 F5, f. 110a.
76 G19, ff. 29b–30a.
77 G9, f. 46a-b.
78 G18, unnumbered folio.
79 G7, pp. 77–8; G8, f. 37a-b.
80 G13, f. 35a; f. 35b.
81 G16, f. 113a-b.
82 G17, pp. 34–5.
83 Jauss 1982, 141.
84 Metre: *hazaj-i musamman-i salim.* G2, pp. 62–3; G3, ff. 20b–21a.
85 Sa'ib 1991, 1:437.
86 Compare Losensky 1998, 166.
87 Sa'ib 1991, 1:438. For a cognate image of plants being bleached to look like quicksilver, see Fani 1342*s*, 22.
88 Sa'ib 1991, 1:438.
89 Metre: *hazaj-i musamman-i salim.* G7, pp. 77–8; G8, f. 37a-b.
90 Metre: *hazaj-i musamman-i salim.* G2, pp. 64–5; G3, ff. 21b–22a.
91 Metre: *hazaj-i musamman.* G7, p. 78; G8, f. 37b.
92 See White 2021.

Conclusion

1   Alighieri 1999, 17.
2   See Mufti 2016, 74–9.
3   See Tavakoli-Targhi 2001.
4   Quoted in Cai 2001, 143.
5   See Prendergast 2004, 12.
6   Prendergast 2004, 7.
7   See Subrahmanyam 2017, 43.
8   See Apter 2013, Part One, Chapter One.
9   For a further example, see D'Hulster 2021, 200–2.
10 Hirschler 2020, 67.
11 Greene 1982, 151.
12 Bhabha 1994, 141.
13 Keshavmurthy 2013, 42.
14 Keshavmurthy 2017, 13.
15 Tagore 2001, 150.
16 See Jauss 1982, 148.

BIBLIOGRAPHY OF PRINT WORKS

Abbreviated Primary Texts

SA = Ibn Ma'sum (2009), *Sulafat al-'Asr fi Mahasin Ahl al-'Asr*, ed. Mahmud Khalaf al-Badi, Damascus: Dar Kinan.

TN = Nasrabadi, Muhammad Tahir (1378s), *Tazkira-yi Nasrabadi*, ed. Muhsin Naji Nasrabadi, Tehran: Asatir.

Further Primary Texts

Agulets'i, Zak'aria (2003), *The Journal of Zak'aria of Agulis (Zak'aria Agulets'u Ōragrut'iwnê)*, trans. George A. Bournutian, Costa Mesa: Mazda.

Ahsan, Zafar Khan (1976), *Zafar Khan Ahsan: Tahqiq dar Ahval va Asar va Afkar va Ash'ar*, ed. Muhammad Aslam Khan, Delhi: Indo-Persian Society.

Alighieri, Dante (1999), *La Divina Commedia: Purgatorio*, ed. Natalino Sapegno, third printing, Florence: La Nuova Italia Editrice.

'Amili, Baha' al-Din (1361s), *Divan-i Kamil-i Shaykh-i Baha'i*, ed. Sa'id Nafisi, Tehran: Nashr-i Chakama.

al-'Amili, Baha' al-Din (1961), *al-Kashkul*, ed. Tahir Ahmad al-Zawi, Cairo: Dar Ihya' al-Kutub al-'Arabiyya.

al-Andalusi, Ibn Hani' (1995), *Diwan Muhammad ibn Hani' al-Andalusi*, ed. Muhammad Yalaoui, second printing, Beirut: Dar al-Gharb al-Islami.

Ansari, Muhammad Rafi' (2002), *Mirza Rafi'a's Dastur al-Muluk: A Manual of Later Safavid Administration. Annotated English Translation, Comments on the Offices and Services, and Facsimile of the Unique Persian Manuscript*, Kuala Lumpur: International Institute of Islamic Thought and Civilization (ISTAC).

'Antara (2018), *Dīwān 'Antarah Ibn Shaddād: A Literary-Historical Study*, ed. James E. Montgomery, New York: New York University Press.

Arzu, Siraj al-Din 'Ali Khan (2006), *Tazkira-yi Majma' al-Nafa'is*, eds. Mihr-i Nur Muhammad Khan and Zib al-Nisa' 'Ali Khan, Islamabad: Markaz-i Tahqiqat-i Farsi-yi Iran va Pakistan.

Asir, Jalal al-Din (2005), *Divan-i Ghazaliyyat-i Asir-i Shahristani*, ed. Ghulam Husayn Sharifi Vildani, Tehran: Miras-i Maktub.

Aslah (1967), *Tazkira-yi Shu'ara'-yi Kashmir, Ta'lif-i Aslah Mutakhallis bi-Mirza ibn Hajji Muhammad Aslam Khan Salim Kashmiri*, ed. Sayyid Husam al-Din Rashidi, Lahore: Iqbal Akadimi-yi Pakistan.

Awhadi (2010), *'Arafat al-'Ashiqin u 'Arasat al-'Arifin*, eds. Amina Fakhr Ahmad and Zabih Allah Sahibkari, Tehran: Miras-i Maktub.

al-'Aydarus, 'Abd al-Qadir (2001), *al-Nur al-Safir 'an Akhbar al-Qarn al-'Ashir*, eds. Ahmad Halu, Mahmud Arna'ut and Akram Bushi, Beirut: Dar Sadir.

'Azimabadi, Husayn Quli Khan (2012), *Tazkira-yi Nishtar-i 'Ishq*, ed. Sayyid Kamal Hajj Sayyid Javadi, Tehran: Miras-i Maktub.

al-Bahrani, Yusuf (1386s), *Kashkul al-Bahrani, aw Anis al-Khatir wa-Jalis al-Safir*, Najaf: Al-Maktaba al-Haydariyya.

al-Bahrani, Yusuf (2008), *Lu'lu'at al-Bahrayn fi Ijazat wa-Tarajim Ahl al-Hadith*, Manama: Maktab Fakhrawi.

Bidil (1962–), *Kulliyat*, Kabul: da Pohani Wizarat.

Bilgrami, Azad (1918), *Ma'asir al-Kiram, Mawsum ba Sarv-i Azad*, Hyderabad: Kitabkhana-yi Asafiyya.

Bilgrami, Azad (2015), *Subhat al-Marjan fi Athar Hindustan*, ed. Muhammad Sa'id Turayhi, Beirut: Dar al-Rafidin li-l-Tiba'a wa-l-Nashr wa-l-Tawzi'.

Damad, Mir Muhammad Baqir (1385s), *Divan-i Ishraq*, ed. Samira Pustin-Duz, Tehran: Miras-i Maktub.

Danish, Mir Razi (2000), *Divan-i Mir Razi Danish Mashhadi*, ed. Muhammad Qahraman, Mashhad: Tasu'a.

Darabi, Shah Muhammad b. Muhammad (2012), *Tazkira-yi Lata'if al-Khayal*, ed. Yusuf Bayg Babapur, Qum: Majma'-i Zakha'ir-i Islami.

Fani (1342s), *Divan-i Muhsin Fani*, ed. G. L. Tiku, Tehran: Anjuman-i Iran u Hind.

Ibn al-Farid, Sharaf al-Din 'Umar (1985), *Diwan*, ed. Ibrahim al-Samarra'i, Amman: Dar al-Fikr li-l-Nashr wa-l-Tawzi'.

Fasa'i, Hajj Mirza Husayn Hasani (1378s), *Farsnama-yi Nasiri*, ed. Mansur Rastagar Fasa'i, Tehran: Amir Kabir.

Fasihi Haravi, Fasih al-Din (1383s), *Divan*, ed. Ibrahim Qaysari, Tehran: Amir Kabir.

Fayzi (1362s), *Divan-i Fayzi (954–1004): Buzurgtarin Sha'ir-i Sada-yi Dahum-i Sarzamin-i Hind*, ed. E. D. Arshad, Tehran: Furughi.

Ghani Kashmiri, Muhammad Tahir (1362s), *Divan*, ed. Ahmad Karami, Tehran: Ma.

Gupamavi, Muhammad Qudrat Allah (1336s), *Tazkira-yi Nata'ij al-Afkar*, Bombay: Chapkhana-yi Sultani.

Hafiz (1362s), *Divan*, ed. Parviz Natil Khanlari, Tehran: Intisharat-i Khvarazmi.

Haravi, Nazim (1374s), *Divan*, ed. Muhammad Qahraman, Mashhad: Astan-i Quds.

Hasan, Muhammad Sadiq (1878), *Subh-i Gulshan*, Bhopal: Matba'a-yi Shah Jahani.

al-Haymi al-Kawkabani, Ahmad b. Muhammad (1986), *Hada'iq al-Nammam fi l-Kalam 'ala Ma Yata'allaqu bi-l-Hammam*, San'a': al-Dar al-Yamaniyya li-l-Nashr wa-l-Tawzi'.

al-Haymi al-Kawkabani, Ahmad b. Muhammad (2002), *Tib al-Samar fi Awqat al-Sahar*, ed. 'Abd Allah Muhammad al-Hibshi, Abu Dhabi: al-Majma' al-Thaqafi.

al-Haymi al-Kawkabani, al-Hasan b. Ahmad (2020), *Ladhdhat al-Wasan*, ed. Nuha 'Abd al-Raziq al-Hifnawi, Beirut: Dar al-Kutub al-'Ilmiyya.

al-Hurr al-'Amili, Muhammad b. al-Hasan (1966), *Amal al-Amil fi Dhikr 'Ulama' Jabal 'Amil*, ed. Sayyid Ahmad Husayni, Baghdad: Maktabat al-Andalus.

al-Husayni, Diya' al-Din Yusuf b. Yahya (2009), *Nasmat al-Sahar bi-Dhikr Man Tashaya'a wa-Sha'ar*, ed. Kamil Salman al-Juburi, Beirut: Dar al-Mu'arrikh al-'Arabi.

al-Ibshihi (1986), *al-Mustatraf fi kull Fann Mustazraf*, ed. Muhammad Mufid Qumayha, second printing, Beirut: Dar al-Kutub al-'Ilmiyya.

'Inayat Khan, Muhammad Tahir (1990), *The Shah Jahan Nama of 'Inayat Khan: An Abridged History of the Mughal Emperor Shah Jahan, Compiled by His Royal Librarian: The Nineteenth-Century Manuscript Translation of A.R. Fuller (British Library, add. 30,777)*, eds. W. E. Begley and Z. A. Desai, Delhi: Oxford University Press.

al-Isfahani, Abu l-Faraj (2010), *Kitab al-Aghani*, ed. Muhammad Abu l-Fadl Ibrahim, Cairo: al-Hay'a al-'Ama al-Misriyya li-l-Kitab.

Ibn Isfandiyar, Muhammad b. al-Hasan (1941), *Tarikh-i Tabaristan*, ed. ʿAbbas Iqbal, Tehran: Khavar.

Jaruni, Salimi (1382s), *Masnavi-yi Shirin u Farhad*, ed. Najaf Jawkar, Tehran: Miras-i Maktub.

Kalim Kashani, Abu Talib (1957), *Divan-i Abu Talib Kalim*, ed. Partaw Bayzaʾi, Tehran: Khayyam.

Kashani, Nur al-Din Muhammad Sharif (2003), *Kulliyat-i Najib Kashani*, eds. Asghar Dadbih and Mahdi Sadri, Tehran: Miras-i Maktub.

Kashani, Nur al-Din Muhammad Sharif (2015), *Tarikh-i Kishikkhana-yi Humayun*, eds. Asghar Dadbih and Mahdi Sadri, Tehran: Miras-i Maktub.

Kashani, Taqi al-Din (2005–), *Khulasat al-Ashʿar va Zubdat al-Afkar*, eds. Muhammad Husayn Kahnamuyi, Adib Barumand, ʿAli Ashraf Sadiqi, Nafisa Irani, Ruqayya Bayram Haqiqi, Sayyid ʿAli Mir Afzali, Muhammad Dabir Siyaqi and Mahdi Malik Muhammadi, Tehran: Miras-i Maktub.

Kashifi, Husayn Vaʿiz (1336s), *Anvar-i Suhayli*, Tehran: Amir Kabir.

al-Khafaji (1967), *Rayhanat al-Alibbaʾ wa-Zahrat al-Hayat al-Dunya*, ed. ʿAbd al-Fattah Muhammad Hulw, Cairo: Matbaʿat ʿIsa al-Babi al-Halabi.

Lahiji, Hazin (1375s), *Tazkirat al-Muʿasirin*, ed. Maʿsuma Salik, Tehran: Saya.

Lahuri, Munir (1977), *Karnama-yi Abu l-Barakat Munir Lahuri va Siraj-i Munir-i Siraj al-Din ʿAli Khan Arzu*, ed. Sayyid Muhammad Akram Ikram, Islamabad: Markaz-i Tahqiqat-i Farsi-yi Iran va Pakistan.

al-Makki, ʿAbbas (1967), *Nuzhat al-Jalis wa-Munyat al-Adib al-Anis*, Najaf: al-Matbaʿa al-Haydariyya.

Maliha-yi Samarqandi, Muhammad Badiʿ (1390s), *Muzakkir al-Ashab*, ed. Muhammad Taqva, Tehran: Kitabkhana, Muzih u Markaz-i Asnad-i Majlis-i Shura-yi Islami.

Manjak Basha, Manjak b. Muhammad (2009), *Diwan*, ed. Muhammad Basil ʿUyun al-Sud, Damascus: al-Hayʾa al-ʿAmma al-Suriyya li-l-Kitab.

Ibn Manzur, Muhammad b. Mukarram (1999), *Lisan al-ʿArab*, third printing, Beirut: Dar Ihyaʾ al-Turath al-ʿArabi.

al-Maqqari (1983), *Rawdat al-Asʿ al-ʿAtirat al-Anfas fi Dhikr man Laqaytuhu min Aʿlam al-Hadratayn Marrakush wa-Fas*, Rabat: al-Matbaʿa al-Makiyya.

al-Maqqari (1988), *Nafh al-Tib min Ghusn al-Andalus al-Ratib*, ed. Ihsan ʿAbbas, Beirut: Dar Sadir.

Ibn Maʿsum, ʿAli Sadr al-Din (1363s), *Takhmis Qasidat al-Burda*, ed. ʿAli Muhaddith, Tehran: Qism Dirasat al-Islamiyya - Muʾassisat al-Baʿtha.

Ibn Maʿsum, ʿAli Sadr al-Din (1962), *al-Darajat al-Rafiʿa fi Tabaqat al-Shiʿa*, ed. Muhammad Sadiq Bahr al-ʿUlum, Najaf: al-Maktaba al-Haydariyya.

Ibn Maʿsum, ʿAli Sadr al-Din (1968), *Anwar al-Rabiʿ fi Anwaʿ al-Badiʿ*, ed. Shakir Hadi Shukr, Najaf: Matbaʿat al-Nuʿman.

Ibn Maʿsum, ʿAli Sadr al-Din (1988a), *Diwan Ibn Maʿsum*, ed. Shakir Hadi Shukr, Beirut: ʿAlam al-Kutub.

Ibn Maʿsum, ʿAli Sadr al-Din (1988b), *Salwat al-gharib wa-uswat al-arib*, ed. Shakir Hadi Shukr, Beirut: ʿAlam al-Kutub.

Ibn Maʿsum, ʿAli Sadr al-Din (1994–95), *Riyad al-Salikin fi Sharh Sahifat al-Sajidin*, Qum: Muʾassisat al-Nashr al-Islami.

al-Miʿmar (2018), *Der Diwān Des Ibrāhīm al-Miʿmār (gest. 749/1348-49): Edition Und Kommentar*, eds. Thomas Bauer, Anke Osigus and Hakan Özkan. Baden-Baden: Ergon Verlag.

al-Muhibbi (1967–69), *Nafhat al-Rayhana wa-Rashhat Tilaʾ al-Hana*, ed. ʿAbd al-Fattah Muhammad Hulw, Cairo: Dar Ihyaʾ al-Kutub al-ʿArabiyya.

Mutribi Samarqandi, Sultan Muhammad (2003), *Tazkirat al-Shu'ara'*, ed. 'Ali Rafi'i 'Ala' Marvdashti, second printing, Tehran: Miras-i Maktub.

Ibn al-Nahhas, Fath Allah (2018), *Diwan Ibn al-Nahhas al-Halabi*, ed. Mahmud Muhammad al-Amudi, Beirut: Dar al-Kutub al-'Ilmiyya.

Nasrabadi (1378s), *Tazkira-yi Nasrabadi*, ed. Ahmad Mudaqqiq Yazdi, Yazd: Intisharat-i Danishgah-i Yazd.

Naziri (1379s), *Divan-i Naziri Nishapuri*, ed. Muhammad Riza Tahiri, Tehran: Nigah.

Nizami Ganjavi, Jamal al-Din Abu Muhammad Ilyas (1366s), *Khusraw u Shirin*, ed. Bihruz Sarvatiyan, Tehran: Tus.

Ibn Nubata, Muhammad b. Muhammad (1905), *Diwan*, ed. Muhammad al-Qalqili, Cairo: n.p.

Abu Nuwas, al-Hasan ibn Hani' al-Hakami (1958–2006), *Diwan Abi Nuwas al-Hasan ibn Hani' al-Hakami*, ed. Ewald Wagner, Wiesbaden: Franz Steiner.

Qazvini, 'Abd al-Nabi Fakhr al-Din (1340s), *Tazkira-yi Maykhana: Ba Tashihi va Tanqih va Takmil-i Tarajim*, ed. Ahmad Gulchin Ma'ani, Tehran: Muhammad Husayn Iqbal.

Qudsi (1996), *Divan-i Muhammad Jan Qudsi Mashhadi*, ed. Muhammad Qahraman, Mashhad: Ferdowsi University Press.

Ram, Kewal (1985), *Tazkiratul-Umara of Kewal Ram: Biographical Account of the Mughal Nobility 1556–1707 AD*, trans. S. M. Azizuddin Husain, New Delhi: Munshiram Manoharlal.

Razi, Amin Ahmad (1999), *Tazkira-yi Haft Iqlim*, ed. Sayyid Muhammad Riza Tahiri, Tehran: Surush.

Razi Artimani, Muhammad (1986), *Divan-i Artimani*, ed. Muhammad 'Ali Imami, second printing, Tehran: Khayyam.

Rudaki (2012), *Divan-i Abu 'Abd Allah Ja'far ibn Muhammad ibn Hakim ibn 'Abd al-Rahman ibn Adam Rudaki Samarqandi*, eds. Qadir Rustam and Hasan Anusha, Tehran: Mu'assisa-yi Farhangi-yi Iku.

Ruh al-Amin, Muhammad (2012a), *Bahramnama (Asman-i Hashtum): Chaharumin Masnavi az Khamsa-yi Mir Jumla*, ed. Gulala Hunari, Bonn: Friedrich-Wilhelms-Universität.

Ruh al-Amin, Muhammad (2012b), *Layli u Majnun: Sivummin Masnavi az Khamsa-yi Mir Jumla*, ed. Stephann Popp, Bonn: Friedrich-Wilhelms-Universität.

al-Sadr, Hasan (1986), *Takmilat Amal al-Amil*, ed. al-Sayyid Ahmad al-Husayni, Qum: Maktabat Ayat Allah al-Mar'ashi.

Sa'ib (1991), *Divan-i Sa'ib Tabrizi*, ed. Muhammad Qahraman, Tehran: 'Ilmi va Farhangi.

Sa'idi Shirazi, Nizam al-Din Ahmad (1961), *Hadiqat al-Salatin*, ed. Sayyid 'Ali Aaghar Bilgrami, Hyderabad: Islamic Publications Society.

Salik Qazvini, Muhammad Ibrahim (1994), *Divan*, ed. Ahmad Karami, Tehran: Ma.

Salim (1349s), *Divan-i Kamil-i Muhammad Quli Salim Tihrani*, ed. Riza Rahim, Tehran: Ibn Sina.

Samit, Sadiq (1393s), *Divan-i Samit Isfahani Darguzashta-yi 1100, bar Asas-i Si Nuskha-yi Khatti*, ed. Ahmad Bihishti Shirazi, Tehran: Intisharat-i Rawzana.

Saydi (1364s), *Divan-i Saydi Tihrani*, ed. Muhammad Qahraman, Tehran: Ittila'at.

Shapur (1382s), *Divan-i Shapur Tihrani*, ed. Yahya Karadgar, Tehran: Kitabkhana, Muzih va Markaz-i Asnad-i Majlis-i Shura-yi Islami.

al-Shawkani (198–), *al-Badr al-Tali' bi-Mahasin Man ba'd al-Qarn al-Sabi'*, Beirut: Dar al-Ma'rifa.

Shawkat (1382s), *Divan-i Shawkat Bukhari*, ed. Sirus Shamisa, Tehran: Firdaws.

Shifa'i (1983), *Divan-i Sharaf al-Din Hasan Hakim Shifa'i Isfahani*, ed. Lutf 'Ali Banan, Tabriz: Idara-yi Kull-i Irshad-i Islami-yi Azarbayjan-i Sharqi.

Shirwani, Ahmad b. Muhammad (2017), *Hadiqat al-Afrah li-Izahat al-Atrah*, Jiddah: Dar al-Minhaj li-l-Nashr wa-l-Tawzi'.

Shushtari, Nur Allah b. 'Abd Allah (1973), *Firdaws: Dar Tarikh-i Shushtar va Barkhi az Mashahir-i An*, Tehran: Bahman.

Talib Amuli, Sayyid Muhammad (1967), *Kulliyat-i Ash'ar-i Malik al-Shu'ara' Talib Amuli*, ed. Tahiri Shihab, Tehran: Kitabkhana-yi Sana'i.

al-Taluwi, Darwish Muhammad (1983), *Sanihat Duma al-Qasr fi Mutarahat Bani al-'Asr*, Beirut: 'Alam al-Kutub.

Ta'sir (1373s), *Divan-i Muhsin Ta'sir Tabrizi*, ed. Amin Pasha Ijlali, Tehran: Markaz-i Nashr-i Danishgahi-yi Tihran.

al-Tha'alibi (2000), *Yatimat al-Dahr fi Mahasin Ahl al-'Asr*, ed. M. M. Qumayha, Beirut: Dar al-Kutub al-'Ilmiyya.

'Urfi (1378s), *Kulliyat-i 'Urfi Shirazi*, ed. Muhammad Vali al-Haqq Ansari, Tehran: Danishgah-i Tihran.

Vahid, Muhammad Tahir (1338s), *Sharh Shawahid Majma' al-Bayan*, Tehran: Dar al-Kutub al-Islamiyya.

Va'iz Qazvini (1359s), *Divan-i Mulla Muhammad Rafi' Va'iz Qazvini*, ed. Sayyid Hasan Sadat Nasiri, Tehran: 'Ali Akbar 'Ilmi.

Valih Daghistani, 'Ali Quli Khan (2006), *Tazkira-yi Riyaz al-Shu'ara'*, ed. Muhsin Naji Nasrabadi, Tehran: Intisharat-i Asatir.

Wazir, 'Abd Allah b. 'Ali (1985), *Ta'rikh al-Yaman Khilala al-Qarn al-Hadi 'Ashar al-Hijri/al-Sabi' al-'Ashar al-Miladi, 1045-1090 H/1635–1680 M, al-Musamma Ta'rikh Tabaq al-Halwa wa-Sihaf al-Mann wa-l-Salwa*, ed. Muhammad 'Abd al-Rahim Jazim, Beirut: Dar al-Masira.

al-Zabidi, Murtada (2001), *Taj al-'Arus min Jawahir al-Qamus*, al-Kuwayt: al-Turath al-'Arabi.

Zuhuri (2011), *Divan-i Zuhuri Turshizi (Ghazaliyyat)*, Tehran: Kitabkhana, Muzih va Markaz-i Asnad-i Majlis-i Shura-yi Islami.

Secondary Scholarship

'Abd al-Muqtadir (1912), *Catalogue of the Arabic and Persian Manuscripts in the Oriental Public Library at Bankipore, Volume 3: Persian Poetry, 17th, 18th and 19th Centuries*, Calcutta: Bengal Secretariat Book Depot.

Abdesselem, A. Ben (2012), 'al-Ṭurṭūshī', in *Encyclopaedia of Islam*, Second Edition, eds. P. Bearman, T. Bianquis, C. E. Bosworth, E. van Donzel and W. P. Heinrichs, http://dx.doi.org/10.1163/1573-3912_islam_SIM_7650.

Abisaab, Rula Jurdi (2015), *Converting Persia: Religion and Power in Safavid Iran*, London: I.B. Tauris.

Ahlwardt, Wilhelm (1887–1899), *Verzeichniss der arabischen Handschriften der königlichen Bibliothek zu Berlin*, Berlin: A.W. Schade's Buchdr. (L. Schade).

Ahmad, Aziz (1976), 'Safawid Poets and India', *IRAN* 14: 117–32.

Ahmad, Zubayd (1978), *al-Adab al-'Arabiyya fi Shibh al-Qara al-Hindiyya*, Baghdad: Wizarat al-Thaqafa.

Ahmed, Shahab (2015), *What Is Islam? The Importance of Being Islamic*, Princeton: Princeton University Press.

Akopyan, Alexander V. (2021), 'Coinage and the Monetary System', in *The Safavid World*, ed. Rudolph P. Matthee, 285–309, London: Routledge.

Ala Amjadi, Maryam (2021), '"The World is an Oyster and Iran, the Pearl": Representations of Iran in Safavid Persian Travel Literature', in *Safavid Persia in the Age of Empires. The Idea of Iran, Volume 10*, ed. Charles Melville, 291–308, London: I.B. Tauris .

Alam, Muzaffar (2003), 'The Culture and Politics of Persian in Precolonial Hindustan', in *Literary Cultures in History: Reconstructions from South Asia*, ed. Sheldon Pollock, 131–98, Berkeley: University of California Press .

Alam, Muzaffar (2015), 'Mughal Philology and Rūmī's *Mathnavī*', in *World Philology*, eds. Sheldon Pollock, Benjamin A. Elman and Ku-ming Kevin Chang, 178–200, Cambridge, MA: Harvard University Press .

Alam, Muzaffar and Sanjay Subrahmanyam (1996), 'Discovering the Familiar: Notes on the Travel Account of Anand Ram Mukhlis, 1745', *South Asia Research* 16, no. 2: 131–54.

Alam, Muzaffar and Sanjay Subrahmanyam (2004), 'The Making of a Munshi', *Comparative Studies of South Asia, Africa and the Middle East* 24, no. 4: 61–72.

Alam, Muzaffar and Sanjay Subrahmanyam (2007), *Indo-Persian Travels in the Age of Discoveries*, Cambridge: Cambridge University Press.

Alam, Muzaffar and Sanjay Subrahmanyam (2017), 'A View from Mecca: Notes on Gujarat, the Red Sea, and the Ottomans, 1517-39/923-946 H', *Modern Asian Studies* 51, no. 2: 268–318.

Alavi, Seema (2015), *Muslim Cosmopolitanism in the Age of Empire*, Cambridge, MA: Harvard University Press.

ʿAli, M. Athar (1966), *The Mughal Nobility Under Aurangzeb*, London: Asia Publishing House.

ʿAli, M. Athar (2012), 'Dāgh u Taṣḥīḥa', in *Encyclopaedia of Islam* , Second Edition, eds. P. Bearman, Th. Bianquis, C. E. Bosworth, E. van Donzel and W. P. Heinrichs, http://dx .doi.org/10.1163/1573-3912_islam_SIM_8451.

Ali, Samer (2010), *Arabic Literary Salons in the Islamic Middle Ages: Poetry, Public Performance, and the Presentation of the Past*, Notre Dame: University of Notre Dame Press.

ʿAlim, Tayka Shuʿayb (1993), *Arabic, Arwi, and Persian in Sarandib and Tamil Nadu: A Study of the Contributions of Sri Lanka and Tamil Nadu to Arabic, Arwi, Persian, and Urdu Languages, Literature, and Education*, Madras: Imamul ʿArus Trust for the Ministry of State for Muslim Religious and Cultural Affairs, Colombo, Sri Lanka.

al-Amin, Muhsin (1979), *A ʿyan al-Shiʿa*, ed. Hasan al-Amin, second printing, Beirut: Dar al-Tabligh al-Islami.

Anderson, Benedict (2016), *Imagined Communities: Reflections on the Origin and Spread of Nationalism*, revised edn, London: Verso.

Andrews, Walter G. and Mehmet Kalpaklı (2005), *The Age of Beloveds: Love and the Beloved in Early-modern Ottoman and European Culture and Society*, Durham: Duke University Press.

Apter, Emily (2013), *Against World Literature: On the Politics of Untranslatability*, London: Verso.

Arberry, Arthur John (1952), *A Second Supplementary Hand-List of the Muhammadan Manuscripts in the University & Colleges of Cambridge*, Cambridge: Cambridge University Press.

Asafiyya (1914), *Fihrist-i Kutub-i ʿArabi va Farsi va Urdu Makhzuna-yi Kutubkhana-yi Asafiyya-yi Sarkar-i ʿAli*, Hyderabad: Akhtar-i Dakkan.

Asif, Manan Ahmed (2020), *The Loss of Hindustan: The Invention of India*, Cambridge, MA: Harvard University Press.

Avery, P., B. G. Fragner and J. B. Simmons (2020), '' Abbāsī', in *Encyclopaedia Iranica Online*, http://dx.doi.org/10.1163/2330-4804_EIRO_COM_4262.

Baalbaki, Ramzi (2001), 'The Historic Relevance of Poetry in the Arab Grammatical Tradition', in *Poetry and History: The Value of Poetry in Reconstructing Arab History*, eds. Ramzi Baalbaki, Salih Sa'id Agha and Tarif Khalidi, 95–120, Beirut: American University of Beirut Press .

Babayan, Kathryn (2021), *The City as Anthology: Eroticism and Urbanity in Early Modern Isfahan*, Stanford: Stanford University Press.

Bahl, Christopher D. (2018a), *Histories of Circulation: Sharing Arabic Manuscripts across the Western Indian Ocean, 1400–1700*, PhD thesis, SOAS, University of London.

Bahl, Christopher D. (2018b), 'Creating a Cultural Repertoire Based on Texts: Arabic Manuscripts and the Historical Practices of a Sufi in 17th-Century Bijapur', *Journal of Islamic Manuscripts* 9, no. 2–3: 132–53.

Bahl, Christopher D. (2020a), 'Arabic Philology at the Seventeenth-Century Mughal Court: Sa'd Allāh Khān's and Shāh Jahān's Enactments of the *Sharḥ al-Raḍī*', *Philological Encounters* 5, no. 2: 190–222.

Bahl, Christopher D. (2020b), 'Transoceanic Arabic Historiography: Sharing the Past of the Sixteenth-Century Western Indian Ocean', *Journal of Global History* 15, no. 2: 203–23.

Balachandran, Jyoti Gulati (2015), 'Exploring the Elite World in the *Siyar al-Awliyā* ', Urban Elites, Their Lineages and Social Networks', *The Indian Economic and Social History Review* 52, no. 3: 241–70.

Balachandran, Jyoti Gulati (2020a), *Narrative Pasts: The Making of a Muslim Community in Gujarat, c. 1400–1650*, New Delhi: Oxford University Press.

Balachandran, Jyoti Gulati (2020b), 'Counterpoint: Reassessing Ulughkhānī's Arabic History of Gujarat', *Asiatische Studien* 74, no. 1: 137–61.

Bandy, Hunter (2021), 'Neẓām al-Din Aḥmad Gilāni', in *Encyclopaedia Iranica Online*, http://dx.doi.org/10.1163/2330-4804_EIRO_COM_336452.

Barthes, Roland (1977), *Image-Music-Text*, trans. S. Heath, London: Fontana.

Basha, 'Umar Musa (1989), *Ta'rikh al-Adab al-'Arabi: al-'Asr al-'Uthmani*, Beirut: Dar al-Fikr al-Mu'asir.

Bauden, Frédéric and Elise Franssen, eds (2020), *In the Author's Hand: Holograph and Authorial Manuscripts in the Arabic Written Tradition*, Leiden: Brill.

Bauer, Thomas (1992), *Altarabische Dichtkunst: Eine Untersuchung ihrer Struktur und Entwicklung am Beispiel der Onagerepisode*, Wiesbaden: Harrassowitz.

Bauer, Thomas (1998), *Liebe und Liebesdichtung in der arabischen Welt des 9. und 10. Jahrhunderts: Eine literatur- und mentalitätsgeschichte des arabischen Ġazal*, Wiesbaden: Harrassowitz.

Bauer, Thomas (2006), 'Die Badī'iyya des Nāṣīf al-Yāzġī und das Problem der spätosmanischen arabischen Literatur', in *Reflections on Reflections: Near Eastern Writers Reading Literature*, eds. Angelika Neuwirth and Andreas Christian Islebe, 49–118, Wiesbaden: Reichert.

Bauer, Thomas (2007), 'The Dawādār's Hunting Party: A Mamluk *Muzdawija Ṭardiyya*, probably by Shihāb al-Dīn Ibn Faḍl Allāh', in *O Ye Gentlemen: Arabic Studies on Science and Literary Culture, in Honour of Remke Kruk*, eds. Arnoud Vrolijk and Jan P. Hogendijk, 291–312, Leiden: Brill.

Bauer, Thomas (2008), 'Ibn Nubātah al-Miṣrī (686–768/1287–1366): Life and Works. Part II: The *Dīwān* of Ibn Nubātah', *Mamluk Studies Review* 12, no. 2: 25–69.

Bauer, Thomas (2014), 'How to Create a Network: Zaynaddīn al-Ātārī and his *Muqarriẓūn*', in *Everything is on the Move: The Mamluk Empire as a Node in (Trans-) Regional Networks*, ed. Stephan Conermann, 205–21, Bonn: University of Bonn Press.

Bausani, Alessandro (1958), ' Contributo a una definizione dello "stile indiano" della poesia persiana', *AIUON*, N.S. vii: 163–91.

Bausani, Alessandro and Antonino Pagliaro (1960), *Storia della letteratura persiana*, Milan: Nuova Accademia Editrice.

Bazmee Ansari, A. S. (2012), 'Burhanpur', in *Encyclopaedia of Islam*, Second Edition, eds. P. Bearman, Th. Bianquis, E. van Donzel and W. P. Heinrichs, http://dx.doi.org/10.1163 /1573-3912_islam_SIM_1547.

Beelaert, Anna Livia (2020), 'Kāqānī Šervānī', *Encyclopædia Iranica Online*, . http://dx.doi .org/10.1163/2330-4804_EIRO_COM_10740.

Beers, Theodore S. (2020), 'The Treatment of Coeval Persian Poetry in Arabic Anthologies of the Eleventh/Seventeenth Century', *al-ʿUṣūr al-Wusṭā* 28: 233–53.

Behl, Aditya (2012), *Love's Subtle Magic: An Indian Islamic Literary Tradition, 1379–1545*, ed. Wendy Doniger, New York and Oxford: Oxford University Press.

Bendrey, V. S. and B. D. Verma (1934), *Satarāvya śatakāntīla Govaḷakoṇḍyācī Kutbaśāhī: kīvā, The History of a Late Revolution in the Kingdom of Golcondah: Chapters VI and VII from 'Hadiqat-u'l alam' by Mir Alam, and Some Account of Akana and Madana, Chief Ministers of Golcondah, with an Historical Sketch of the Qutbshahi of Golcondah by the Editor*, Pune: Bharatiya Itihasa Sasodhaka Mandala.

Bernard, Anna (2018), 'Nation, Transnationalism, and Internationalism', in *The Cambridge Companion to World Literature*, eds. Ben Etherington and Jarad Zimbler, 37–51, Cambridge: Cambridge University Press.

Bertel's, Evgenii Eduardovich (1956), ' K voprosu ob "Indiyskom stile" v persidskoy poezii', in *Charisteria Orientalia*, ed. F. Tauer, Věra Kubičková and Ivan Hrbek, 56–9, Prague: Czech Academy of Sciences .

Bhabha, Homi (1994), *The Location of Culture*, London and New York: Routledge.

Bhatti, Anil (2015), 'Language, Heterogeneities, Homogeneities and Similarities: Some Reflections', in *'Impure Languages': Linguistic and Literary Hybridity in Contemporary Cultures*, eds. Rama Kant Agnihotri, Claudia Benthien and Tatiana Oranskaia, 3–25, New Delhi: Orient Blackswan.

Binbaş, İlker Evrim (2018), *Intellectual Networks in Timurid Iran: Sharaf al-Dīn ʿAlī Yazdī and the Islamicate Republic of Letters*, Cambridge: Cambridge University Press.

de Blois, François (2004), *Persian Literature: A Bio-Bibliographical Survey. Volume V: Poetry of the Pre-Mongol Period*, London and New York: RoutledgeCurzon.

Bloom, Harold (1997), *The Anxiety of Influence: A Theory of Poetry*, 2nd edn, Oxford: Oxford University Press.

Boehmer, Elleke (2005), *Colonial and Postcolonial Literature: Migrant Metaphors*, 2nd edn, New York: Oxford University Press.

Bollack, Jean (2016), *The Art of Reading: From Homer to Paul Celan*, trans. C. Porter and S. Tarrow with B. King, eds. C. Koenig, L. Muellner, G. Nagy and S. Pollock, Washington, DC: Center for Hellenic Studies.

Bosworth, Clifford Edmund (1989), *Bahāʾ al-Dīn al-ʿĀmilī and His Literary Anthologies*, Manchester: University of Manchester.

Bray, Julia (2000), 'Al-Muʿtaṣim's 'Bridge of Toil' and Abū Tammām's Amorium *qaṣīda*', in *Studies in Islamic and Middle Eastern Texts and Traditions in Memory of Norman*

Calder, eds. G. R. Hawting, J. A. Mojaddedi and A. Samely, 31–73, Oxford: Oxford University Press .

Bray, Julia (2010), 'Literary Approaches to Medieval and Early Modern Arabic Biography', *Journal of the Royal Asiatic Society* n.s. 20, no. 3: 237–53.

Brockelmann, Carl (1902), *Geschichte der arabischen Litteratur*, Berlin: E. Felber.

Brockelmann, Carl (1938), *Geschichte der arabischen Litteratur* [Supplement], Leiden: E.J. Brill.

Brookshaw, Dominic P. (2003), 'Palaces, Pavilions and Pleasure-Gardens: The Context and Setting of the Medieval Majlis', *Middle Eastern Literatures* 6, no. 2: 199–223.

Brookshaw, Dominic P. (2014), 'Lascivious Vines, Corrupted Virgins, and Crimes of Honor: Variations on the Wine-Production Myth as Related in Early Persian Poetry', *Iranian Studies* 47, no. 1: 87–129.

Brookshaw, Dominic P. (2019), *Hafiz and His Contemporaries: Poetry, Performance and Patronage in Fourteenth-Century Iran*, London: I.B. Tauris.

Brouwer, C. G. (2006), *Al-Mukhā: The Transoceanic Trade of a Yemeni Staple Town as Mapped by Merchants of the VOC, 1614–1640: Coffee, Spices and Textiles*, Amsterdam: D'Fluyte Rarob.

Browne, Edward (1924), *A History of Persian Literature in Modern Times (A.D. 1500 –1924)*, Cambridge: Cambridge University Press.

Burke, Peter (2004), *Languages and Communities in Early Modern Europe*, Cambridge: Cambridge University Press.

Burton-Page, J. et al. (2012), 'Mughals', in *Encyclopaedia of Islam, Second Edition*, eds. P. Bearman, Th. Bianquis, C. E. Bosworth, E. van Donzel and W. P. Heinrichs, http://dx .doi.org/10.1163/1573-3912_islam_COM_0778.

Busch, Allison (2011), *Poetry of Kings: The Classical Hindi Literature of Mughal India*, Oxford: Oxford University Press.

Cai, Zong-qi (2001), *Configurations of Comparative Poetics: Three Perspectives on Western and Chinese Literary Criticism*, Honolulu: University of Hawai'i Press.

Calmard, Jean (2000), 'Safavid Persia in Indo-Persian Sources and in Timurid-Mughal Perception', in *The Making of Indo-Persian Culture: Indian and French Studies*, eds. Muzaffar Alam, Françoise 'Nalini' Delvoye and Marc Gaborieau, 351–91, New Delhi: Manohar Publishers & Distributors.

Casanova, Pascale (2004), *The World Republic of Letters*, trans. M. B. Debevoise, Cambridge, MA and London: Harvard University Press.

Caton, Steven C. (1990), *Peaks of Yemen I Summon: Poetry as Cultural Practice in a North Yemeni Tribe*, Berkeley: University of California Press.

Chen, Jing (2017), 'Reinventing the Pre-Tang Tradition: Compiling and Publishing Pre-Tang Poetry Anthologies in Sixteenth-Century China', *Journal of Chinese Literature and Culture* 4, no. 1: 91–128.

Clayton, Jay and Eric Rothstein, eds. (1991), *Influence and Intertextuality in Literary History*, Madison: University of Wisconsin Press.

Collot, Michel (2014), *Pour une géographie littéraire*, Paris: Corti.

Culler, Jonathan (2015), *Theory of the Lyric*, Cambridge, MA: Harvard University Press.

Cureton, William and Charles Rieu (1846–71), *Catalogus codicum manuscriptorum orientalium qui in Museo Britannico asservantur: Pars secunda, codices arabicos amplectens*, London: The British Museum.

Dabashi, Hamid (2012), *The World of Persian Literary Humanism*, Cambridge, MA and London: Harvard University Press.

Dadvar, Abolghasem (1999), *Iranians in Mughal Politics and Society 1606–1658*, New Delhi: Gyan Publication House.

Dafari, J. A. (1966), 'Ḥumainī Poetry in South Arabia', PhD thesis, London: University of London.

Dale, Stephen Frederic (1994), *Indian Merchants and Eurasian Trade, 1600–1750*, Cambridge: Cambridge University Press.

Dale, Stephen Frederic (2003), 'A Safavid Poet in the Heart of Darkness: The Indian Poems of Ashraf Mazandarani', *Iranian Studies* 36, no. 2: 197–212.

Damrosch, David (2018), *How to Read World Literature*, 2nd edn, Hoboken: Wiley Blackwell.

Danishpazhuh, Muhammad Taqi (1358s), 'Sih Jung-i Khutut-i Danishmandan-i Irani az Sada-yi Yazdahum, *Tahqiqat-i Kitabdari va Ittila'-Risani-yi Danishgahi* 7: 66–111.

Dayal, Subah (2017), 'Vernacular Conquest? A Persian Patron and His Image in the Seventeenth-Century Deccan', *Comparative Studies of South Asia, Africa and the Middle East* 37, no. 3: 549–69.

Dayal, Subah (2020), 'On Heroes and History: Responding to the *Shahnama* in the Deccan', in *Iran and the Deccan: Persianate Art, Culture and Talent in Circulation, 1400–1700*, ed. Keelan Overton, 421–46, Bloomington: Indiana University Press .

Dehoux, Amaury (2019), 'Liquid Spaces: (Re)thinking Transnationalism in an Era of Globalization', in *Literary Transnationalism(s)*, eds. Dagmar Vandenbosch and Theo D'haen, 28–36, Leiden: Brill.

Denecke, Wiebke (2014), *Classical World Literatures: Sino-Japanese and Greco-Roman Comparisons*, Oxford: Oxford University Press.

Devare, T. N. (2018), *A Short History of Persian Literature: At the Bahmani, the 'Adilshahi and the Qutbshahi Courts – Deccan*, London: Routledge.

Dhavan, Purnima (2020), 'Networks and Fault Lines in Eighteenth-Century Deccani Literary Communities: Lachmī Narāyān 'Shafīq' and His Circle', *The Indian Economic and Social History Review* 57, no. 4: 461–80.

Digby, Simon (1993), 'Some Asian Wanderers in Seventeenth-Century India: An Examination of Sources in Persian', *Studies in History* n.s. 9, no. 2: 247–64.

Dimock, Wai Chee (2008), *Through Other Continents: American Literature Across Deep Time*, Princeton: Princeton University Press.

Dirayati, Mustafa (2010), *Fihristvara-yi Dastnivisht-ha-yi Iran* (DENA), Tehran: Majlis-i Shura.

Duda, Herbert W. (1933), *Ferhād und Schīrīn: die literarische Geschichte eines persischen Sagenstoffes*, Prague: Orientální ústav.

Dufour, Julien (2011), *Huit siècles de poésie chantée au Yémen: Langue, mètres, et formes du ḥumaynī*, Strasbourg: Presses Universitaires de Strasbourg.

Eaton, Richard (1978), *Sufis of Bijapur: Social Roles of Sufis in Medieval India*, Princeton: Princeton University Press.

Eaton, Richard (2005), *A Social History of the Deccan, 1300–1761: Eight Indian Lives*, Cambridge: Cambridge University Press.

Eaton, Richard (2020), *India in the Persianate Age: 1000–1765*, London: Penguin.

Emami, Farshid (2016), 'Coffeehouses, Urban Spaces, and the Formation of a Public Sphere in Safavid Isfahan', *Muqarnas: An Annual on the Visual Culture of the Islamic World* 33: 177–220.

Emami, Farshid (2018), 'Discursive Images and Urban Itineraries: Literary Form and City Experience in Early Modern Iran', *Journal for Early Modern Cultural Studies* 18, no. 3: 154–86.

Ernst, Carl W. (2013), 'Indian Lovers in Arabic and Persian Guise: Azad Bilgrami's Depiction of Nayikas', *Journal of Hindu Studies* 6, no. 1: 37–51.

Ethé, Hermann and Edward Edwards (1903–), *Catalogue of Persian Manuscripts in the Library of the India Office*, Oxford: Printed for the India Office by H. Hart, Printer to the University.

Fakhreddine, Huda (2015), *Metapoesis in the Arabic Tradition: From Modernists to Muḥdathūn*, Leiden: Brill.

Faruqi, Shamsur Rahman (2004), 'A Stranger in the City: The Poetics of *Sabk-e Hindi*', *Annual of Urdu Studies* 19: 1–93.

Feener, R. Michael and Joshua Gedacht (2018), 'Hijra, Ḥajj and Muslim Mobilities: Considering Coercion and Asymmetrical Power Dynamics in Histories of Islamic Cosmopolitanism', in *Challenging Cosmopolitanism: Coercion, Mobility and Displacement in Islamic Asia*, eds. R. Michael Feener and Joshua Gedacht, 1–29, Edinburgh: Edinburgh University Press.

Fischel, Roy (2020a), '*Ghariban* in the Deccan: Migration, Elite Mobility, and the Making and Unmaking of an Early Modern State', in *Iran and the Deccan: Persianate Art, Culture and Talent in Circulation, 1400–1700*, ed. Keelan Overton, 127–44, Bloomington: Indiana University Press.

Fischel, Roy (2020b), *Local States in an Imperial World: Identity, Society and Politics in the Early Modern Deccan*, Edinburgh: Edinburgh University Press.

Flatt, Emma (2019), *The Courts of the Deccan Sultanates: Living Well in the Persian Cosmopolis*, Cambridge: Cambridge University Press.

Floor, Willem (2000), *The Economy of Safavid Persia*, Wiesbaden: Reichert.

Floor, Willem (2021), 'Trade in Safavid Iran', in *The Safavid World*, ed. Rudolph P. Matthee, 264–84, London: Routledge.

Floor, Willem and Hasan Javadi (2013), 'The Role of Azerbaijani Turkish in Safavid Iran', *Iranian Studies* 46, no. 4: 569–81.

Floor, Willem M. (2006), *The Persian Gulf: A Political and Economic History of Five Port Cities, 1500–1730*, Washington, D.C.: Mage.

Fotoohi, Mahmoud (2020), 'Tadkera-ye Naṣrābādī', *Encyclopaedia Iranica Online*, http://dx.doi.org/10.1163/2330-4804_EIRO_COM_10916.

Frolov, D. V. (1999), *Classical Arabic Verse: History and Theory of ʿArūḍ*, Leiden: Brill.

Futuhi, Mahmud (2000), *Naqd-i Adabi dar Sabk-i Hindi*, second printing, Tehran: Sukhan.

Gabbay, Alyssa (2009), 'Love Gone Wrong, Then Right Again: Male-Female Dynamics in the Bahrām Gūr-Slave Girl Story', *Iranian Studies* 42, no. 5: 677–92.

Gabbay, Alyssa (2010), *Islamic Tolerance: Amir Khusraw and Pluralism*, Abingdon: Routledge.

van Gelder, Geert Jan (2003), 'The Classical Arabic Canon of Polite (and Impolite) Literature', in *Cultural Repertoires: Structure, Function, and Dynamics*, eds. Gillis J. Dorleijn and Herman L. J. Vanstiphout, 45–57, Leuven: Peeters.

van Gelder, Geert Jan (2008), '"A Good Cause": Fantastic Etiology (*Ḥusn al-Taʿlīl*) in Arabic Poetics', in *Takhyīl: The Imaginary in Classical Arabic Poetics*, eds. Geert Jan van Gelder and Marlé Hammond, 221–37, Cambridge: Gibb Memorial Trust.

van Gelder, Geert Jan (2009), 'Shihāb al-Dīn al-Khafājī', in *Essays in Arabic Literary Biography, 1350–1850*, eds. Joseph E. Lowry and Devin J. Stewart, 251–62, Wiesbaden: Harrassowitz.

van Gelder, Geert Jan (2012), *Sound and Sense in Classical Arabic Poetry*, Wiesbaden: Harrassowitz.

van Gelder, Geert Jan (2013), *Classical Arabic Literature: A Library of Arabic Literature Anthology*, New York: New York University Press.

Gilliot, Claude (1996), 'Les citations probantes (šawāhid) en langue', *Arabica* 43: 297–356.

Gordon, Stewart (1988), 'Burhanpur: Entrepot and Hinterland, 1650–1750', *Indian Economic and Social History Review* 25, no. 4: 425–42.

Green, Nile (2011), *Bombay Islam: The Religious Economy of the West Indian Ocean, 1840–1915*, Cambridge and New York: Cambridge University Press.

Green, Nile (2012), *Making Space: Sufis and Settlers in Early Modern India*, New Delhi: Oxford University Press.

Green, Nile (2014), 'Rethinking the "Middle East" after the Oceanic Turn', *Comparative Studies of South Asia, Africa and the Middle East* 34, no. 3: 556–64.

Green, Nile (2018), 'The Waves of Heterotopia: Toward a Vernacular Intellectual History of the Indian Ocean', *The American Historical Review* 123, no. 3: 846–74.

Green, Nile, ed. (2019), *The Persianate World: Frontiers of a Eurasian Lingua Franca*, Oakland: University of California Press.

Greene, Thomas M. (1982), *The Light in Troy: Imitation and Discovery in Renaissance Poetry*, New Haven and London: Yale University Press.

Gruendler, Beatrice (2003), *Medieval Arabic Praise Poetry: Ibn al-Rumi and the Patron's Redemption*, Abingdon: Routledge.

Gruendler, Beatrice (2008a), 'Qasida: Its Reconstruction in Performance', in *Classical Arabic Humanities in their Own Terms*, ed. Beatrice Gruendler, 325–89, Leiden: Brill.

Gruendler, Beatrice (2008b), 'Originality in Imitation: Two *Muʿāraḍas* By Ibn Darrāj al-Qasṭallī', *al-Qanṭara* 29, no. 2: 437–365.

Guillory, John (1993), *Cultural Capital: The Problem of Literary Canon Formation*, Chicago: University of Chicago Press.

Gulchin Maʿani, Ahmad (1364s), *Farhang-i Ashʿar-i Saʾib*, Muʾassasa-yi Mutalaʿat va Tahqiqat-i Farhangi.

Gulchin Maʿani, Ahmad (1369s), *Karvan-i Hind*, first printing, Mashhad: Astan-i Quds.

Gulchin Maʿani, Ahmad (1969–1971), *Tarikh-i Tazkira-ha-yi Farsi*, Tehran: Danishgah-i Tehran.

Hafiziyan, Abu l-Fazl (1383s), *Nuskha-Pazhuhi: Daftar-i Yikum*, Qum: Muʾassisa-yi Ittilaʿ-Risani-yi Marjaʿ.

Hamori, Andras (1981), 'Reading al-Mutanabbī's Ode on the Siege of al-Ḥadath', in *Studia Arabica et Islamica: Festschrift for Iḥsān ʿAbbās on His Sixtieth Birthday*, ed. Wadad al-Qadi, 195–208, Beirut: American University of Beirut.

Hamori, Andras (1992), *The Composition of al-Mutanabbī's Panegyrics to Sayf al-Dawla*, Leiden: Brill.

Haneda, Masashi (1989), 'The Evolution of the Safavid Royal Guard', *Iranian Studies* 22, no. 2–3: 57–85.

Haneda, Masashi (1997), 'Emigration of Iranian Elites to India during the 16–18th Centuries', *Cahiers d'Asie centrale* 3, no. 4: 129–43.

Harb, Lara (2017), 'Beyond the Known Limits: Ibn Dāwūd al-Iṣfahānī's Chapter on "Intermedial" Poetry', in *Arabic Humanities, Islamic Thought: A Festschrift for Everett K. Rowson*, eds. Shawkat Toorawa and Joseph Lowry, 122–49, Leiden: Brill.

Harb, Lara (2020), *Arabic Poetics: Aesthetic Experience in Classical Arabic Literature*, Cambridge: Cambridge University Press.

al-Hasani, ʿAbd al-Hayy b. Fakhr al-Din (1978), *Nuzhat al-Khawatir wa-Bahjat al-Masamiʿ wa-l-Nawazir*, second printing, Hyderabad: Daʾirat al-Maʿarif.

Haykel, Bernard (2003), *Revival and Reform in Islam: The Legacy of Muhammad al-Shawkānī*, Cambridge: Cambridge University Press.

Heinz, Wilhelm (1973), *Der indische Stil in der persischen Literatur*, Wiesbaden: Franz Steiner.

al-Hibshi, ʿAbd Allah (1986), *al-Adab al-Yamani: ʿAsr Khuruj al-Atrak al-Awwal min al-Yaman*, Beirut: al-Dar al-Yamani li-l-Nashr wa-l-Tawziʿ.

Hidayet Hosain, M. (2012), 'Nūr Allāh', in *Encyclopaedia of Islam*, Second Edition, eds. P. Bearman, T. Bianquis, C. E. Bosworth, E. van Donzel and W. P. Heinrichs, http://dx.doi.org/10.1163/1573-3912_islam_SIM_5981.

Hijazi, Hasan ʿAbd al-Karim (1999), *Bahaʾ al-Din al-ʿAmili Shaʾiran 953–1030/1547-1621*, Beirut: s.n.

Hirschler, Konrad (2020), *A Monument to Medieval Syrian Book Culture: The Library of Ibn ʿAbd al-Hādī*, Edinburgh: Edinburgh University Press.

Ho, Engseng (2006), *The Graves of Tarim: Genealogy and Mobility across the Indian Ocean*, Berkeley: University of California Press.

Ho, Engseng (2007), 'The Two Arms of Cambay: Diasporic Texts of Ecumenical Islam in the Indian Ocean', *Journal of the Economic and Social History of the Orient* 50, no. 2/3: 347–61.

d'Hubert, Thibaut (2018), *In the Shade of the Golden Palace: Alaol and Middle Bengali Poetics in Arakan*, New York: Oxford University Press.

d'Hulster, Kristof (2021), *Browsing Through the Sultan's Bookshelves: Towards a Reconstruction of the Library of the Mamluk Sultan Qāniṣawh al-Ghawrī (r. 906-922/1501-1516)*, Bonn: V&R unipress.

Hussein, Ali A. (2011), 'One *Qaṣīda* with Several Chaste Love Affairs in Light of al-*Mufaḍḍaliyyāt* and al-*Aṣmaʿiyyāt*', *Middle Eastern Studies* 14, no. 1: 1–19.

Hutcheon, Linda (1985), *A Theory of Parody: The Teachings of Twentieth-Century Art Forms*, London: Methuen.

Ingenito, Domenico (2021), *Beholding Beauty: Saʿdi of Shiraz and the Aesthetics of Desire in Medieval Persian Poetry*, Leiden: Brill.

Islam, Riazul (1970), *Indo-Persian Relations*, Tehran: Iranian Culture Foundation.

Jacobi, Renate (1971), *Studien zur Poetik der altarabischen Qaṣide*, Universität des Saarlandes, Saarbrücken.

Jauss, Hans Robert (1982), *Toward an Aesthetic of Reception*, Minneapolis: University of Minnesota Press.

Jayyusi, Salma Khadra (2006), 'Arabic Poetry in the Post-Classical Age', in *Arabic Literature in the Post-Classical Age*, eds. Roger Allen and D. S. Richards, 25–59, Cambridge: Cambridge University Press.

al-Kaʿbi, Karim ʿAlkam (2008), *Ibn Maʿsum al-Madani Adiban wa-Naqidan*, Najaf: Dar al-Diyaʾ li-l-Tibaʿa wa-l-Tasmim.

Kaempfer, Engelbert (2018), *Exotic Attractions in Persia, 1684–1688: Travels and Observations*, trans. Willem Floor and Colette Ouahes, Washington, D.C.: Mage.

Kaicker, Abhishek (2018), 'The Promises and Perils of Courtly Poetry: The Case of Mir ʿAbd al-Jalil Bilgrami (1660–1725) in the Late Mughal Empire', *Journal of the Economic and Social History of the Orient* 61, no. 3: 327–60.

Kamens, Edward (1997), *Utamakura, Allusion, and Intertextuality in Traditional Japanese Poetry*, New Haven: Yale University Press.

Keegan, Matthew L. (2020), 'Levity Makes the Law: Islamic Legal Riddles', *Islamic Law and Society* 27, no. 3: 214–39.

Kennedy, Philip (1997), *The Wine Song in Classical Arabic Poetry: Abū Nuwās and the Literary Tradition*, Oxford: Clarendon Press.

Keshavmurthy, Prashant (2013), 'The Local Universality of Poetic Pleasure: Sirājuddin ʿAli Khān Ārzu and the Speaking Subject', *The Indian Economic and Social History Review* 50, no. 1: 27–45.

Keshavmurthy, Prashant (2017), 'Khushgū's Dream of Ḥāfiẓ: Authorship, Temporality and Canonicity in Late Mughal India', in *Urdu and Indo-Persian Thought, Poetics, and Belles Lettres*, ed. Alireza Korangy, 1–22, Leiden: Brill.

Key, Alexander (2018), *Language between God and the Poets: Maʿnā in the Eleventh Century*, Berkeley: University of California Press.

Khalidi, Omar (2004), 'Sayyids of Hadhramaut in Early Modern India', *Asian Journal of Social Science* 32, no. 3: 329–52.

Khan, Yusuf Husain (1953), *Selected Waqaʾiʿ of the Deccan (1660–1671 A.D.)*, Hyderabad: Central Records Office.

Kia, Mana (2020), *Persianate Selves: Memories of Place and Origin Before Nationalism*, Stanford: Stanford University Press.

Kilpatrick, Hilary (2003), *Making the Great Book of Songs: Compilation and the Author's Craft in Abū l-Faraj al-Iṣbahānī's Kitāb al-aghānī*, London: RoutledgeCurzon.

Kilpatrick, Hilary (2008), 'Visions of Distant Cities: Travellers as Poets in the Early Modern Period', *Quaderni di Studi Arabi* n.s. 3: 67–82.

Kilpatrick, Hilary (2011a), 'The Inter-communal Poetry of Niqūlāwus aṣ-Ṣāʾiġ (1692–1756)', *Rocznik Orientalistyczny* 64, no. 1: 60–79.

Kilpatrick, Hilary (2011b), 'Poetry on Political Events in the Mamluk and Early Ottoman Periods', in *A Festschrift for Nadia Anghelescu*, eds. Andrei A. Avram, Anca Focşeneanu and George Grigore, 297–304, Bucharest: Editura Universităţii din Bucureşti.

Kim, Sooyong (2022), 'The Poet Nefʿī, Fresh Persian Verse, and Ottoman Freshness', *Iranian Studies* 55, no. 2: 551–73.

Kinra, Rajeev (2015), *Writing Self, Writing Empire: Chandar Bhan Brahman and the Cultural World of the Indo-Persian State Secrtary*, Oakland: University of California Press.

Kinra, Rajeev (2007), 'Fresh Words for a Fresh World: *Tāza-Gūʾī* and the Poetics of Newness in Early Modern Persian Poetry', *Sikh Formations* 3, no. 2: 125–49.

Kohlberg, Ethan (2012), 'al-Shahīd al-Thānī', in *Encyclopaedia of Islam*, Second Edition, eds. P. Bearman, Th. Bianquis, C. E. Bosworth, E. van Donzel and W. P. Heinrichs, http://dx.doi.org/10.1163/1573-3912_islam_SIM_6763.

Krenkow, Fritz (1910), 'The Diwan of Abu Dahbal al-Gumahi', *Journal of the Royal Asiatic Society* 42, no. 4: 1017–75.

Kristeva, Julia (1969), *Sēmiōtikē: Récherches pour une sémanalyse*, Paris: Éditions du Seuil.

Kugle, Scott A. (2021), *Hajj to the Heart: Sufi Journeys Across the Indian Ocean*, Chapel Hill: University of North Carolina Press.

Latham, J. Derek (1979), 'Towards a Better Understanding of al-Mutanabbī's Poem on the Battle of al-Ḥadath', *Journal of Arabic Literature* 10: 1–22.

Leese, Simon (2021), 'Arabic Utterances in a Multilingual World: Shāh Walī-Allāh and Qurʾanic Translatability in North India', *Translation Studies* 14, no. 2: 242–61.

Lefèvre, Corinne (2012), 'Āṣaf Khān', in *Encyclopaedia of Islam, THREE*, eds. K. Fleet, G. Krämer, D. Matringe, J. Nawas and E. Rowson, http://dx.doi.org/10.1163/1573-3912_ei3_COM_26356.

Lefèvre, Corinne (2014), 'The Court of ʿAbd-ur-Raḥīm Khān-i Khānān as a Bridge between Iranian and Indian Cultural Traditions', in *Culture and Circulation: Literature in Motion in Early Modern India*, eds. Thomas de Bruijn and Allison Busch, 75–106, Leiden and Boston: Brill.

Lefèvre, Corinne (2017), 'Messianism, Rationalism, and Inter-Asian Connections: The *Majalis-i Jahangiri* (1608– 11) and the Socio-Intellectual History of the Mughal ʿulama', *Indian Economic and Social History Review* 54, no. 3: 317–38.

Levi, Scott C. (2002), *The Indian Diaspora in Central Asia and Its Trade, 1550 – 1900*, Leiden: Brill.

Lewis, Franklin (1994), 'The Rise and Fall of a Persian Refrain: The Radif "Atash u Ab"', in *Reorientations/Arabic and Persian Poetry*, ed. Suzanne Pinckney Stetkevych, 199–226, Bloomington: Indiana University Press.

Lewis, Franklin (2010), 'The Semiotic Horizons of Dawn in the Poetry of Ḥāfiẓ', in *Hafiz and the Religion of Love in Classical Persian Poetry*, ed. Leonard Lewisohn, 251–77, London: I.B. Tauris.

Lewis, Franklin (2018), 'To Round and Rondeau: Jāmī and Fānī's Reception of the Persian Lyrical Tradition', in *Jāmī in Regional Contexts: The Reception of ʿAbd al-Raḥmān Jāmī's Works in the Islamicate World, circa 9th/15th – 14th/20th Century*, eds. Thibaut d'Hubert and Alexandre Papas, 463–567, Leiden: Brill.

Löfgren, O. (2012), 'al-Ahdal', in *Encyclopaedia of Islam*, Second Edition, eds. P. Bearman, T. Bianquis, C. E. Bosworth, E. van Donzel, and W. P. Heinrichs, http://dx.doi.org/10.1163/1573-3912_islam_SIM_0372.

Losensky, Paul (1994), '"The Allusive Field of Drunkenness": Three Safavid-Moghul Responses to a Lyric by Baba Fighani', in *Reorientations/Arabic and Persian Poetry*, ed. Suzanne Pinckney Stetkevych, 227–62, Bloomington: Indiana University Press.

Losensky, Paul E. (1998), *Welcoming Fighānī: Imitation and Poetic Individuality in the Safavid-Mughal Ghazal*, Costa Mesa: Mazda.

Losensky, Paul E. (2004), '"The Equal of Heaven's Vault": The Design, Ceremony, and Poetry of the Hasanabad Bridge', in *Writers and Rulers: Perspectives on Their Relationship from Abbasid to Safavid Times*, eds. Beatrice Gruendler and Louise Marlow, 195–215, Wiesbaden: Reichert Verlag.

Losensky, Paul E. (2014), 'Vintages of the *Sāqī-nāma*: Fermenting and Blending the Cupbearer's Song in the Sixteenth Century', *Iranian Studies* 47, no. 1: 131–57.

Losensky, Paul E. (2015), '"Square Like a Bubble": Architecture, Power and Poetics in Two Inscriptions by Kalim Kāshānī', *Journal of Persianate Studies* 8: 42–70.

Losensky, Paul E. (2018), '"Utterly Fluent, but Seldom Fresh": Jāmī's Reception among the Safavids', in *Jāmī in Regional Contexts: The Reception of ʿAbd al-Raḥmān Jāmī's Works in the Islamicate World, circa 9th/15th – 14th/20th Century*, eds. Thibaut d'Hubert and Alexandre Papas, 568–601, Leiden: Brill.

Losensky, Paul E. (2020a), 'Ṣāʾeb Tabrizi', in *Encyclopaedia Iranica Online*, http://dx.doi.org/10.1163/2330-4804_EIRO_COM_1089.

Losensky, Paul E. (2020b), 'Vahši Bāfqi', in *Encyclopaedia Iranica Online*, http://dx.doi.org/10.1163/2330-4804_EIRO_COM_1251.

Losensky, Paul E. (2020c), 'ʿOrfi Širazi', in *Encyclopaedia Iranica Online*, http://dx.doi.org/10.1163/2330-4804_EIRO_COM_1084.

Losensky, Paul E. (2021a), 'Not All the Poets Went to India: Literary Culture in Iran Under Safavid Rule', in *The Safavid World*, ed. Rudolph P. Matthee, 447–68, London: Routledge.

Losensky, Paul E. (2021b), 'Biographical Writing: *Tadhkere* and *Manâqeb*', in A *History of Persian Literature. Volume Five: Persian Prose*, ed. Bo Utas, 339–78, London: I.B. Tauris.

Lowry, Joseph (2009), 'Ibn Maʿṣūm', in *Essays in Arabic Literary Biography, 1350–1850*, eds. Joseph E. Lowry and Devin J. Stewart, 174–84, Wiesbaden: Harrassowitz.

Maeda, Hirotake (2003), 'On the Ethno-Social Background of Four *Gholām* Families from Georgia in Safavid Iran', *Studia Iranica* 32: 243–78.

al-Maqhafi, Ibrahim Ahmad (2002), *Muʿjam al-Buldan wa-l-Qabaʾil al-Yamaniyya*, Sanʿaʾ: Dar al-Kalima.

Matthee, Rudi (2020), 'Safavid Dynasty', in *Encyclopaedia Iranica Online*, http://dx.doi.org/10.1163/2330-4804_EIRO_COM_509.

Matthee, Rudolph (2006), 'Between Arabs, Turks and Iranians: The Town of Basra, 1600–1700', *BSOAS* 69, no. 1: 53–78.

Matthee, Rudolph (2009), 'Boom and Bust: The Port of Basra in the Sixteenth and Seventeenth Centuries', in *The Persian Gulf in History*, ed. Lawrence G. Potter, 105–27, New York: Palgrave.

Matthee, Rudolph (2012), *Persia in Crisis: Safavid Decline and the Fall of Isfahan*, London: I.B. Tauris.

Matthee, Rudolph, Willem Floor and Patrick Clawson (2013), *The Monetary History of Iran: From the Safavids to the Qajars*, London: I.B. Tauris.

McChesney, Robert D. (1990), 'The Biography of Poets: *Muzakkir al-Ashab* as a Source for the History of Seventeenth-Century Central Asia', in *Intellectual Studies on Islam: Studies in Honor of Martin B. Dickson*, eds. Michel M. Mazzaoui and Vera B. Moreen, 57–84, Salt Lake City: University of Utah Press.

McLaughlin, Martin L. (1995), *Literary Imitation in the Italian Renaissance: The Theory and Practice of Literary Imitation in Italy from Dante to Bembo*, Oxford: Clarendon Press.

Meisami, Julie S. (1987), *Medieval Persian Court Poetry*, Princeton: Princeton University Press.

Meisami, Julie S. (2003), *Structure and Meaning in Medieval Arabic and Persian Poetry: Orient Pearls*, London: RoutledgeCurzon.

Meredith-Owens, Glyn M. (1968), *Handlist of Persian manuscripts: [acquired by the British Museum] 1805–1966*, London: British Museum.

Mikkelson, Jane (2017), 'Of Parrots and Crows: Bīdil and Ḥazīn in Their Own Words', *Comparative Studies of South Asia, Africa and the Middle East* 37, no. 3: 510–30.

Miner, Earl (1990), *Comparative Poetics: An Intercultural Essay on Theories of Literature*, Princeton: Princeton University Press.

Montgomery, James E. (2015), *The Vagaries of the Qasidah: The Tradition and Practice of Early Arabic Poetry*, paperback reprint, Haverton, Pennsylvania: Gibb Memorial Trust.

Moosvi, Shireen (2015), *The Economy of the Mughal Empire, c. 1595: A Statistical Study*, revised and enlarged edition, New Delhi: Oxford University Press.

Mortel, Richard T. (1997), 'Madrasas in Mecca during the Medieval Period: A descriptive Study Based on Literary Sources', *Bulletin of the School of Oriental and African Studies* 60, no. 2: 236–52.

Mufti, Aamir (2016), *Forget English! Orientalisms and World Literatures*, Cambridge, MA: Harvard University Press.

Muhanna, Elias (2018), *The World in a Book: al-Nuwayri and the Islamic Encyclopedic Tradition*, Princeton: Princeton University Press.

Muʿid Khan, M. A. (1963), *The Arabian Poets of Golconda*, Mumbai: University of Bombay Press.

Muinuddin, Nadwi (1939), *Catalogue of the Arabic and Persian Manuscripts in the Oriental Public Library at Bankipore. Vol. 23: Poetry and Elegant Prose*, Patna: Government of Bihar.

Musawi, Muhsin Jasim (2015), *The Medieval Islamic Republic of Letters: Arabic Knowledge Construction*, Notre Dame: University of Notre Dame Press.

Naim-Siddiqi, M. Asif (2020), 'Elāhī Hamadānī, Sayyed Mīr ʿEmād al-Dīn Mahmūd', in *Encyclopaedia Iranica Online*, http://dx.doi.org/10.1163/2330-4804_EIRO_COM_8961.

Nancy, Jean-Luc (1991), *The Inoperative Community*, Minneapolis and Oxford: University of Minnesota Press.

Neuwirth, Angelika (2014), *Scripture, Poetry, and the Making of a Community: Reading the Qur'an as a Literary Text*, Oxford: Oxford University Press.

Newman, Andrew J. (1993), 'The Myth of the Clerical Migration to Safawid Iran: Arab Shiite Opposition to ʿAlī al-Karakī and Safawid Shiism', *Welt des Islams* 33, no. 1: 66–112.

Newman, Andrew J. (1999), 'The Role of the *Sādāt* in Safavid Iran: Confrontation or Accommodation?', *Oriente Moderno* 18 (79), no. 2: 577–96.

Newman, Andrew J. (2009), *Safavid Iran: Rebirth of a Persian Empire*, London: I.B. Tauris.

Newman, Andrew J. (2010), 'Clerical Perceptions of Sufi Practices in Late Seventeenth-Century Persia, II: Al– Hurr al-ʿAmili (d. 1693) and the Debate on the Permissibility of *Ghina*', in *Studies in Living Islamic History: Essays in Honour of Professor Carole Hillenbrand*, ed. Suleiman Yasir, 192–208, Edinburgh: Edinburgh University Press.

Nuʿmani, Shibli (1948–55), *Shiʿr al-ʿAjam, ya Tarikh-i Shuʿara' va Adabiyat-i Iran*, trans. Muhammad Taqi Daʿi Gilani, Tehran: Shirkat-i Sihami-yi Chap-i Rangin.

Orfali, Bilal (2011), 'Ghazal and Grammar: al-Bāʿūnī's *taḍmīn Alfiyyat Ibn Mālik fī l-ghazal*', in *In the Shadow of Arabic: The Centrality of Language to Arabic Culture. Studies presented to Ramzi Baalbaki on the Occasion of His Sixtieth Birthday*, ed. B. Orfali, 445–93, Leiden: Brill.

Orfali, Bilal (2016), *The Anthologist's Art: Abū Manṣūr al-Thaʿālibī and His Yatīmat al-dahr*, Leiden: Brill.

Orsatti, Paola (2020), 'Kosrow o Širin', in *Encyclopaedia Iranica Online*, http://dx.doi.org/10.1163/2330-4804_EIRO_COM_222.

Orsini, Francesca (2015), 'The Multilingual Local in World Literature', *Comparative Literature* 67, no. 4: 345–74.

Overton, Keelan and Jake Benson (2019), 'Deccani Seals and Scribal Notations: Sources for the Study of Indo-Persian Book Arts and Collecting (c. 1400–1680)', in *The Empires of the Near East and India: Source Studies of the Safavid, Ottoman, and Mughal Literate Communities*, ed. Hani Khafipour, 544–96, New York: Columbia University Press.

Özkan, Hakan (2020a), *Geschichte des östlichen zaǧal: dialektale arabische Strophendichtung aus dem Osten der arabischen Welt - von den Anfängen bis zum Ende der Mamlukenzeit*, Baden-Baden: Ergon Verlag.

Özkan, Hakan (2020b), 'Donkey or Thief, Defamation or Well-Deserved Criticism? An-Nawāǧī and His Treatise *al-Ḥuǧǧah fī sariqāt Ibn Ḥiǧǧah*', in *The Racecourse of Literature: An-Nawāǧī and His Contemporaries*, eds. Alev Marsawa and Hakan Özkan, 83–95, Würzburg: Ergon Verlag.

Papoutsakis, Nefeli (2017), *Classical Arabic Begging Poetry and Šakwā, 8th–12th Centuries*, Wiesbaden: Harrassowitz.

Papoutsakis, Nefeli (2022), 'Ibrāhīm Ibn al-Mullā's (d. 1032/1623) Ḥalbat al-mufāḍala wa-ḥilyat al-munāḍala: The Correspondence of an Ottoman-Era Aleppine Littérateur', in *Doing Justice to a Wronged Literature: Essays on Arabic Literature and Rhetoric of the 12th–18th Centuries in Honour of Thomas Bauer*, 366–86, Leiden: Brill.

Ragıp Paşa. (1868), *Defter-i Kütüphane-i Ragıp Paşa*, Constantinople.

Peacock, A. C. S (2020), 'Remembering Turkish Origins in the Sixteenth- and Seventeenth-Century Deccan: The Qaraqoyunlu Past in the Persian Chronicles of the Qutbshahi Dynasty', in *Turkish History and Culture in India: Identity, Art and Transregional Connections*, eds. A. C. S. Peacock and Richard Piran McClary, 152–200, Leiden: Brill.

Peacock, A. C. S. (2021), ''Iyani, A Shirazi Poet and Historian in the Bahmani Deccan', *IRAN* 59, no. 2: 169–86.

Pellò, Stefano (2012), *Ṭūṭiyān-i Hind: Specchi identitari e proiezioni cosmopolite indo-persiane (1680 – 1856)*, Florence: Società Editrice Fiorentina.

Pellò, Stefano (2015), 'Persian Poets on the Streets: The Lore of Indo-Persian Poetic Circles in Late Mughal India', in *Tellings and Texts: Music, Literature and Performance in North India*, eds. Francesca Orsini and Katherine Butler Schofield, 303–25, Cambridge: Open Book Publishers.

Péri, Benedek (2020), 'Yavuz Sultan Selīm (1512–1520) and His Imitation Strategies: A Case Study of Four Ḥāfiẓ *ghazals*', *Acta orientalia Academiae Scientiarum Hungaricae* 73, no. 2: 233–51.

Pertsch, Wilhelm (1888), *Verzeichniss der persischen Handschriften der Königlichen Bibliothek zu Berlin*, Berlin: A. Asher.

Pfeifer, Helen (2022), *Empire of Salons: Conquest and Community in Early Modern Ottoman Lands*, Princeton: Princeton University Press.

Piamenta, Moshe (1990), *A Dictionary of Post-Classical Yemeni Arabic*, Leiden: Brill.

de Planhol, Xavier et al. (2020), 'Kandahar', in *Encyclopaedia Iranica* Online, http://dx.doi.org/10.1163/2330-4804_EIRO_COM_10716.

Pollock, Sheldon (1998), 'The Cosmopolitan Vernacular', *The Journal of Asian Studies* 57, no. 1: 6–37.

Pollock, Sheldon (2006), *The Language of the Gods in the World of Men: Sanskrit, Culture, and Power in Premodern India*, Berkeley: University of California Press.

Popp, Stephan (2018), ''Ināyat Khān', in *Encyclopaedia of Islam, THREE*, eds. Kate Fleet, Gudrun Krämer, Denis Matringe, John Nawas and Everett Rowson. http://dx.doi.org/10.1163/1573-3912_ei3_COM_32462.

Prange, Sebastian R. (2018), *Monsoon Islam: Trade and Faith on the Medieval Malabar Coast*, Cambridge: Cambridge University Press.

Prendergast, Christopher (2004), 'The World Republic of Letters', in *Debating World Literature*, ed. Christopher Prendergast, 1–25, London: Verso.

Al Qays, Qays (1984–), *Al-Iraniyyun wa-l-Adab al-'Arabi*, Tehran: Mu'assisat al-Buhuth wa-al-Tahqiqat al-Thaqafiyya.

Quinn, Sholeh A. (2021), *Persian Historiography Across Empires: The Ottomans, Safavids and Mughals*, Cambridge: Cambridge University Press.

Qutbuddin, Tahera (2005), *Al-Mu'ayyad al-Shīrāzī and Fatimid Da'wa Poetry: A Case of Commitment in Classical Arabic Literature*, Leiden: Brill.

Qutbuddin, Tahera (2007), 'Arabic in India: A Survey and Comparison of Its Uses, Compared with Persian', *Journal of the American Oriental Society* 127, no. 3: 315–38.

Qutbuddin, Tahera (2021), 'Karbala Mourning among the Fāṭimid-Ṭayyibī Shī'a of India: Doctrinal and Performative Aspects of Sayyidnā Ṭāhir Sayf al-Dīn's Arabic

Marthiya, "O King of Martyrs" (*Yā Sayyida l-Shuhadā ʾī*)ʾ, *Shii Studies Review* 5, no. 1–2: 3–46.

Rahman, Munibur (2012), 'Shawkat Bukhārīʾ, in *Encyclopaedia of Islam, Second Edition*, eds. P. Bearman, Th. Bianquis, C. E. Bosworth, E. van Donzel and W. P. Heinrichs, http://dx.doi.org/10.1163/1573-3912_islam_SIM_6877.

Ranjbar, Muhammad ʿAli (1377s), 'Mutavalliyan-i Madrasa-yi Mansuriyya-yi Shiraz: Bazkhvani-yi Shish Sanadʾ, *Ganjina-yi Asnad* 31, no. 32: 48–61.

Rao, Velcheru Narayana (2003), 'Multiple Literary Cultures in Telugu: Court, Temple, and Publicʾ, in *Literary Cultures in History: Reconstructions from South Asia*, ed. Sheldon Pollock, 383–436, Berkeley: University of California Press.

Rashidi, Sayyid Husam al-Din (1967–), *Tazkira-yi Shuʿaraʾ-yi Kashmir*, Lahore: Iqbal Akadimi-yi Pakistan.

Reichmuth, Stefan (2009), *The World of Murtaḍā al-Zabīdī (1732–91): Life, Network, and Writings*, Cambridge: E.J.W. Gibb Memorial Trust.

Ricci, Ronit (2011), *Islam Translated: Literature, Conversion, and the Arabic Cosmopolis of South and Southeast Asia*, Chicago: University of Chicago Press.

Richardson, Kristina L. (2012), *Difference and Disability in the Medieval Islamic World: Blighted Bodies*, Edinburgh: Edinburgh University Press.

Rieu, Charles (1879–1883), *Catalogue of the Persian Manuscripts in the British Museum*, London: British Museum.

Rieu, Charles (1894), *Supplement to the Catalogue of the Arabic Manuscripts in the British Museum*, London: British Museum.

Rieu, Charles (1895), *Supplement to the Catalogue of the Persian Manuscripts in the British Museum*, London: British Museum.

Riffaterre, Michael (1978), *Semiotics of Poetry*, Bloomington: Indiana University Press.

Robbins, Bruce, Paulo Lemos Horta and Kwame Anthony Appiah, eds (2018), *Cosmopolitanisms*, New York: New York University Press.

Robinson, Francis (1997), 'Ottomans-Safavids-Mughals: Shared Knowledge and Connective Systemsʾ, *Journal of Islamic Studies* 8, no. 2: 151–84.

el-Rouayheb, Khaled (2005), *Before Homosexuality in the Arab-Islamic World, 1500–1800*, Chicago: University of Chicago Press.

el-Rouayheb, Khaled (2015a), *Islamic Intellectual History in the Seventeenth Century: Scholarly Currents in the Ottoman Empire and the Maghrib*, Cambridge: Cambridge University Press.

el-Rouayheb, Khaled (2015b), 'The Rise of "Deep Reading" in Early Modern Ottoman Scholarly Cultureʾ, in *World Philology*, eds. Sheldon Pollock, Benjamin A. Elman and Ku-ming Kevin Chang, 201–24, Cambridge, MA: Harvard University Press .

Rypka, Jan (1968), *History of Iranian Literature*, Dordrecht: D. Reidel.

Sachau, Ed. and Hermann Éthé (1889), *Catalogue of the Persian, Turkish, Hindûstânî, and Pushtû Manuscripts in the Bodleian Library*, Oxford: The Clarendon Press.

Safa, Zabih Allah (1364s), *Tarikh-i Adabiyat-i Iran*, Vol. 5:2, Tehran: Ibn Sina.

Salati, Marco (1999a), *Il passaggio in India di ʿAlī Khān al-Shīrāzī al-Madanī*, Padova: CLEUP.

Salati, Marco (1999b), 'Presence and Role of the Sādāt in and from Ğabal ʿĀmil (14th –18th Centuries)ʾ, *Oriente Moderno* 79, no. 2: 597–627.

Sardar, Marika (2010), 'Golkonda and Hyderabadʾ, in *Silent Splendour: Palaces of the Deccan, 14th-19th Centuries*, ed. Helen Philon, 78–87, Mumbai: Marg Publications.

Sarkar, Sir Jadunath (1930), *History of Aurangzeb*, 2nd edn, Calcutta: M.C. Sarkar.

Sarkar, Jagadish Narayan (1979), *The Life of Mir Jumla: The General of Aurangzeb*, second and revised edition, Delhi: Rajesh Publications.

Scarcia, G. (2012), 'al-Ḥurr al-ʿĀmilī', in *Encyclopaedia of Islam*, Second Edition, eds. P. Bearman, Th. Bianquis, C. E. Bosworth, E. van Donzel and W. P. Heinrichs, http://dx.doi.org/10.1163/1573-3912_islam_SIM_2969.

Schimmel, Annemarie (1973), *Islamic Literatures of India*, Wiesbaden: Harrassowitz.

Schoeler, Gregor (1974), *Arabische Naturdichtung: die Zahrīyāt, Rabīʿīyāt und Rauḍīyāt von ihren Anfängen bis aṣ-Ṣanaubarī: eine gattungs-, motiv- und stilgeschichtliche Untersuchung*, Beirut: Orient-Institut der Deutschen Morgenländischen Gesellschaft.

Schwartz, Kevin L. (2020), *Remapping Persian Literary History, 1700–1900*, Edinburgh: Edinburgh University Press.

Serjeant, Robert Bertram (1963), *The Portuguese Off the South Arabian Coast: Ḥaḍramī Chronicles*, Oxford: Clarendon Press.

Shafieioun, Saeid (2019), 'Some Critical Remarks on the Migration of Iranian Poets to India in the Safavid Era', *Journal of Persianate Studies* 11, no. 2: 155–74.

Shafir, Nir (2020), 'In an Ottoman Holy Land: The Hajj and the Road from Damascus, 1500–1800', *History of Religions* 60, no. 1: 1–36.

Shakeb, M. Z. A. (2017), *Relations of Golkonda with Iran: Diplomacy, Ideas and Commerce, 1518–1687*, Delhi: Primus Books.

Sharma, Sunil (2000), *Persian Poetry at the Indian Frontier: Masʿud Saʿd Salman of Lahore*, New Delhi: Permanent Black.

Sharma, Sunil (2002), 'Hāfiz's *Sāqīnāmeh*: The Genesis and Transformation of a Classical Poetic Genre', *Persica* 18: 75–83.

Sharma, Sunil (2004), 'The City of Beauties in Indo-Persian Poetic Landscapes', *Comparative Studies of South Asia, Africa and the Middle East* 24: 73–81.

Sharma, Sunil (2009), 'From ʿAʾesha to Nur Jahan: The Shaping of a Classical Persian Poetic Canon of Women', *Journal of Persianate Studies* 2: 148–64.

Sharma, Sunil (2011), '"If There is a Paradise on Earth, It Is Here": Urban Ethnography in Indo-Persian Poetic and Historical Texts', in *Forms of Knowledge in Early Modern Asia: Explorations in the Intellectual History of India and Tibet, 1500–1800*, ed. Sheldon Pollock, 240–56, Durham: Duke University Press.

Sharma, Sunil (2012a), 'The Nizamshahi Persianate Garden in Zuhūrī's *Sāqīnāma*', in *Garden and Landscape Practice in Pre-Colonial India*, eds. Daud Ali and Emma J. Flatt, 159–71, New Delhi: Routledge.

Sharma, Sunil (2012b), 'The Function of the Catalogue of Poets in Persian Poetry', in *Metaphor and Imagery in Persian Poetry*, ed. Ali Asghar Seyed Gohrab, 231–47, Leiden: Brill.

Sharma, Sunil (2017), *Mughal Arcadia: Persian Literature in an Indian Court*, Cambridge, MA: Harvard University Press.

Sharma, Sunil (2020), 'Forging a Canon of Dakhni Literature: Translations and Retellings from Persian', in *Iran and the Deccan: Persianate Art, Culture and Talent in Circulation, 1400–1700*, ed. Keelan Overton, 401–20, Bloomington: Indiana University Press.

Sharma, Sunil (2021), 'Local and Transregional Places in the Works of Safavid Men of Letters', in *Safavid Persia in the Age of Empires: The Idea of Iran*, ed. Charles Melville, 309–30, London: I.B.Tauris.

Sherwani, Haroon Khan (1974), *History of the Qutb Shāhī Dynasty*, New Delhi: Munshiram Manoharlal Publishers.

Siddiqi, W. H. (1997), *Fihrist-i Nuskha-ha-yi Khatti-yi Kitabkhana-yi Raza Rampur*, vol. 2, Rampur: Kitabkhana-yi Raza Rampur.

Siddiqi, Muhammad Suleman (2014), *The Junaydī Sufis of the Deccan: Discovery of a Seventeenth Century Scroll*, Delhi: Primus Books.

Siddiqua, Najma (2011), *Persian Language and Literature in Golconda*, New Delhi: Adam Publishers.

Siebertz, Roman (2013), *Preise, Löhne und Lebensstandard im safavidischen Iran: eine Untersuchung zu den Rechnungsbüchern Wollebrand Geleynssen de Jonghs (1641-1643)*, Vienna: Verlag der Österreichischen Akademie der Wissenschaften.

Sing, Manfred (2017), 'The Decline of Islam and the Rise of *Inḥiṭāṭ*: The Discrete Charm of Language Games about Decadence in the 19th and 20th Centuries', in *Inḥiṭāṭ - The Decline Paradigm: Its Influence and Persistence in the Writing of Arab Cultural History*, ed. Syrinx von Hees, 11–70, Würzburg: Egon Verlag.

Smith, G. R. et al. (2012), '' Umān', in *Encyclopaedia of Islam*, Second Edition, eds. P. Bearman, Th. Bianquis, C. E. Bosworth, E. van Donzel and W. P. Heinrichs, http://dx.doi.org/10.1163/1573-3912_islam_COM_1281.

Smoor, Pieter (1991), 'Fatimid Poets and the *Takhallus* That Bridges the Nights of Time to the Imam of Time', *Der Islam* 68: 232–62.

Spivak, Gayatri Chakravorty (2003), *Death of a Discipline*, New York: Columbia University Press.

Sprenger, Aloys (1854), *A Catalogue of the Arabic, Persian and Hindustany Manuscripts of the Libraries of the King of Oudh*, Calcutta: J. Thomas at the Baptist Mission Press.

Stetkevych, Jaroslav (1993), *The Zephyrs of Najd: The Poetics of Nostalgia in the Classical Arabic Nasib*, Chicago: University of Chicago Press.

Stetkevych, Suzanne Pinckney (1991), *Abū Tammām and the Poetics of the ʿAbbāsid Age*, Leiden: Brill.

Stetkevych, Suzanne Pinckney (2002), *The Poetics of Islamic Legitimacy: Myth, Gender, and Ceremony in the Classical Arabic Ode*, Bloomington: Indiana University Press.

Stetkevych, Suzanne Pinckney (2010), *The Mantle Odes: Arabic Praise Poems to the Prophet Muhammad*, Bloomington: Indiana University Press.

Stewart, Devin (1996a), '*Taqiyyah* as Performance: The Travels of Bahāʾ al-Dīn al-ʿĀmilī in the Ottoman Empire (991-93/1583-85)', *Princeton Papers in Near Eastern Studies* 4: 1–70.

Stewart, Devin (1996b), 'Notes on the Migration of ʿĀmilī scholars to Safavid Iran', *Journal of Near Eastern Studies* 55, no. 2: 81–103.

Stewart, Devin (1998), 'The Lost Biography of Bahāʾ al-Dīn al-ʿĀmilī and the Reign of Shah Ismāʿīl II in Safavid Historiography', *Iranian Studies* 31: 1–29.

Stewart, Devin (2006), 'An Episode in the ʿAmili Migration to Safavid Iran: Husayn b. ʿAbd al-Samad al-ʿAmili's Travel Account', *Iranian Studies* 39, no. 4: 481–508.

Stewart, Devin (2008), 'The Ottoman Execution of Zayn al-Dīn al-ʿĀmilī', *Welt des Islams* 48, no. 3: 289–347.

Stewart, Devin (2009), 'Bahāʾ al-Dīn Muḥammad al-ʿĀmilī', in *Essays in Arabic Literary Biography, 1350–1850*, eds. Joseph E. Lowry and Devin J. Stewart, 27–48, Wiesbaden: Harrassowitz.

Stewart, Devin (2010), 'Notes on Zayn al-Dīn al-ʿĀmilī's *Munyat al-murīd fī ādāb al-mufīd wa-l-mustafīd*', *Journal of Islamic Studies* 21, no. 2: 230–70.

Stewart, Devin (2017), 'Zayn al-Dīn al-ʿĀmilī's *Kashf al-Rība ʿan Aḥkām al-Ghība* and Abū Ḥāmid al-Ghazālī's *Iḥyāʾ ʿUlūm al-Dīn*', *Shii Studies Review* 1, no. 1–2: 130–50.

Storey, Charles A. (1953), *Persian Literature: A Bio-Bibliographical Survey. Volume 1, Part 2: Biography, Additions and Corrections, Indices*, London: Luzac and Co.

Subrahmanyam, Sanjay (1988), 'Persians, Pilgrims and Portuguese: The Travails of Masulipatnam Shipping in the Western Indian Ocean, 1590–1665', *Modern Asian Studies* 2, no. 3: 503–30.

Subrahmanyam, Sanjay (1992), 'Iranians Abroad: Intra-Asian Elite Migration and Early Modern State Formation', *The Journal of Asian Studies* 51, no. 2: 340–63.

Subrahmanyam, Sanjay (2011), *Mughals and Franks: Explorations in Connected History*, second printing, New Delhi: Oxford University Press.

Subrahmanyam, Sanjay (2017), 'Beyond the Usual Suspects: On Intellectual Networks in the Early Modern World', *Global Intellectual History* 2, no. 1: 30–48.

Subrahmanyam, Sanjay (2018), 'The Hidden Face of Surat: Reflections on a Cosmopolitan Indian Ocean Center, 1540–1750', *Journal of the Economic and Social History of the Orient* 61: 205–55.

Suleiman, Susan R. (1998), 'Introduction', in *Exile and Creativity: Signposts, Travelers, Outsiders, Backward Glances*, ed. Susan R. Suleiman, 1–6, Durham and London: Duke University Press.

Szuppe, Maria (2004), 'Circulation des lettrés et cercles littéraires. Entre Asie Centrale, Iran et Inde du Nord (XVe-XVIIIe siècle)', *Annales: Histoire, Sciences Sociales* 59, no. 5–6: 997–1018.

Szuppe, Maria (2011), 'A Glorious Past and an Outstanding Present: Writing a Collection of Biographies in Late Persianate Central Asia', in *The Rhetoric of Biography: Narrating Lives in Persianate Societies*, ed. Louise Marlow, 41–88, Cambridge, MA: Harvard University Press.

Tabor, Nathan Lee Marsh (2019), 'Heartless Acts: Literary Competition and Multilingual Association at a Graveside Gathering in Eighteenth-Century Delhi', *Comparative Studies of South Asia, Africa, and the Middle East* 39, no. 1: 81–95.

Tagore, Rabindranath (2001), *Selected Writings on Literature and Language*, New Delhi: Oxford University Press.

Talib, Adam (2018a), *How Do You Say Epigram in Arabic? Literary History at the Limits of Comparison*, Leiden: Brill.

Talib, Adam (2018b), 'Citystruck', in *The City in Premodern and Modern Arabic Literature*, eds. Nizar F. Hermes and Gretchen Head, 138–64, Edinburgh: Edinburgh University Press.

Talib, Adam (2019), 'Al-Ṣafadī, His Critics, and the Drag of Philological Time', *Philological Encounters* 4: 109–34.

Tavakoli-Targhi, Mohamad (2001), 'The Homeless Texts of Persianate Modernity', *Cultural Dynamics* 13, no. 3: 263–91.

Tavernier, Jean-Baptiste (1889), *Travels in India*, trans. Valentine Ball, London: Macmillan & Co.

Thackston, Wheeler M. (2020), 'Adham, Mīrzā Ebrāhīm', in *Encyclopaedia Iranica* Online, http://dx.doi.org/10.1163/2330-4804_EIRO_COM_4767.

Thiesen, Finn (1982), *A Manual of Classical Persian Prosody: With Chapters on Urdu, Karakhanidic, and Ottoman Prosody*, Wiesbaden: Harrassowitz.

Thornber, Karen Laura (2009), *Empire of Texts in Motion: Chinese, Korean and Taiwanese Transculturations of Japanese Literature*, Cambridge, MA: Harvard University Press.

Tomasello, Michael (1999), *The Cultural Origins of Human Cognition*, Cambridge, MA: Harvard University Press.

Toorawa, Shawkat (2008), 'The *Shifā' al-'Alīl* of Āzād Bilgrāmī (d. 1200/1786): Introducing an Eighteenth-Century Indian Work on al-Mutanabbī's Poetry', *Middle Eastern Literatures* 11, no. 2: 249–64.

Toorawa, Shawkat (2009), 'Āzād Bilgrāmī', in *Essays in Arabic Literary Biography, 1350–1850*, eds. Joseph E. Lowry and Devin J. Stewart, 91–7, Wiesbaden: Harrassowitz.

Toutant, Marc (2016), *Un empire des mots: pouvoir, culture et soufisme à l'époque des derniers Timourides au miroir de la Khamsa de Mīr 'Alī Shīr Nawā'ī*, Paris: Peeters.

Truschke, Audrey (2021), *The Language of History: Sanskrit Narratives of Indo-Muslim Rule*, New York: Columbia University Press.

Truschke, Audrey (2016), *Culture of Encounters: Sanskrit at the Mughal Court*, New York: Columbia University Press.

Um, Nancy (2009), *The Merchant Houses of Mocha: Trade and Architecture in an Indian Ocean Port City*, Seattle: University of Washington Press.

Veseley, Rudolf (2003), 'Das Taqrīẓ in der arabischen Literatur', in *Die Mamluken. Studien zu ihrer Geschichte und Kultur. Zum Gedenken an Ulrich Haarmann (1942 – 1999)*, eds. Stephan Conermann and Anja Pistor-Hatam, 379–85, Hamburg: EB-Verlag.

Virani, Nargis (2008), '*Mulamma'* in Islamic Literatures', in *Classical Arabic Humanities in their Own Terms: Festschrift for Wolfhart Heinrichs on His 65th Birthday*, ed. Beatrice Gruendler with Michael Cooperson, 291–324, Leiden: Brill.

Wagner, Mark S. (2009), *Like Joseph in Beauty: Yemeni Vernacular Poetry and Arab-Jewish Symbiosis*, Leiden: Brill.

Wagoner, Philip B. (2011), 'The Multiple Worlds of Amin Khan: Crossing Persianate and Indic Cultural Boundaries in the Qutb Shahi Kingdom', in *Sultans of the South: Arts of India's Deccan Courts, 1323 – 1687*, 90–101, New York: Metropolitan Museum of Art.

Walravens, Meia (2020), 'Arabic as a Language of the South Asian Chancery: Bahmani Communications to the Mamluk Sultanate', *Arabica* 67, no. 4: 409–35.

Watt, W. Montgomery et al. (2012), 'Makka', in *Encyclopaedia of Islam, Second Edition*, eds. P. Bearman, Th. Bianquis, C. E. Bosworth, E. van Donzel and W. P. Heinrichs, http://dx.doi.org/10.1163/1573-3912_islam_COM_0638.

Webb, Peter (2017), *Imagining the Arabs: Arab Identity and the Rise of Islam*, Edinburgh: Edinburgh University Press.

White, James (2021), 'Textual Culture Between Iran and India: The Reproduction of Verse in Nasrabadi's Biographical Anthology', *IRAN* 59, no. 2: 263–86.

Wink, André (2004), *Al-Hind: The Making of the Indo-Islamic World. Volume 3: Indo-Islamic Society, 14th-15th Centuries*, Leiden: Brill.

Winter, Stefan (2010), *The Shiites of Lebanon Under Ottoman Rule, 1516–1788*, Cambridge: Cambridge University Press.

Wormser, Paul (2015), 'L'expérience paradoxale de Nuruddin ar-Raniri dans l'océan Indien du XVIIᵉ siècle', in *Cosmopolitismes en Asie du Sud: Sources, itinéraires, langues (XVIe-XVIIIe siècle)*, eds. Corinne Lefèvre, Ines G. Županov and Jorge Flores, 171–83, Paris: Éditions de l'École des hautes études en sciences sociales.

Yalaoui, Muhammad (1976), *Un poète chiite d'Occident au IVème-Xème siècle, 'Ibn Hâni' al-'Andalusî*, Tunis: Université de Tunis, Faculté des lettres et sciences humaines.

Yarshater, Ehsan (1974), 'Safavid Literature: Progress or Decline?', *Iranian Studies* 7, no. 1–2: 217–70.

Zabara, Muhammad b. Muhammad (1957), *Nashr al-'Arf li-Nubala' al-Yaman ba'da l-Alf ila Sanat 1375 Hijriyya*, Cairo: al-Matba'a al-Salafiyya.

Zajączkowski, Ananiasz (1958), *Najstarsza wersja turecka Ḫusräv u Šīrīn Quṭba*, Warsaw: Państwowe Wydawnictwo Naukowe.

Zakir al-Husayni, Muhsin (1393s), 'Ash'ari az Nasrabadi', *Guzarish-i Miras*, Series 2, Year
    8, Nos. 3–4: 72–4.

Zipoli, Riccardo (1981), 'Fra Ṣā'eb e G̲h̲āleb: Appunti per una storia filologica dell'estetica
    "Indo-Persiana"', in *La Bisaccia dello Sheikh: omaggio ad Alessandro Bausani islamista
    nel sessantesimo compleanno: Venezia, 29 maggio 1981*, 275–89, Rome: n.p.

Zipoli, Riccardo (1993), *The Technique of the Ǧawab: Replies by Nawa'i to Hafiz and Ǧami*,
    Venice: Cafoscarina.

INDEX